ZAGATSURVEY®

1999

AMERICA'S TOP RESTAURANTS

Published and distributed by
ZAGAT SURVEY, LLC
4 Columbus Circle
New York, New York 10019
Tel: 212 977 6000
E-mail: zagat@zagatsurvey.com
Web site: www.zagat.com

Acknowledgments

Our special thanks to the thousands of surveyors who have shared their views with us and made this nationwide *Survey* possible. We would also like to thank our editors in each city: Karen Berk, Anthony Dias Blue, Olga Boikess, Mark Brown, Teresa Byrne-Dodge, Jon Christensen, Providence Cicero, Maureen Clancy, Millard Cohen, Chris Cook, Cass Davies, Pat Denechaud, Victoria Pesce Elliott, John Farrell Jr., Carrie Floyd, Hal Foster, Valerie Foster, William Fox, Connie Frost, David Gadd, Anthony Giglio, Norma Gottlieb, Angela Hagen, Lisa Shara Hall, Barbara Herring, Robert Hosmon, Suzanne Hough, Bobbye Hughes, Janet K. Johnson, Ed Jonna, Marty Katz, Joan Keane, Michael Klein, Sandy Kupfer, Gretchen Kurz, Jane Heald Lavine, Nancy Leson, Sharon Litwin, John Long, Charles Malody, Myrna Marston, John Martellaro, John McDermott, Carolyn McGuire, Charles Monaghan, M. F. Munday, David Nelson, Kristine Nickel, Ann Orton, Michael Paskevich, Ann Lemons Pollack, Joe Pollack, Joan Reminick, June Naylor Rodriguez, Susan Safronoff, Shelley Skiles Sawyer, John Schell, Carol Seibert, Merrill Shindler, Victoria Spencer, Mary Stagaman, Al Stankus, Muriel Stevens, Susan Stiger, Bill St. John, Steve Stover, Polly Summar, Alan Thompson, Suzanne Thompson, Paul Uhlmann III, Jill Van Cleave, Phil Vettel, Carla Waldemar, Julie Wilson, Jami Yuspa and Terry Zarikian.

ISBN 1-57006-151-3

Contents

Introduction

Here are the results of our *1999 Zagat Survey of America's Top Restaurants,* covering 1,140 restaurants in 38 US cities and states. This book represents a compilation of the best restaurants selected by thousands of local *Survey* participants. For each area, we have included a list of the top restaurants (based on the results of our most recent *Surveys* in that area) as well as a list of other "important places" chosen by our local editors.

The cities covered were chosen mainly because they are leading culinary centers. However, this is still a "work in progress." Each year we add more areas of the country, but we still have more to cover.

By regularly surveying large numbers of local restaurant-goers across the country, we think we have achieved a uniquely reliable guide. We hope you agree. On the assumption that most people want a "quick fix" on the places at which they are considering eating, we've tried to be concise, and have provided a handy cuisine index.

Knowing that the quality of this *Survey* is the direct result of their voting and commentary, we sincerely thank each participant. They include numerous professionals, business executives and just plain folks – food lovers all. We also thank our local editors. It was they who helped us choose the restaurants to be surveyed and edited the *Survey* results.

We invite you to be a reviewer in our city *Restaurant Surveys* or in our nationwide *Hotel Survey*. So that we can contact you at the time of the next *Survey*, send a stamped, self-addressed, business-size envelope to ZAGAT SURVEY, 4 Columbus Circle, New York, NY 10019 indicating the *Survey* in which you would like to participate, e.g. "LA" or "Hotel." Each participant will receive a free copy of the resulting *Survey* when it's published.

Your comments, suggestions and criticisms of this *Survey* are also solicited. There is always room for improvement – with your help.

New York, New York — Nina and Tim Zagat
November 17, 1998

Foreword

When we published our first restaurant *Survey* 20 years ago, the country's culinary landscape looked very different than it does today.

Back then, 'fine dining' was equated almost exclusively with French and Italian cuisine. The nation's best restaurants were clustered in New York and a handful of other cities, and their kitchens were largely manned by Europeans who, with few exceptions, remained anonymous.

That picture has undergone dramatic changes, as this *1999 Zagat Survey of America's Top Restaurants* illustrates. French and Italian have been joined by a global gamut of cuisines that reflect the country's ethnic diversity as well as the increasingly sophisticated tastes of its well-traveled diners. Many of today's top chefs are American-born or American-trained, and the position of chef has reached celebrity status.

Most significantly for this guide, just about every American city now boasts world-class restaurants – there's no better example than Las Vegas, once a culinary desert and now home to ventures by such superstar restaurateurs as Emeril Lagasse, Sirio Maccioni, Wolfgang Puck and Jean-Georges Vongerichten.

Naturally, the revolution that has reshaped the American restaurant industry has been echoed in our *Surveys.* What began as a hobby in 1979 – when we collected the opinions of 175 of our gourmet friends on roughly 100 New York restaurants – has grown into a guidebook business covering over 45 cities including, most recently, London and Paris, and involving over 100,000 surveyors.

We feel privileged to have served as a means of reflecting the country's growing interest in, and sophistication about, dining out in this period. Looking to the future, we're developing an electronic voting feature on our web site to make it easier for people to participate in our *Surveys.* Come visit us at www.zagat.com. We're beta-testing the system and can use as much input as possible.

New York, New York
November 17, 1998

Nina and Tim Zagat

Key to Ratings/Symbols

This sample entry identifies the various types of information contained in your Zagat Survey.

(1) Restaurant Name, Address & Phone Number

(2) Hours & Credit Cards

(3) ZAGAT Ratings

F	D	S	C
23	5	9	$19

Tim & Nina's ◐ S ⊄

4 Columbus Circle (8th Ave.), 212-977-6000

◪ "What a dump!" – open 7 days a week, 24 hours a day, this successful "deep dive" started the "deli-tapas craze" (i.e., tidbits of pastrami, corned beef, etc. on cracker-size pieces of stale rye); though the place looks like a "none-too-clean garage" and T & N "never heard of credit cards or reservations", "dirt cheap" prices for "great eats" draw demented crowds.

(4) Surveyors' Commentary

(2) Hours & Credit Cards

After each restaurant name you will find the following courtesy information:

◐ .... ***serving after 11 PM***

S .... ***open on Sunday***

⊄ .... ***no credit cards accepted***

(3) ZAGAT Ratings

Food, Decor and **Service** are each rated on a scale of **0** to **30**:

F	D	S	C

F .... *Food*
D .... *Decor*
S .... *Service*
C .... *Cost*

23	5	9	$19

0 - 9 .... *poor to fair*
10 - 15 .... *fair to good*
16 - 19 .... *good to very good*
20 - 25 .... *very good to excellent*
26 - 30 .... *extraordinary to perfection*

▽23	5	9	$19

▽ .... *Low number of votes/less reliable*

The **Cost (C)** column reflects the estimated price of a dinner with one drink and tip. Lunch usually costs 25% less.

A restaurant listed without ratings is either an important **newcomer** or a popular **write-in**. The estimated cost, with one drink and tip, is indicated by the following symbols.

–	–	–	VE

I .... *$15 and below*
M .... *$16 to $30*
E .... *$31 to $50*
VE .... *$51 or more*

(4) Surveyors' Commentary

Surveyors' comments are summarized, with literal comments shown in quotation marks. The following symbols indicate whether responses were mixed or uniform.

◪ .... *mixed*
■ .... *uniform*

Top Five Food Rankings by Area

Atlanta
1. Bacchanalia
2. Ritz-Carlton Din. Rm.
3. Soto
4. Pano's & Paul's
5. Chops

Atlantic City
1. Le Palais
2. White House
3. Capriccio
4. Savaradio
5. Chef Vola's

Baltimore/Annapolis
1. Prime Rib
2. Hampton's
3. Linwood's
4. 208 Talbot
5. Charleston

Boston
1. Aujourd'hui
2. L'Espalier
3. Olives
4. Hamersley's Bistro
5. Saporito's

Chicago
1. Le Français
2. Ambria
3. Carlos'
4. Tallgrass
5. Le Titi de Paris

Cincinnati
1. Maisonette
2. Palace
3. Precinct
4. BonBonerie
5. Phoenix

Cleveland
1. Johnny's Bar/Fulton
2. Sans Souci
3. Chez François
4. Hyde Park Grille
5. Baricelli Inn

Columbus
6. L'Antibes
7. Handke's
8. Refectory
9. Rigsby's
10. Rotolo's Pizza

Dallas
1. French Room
2. Riviera
3. Mansion on Turtle Creek
4. Pyramid Room
5. Cafe Pacific

Denver/Mountain Resorts
1. Piñons
2. Q's
3. Papillon Cafe
4. Keystone Ranch
5. Highlands Garden Cafe

Detroit
1. Lark
2. Golden Mushroom
3. Opus One
4. Zingerman's Deli
5. Cafe Bon Homme

Fort Lauderdale
1. Darrel & Oliver's Cafe
2. Eduardo de San Angel
3. Primavera
4. Mark's Las Olas
5. La Brochette Bistro

Fort Worth
1. Cacharel
2. Del Frisco's
3. Saint-Emilion
4. Bistro Louise
5. Railhead Smokehouse

Honolulu
1. Alan Wong's
2. La Mer
3. Roy's
4. Cliquo
5. Hoku's

Houston
6. La Réserve
7. Chez Nous
8. Ruggles Grill
9. Cafe Annie
10. Rotisserie/Beef & Bird

Kansas City
1. Cafe Allegro
2. American Restaurant
3. Bristol Bar & Grill
4. Peppercorn Duck Club
5. Tatsu's

Las Vegas
1. Emeril's New Orleans
2. Sterling Brunch
3. Andre's
4. Michael's
5. Steak Hse. (Circus Circus)

Los Angeles
1. Patina
2. Matsuhisa
3. Sushi Nozawa
4. Chinois on Main
5. Shiro

Miami/Miami Beach
1. Chef Allen's
2. Palm
3. Hy-Vong
4. Joe's Stone Crab
5. Giacosa

Minneapolis/St. Paul
1. Goodfellow's
2. Ristorante Luci
3. D'Amico Cucina
4. Manny's
5. St. Paul Grill

New Jersey
1. Saddle River Inn
2. Sagami
3. Ryland Inn
4. Chez Madeleine
5. Scalini Fedeli

New Orleans
1. Grill Room
2. Peristyle
3. Gabrielle
4. Brigtsen's
5. Ruth's Chris

New York City
6. Le Bernardin
7. Daniel
8. Lespinasse
9. Chanterelle
10. Nobu

Orange County
1. Troquet
2. Ritz
3. Pascal
4. Pavilion
5. Gustaf Anders

Orlando
1. Victoria & Albert's
2. La Coquina
3. Del Frisco's
4. Le Coq au Vin
5. California Grill

Palm Beach
1. Cafe Chardonnay
2. La Vieille Maison
3. Auberge Le Grillon
4. Kathy's Gazebo
5. Chef Reto's

Philadelphia
1. Le Bec-Fin
2. Fountain
3. Le Bar Lyonnais
4. Sagami
5. Brasserie Perrier

Phoenix/Scottsdale
1. Pizzeria Bianco
2. Vincent Guerithault
3. Mary Elaine's
4. Los Dos Molinos
5. Ruth's Chris

Portland
1. Cafe des Amis
2. Genoa
3. Wildwood
4. Heathman
5. Zefiro

Salt Lake City
1. Mariposa
2. New Yorker Club
3. Fresco Italian Cafe
4. Chez Betty
5. Metropolitan

San Diego
6. El Bizcocho
7. WineSellar & Brasserie
8. Sushi Ota
9. Mille Fleurs
10.Azzura Point

San Francisco
1. French Laundry
2. La Folie
3. Masa's
4. Ritz-Carlton Din. Rm.
5. Chez Panisse

Santa Fe
1. Santacafe
2. Cafe Pasqual's
3. Coyote Cafe
4. Carlos' Gosp'l Cafe
5. India Palace

Seattle
1. Rover's
2. Campagne
3. Shiro's
4. Georgian Room
5. Shoalwater

St. Louis
1. Tony's
2. Fio's La Fourchette
3. Cafe de France
4. Giovanni's
5. Al's

Tampa Bay/Sarasota
1. Mise en Place
2. Beach Bistro
3. Bern's Steak House
4. Blue Heron
5. Euphemia Haye

Tucson
1. Ventana Room
2. Janos
3. Vivace
4. Le Rendez-Vous
5. Gold Room

Washington, D.C.
1. Inn at Little Washington
2. Kinkead's
3. Makoto
4. L'Auberge Chez Francois
5. Obelisk

Most Popular by Area

Atlanta
1. Bacchanalia
2. Brasserie Le Coze
3. Nava
4. Canoe
5. Bone's

Atlantic City
1. Chef Vola's
2. Ram's Head Inn
3. Gary's Little Rock Cafe
4. Le Palais
5. Capriccio

Baltimore/Annapolis
1. Tio Pepe
2. Prime Rib
3. Linwood's
4. Ruth's Chris
5. Cheesecake Factory

Boston
1. Olives
2. Aujourd'hui
3. Hamersley's Bistro
4. Rialto
5. Elephant Walk

Chicago
1. Charlie Trotter's
2. Le Français
3. Ambria
4. Everest
5. Frontera Grill

Cincinnati
1. Maisonette
2. Precinct
3. Montgomery Inn
4. Palace
5. Grand Finale

Cleveland
1. Classics
2. Johnny's Bar/Fulton
3. Baricelli Inn
4. Sans Souci
5. Giovanni's

Columbus
1. Refectory
2. Lindey's
3. Rigsby's
4. Handke's
5. Cameron's

Dallas
1. Mansion on Turtle Creek
2. Cafe Pacific
3. Riviera
4. Star Canyon
5. French Room

Denver/Mountain Resorts
1. Strings
2. Briarwood Inn
3. Tante Louise
4. Papillon Cafe
5. Flagstaff House

Detroit
1. Lark
2. Golden Mushroom
3. Opus One
4. Rattlesnake Club
5. Whitney

Fort Lauderdale
1. Darrel & Oliver's Cafe
2. Mark's Las Olas
3. Cafe Arugula
4. Brooks
5. Armadillo Cafe

Fort Worth
1. Bistro Louise
2. Del Frisco's
3. Reata
4. La Piazza
5. Saint-Emilion

Honolulu
1. Alan Wong's
2. Roy's
3. Sam Choy's Diamond
4. 3660 on the Rise
5. Hy's Steak House

Houston
1. Cafe Annie
2. Ruggles Grill
3. Brennan's
4. Anthony's
5. Rotisserie/Beef & Bird

Kansas City
1. Cafe Allegro
2. American Restaurant
3. Plaza III
4. Grand St. Cafe
5. Houston's

Las Vegas
1. Spago
2. Andre's
3. Tillerman
4. Hugo's Cellar
5. Mayflower Cuisinier

Los Angeles
1. Patina
2. Cafe Bizou
3. Chinois on Main
4. Bel-Air Hotel
5. Campanile

Miami/Miami Beach
1. Chef Allen's
2. Joe's Stone Crab
3. Caffe Abbracci
4. Forge
5. Christy's

Minneapolis/St. Paul
1. Goodfellow's
2. D'Amico Cucina
3. Palomino
4. St. Paul Grill
5. Kincaid's

New Jersey
1. Saddle River Inn
2. Ryland Inn
3. Chez Madeleine
4. Manor
5. Cafe Panache

New Orleans
1. Commander's Palace
2. Galatoire's
3. Emeril's
4. Bayona
5. Brennan's

New York City
1. Union Square Cafe
2. Aureole
3. Gramercy Tavern
4. Gotham Bar/Grill
5. Le Bernardin

Orange County
1. Ritz
2. Pascal
3. Gustaf Anders
4. Five Crowns
5. Troquet

Orlando
1. California Grill
2. Le Coq au Vin
3. Pebbles
4. Maison et Jardin
5. Enzo's on the Lake

Palm Beach
1. La Vieille Maison
2. Max's Grille
3. Cafe L'Europe
4. Auberge Le Grillon
5. Cafe Chardonnay

Philadelphia
1. Le Bec-Fin
2. Fountain
3. Susanna Foo
4. Brasserie Perrier
5. Striped Bass

Phoenix/Scottsdale
1. Vincent Guerithault
2. Ruth's Chris
3. RoxSand
4. Lon's at the Hermosa
5. Eddie's Grill

Portland
1. Wildwood
2. Heathman
3. Zefiro
4. Cafe des Amis
5. Esparza's

Salt Lake City
1. New Yorker Club
2. Fresco Italian Cafe
3. Chez Betty
4. Market St. Broiler/Grill
5. Metropolitan

San Diego
1. George's at the Cove
2. Mille Fleurs
3. Laurel
4. Pamplemousse Grill
5. WineSellar & Brasserie

San Francisco
1. Boulevard
2. Postrio
3. French Laundry
4. Aqua
5. Fleur de Lys

Santa Fe
1. Coyote Cafe
2. Santacafe
3. Inn of the Anasazi
4. Geronimo
5. La Casa Sena

Seattle
1. Wild Ginger
2. Dahlia Lounge
3. Campagne
4. Etta's Seafood
5. Kaspar's

St. Louis
1. Tony's
2. Fio's La Fourchette
3. Sidney Street Cafe
4. Cardwell's
5. Malmaison

Tampa Bay/Sarasota
1. Michael's on East
2. Bern's Steak House
3. Bijou Café
4. Mise en Place
5. Café L'Europe
   Euphemia Haye*

Tucson
1. Janos
2. Vivace
3. Arizona Inn
4. Anthony's
5. Ventana Room

Washington, D.C.
1. L'Auberge Chez Francois
2. Kinkead's
3. Inn at Little Washington
4. Galileo
5. Vidalia

* Tied with the restaurant listed directly above it.

Alphabetical Directory of Restaurants

Atlanta

TOP 20 FOOD RANKING

	Restaurant	Cuisine Type
28	Bacchanalia	New American
	Ritz-Carlton Buck. Din. Rm.	Mediterranean
27	Soto	Japanese
	Pano's & Paul's	Continental/New Amer.
	Chops	Steakhouse
	Ciboulette	Classic French
26	Bone's	Steakhouse
	Brasserie Le Coze	French Bistro
	Seeger's	New American
	Sushi Huku	Japanese
	La Grotta	N/S Italian
	Riviera	New French
	Four Seasons Cafe	New American
	Ritz-Carlton Buck. Cafe	Continental/French
	Bread Garden	Bakery/Sandwiches
	Nikolai's Roof	Continental/Russian
25	Hedgerose	New American
	Morton's of Chicago	Steakhouse
	Nava	Southwestern
	103 West	Continental/French

OTHER IMPORTANT PLACES

Abruzzi	N/S Italian
Babette's Cafe	French Bistro
Bistro	French Bistro
Buckhead Diner	New American
Canoe	Continental/New Amer.
Chopstix	Chinese
dick & harry's	New American
Flying Biscuit Cafe	Southern/Vegetarian
Floataway Cafe	French/Italian
Food Studio	New American
Mumbo Jumbo	New American
Palm	Seafood/Steakhouse
Prime	Seafood/Steakhouse
Ritz-Carlton Atlanta Rest.	Classic/New French
South City Kitchen	Southern
Tamarind	Thai
Van Gogh's	New American
Veni Vidi Vici	Northern Italian

	F	D	S	C
Abruzzi	24	20	24	$41

Peachtree Battle Shopping Ctr., 2355 Peachtree Rd. (Peachtree Battle Ave.), 404-261-8186

◪ You'll find "a bit of NY" at this "upscale Italian" "favorite" in Buckhead where the "well-heeled retired set" goes for "timeless" food and "personal attention" by "old-school waiters"; but even admirers admit the interior "needs to be renovated" and a minority maintains that "service can be snobby if you're not a regular."

Babette's Cafe S | 24 | 20 | 22 | $26

471 N. Highland Ave. (bet. Colquitt Ave. & Freedom Pkwy.), 404-523-9121
■ "Success has not spoiled anything" at this "charming country French" that adds a "European touch to Poncey-Highlands" with its "romantic", "cozy" atmosphere and "affordable", "creative" cuisine, including "theme meals" like the re-creation of *Babette's Feast*; loyal followers lament "if only they would take reservations."

Bacchanalia | 28 | 25 | 27 | $51

3125 Piedmont Rd. (Martina Dr.), 404-365-0410
■ Anne Quatrano and Clifford Harrison's "intimate" prix fixe New American in a "beautiful Victorian home" "continues to hit all the notes", delivering a "flawless", "unparalleled", "A++" experience "without the Buckhead attitude" and earning the No. 1 food score in our *Atlanta Survey* once again; no wonder it's "difficult to get a reservation on weekends."

Bistro, The | 24 | 21 | 23 | $36

Andrews Sq., 56 E. Andrews Dr. NW (Cains Hill Pl.), 404-231-5733
■ There's "never a wait" at this "hidden gem" in Buckhead, "Atlanta's best-kept secret" for "consistently excellent" "cooked to order" French bistro food served in a "warm", "understated" setting by a "competent" staff; chef-owner Jim Brown also has cultivated a "fabulous wine cellar" here.

Bone's S | 26 | 23 | 25 | $45

3130 Piedmont Rd. (Peachtree Rd.), 404-237-2663
■ "No bones about it" – this "pricey" Buckhead beef "bastion" is a "man's delight" with its "great drinks", "major league steaks", "cigar chomping" and "clubby" ambiance that "make you want to do a deal"; a few nonmembers claim "regulars get the best service."

Brasserie Le Coze | 26 | 24 | 23 | $34

Lenox Sq., 3393 Peachtree Rd. (Lenox Rd.), 404-266-1440
■ "Close my eyes and I'm in France" gush devotees of this "sophisticated" "country French bistro" in Buckhead with "Le Bernardin [NYC] lineage" where they turn out "fabulous" seafood dishes and "soups that are good to the last drop"; only the "Neiman Marcus bags" remind you that "you're in a mall" – the "only drawback" for some, but others add "deafening" "noise."

Bread Garden S ⇏ | 26 | 11 | 16 | $8

549 Amsterdam Ave. (Monroe Dr.), 404-875-1166
1035 N. Highland Ave. (Virginia Ave.), 404-875-5599
■ Everyone agrees this Va-Highlands duo doles out the "best bread in the city"; chef-owner Catherine Krasnow's creations are "too good to be true", with the "best sandwiches" and "amazing desserts" flying out the door of these takeout-only, no-frills bakeries where everything is "fresh, delightful and different."

Buckhead Diner ◐ S | 24 | 23 | 21 | $26

3073 Piedmont Rd. NE (Pharr Rd.), 404-262-3336
◪ When it comes to "upscale diner" food, "nobody does it better" than this "glitzy", "see and be seen" Buckhead American (the most highly trafficked restaurant in our *Atlanta Survey*) where locals, out-of-towners and celebs go for veal meat loaf, homemade potato chips and the like; not everyone is willing to endure "long waits", however, especially those who find it "the original Snobs R Us."

Canoe S | 23 | 26 | 22 | $34

Vinings on the River, 4199 Paces Ferry Rd. (I-75), 770-432-2663

◪ "How sublime!" gush enthusiasts of this New American–Continental boasting "beautiful architecture and design" and a "wonderful terrace" overlooking the Chattahoochee River where "beautiful people" flock to "see and be seen" while dining on "fabulous creative cuisine"; for most, this "stunning" spot "hits all the senses" ("earplugs necessary"), but a boatload of patrons gripe that "sometimes the waiters forget one has an option to tip" and that, "unless you're the mayor, expect a wait."

Chops S | 27 | 25 | 25 | $42

Buckhead Plaza, 70 W. Paces Ferry Rd. (Peachtree Rd.), 404-262-2675

■ For "melt in your mouth steaks" or a "lobster feast with finesse" at the "excellent" lobster bar downstairs, this Buckhead "boys' club" is the "best in Atlanta, bar none"; a few beef about "haughty service", but for most the "masculine decor" and "comfortable", "relaxing" atmosphere bolster this "pricey but worth it" power scene; after all, "sometimes it's ok to pay a lot for meat."

Chopstix S | 24 | 20 | 22 | $29

Chastain Sq., 4279 Roswell Rd. (Wieuca Rd.), 404-255-4868

■ The No. 1 Chinese in our *Atlanta Survey* is a "gourmet" operation in Buckhead offering candlelight, white tablecloths, a "relaxing pianist" and "outstanding" "upscale Hong Kong–style" fare to a "dressed-up clientele"; it's "expensive but worth it" – owner "Philip Chan really knows what he's doing."

Ciboulette | 27 | 23 | 24 | $41

Clear Creek Shopping Ctr., 1529 Piedmont Ave. (Monroe Dr.), 404-874-7600

■ Surveyors say "très bon" to this "exquisite" Midtowner and its "inventive food" bathed in "artery-busting sauces so good they should be illegal", "impeccable service" and "beautiful and intimate" setting, rating it the No. 1 Classic French in our *Atlanta Survey*; "elbow to elbow" dining and "long waits" in the "crowded" bar area (despite accepting reservations) are "the only drawbacks."

dick and harry's | 25 | 20 | 22 | $33

Holcomb Woods Village, 1570 Holcomb Bridge Rd. (½ mi. east of GA 400), Roswell, 770-641-8757

■ There's "well-deserved praise" for this New American with "innovative", "excellent food" that's "the best thing to happen to the suburbs" in a long time; it's a "very loud", "fun, in-place" for locals and Intowners who think this "treat by any standard" is "worth every minute of the long drive to Roswell."

Floataway Cafe S | – | – | – | M

1123 Zonolite Rd., Ste. 15 (Briarcliff & Johnson Rds.), 404-892-1414

In a renovated warehouse on a dead-end road near Emory, this casual newcomer is drawing crowds thanks to the top-quality rustic French-Italian cooking of Annie Quatrano (who also remains involved with Bacchanalia); brushed chrome, sheer curtains and milk bottle light fixtures create a contemporary mood, and the wine list is culled from far-flung corners of the world; reservations highly recommended, or try lunch Wednesday–Friday and Sunday.

Flying Biscuit Cafe S | 23 | 19 | 19 | $15

1655 McLendon Ave. (Clifton Rd.), 404-687-8888

■ Breakfast lovers unite over this "warm and fuzzy" "bohemian delight" in Candler Park offering "homemade everything" on a "healthy, creative" Southern-Vegetarian menu; while the weekend "wait can be unbearable", most line up because the "sage turkey sausage and biscuits are as good as champagne and caviar."

Food Studio S | 23 | 27 | 22 | $34

887 W. Marietta St. (Howell Mill Rd.), 404-815-6677

■ Dinner at this "stunning" New American in an "out-of-the-way" 1902 farm equipment factory west of Georgia Tech is "like sitting in a feature article of *Architectural Digest*"; while a few cynics snipe "beauty is only skin deep" and "the food can't live up to the great decor", the majority maintains the "creative" menu and "hip, warm and artsy" atmosphere are "way ahead of the Atlanta scene."

Four Seasons Cafe S | 26 | 25 | 24 | $34

Four Seasons Atlanta, 75 14th St. (Peachtree St.), 404-881-9898

■ "A true dining experience, even if you're just dropping by for a snack", this "lovely cafe" that's "good for business lunches" or pre-theater dining is now the only restaurant at the Four Seasons in Midtown; menu changes by new management and chef Brooke Vosika bring a wide variety of New American choices – from burgers to lobster to rack of lamb.

Hedgerose S | 25 | 26 | 26 | $52

490 E. Paces Ferry Rd. (Maple Dr.), 404-233-7673

◪ This Buckhead New American is a "top to bottom" remake (from decor and owners to chef and cuisine) of the former Hedgerose Heights Inn and some who have paid a visit to this "romantic" prix fixe affair praise it as "a rose in Atlanta's culinary garden" thanks to "beautiful food" and "attentive" service in "elegantly comfortable" surroundings; others, however, cite "overpriced" fare that's a "mixed success" and an atmosphere that's a "little stiff"; still, no one can deny that it "shows a lot of promise."

La Grotta | 26 | 23 | 25 | $40

2637 Peachtree Rd. (bet. Lindbergh Dr. & W. Wesley Rd.), 404-231-1368
Crowne Plaza Ravinia Hotel, 4355 Ashford Dunwoody Rd. (I-285), 770-395-9925

■ The No. 1 Italian in our *Atlanta Survey*, presided over by "primo padrone" Sergio Favalli, is "what fancy Italian restaurants used to be" with its "dark" and "romantic" setting, "very attentive service" and "beautiful food"; the original Buckhead location "hidden in the basement of a condo" is dinner only, while the newer branch in the Crowne Plaza Ravinia also serves lunch to a largely business crowd.

Morton's of Chicago S | 25 | 22 | 23 | $42

3379 Peachtree Rd. (Lenox Rd.), 404-816-6535
303 Peachtree Ctr. Ave. (Baker St.), 404-577-4366

◪ "If you want lots of beef", put on your "power suit" and head to one of these "deluxe" "carnivore feeding grounds" that supporters swear "can compete with any steakhouse in town"; both the Downtown and Buckhead branches are "very good" for business meals, but some grumble about the practice of peddling the cuts tableside – "the servers need to be told this is food, not Broadway."

Mumbo Jumbo S
22 | 25 | 20 | $32

89 Park Pl. NE (Auburn Ave.), 404-523-0330

◪ This "sexy, sassy" Downtown New American is "a delicious feast for the senses" with its "global menu" featuring "cutting-edge food" courtesy of "genius" chef Shawn Doty, "incredible" "eccentric" decor and "glitzy, preening" servers; but it can be more than "a bit of a scene" for the fainthearted who find "too much attitude" and "overpriced" "small portions."

Nava S
25 | 27 | 22 | $33

Buckhead Plaza, 3060 Peachtree Rd. NW (W. Paces Ferry Rd.), 404-240-1984

■ The No. 1 Southwestern in our *Atlanta Survey* is an "awesome experience" with "one of the more innovative kitchens in town" steered by Kevin Rathbun, "stunning" decor that matches the "food as art" and "awesome" margaritas that make the "great people-watching" even better; aside from an occasional slam of the decor ("Santa Fe on steroids"), the main complaint from the few critics is "snooty hostesses"; everyone else "can't get enough of Nava."

Nikolai's Roof S
26 | 26 | 26 | $59

Atlanta Hilton, 255 Courtland St., 30th fl. (bet. Baker & Harris Sts.), 404-221-6362

■ After more than 20 years, this Russian-Continental is "still one of Atlanta's best" for "special" "romantic" evenings, "superb" expense-account dining or just a "unique night out"; an "elegant" prix fixe featuring "authentic" cuisine is "beautifully presented" by old-world waiters in front of an "awesome view" of Downtown, but even the vista can't make a few forget how "expensive" it is.

103 West
25 | 23 | 25 | $45

103 W. Paces Ferry Rd. (Peachtree St.), 404-233-5993

◪ Surveyors in search of "excellent" cuisine, "attentive service" and an "opulent" setting frequent this Buckhead Life Group French-Continental "landmark" "best known for fried lobster tails"; a few find the "menu stale", the service "stuffy" and the "red velvet" "New Orleans brothel" decor "dated", but many more swear it's "expensive but worth it" for "special occasion dining."

Palm Restaurant S
23 | 20 | 22 | $45

Swissôtel Atlanta, 3391 Peachtree Rd. NE (Lenox Rd.), 404-814-1955

◪ For "an infusion of cholesterol", devotees of "tasty" steaks, "gargantuan" lobsters and basically "big everything" mosey on over to this "classy, sassy" à la carte steakhouse/seafooder "hidden" in Buckhead's Swissôtel; "at these prices it better be perfect", but foes feel it's not, beefing "too loud", "overrated" and "doesn't measure up to the original" in New York.

Pano's & Paul's
27 | 23 | 26 | $45

W. Paces Ferry Shopping Ctr., 1232 W. Paces Ferry Rd. (Northside Pkwy.), 404-261-3662

■ The original "star" in the Buckhead Life Group's ever-expanding universe, this "sumptuous" and "scrumptious" Continental–New American is still a shining example of special occasion dining; "as soon as you step inside, you're in a different century" with piano music, "private, cozy booths" and "ornate" decor as the backdrop to "divine" fried lobster tail and other "marvelous" creations; while a few fuss about "rushed" service and "house of ill repute" decor, most maintain it "lives up to its reputation."

Prime 🅂 — 24 | 24 | 23 | $39

Lenox Sq., 3393 Peachtree Rd. (Lenox Rd.), 404-812-0555

■ What a "great concept" – a "stylish mix" of "excellent steaks" and "flawless sushi" ensures there's "something for everyone" who's willing to pay "high prices"; it's "too bad it's in a mall", but this "extremely enjoyable" "oasis" "overcomes" its Lenox location with a "pampering" staff, "hip" clientele and "cool" decor.

Ritz-Carlton Atlanta Restaurant — – | – | – | VE

Ritz-Carlton Atlanta, 181 Peachtree St. NE (Ellis St.), 404-659-0400

There's been a buzz about this "classy" Downtown dining room since chef Olivier Gaupin (ex Provence in Washington, DC) took over the stoves in October 1997; he's created a seasonal Provençal menu featuring seafood and game specialties finished with unique sauces as well as a three-course vegetarian menu and four-course tasting menu; early reviewers rave "the Ritz at its best."

Ritz-Carlton Buckhead Cafe 🅂 — 26 | 26 | 26 | $41

Ritz-Carlton Buckhead, 3434 Peachtree Rd. NE (Lenox Rd.), 404-237-2700

■ Admirers of this "civilized" Buckhead French-Continental consider it "a real treat for special occasions", an afternoon "tea date", Saturday-night dancing or for "a brilliant Sunday buffet" – all done in the "extraordinary" style (and at the "incredible prices") of the Ritz; "unwind, relax and let the luxury begin."

Ritz-Carlton Buckhead Dining Room — 28 | 27 | 28 | $68

Ritz-Carlton Buckhead, 3434 Peachtree Rd. NE (Lenox Rd.), 404-237-2700

■ "Yes, yes and oh yes!" moan enthusiasts about the "most exquisite taste sensations ever" created by chef Joel Antunes in this "inspired" Mediterranean in the Buckhead Ritz; while a few sniff "stuffy" and warn "bring your wallet", an "excellent wine list", the "best sommelier in the city", "polished service" and an "elegant atmosphere" all add up to one of Atlanta's "crème de la crème dining" experiences.

Riviera, The — 26 | 24 | 23 | $48

519 E. Paces Ferry Rd. (Piedmont Rd.), 404-262-7112

◪ "Beautiful people eating beautiful food" in a "beautiful setting" is the majority view of this "intimate" Buckhead Contemporary French in an "elegant yet comfortable" converted home; fans toss "bouquets to the chef" for his "world-class" creations like "lobster ravioli to die for", but hurl "brickbats at the condescending waiters" who "take their cue from Paris"; critics feel it's "just not the same" under the new chef and owners.

Seeger's — 26 | 26 | 26 | $72

111 W. Paces Ferry Rd. (E. Andrews Dr.), 404-846-9779

■ Guenter Seeger (ex Ritz-Carlton Buckhead Dining Room), a "genius" who's "in a class by himself", created this New American "hot spot" in Buckhead where "food as art" is only a part of the "visual feast"; the "beautiful contemporary" decor and "best service we have ever seen" complete a "sophisticated" picture that "real food lovers" are "really excited about"; but fans and foes alike are hungry for "more, more, more", claiming the portions are "way too small" and the prices are "astronomical."

Soto ◐ 27 | 14 | 14 | $29

Kroger Shopping Ctr., 3330 Piedmont Rd. (Peachtree Rd.), 404-233-2005

■ "There is no better sushi and there is only one Soto!" declare zealots of the No. 1 Japanese in Atlanta and its eponymous "genius" who creates "amazingly fresh and inventive" fare that "makes others pale in comparison"; even the most ardent boosters acknowledge that the "quirky strip mall" spot in Buckhead has "no ambiance" and service is "painfully slow", but once you get your food, it's "just heaven."

South City Kitchen S 23 | 22 | 20 | $28

1144 Crescent Ave. (bet. 14th & Peachtree Sts.), 404-873-7358

■ This "upscale twist" on Southern cuisine ("mama don't cook like this") comes "highly recommended", and the "snazzy" "innovative" fare benefits from a "terrific" and "reasonable" wine list and "urban chic" setting in a renovated Midtown house fronted by a "very well done" patio; it's an "in vogue" place for people-watching and, as a result, often "loud", "crowded" and loaded with "attitude."

Sushi Huku S 26 | 19 | 20 | $28

Powers Ferry Landing, 6300 Powers Ferry Rd. (Northside Dr.), 770-956-9559

■ The "best sushi on the Northside" and "in Atlanta" declare devotees of this highly rated "authentic" Japanese where you can "sit at the bar and watch the show" starring "entertaining sushi chefs" who "consistently" turn out "high-quality" fare to a "largely Japanese clientele"; it's "smoky" and certainly "not cheap", but the "great hospitality" and "marvelous" cuisine make it a "favorite."

Tamarind S – | – | – | M

80 14th St. (bet. Spring & Williams Sts.), 404-873-4888

New, sophisticated Thai in Midtown near Georgia Tech, where a velo taxi parked by the front door is the first sign of a truly authentic experience; owners Charlie and Nan Nikomkul, who owned a restaurant in New York, have everything running smoothly – from bite-sized appetizers served on banana leaves to unbelievably good dishes beyond the traditional curries and pad Thai; don't let the unassuming exterior and inconvenient parking deter you.

Van Gogh's S 25 | 23 | 22 | $31

70 W. Crossville Rd. (Crabapple Rd.), Roswell, 770-993-1156

■ "Consistently excellent", "carefully prepared food" that's "clearly a work of art" is the draw at this Roswell New American, which is our *Atlanta Survey's* top-rated spot in its northern environs; "good service", a "great wine list" and "prime" paintings on the walls enhance the "upscale" atmosphere; P.S. news flash for surveyors who say they "need to take reservations" – they do now.

Veni Vidi Vici S 24 | 24 | 22 | $33

41 14th St. (bet. Spring & W. Peachtree Sts.), 404-875-8424

◪ Formerly the brainchild of Marcella Hazan, the diva of Italian cuisine, this "fabulous", "upscale" Midtown Northern Italian has been under the aegis of the Buckhead Life kingdom for a while; chef Jamie Adams' "brilliant" cooking, the "sexy" postmodern interior and "smooth" service keep it a "favorite for business lunches" and "sophisticated" dinners; even dissenters who dub it "inconsistent" and "noisy" admit it's still "enjoyable."

TOP 10 FOOD RANKING

	Restaurant	Cuisine Type
27	Le Palais	New French
26	White House	Sandwiches
	Capriccio	N/S Italian
25	Savaradio	Eclectic
24	Chef Vola's	N/S Italian
	Medici	N/S Italian
	Gary's Little Rock Cafe	Eclectic
	Tre Figlio	N/S Italian
23	Ram's Head Inn	Traditional American
	Little Saigon	Vietnamese

F | D | S | C

Capriccio S — 26 | 26 | 24 | $42

Resorts Casino Hotel, Boardwalk & North Carolina Ave., AC, 609-340-6789

■ "Watch high-stakes characters" soaking up the "delicious" food, "super service" and Boardwalk views at this "classy" Italian in Resorts; perhaps they're the same patrons who sometimes "sing with the musician" who strolls through the "beautiful surroundings."

Chef Vola's S ⊄ — 24 | 11 | 23 | $39

111 S. Albion Pl. (Pacific Ave.), 609-345-2022

◪ "You practically have to submit a resume" to get a reservation at this Italian BYO in the "cramped" "basement of an old house" in Atlantic City; most find the Espositos' home cooking "superb" and say you'll take home a "shopping bag full of leftovers"; negativists insist it "thrives on its mystique of inaccessibility"; N.B. bring cash.

Gary's Little Rock Cafe S — 24 | 15 | 20 | $32

5214 Atlantic Ave. (bet. Little Rock & Weymouth Aves.), Ventnor, 609-823-2233

■ It's "hard to get a reservation", there are "long waits" and it's "cramped" and "too noisy", but this Ventnor Eclectic BYO continues to reign as one of the "best noncasino restaurants on the island", with an "inspired", "creative menu" packed with "amazing flavors – try the warm duck salad."

Le Palais S — 27 | 27 | 27 | $47

Resorts Casino Hotel, Boardwalk & North Carolina Ave., 609-340-6400

■ Merv's really cooking at his "gorgeous", classy New French at Resorts, where "exquisite", "luscious" food ("best foie gras and chocolate soufflé") and an "elegant" ambiance are complemented by an "outstanding" staff that "treats you royally every time"; Sunday brunch is "beautiful."

Little Saigon S ⊄ — 23 | 11 | 22 | $20

Arctic & Iowa Aves., 609-347-9119

■ This Vietnamese BYO in AC has finally been "discovered" as a "wonderful alternative to casino rip-offs" since the "terrific" food is a "shore bargain" – "little in name, grand in quality."

Medici — 24 | 25 | 25 | $44

Sands Hotel & Casino, Brighton Park & Indiana Ave., 609-441-4300

■ This Sands high-end Italian offers one of AC's lovelier rooms, with superb food and a dazzling ocean view, though you might hanker for a comp to foot the tab.

Ram's Head Inn S | 23 | 26 | 23 | $40

9 W. White Horse Pike (Garden State Pkwy. & Rte. 30), Absecon, 609-652-1700

■ A "favorite for many years", this "good place to spend an entire evening" is an "old-fashioned, dressy" American in Absecon that "continues to hold its own" with "superb" food, "elegant" atmospherics and "fine" service.

Savaradio S ⊄ | 25 | 16 | 21 | $30

5223 Ventnor Ave. (Little Rock Ave.), Ventnor, 609-823-2110

■ Just "try to get in" to this Ventnor BYO "gem" during high season when everyone's clamoring for the "delicious", "beautifully served", "cutting-edge" Eclectic food; even if the "comfort level is low", it's "worth going back to again."

Tre Figlio S | 24 | 19 | 22 | $36

500 W. White Horse Pike (bet. Manheim Ave. & Rte. 30), Egg Harbor, 609-965-3303

◪ "Slow down or you'll drive right by" this family Italian that's "a must" on the way to the shore; while "outstanding dishes are enhanced by great service", some quibble that the "tables are too close" together.

White House S ⊄ | 26 | 9 | 16 | $10

2301 Arctic Ave. (Mississippi Ave.), 609-345-1564

■ "Ultimate" "hoagies to die for" draw crowds (including Philadelphians who willingly "travel 55 miles") to this "noisy" institution off the AC casino track; aficionados who "wish the D.C. White House were as dependable" assert that the secret to these "cheap" treats is "the bread."

TOP 10 FOOD RANKING

	Restaurant	Cuisine Type
28	Prime Rib	Steakhouse
27	Hampton's	New American
	Linwood's	Cal./New American
	208 Talbot/A	New American
	Charleston	American/Southern
	Inn at Perry Cabin/A	Continental
26	Milton Inn	Regional American
	Lenny's Chop House	Seafood/Steakhouse
	Lewnes' Steakhouse/A	Steakhouse
	Boccaccio	Northern Italian

OTHER IMPORTANT PLACES

Black Olive	Greek/Seafood
Cantler's Riverside Inn/A	Crab House/Seafood
Cheesecake Factory	Californian
Marconi's	Traditional American
McCormick & Schmick's	Seafood
Oregon Grill	Regional American
Pierpoint	New American/Seafood
Polo Grill	New American
Rudys' 2900	Continental/New Amer.
Ruth's Chris	Steakhouse
Tersiguel's	Classic French
Tio Pepe	Continental/Spanish

F | D | S | C

Black Olive S — 26 | 18 | 21 | $38

814 S. Bond St. (Shakespeare St.), 410-276-7141

■ "Great everything" – no wonder this young Greek scored high food ratings on its first try, proving that in Fells Point, as on the Aegean, classically "simple" cuisine and hands-on "hospitality" impress; its white brick and wood decor "is like being in a Greek fishing village", yet a few feel entitled to more "for the price."

Boccaccio S — 26 | 23 | 24 | $41

925 Eastern Ave. (bet. Exeter & High Sts.), 410-234-1322

■ The "chef receives in the kitchen" of this "high-end", "real [Northern] Italian" where he shows Baltimore that there is more to Little Italy than "red sauce" pastas; perhaps "reservations are not always on time", but the "wonderful" veal chop is.

Cantler's Riverside Inn S — 22 | 15 | 18 | $20

458 Forest Beach Rd. (Brown's Wood Rd.), Annapolis, 410-757-1311

■ "It's worth getting lost to find" this "wonderful, on the river" site near Annapolis for "elbow-to-elbow crab picking"; the seafood arrives daily, and diners can enjoy a "great" open-air deck overlooking a wooded creek; maybe it's "not perfect" ("needs better parking"), but it's one of the "most relaxed crab places" in the vicinity; N.B. call for directions.

	F	D	S	C
Charleston S	27	25	26	$40

1000 Lancaster St. (bet. Central & Exeter Sts.), 410-332-7373

■ Even though it only opened shortly before our *Baltimore Survey* was conducted, this "stunning" Southern American vaulted to No. 5 for Food, 3 for Service and 10 for Decor; chef-owner Cindy Wolf and her husband Tony Forman's stellar performance at the defunct Savannah continues here with "unique, delicious" takes on "Low Country delicacies" and one of the "best wine cellars in town"; even the harbor-view office building location is "smashing."

	F	D	S	C
Cheesecake Factory ◐ S	21	18	18	$21

Harborplace, Pratt St. Pavilion (Calvert St.), 410-234-3990

◪ There are no just-in-time arrivals at this chain Big Food factory – with no reserving, "humongous" servings and an "overwhelming" Californian menu (most of it deemed "consistently good"), near "unbearable" noise and waits are routine.

	F	D	S	C
Hampton's S	27	28	27	$54

Harbor Court Hotel, 550 Light St. (bet. Conway & Lee Sts.), 410-347-9744

■ Voted No. 1 for Decor and Service in Baltimore, this premier "event restaurant" offers "first-class" formal dining that "doesn't get any better"; the breathtaking harbor views and "top-quality" New American menu leave patrons feeling "pampered"; P.S. "a drink in the Explorer's Lounge" starts the evening off in style.

	F	D	S	C
Inn at Perry Cabin S	27	28	26	$54

Inn at Perry Cabin, 308 Watkins Ln. (Talbot St.), St. Michaels, 410-745-2200

■ Join luminaries looking for privacy at this "elegant" Eastern Shore getaway; though the "dinner 'production'" strikes some as "pretentious", the modern Continental food, "great wine list" and "professional" service "befit the lovely surroundings" and do justice to the spectacular water view from the lovely patio.

	F	D	S	C
Lenny's Chop House S	26	27	23	$46

Harbor Inn Pier 5, 711 Eastern Ave. (President St.), 410-843-5555

■ When consummate restaurateur Lenny Kaplan (of Polo Grill and Classic Catering repute) inaugurated this "sleek", "classy" Inner Harbor steak and seafood house – acclaimed as the "most handsome room" in town, with the "best steak" – folks were primed for it to become a "place to see, be seen and feel important"; the above ratings bear this out, but the debut of nearby McCormick & Schmick's may bust a few of Lenny's chops.

	F	D	S	C
Lewnes' Steakhouse S	26	19	21	$48

401 Fourth St. (Severn Ave.), Annapolis, 410-263-1617

■ For "great steaks in a seafood town", Annapolis carnivores proudly point to this "classic", which boasts "humongous" portions of "outstanding meat" and men's-clubby vibes; devotees swear it's every bit "as good as the Palm" and, some say, just as "expensive."

	F	D	S	C
Linwood's S	27	26	25	$41

McDonough Crossroads, 25 Crossroads Dr. (McDonough & Reisterstown Rds.), Owings Mills, 410-356-3030

■ A "class act", this "elegant" bistro is "amazingly consistent" for an "imaginative" Cal-style menu; this is where Owings Mills goes "for a celebration" overseen by a "well-trained staff", or to "watch all the action" from the bar; there's never "too much table-hopping" for its steady customers, who go to "eat well, see and be seen."

Marconi's | 23 | 18 | 24 | $30 |

106 W. Saratoga St. (bet. Cathedral St. & Park Ave.), 410-727-9522
■ "Like Gibraltar, a sturdy Baltimore tradition"– this American's "delicious signature dishes" ("great lobster cardinale" and hot fudge sundaes) are still a "draw"; also compelling is the "old Baltimore atmosphere", which harks back to "H. L Mencken's time", not to mention the servers ("average age only 65"); but, yes, there are a couple of curmudgeons who "never did like grainy chocolate sauce."

McCormick & Schmick's S | – | – | – | M |

Harbor Inn Pier 5, 711 Eastern Ave. (President St.), 410-234-1300
Floor-to-ceiling windows, sweeping waterfront views and a dockside outdoor cafe distinguish Baltimore's link in this high-end, Edwardian-feeling West Coast seafood chain; virtually a clubroom for Downtown since day one, its open, yet workmanlike, manners are reflected in the clientele's loosened ties and rolled-up sleeves, but tourists tout it too.

Milton Inn S | 26 | 26 | 25 | $48 |

14833 York Rd. (2½ mi. north of Shawan Rd.), Sparks, 410-771-4366
■ New owners (Brass Elephant, King's Contrivance) have brightened this 18th-century destination without disturbing its "country atmosphere" or its tradition of "excellent" Maryland regional food and service; as "rustic and romantic" as ever, it's a premier special occasion place – the lovely "walk to the door", the smell of wood smoke from the hearth room and the glow of candlelight are "only a hint of the wonderful things to come."

Oregon Grill S | 24 | 27 | 22 | $47 |

1201 Shawan Rd. (Beaver Dam Rd.), Hunt Valley, 410-771-0505
◪ This "classy, clubby" Hunt Country "high roller" showcasing chef Mark Henry's "genius" with Regional American cuisine is "fast becoming one of the best formal restaurants" in the area; though a minority feels it "still needs work", "when it's good, it's great"; the help may be "a bit young", but rest assured the "expensive" wines are not.

Pierpoint S | 25 | 17 | 21 | $35 |

1822 Aliceanna St. (bet. Ann & Wolfe Sts.), 410-675-2080
■ "Sophisticated and intimate" Fells Point boîte that spotlights chef-owner Nancy Longo's "innovative Maryland cuisine"; her fans "love its smallness", which lets her produce "tremendous food without the prices and atmosphere of a high-class restaurant"; while some respondents regret the "tight quarters", virtually all agree that "when it's good, it's very good", especially at brunch.

Polo Grill S | 26 | 25 | 24 | $42 |

Inn at the Colonnade, 4 W. University Pkwy. (bet. Canterbury & Charles Sts.), 410-235-8200
■ A "really classy", "clubby", "truly professional operation" in a Homewood location, where Charm City's "big dogs" and "power players" come to nod and "be seen" (not heard – it's "too noisy"); the atmosphere is a bit "stuffy", but the "kitchen turns out well-done innovations on classic Continentals" that earn raves.

Prime Rib 🅂 28 | 25 | 25 | $46

Horizon House, 1101 N. Calvert St. (Chase St.), 410-539-1804

■ The town "never tires" of this "swank", "old-fashioned supper club" (our version of the "Stork Club"), with its "sexy bar", glass-topped baby grand and "retro-chic decor"; "butter-soft steak" and the "best crab imperial around" win it top ratings for food (it's No. 2 for Popularity) in this year's *Baltimore Survey*; devotees say it "blows away the chains" by making each diner "feel special."

Rudys' 2900 🅂 26 | 22 | 24 | $39

2900 Baltimore Blvd. (Rte. 91), Finksburg, 410-833-5777

■ At their "marvelous" Continental-American "classic" in Finksburg, the "two Rudys are always on their toes": Rudy Speckamp, a "champion" chef, keeps his "consistently fine food" fresh with regional and "Austrian innovations", while Rudy Paul and his "very knowledgeable staff" orchestrate a "special dining experience" for each table; though a few shrug "too far from town", most maintain it's "worth the trip."

Ruth's Chris Steak House 🅂 24 | 22 | 23 | $44

600 Water St. (bet. Gay St. & Market Pl.), 410-783-0033

■ "You get what you pay for" at this chain cow palace: butter-drenched beef, "fancy" New Orleans decor and "extraordinary" courtesy; but some seem to find Ruth's "formula" a little too "different tasting", "pricey" or "not personally engaging."

Tersiguel's 🅂 25 | 23 | 24 | $40

8293 Main St. (Old Columbia Pike), Ellicott City, 410-465-4004

■ At their "charming", lace-curtained 1890 townhouse in Ellicott City, the Tersiguel family, which "has and meets high standards", "makes dining out a special warm occasion" that captures the spirit of the French countryside; their "wonderful cooking" is served in a "take-your-time atmosphere" that lets diners savor the meal and "excellent" wines; if it seems a bit "stuffy" at first, it soon "thaws."

Tio Pepe 🅂 25 | 22 | 22 | $38

10 E. Franklin St. (bet. Charles & St. Paul Sts.), 410-539-4675

◪ An "institution" and the *Baltimore Survey*'s favorite restaurant, this Downtown Spanish-Continental is one of those places people love to hate – they complain about being "treated like cattle" and made to "wait with reservations" in a "whitewashed dungeon"; however, loyalists like the "great garlic shrimp", roast pig and "excellent" sangria served in "cozy nooks" that are synonymous with "classy" "celebrations" and "fun."

208 Talbot 🅂 27 | 23 | 24 | $39

208 N. Talbot St. (bet. Dodson Ave. & North St.), St. Michaels, 410-745-3838

■ "Superb" is how surveyors summarize this St. Michaels New American whose "fine kitchen" exemplifies "culinary creativity at its best"; set in a "romantic" townhouse, diners feel like they're "eating in a private home", albeit one that's overseen by a "great" staff; overall, it's considered "the greatest treat", "très chic and worth every penny."

TOP 20 FOOD RANKING

	Restaurant	Cuisine Type
28	Aujourd'hui	New American
	L'Espalier	Classic French
	Olives	Eclectic
27	Hamersley's Bistro	French Bistro/New Amer.
	Saporito's	Northern Italian
	Rialto	Mediterranean
	Caffe Bella	Mediterranean
26	Julien	Classic French
	Il Capriccio	Northern Italian
	White Rainbow	Continental/New Amer.
	Morton's of Chicago	Steakhouse
	Marcuccio's	N/S Italian
	Cafe Louis	New French
	Grill 23 & Bar	Seafood/Steakhouse
	Ginza	Japanese
	Icarus	New American
	Salamander	Asian/Eclectic
	Terramia	N/S Italian
25	Anago	New American
	Biba	Eclectic/New American

OTHER IMPORTANT PLACES

Ambrosia	Asian/New French
Blue Ginger	Asian/Eclectic
Clio	New French
Elephant Walk	Cambodian/New French
La Bettola	Eclectic/Italian
Legal Sea Foods	Seafood
Maison Robert	Classic French
Mistral	New French
No. 9 Park	Eclectic/New American
Pignoli	N/S Italian
Pomodoro	N/S Italian
Ritz-Carlton Din. Rm.	Classic French
Rowes Wharf	Regional American
Seasons	New American
Silks	New French
Tremont 647	Eclectic
Zinc	New French

	F	D	S	C
Ambrosia on Huntington S	25	25	23	$45

116 Huntington Ave. (opposite Marriott Copley), 617-247-2400

◪ The decor is "fabulous" and Tony Ambrose's "beautifully sculpted" French-Asian fusion fare is equally "eye-pleasing" at this Back Bay standout; though an insistent minority finds it "pretentious all-around", even they agree that this "grand dining room" is "good for impressing" anyone from a client to a date.

Anago S | 25 | – | 23 | $36

Lenox Hotel, 65 Exeter St. (Boylston St.), 617-266-6222

■ Now in new quarters in the Lenox Hotel (thus outdating its decor rating), this New American owned by husband and wife team Bob Calderone and Susan Finegold may no longer be the small hidden "gem" that it was in its former Cambridge home, but admirers hope that its knack for turning "superb ingredients" into "delicious" bistro fare will "survive the move" to the Back Bay.

Aujourd'hui ◐ S | 28 | 28 | 29 | $56

Four Seasons Hotel, 200 Boylston St. (bet. Arlington & S. Charles Sts.), 617-351-2071

■ "Elegant and sublime", this New American in the Four Seasons Hotel takes the triple crown as Boston's No. 1 for Food, Decor and Service; exuding "pure class", it offers a "beautiful experience" complete with "heavenly flavors", "exquisite service", "peace and quiet" and a "wonderful view of the Public Garden"; naturally, such "blissful indulgence" is "expensive", but savvy surveyors say "try the prix fixe."

Biba S | 25 | 25 | 22 | $46

272 Boylston St. (bet. Arlington & S. Charles Sts.), 617-426-7878

◪ Lydia Shire and Susan Regis' Back Bay Eclectic–New American combines "urban chic" with an "exotic, creative menu"; meals begin with the "best bread" and continue with "unusual" dishes served in a "dramatic" Adam Tihany–designed setting; on the downside, service still earns a "snobby" label and some feel the kitchen "tries too hard to be avant-garde."

Blue Ginger S | – | – | – | E

583 Washington St. (Rte. 16), Wellesley, 781-283-5790

East meets West in Wellesley where Ming Tsai (ex Santa Fe's Santacafe) is wowing 'em with such strikingly presented Asian-Eclectic dishes as duck with chile-laced raisin chutney; an open kitchen occupies a large corner of the rectangular room whose design received heavy input from a feng shui master who obviously understood the gestalt of the chef because, like the fare, the space manages to be simultaneously soothing and stimulating.

Cafe Louis | 26 | 21 | 23 | $39

234 Berkeley St. (Newbury St.), 617-266-4680

■ "A little gem in a clothing store" (Louis of Boston), this Back Bay New French may be "cramped" but the "superb" fare wins raves, as do the "great presentations" ("gives tall food a good name"); since it's now under the guidance of George Germon and Johanne Killeen of Providence's Al Forno fame, things can only get better.

Caffe Bella | 27 | 19 | 22 | $33

19 Warren St. (Main St. & Rte. 139), Randolph, 781-961-7729

■ Though "no longer a secret", Patrick Barnes' "excellent" Mediterranean fare still has fans shaking their heads and saying "I can't believe it's in Randolph"; the strip mall location means it's "tiny", "crowded" and "noisy", and no reserving means a "long wait", but it's "worth it" to enjoy "wonderfully fresh", "real Tuscan food" and other delights that earn it "best on the South Shore" accolades; special note is made of the "super wine list."

	F	D	S	C
Clio S ▽	26	27	26	$47

Eliot Hotel, 370 Commonwealth Ave. (Mass Ave.), 617-536-7200
■ "Destined to be a big star" is the word on this swank Parisian-style supper club in the Eliot Hotel, where a plush bar leads to the dining room decked out in banquettes and a leopard skin rug; Ken Oringer (ex Silks in San Francisco) uses big flavors to expand on New French fare; all in all, it's "somewhat expensive" but "superb."

	F	D	S	C
Elephant Walk S	24	21	20	$28

900 Beacon St. (Park Dr.), 617-247-1500
2067 Mass Ave. (bet. Hadley & Russell Sts.), Cambridge, 617-492-6900
◪ A "unique" French-Cambodian blend yields "exotic atmosphere, tastes and textures" at this "attractive", family-run Kenmore Square and Porter Square duo where "novel" fare (including *mee siem*, a noodle dish, and "mind-blowing tuna with chile") plus a "great" beer list "reward the adventurous diner"; though dissenters cite "arrogant staff" and feel it's "slipping", the majority says "wild elephants couldn't keep us away" from such "intriguing" flavors.

	F	D	S	C
Ginza S	26	18	19	$26

16 Hudson St. (bet. Beach & Kneeland Sts.), 617-338-2261 ◐
1002 Beacon St. (St. Mary's St.), Brookline, 617-566-9688
■ Bringing a "bit of Tokyo to Beantown", this "crowded" Chinatown Japanese and its younger Beacon Street sibling earn plaudits for their "inventive", "work of art" fare, with the lion's share of praise going to "awesome", "sublime sushi" that's "whimsical" and "dazzlingly prepared"; kudos also go to the "helpful staff", good sake, "late" hours in Chinatown and easier parking in Brookline.

	F	D	S	C
Grill 23 & Bar S	26	23	25	$42

161 Berkeley St. (Stuart St.), 617-542-2255
◪ "What an experience – from the meat to the cigars" say fans of this "brassy" Back Bay steak and seafooder offering "excellent steak and fish" along with "superb service" and a "great wine list"; if some find the "noise" and smoke "intolerable", most say that for "old-fashioned red meat" dining you "can't go wrong" – just bring an "expense account" and "your 'old boy network' friends."

	F	D	S	C
Hamersley's Bistro S	27	24	24	$44

553 Tremont St. (Clarendon St.), 617-423-2700
■ Gordon Hamersley's South End French-American bistro is even "better since it expanded" according to its many admirers; the "sublime seasonal" fare, including the never-out-of-season "garlic chicken", is backed up by "gorgeous" decor, "impeccable service" and an "interesting wine list"; a few dissenters find it "overrated" and pricey, but for most it's "worth every cent."

	F	D	S	C
Icarus S	26	25	24	$41

3 Appleton St. (bet. Arlington & Berkeley Sts.), 617-426-1790
■ "Lovely" sums up this South End New American that has long been considered a "romantic" "date place" as well as a "clubby", "special event celebration" venue; "the best game preparations" are a highlight of the "gussied-up", "adventurous" menu, which is served in a "charming", "soothing" setting by a "helpful" staff; what more could one ask for? – how about "very good brunches" and "great" Friday night jazz in the lounge.

Il Capriccio
26 | 21 | 23 | $40

888 Main St. (Prospect St.), Waltham, 781-894-2234

■ "A jewel in the suburbs"; Richard Barron's "consistently excellent" Northern Italian fare and Jeanne Rogers' wine expertise earn this "romantic hideaway" votes as "best of the many in Waltham"; a "stylish" art deco setting that "feels like Downtown" serves as backdrop for food that's "serious" and "quite inspired"; toss in "intelligent" wine events and you have real "Boston quality", with "prices to match."

Julien
26 | 27 | 26 | $53

Le Meridien Hotel, 250 Franklin St. (bet. Oliver & Pearl Sts.), 617-451-1900

◪ "Prepare to be pampered" at this "elegant", "very French" hotel dining room; a bastion of "fine dining", it offers "sophisticated food in a sophisticated setting", but you'd better have a "sophisticated wallet" as well; still, given the "superb" French fare, "outstanding service" ("everything is done right") and one of "the most beautiful" rooms in town, the majority deems it "worth every penny."

La Bettola ◐ S
– | – | – | E

480A Columbus Ave. (W. Newton St.), 617-236-5252

The owners of Galleria Italiana have brought in Rene Michelina (ex NYC's Sign of the Dove) to oversee this small, noisy South End Eclectic-Italian designed to resemble a hidden Roman alley; the name means 'little neighborhood place', but the ambitious menu covers wider ground, with many Asian nuances (i.e. turmeric-scented pesto, gingered caponata); the third restaurant in this space, it looks like it has strong enough legs to last the course.

Legal Sea Foods S
22 | 15 | 18 | $27

Prudential Ctr., 800 Boylston St. (bet. Fairfield & Gloucester Sts.), 617-266-6800
Copley Pl., 100 Huntington Ave. (bet. Dartmouth & Exeter Sts.), 617-266-7775
Park Plaza Hotel, 35 Columbus Ave. (Arlington St.), 617-426-4444
Burlington Mall, 1131 Middlesex Tpke. (Rte. 128), Burlington, 781-270-9700
5 Cambridge Ctr. (bet. Ames & Main Sts.), Cambridge, 617-864-3400
43 Boylston St. (Hammond Pond Pkwy.), Chestnut Hill, 617-277-7300
Miltons Plaza, 1400 Worcester Rd. (bet. Speen St. & Rte. 126), Natick, 508-820-1115
Northshore Mall, Rtes. 114 & 128, Peabody, 978-532-4500

◪ Boston's top vote-getter, this seafood chain under the command of Roger Berkowitz and newly installed exec chef Jasper White is a true "institution"; "consistent" and "comfortable like an old shoe", it has always excelled at "fresh fish, done simply", and fans feel that White's menu tinkering has "made a great thing better"; faultfinders cite "mall atmosphere", "high prices" and "boring" fare, but they're a minority – expect a "wait" at every branch.

L'Espalier
28 | 27 | 27 | $63

30 Gloucester St. (bet. Commonwealth Ave. & Newbury St.), 617-262-3023

■ Like dining in someone's "elegant" parlor, Frank McClelland's Back Bay French provides "incredible" food (rated No. 2 in Boston) and "superb service" to go along with the "exquisite" townhouse setting; though the "limited menu" is "prix fixe only" and "perfection comes with a serious price tag", for "special occasions" devotees place it "in a class by itself"; a few find it "stiff" and "precious" ("we had to whisper"), but such is life in "heaven's dining hall."

Maison Robert 24 24 24 $43

Old City Hall, 45 School St. (bet. Tremont & Washington Sts.), 617-227-3370

◪ "Classy" and "trustworthy" describes the Robert family's Old City Hall French, "a Boston institution" known for "impeccable, traditional food", yet there have been "changes" lately – namely, installing Jacky Robert as chef, which admirers say has resulted in an "improved" menu; foes find the place "stuffy" and "overrated", but to most, its "calm", "protected" "elegance" makes it "special"; P.S. Ben's Cafe downstairs "has to be the best value in town."

Marcuccio's S ⊄ 26 21 20 $30

125 Salem St. (bet. Parmenter & Prince Sts.), 617-723-1807

◪ At this North Ender, Charles Draghi's modern slant on Italian cuisine produces "innovative", "New Age" creations as well as "wonderful" traditional dishes; though it may "still be working out some service kinks", the "nouvelle" fare, "great tasting menu" (a bargain) and "imaginative decor" have many surveyors proclaiming Draghi "a rising star" and his restaurant "a terrific new find."

Mistral S 23 25 23 $41

223 Columbus Ave. (Berkeley St.), 617-867-9300

◪ The long-awaited venture of chef Jamie Mammano (formerly of Aujourd'hui) and nightclub impresario Seth Greenberg, this South End Provençal has quickly impressed fans who say it's "soon to be the hottest spot" in town thanks to "very good food" from a menu with "excellent variety" and "beautiful" decor likened to the "Delano Hotel in South Beach"; even with what some see as "too much attitude" and inconsistency, it's "already a place to be seen."

Morton's of Chicago S 26 18 23 $44

1 Exeter Plaza (Boylston St.), 617-266-5858

■ "Excellent steaks in a basement" sums up this Back Bay subterranean outpost of the Chicago chain; while the room doesn't thrill, it has the requisite "old boys' club feel" plus "terrific meat", a "solid wine list" and "great service"; some feel there's too much noise and too little space between tables, but for most this is "what steak and potatoes ought to be" – "if your company pays."

No. 9 Park – – – E

9 Park St. (bet. Beacon & Tremont Sts.), 617-742-9991

It didn't take long for Barbara Lynch's (ex Galleria Italiana and Figs) much-anticipated New American–Eclectic close to the State House to become hot; grab a table in one of the two dining rooms – an airy one in the back or the tightly packed one up front with a lovely view of the Common – then tuck into one of her daring, busy plates; the wine list is a treasure trove of bottles and, thanks to a well-schooled staff, simple enough to decipher.

Olives 28 22 22 $43

10 City Sq. (bet. Main & Park Sts.), Charlestown, 617-242-1999

◪ With "extremely creative" food, Todd English's Charlestown Eclectic is again Boston's Most Popular restaurant; sure, there are "drawbacks" – "noise", crowds and "nearly intolerable" waits due to no reserving except for large groups – but most feel it's "worth the discomfort" to enjoy "beautifully presented" food; dissenters who find "too many tastes" on the plate and "rushed service" are easily outvoted by those who say "everything works."

Pignoli S | 24 | 24 | 22 | $41

79 Park Plaza (Arlington St.), 617-338-7500

◪ Lydia Shire's 'other' restaurant (besides Biba) brings "refined" modern Italian dining and "sizzling decor" to Park Square; to most the "electric atmosphere" is "cool" and the menu is "different" and "bold", but some call it "poshly sterile" and object to paying "big bucks for tiny portions" of food that's "occasionally too weird."

Pomodoro S⊄ | 25 | 13 | 18 | $28

319 Hanover St. (bet. Prince & Richmond Sts.), 617-367-4348

◪ A "hole-in-the-wall" Italian North Ender where "tight quarters" ("packed like sardines") and bathrooms two doors down don't deter those seeking "great, simple, fresh food", from seafood to "perfect pasta"; if the specials sometimes "try too hard", it's still "a cut above most in the North End", which explains the "long lines."

Rialto S | 27 | 26 | 25 | $46

Charles Hotel, 1 Bennett St. (Harvard Sq.), Cambridge, 617-661-5050

■ Jody Adams' "big, bold" Mediterranean fare is offered in a "swank" Harvard Square setting, making for an evening that's both "comforting and elegant"; "invigorating" and "intriguing" are typical comments on the menu, and though some cite "high-attitude staff", most consider it "one of the best, and getting better."

Ritz-Carlton Dining Room S | 24 | 26 | 26 | $52

Ritz-Carlton, 15 Arlington St. (Newbury St.), 617-536-5700

■ "Old-world charm", fine Classic French food courtesy of chef Mark Allen (ex Ritz Cafe) and "gracious service" await diners at this classy hotel's second-floor dining room overlooking the Public Garden; perhaps the kitchen "isn't the ultimate, but the elegance is", and though it may be "a bit stuffy" and more than a bit pricey, surveyors agree it's "worth it" – after all, "this is the Ritz."

Rowes Wharf S | 25 | 26 | 24 | $47

Boston Harbor Hotel, 70 Rowes Wharf (Atlantic Ave.), 617-439-3995

■ "Fabulous views" across the Harbor enhance Daniel Bruce's "imaginative", modern New England cooking at this "elegant" hotel dining room; his "seasonal" menus are "daring but never silly", and though opinions on the service vary ("pleasant" vs. "stiff"), all like the "beautiful decor" and "luscious Sunday brunch."

Salamander | 26 | 24 | 23 | $42

1 Athenaeum St. (1st St.), Cambridge, 617-225-2121

◪ "Zesty" describes both the food and open kitchen setting at this Cambridge Asian-Eclectic where Stan Frankenthaler's "unthought-of food combinations" provide "a festival of tastes" "bursting with good ideas"; while most enjoy his "party on a plate" creations, critics feel they can be "too busy", but "creative" is the key word and fans wish the "limited menu" offered more choice.

Saporito's S | 27 | 19 | 24 | $33

11 Rockland Circle (George Washington Blvd.), Hull, 781-925-3023

◪ "Creative but not annoyingly trendy", this husband-and-wife-run Tuscan in Hull offers "Boston quality" at "Hull prices"; one diner's "cozy", "casual" decor is another's "no atmosphere", but quibbles over "plain booths" and "uncomfortable chairs" fade in the face of "inventive" fare that "gets better and better"; "friendly staff" is another plus at this "quirky spot" that's "worth the drive."

Seasons S 25 | 24 | 24 | $46

Regal Bostonian Hotel, 9 Blackstone St. N. (North St.), 617-523-4119

◪ A "comfortable" yet "truly elegant" "dining experience" is what most enjoy at Michael Taylor's New American with a "lovely view" of Faneuil Hall; it offers "fancy food" and "fancy service" at "fancy prices", but supporters say "you get your money's worth"; if "not quite as good as it was", it's still "special" for a "celebratory" meal.

Silks S 24 | 26 | 23 | $46

Stonehedge Inn, 160 Pawtucket Blvd. (Rte. 113), Tyngsboro, 978-649-4400

■ This "stylish" restaurant/inn "in Tyngsboro of all places" is "worth the ride from Boston" (45 minutes) for "fine" New French dining enhanced by an "outstanding wine list"; its brand of "European country elegance" comes with fireplaces, good service and extras like wine tasting dinners; though this "sleeper" can be a bit sleepy, it's a "charming" place to take "that special someone."

Terramia S 26 | 18 | 21 | $31

98 Salem St. (Parmenter St.), 617-523-3112

■ Surveyors are uniform in their praise for Mario Nocera's "simple, upscale gourmet Italian" fare at this North Ender that seems to be "outside the [North End] mold"; though "small and noisy", its food "stands above the rest", even if the "lack of coffee and dessert" (typical in the North End) strikes some as "a real pain."

Tremont 647 S 22 | 19 | 20 | $32

647 Tremont St. (W. Brookline St.), 617-266-4600

◪ Andy Husbands' "superb" Eclectic is a "hot", "happening South End gathering place" where diners begin with "the best martinis in town" and move on to "exciting" food from an open kitchen; doubters say it sometimes "tries a little too hard" and complaints are aimed at "noise" and "attitude with a capital A", yet most consider it a "nice new find."

White Rainbow S 26 | 22 | 25 | $41

65 Main St. (Rogers St.), Gloucester, 978-281-0017

■ "Gloucester's best", this Continental–New American in a "historic" building offers outstanding food and wines in a "fantastic setting" with a "quiet ambiance"; it's "unique" and the "new owner seems to be maintaining consistency", so while it may be "hard to find", it's well worth the effort.

Zinc ◐ S 21 | 20 | 19 | $40

35 Stanhope St. (bet. Berkeley & Clarendon Sts.), 617-262-2323

◪ This Back Bay New French near the Mass Pike is a "happening", with all the pluses and minuses that implies; while most surveyors praise Nick Tischler's food ("crystal clear flavors", "good bistro fare like you'd find in Paris"), many report that "small portions", high prices and "large doses of attitude" and "noise" make it "less desirable"; "handsome decor" and a "sleek bar" are pluses.

Chicago

TOP 20 FOOD RANKING

	Restaurant	Cuisine Type
29	Le Français	Classic French
28	Ambria	New French
	Carlos'	New French
	Tallgrass	New French
27	Le Titi de Paris	New French
	Topolobampo	Mexican
	Ritz-Carlton Din. Rm.	New French
	Arun's	Thai
	Charlie Trotter's	New American
	Everest	New French
	Trio	Eclectic
	Seasons	New American
26	Frontera Grill	Mexican
	Morton's of Chicago	Steakhouse
	Mesón Sabika	Spanish/Tapas
	Bistro Banlieue	French Bistro
25	Courtright's	New American
	Fond de la Tour	Classic French
	Gabriel's	Italian/New French
	Gordon	New American

OTHER IMPORTANT PLACES

Aubriot	New French
Cafe 36	Classic French
Coco Pazzo	Northern Italian
Crofton on Wells	New American
Emilio's Tapas Bar	Spanish/Tapas
Entre Nous	Regional American
Gibsons Steakhse.	Steakhouse
Harvest on Huron	New American
KiKi's Bistro	French Bistro
Le Bouchon	French Bistro
Les Nomades	Classic French
Le Vichyssois	New French
Mango	American/Eclectic
Mia Francesca	Northern Italian
Montparnasse	Classic French
Nick's Fishmarket	Seafood
one sixtyblue	New American
Park Avenue Cafe	New American
Pasteur Cafe	Vietnamese
Printer's Row	New American
Rhapsody	New American
Spago	Californian
Spiaggia	N/S Italian
Spruce	New American
302 West	New American
Va Pensiero	N/S Italian
Zealous	New American

Ambria | 28 | 27 | 28 | $62

2300 N. Lincoln Park W. (Belden Ave.), 773-472-5959

■ This Contemporary French "special occasion" jewel garnered the No. 2 spot across the board for Food, Decor and Service in our *Chicago Survey* and requires both jackets and (far in advance) reservations for entry; surveyors rave about chef Gabino Sotelino's "superb" cuisine, an art nouveau interior that's "classy but unpretentious" and service so attentive, one person testifies "I was afraid to scratch my nose for fear that three waiters would appear with Kleenex"; and romantics, listen up – this is *the* place "for a middle-aged man to propose marriage."

Arun's S | 27 | 24 | 25 | VE

4156 N. Kedzie Ave. (2 blocks north of Irving Park Rd.), 773-539-1909

■ An "awesome culinary experience" awaits those who trek to this North Side Thai where Arun Sampanthavivat offers "impeccable", "top-drawer" cuisine so beautifully presented that "you eat with your eyes first"; while at the time of our *Chicago Survey*, many respondents recommended the $75 tasting menu, raving that "there's nothing else like it in North America", it's now the only way to order, which will further disappoint the minority that already gripes about "astronomical prices" and "microscopic portions."

Aubriot S | – | – | – | E

1962 N. Halsted St. (Armitage Ave.), 773-281-4211

Simplicity and clean flavors are the hallmarks of this ambitious Contemporary French from ex Carlos' chef Eric Aubriot; the small dining room is unfussy and very attractive, as are the relatively friendly prices, both of which are finding favor among the Halsted Street restaurant crowd.

Bistro Banlieue S | 26 | 20 | 23 | $31

44 Yorktown Convenience Ctr. (Butterfield Rd. & Highland Ave.), Lombard, 630-629-6560

■ For the third straight year, this "outpost of taste" in DuPage County is the highest-rated bistro in the *Chicago Survey*, earning raves for "terrific food" with "well-layered flavors" and such customer-friendly touches as petite portions of some entrees and monthly wine dinners; the "improbable" strip mall location aside, this "real suburban treasure" "could be a star even in the city."

Cafe 36 S | 24 | 18 | 22 | $33

365 La Grange Rd. (Harris St.), La Grange, 708-354-5722

■ "A real sleeper", this "underrated" ("I don't know of a restaurant that tries harder") West Suburban French specializes in wild game and "extraordinary sauces"; it garners kudos for a menu that "runs with the big dogs in the city" and might be "too great for its setting."

Carlos' S | 28 | 24 | 27 | $63

429 Temple Ave. (bet. Green Bay & Half Day Rds.), Highland Park, 847-432-0770

■ Despite the "ups and downs" of a "chef shuffle", this "small, romantic" North Shore French still remains "a treasure" – "everyone is treated like royalty" by owners Carlos and Debbie Nieto and "every meal is a special occasion"; there are a few scattered quibbles about the high prices, but consistently high marks bear out the sentiment that it's "still one of the best" for "a memorable evening"; N.B. there's no corkage fee on Mondays.

Charlie Trotter's 27 | 26 | 27 | $92

816 W. Armitage Ave. (Halsted St.), 773-248-6228

◪ Voted the most popular restaurant in our *Chicago Survey*, Charlie Trotter's Lincoln Park temple to New American dining wins raves for his "master of his own domain", never-repeat-a-dish approach and painstakingly presented dishes that are "like going to an art show on plates"; while some find it all "too precious" and "stuffy", many others opine "we will never have a better meal."

Coco Pazzo S 24 | 22 | 22 | $38

300 W. Hubbard St. (Franklin St.), 312-836-0900

■ "A sure winner" say fans of this NYC import where "amazing", "sophisticated" Tuscan cuisine and a "classy but homey" atmosphere add up to a "topflight" dining experience Downtown; the food is "about as good as Italian gets in this town" and the "attentive", "well-informed" service makes it a "fine celebratory choice", though some wish it would "lose the New York prices."

Courtright's S 25 | 26 | 24 | $41

8989 S. Archer Ave. (2 blocks west of Willow Springs Rd.), Willow Springs, 708-839-8000

■ "A perfect 10" "headed for four stars" enthuse supporters of this South Suburban American that's a "high aspiration" operation with "wonderful food", a "top-notch" (600-label) wine list and a "unique" setting featuring double-height windows that showcase forest preserve vistas; "what one expects and doesn't always get Downtown" says one convert to this "gem in the 'burbs."

Crofton on Wells 24 | 19 | 20 | $40

535 N. Wells St. (bet. Grand Ave. & Ohio St.), 312-755-1790

■ This River North American marked chef Suzy Crofton's "dazzling debut" in mid-'97 and praise for her "world-class", "nuanced cooking" continues to build, even though her "very tasteful" dining room – which seats fewer than 75 – makes reservations mandatory and difficult to obtain; some suggest that the place "needs polish", particularly on the service end, but overall, this "jewel among newcomers" is a "keeper."

Emilio's Tapas Bar & Restaurant S 22 | 19 | 20 | $26

444 W. Fullerton Ave. (Clark St.), 773-327-5100
4100 W. Roosevelt Rd. (Mannheim Rd.), Hillside, 708-547-7177

■ These Lakeview and West Suburban flagships of Emilio Gervilla's empire inspire fierce loyalty among fans who laud the "superb", "always interesting menu choices" and swear that "no other tapas compare"; scattered complaints that "it gets pretty expensive" are countered with "it's cheaper than a plane ticket to Spain."

Entre Nous 25 | 26 | 25 | $51

Fairmont Hotel, 200 N. Columbus Dr. (Wacker Dr.), 312-565-7997

■ For "lovely hotel dining", it's hard to outdo this "elegant" Regional American room east of Michigan Avenue, whose lavish appointments and soft piano music make it "a place for a special dinner"; although "it looks like it needs people", the atmosphere is "so romantic, you can recharge your love here" (or slip over to the gift shop for new batteries).

Everest 27 | 27 | 27 | $73

One Financial Plaza, 440 S. LaSalle St., 40th fl. (Congress Pkwy.), 312-663-8920

■ A Top 10 scorer in Food and Service and No. 1 in Decor, this Downtown New French showcases "the most beautiful view in Chicago" from its 40th-floor aerie; chef Jean Joho's "attention to subtle detail shines through" a "wonderfully creative" menu that's tempered with a "touch of Alsace"; factor in "impeccable service", "superb wines" and it's "clearly at the top of the mountain"; the only question that remains: "how do you get a window table?"

Fond de la Tour 25 | 24 | 24 | $42

40 N. Tower Rd. (bet. Butterfield & Meyers Rds.), Oak Brook, 630-620-1500

■ West Suburbanites in the mood to play dress-up head to this jacket-required Classic French, an "elegant, special" place where the food "is rich and fattening but oh, so good"; though some feel that the "menu is in a time warp" and the "decor is lagging behind 20 years", where else can you count on "an experience" like this?

Frontera Grill 26 | 21 | 22 | $29

445 N. Clark St. (bet. Hubbard & Illinois Sts.), 312-661-1434

■ "There aren't enough superlatives" to describe Rick Bayless' seminal River North restaurant, but that doesn't stop surveyors from trying; the praise rolls in for "the best Mexican in the US (take that, LA)" whose "imaginative", "scrumptious" food is "damn near perfect"; Bayless may be "a sorcerer", but he can't conjure up enough seats: "you could qualify for Social Security waiting."

Gabriel's 25 | 21 | 24 | $47

310 Green Bay Rd. (Highwood Ave.), Highwood, 847-433-0031

■ "As good as it gets" on the North Shore, this French-Italian hybrid marries a "first-class atmosphere" with "creative" food by "meticulous" chef-owner Gabriel Viti that "meets all expectations"; aesthetes add that the "open kitchen concept works well here."

Gibsons Steakhouse ◑ S 24 | 19 | 21 | $44

1028 N. Rush St. (bet. Bellevue Pl. & Oak St.), 312-266-8999

■ "Big steaks, tall martinis, long cigars and short skirts" make up the "good show" at this "loud", "glamorous" Rush Street steakhouse that draws a "colorful" mix of "who's who in Chicago" and conventioneers; there's also "wonderful" food, especially dessert, which consists of the "largest pieces of cake in the city."

Gordon S 25 | 25 | 24 | $48

500 N. Clark St. (Illinois St.), 312-467-9780

■ Gordon Sinclair's "cutting-edge" River North New American still wows 'em after 23 years with an "elegant" ambiance where an "oh so cool" crowd dons (required) jackets for dinner and the entrees are available in full and half-portions to encourage nibbling; it "gets better with age no matter who the chef is" (and there've been many) and Gordon himself "still has the magic touch."

Harvest on Huron ◑ S 24 | 21 | 20 | $40

217 W. Huron St. (bet. Franklin & Wells Sts.), 312-587-9600

◪ Chef Alan Sternweiler's "delicious", "interesting" New American fare and an interior that's "pure elegance" are why many dub this River North spot a "best newcomer", "along with Crofton on Wells"; but the Harvest also yields more than a few complaints of "inattentive" service and "unacceptably loud" noise.

	F	D	S	C
KiKi's Bistro	24	22	23	$35

900 N. Franklin St. (bet. Chicago Ave. & Oak St.), 312-335-5454

■ There's beaucoup praise for this "très, très bien" bistro, just north of River North, with cooking "so wonderful you can't wait to go back" and "superb service"; a "real charmer", its "cozy" ambiance makes some feel they're in Provence and it's so "ideal for a romantic date" that many devotees wish "it stayed open later."

	F	D	S	C
Le Bouchon	24	18	21	$33

1958 N. Damen Ave. (Armitage Ave.), 773-862-6600

■ "Pinch me, I'm in Paris" marvel those who secure a table in this "tiny", "cozy" Bucktown bistro, which the smitten promote as home to "the best French food in the city", citing the "great" onion tart and "amazing" roast duck for two; though the noise level makes the "cramped" dining room "no place for conversation", fans shrug "who cares – I love this place."

	F	D	S	C
Le Français	29	27	28	$77

269 S. Milwaukee Ave. (bet. Dundee & Willow Rds.), Wheeling, 847-541-7470

■ Once again, surveyors rate this Wheeling wonder the "epitome of good taste and tastes" and Chicago's No. 1 in Food and Service; it's "what the Bulls are to basketball", thanks to Roland Liccioni's "incomparable" French cooking and his wife and pastry chef Mary Beth's supervision of an "excellent" dining room staff that sees everything ("they even have reading glasses for people who forget"); while "perfection" doesn't come cheap, lunch and the early bird are relative bargains.

	F	D	S	C
Les Nomades	25	23	24	$58

222 E. Ontario St. (1½ blocks east of Michigan Ave.), 312-649-9010

◪ Owned by the Liccionis of Le Français, this city sibling just off the Mag Mile earns stellar, if not as spectacular, marks from surveyors who call the Classic French cooking "luscious" and the cheese course "the best in town"; "the sophisticated ambiance" lends a "secluded feeling" – not unlike the private club it used to be – so while a few find it "snooty" and "stuffy" (jacket required and "hushed tones necessary here"), that's how regulars like it.

	F	D	S	C
Le Titi de Paris	27	25	26	$55

1015 W. Dundee Rd. (Kennicott St.), Arlington Heights, 847-506-0222

■ "How does Pierre Pollin do it?" ask awestruck surveyors who find this more than 25-year-old Northwest Suburban French "still alive with new ideas" – well, let's give chef de cuisine Michael Maddox some credit; in addition, a "wonderful welcome at the door", a "warm", "attentive" staff and prices that are, relatively speaking, an "amazing bargain" contribute to the "fond memories."

	F	D	S	C
Le Vichyssois S	24	22	22	$47

220 W. Rte. 120 (2 mi. west of Rte. 12), Lakemoor, 815-385-8221

■ Bernard Cretier's pioneering Far Northwest Suburban is "a long trip from anywhere", but acolytes happily fill up their gas tanks for "superb" Contemporary French in a charming country setting – a freestanding building that makes some proclaim "now *this* is a roadhouse!"; the atmosphere is "romantic" and it's "the best value in the area."

Mango 🅂 22 | 18 | 20 | $33

712 N. Clark St. (Superior St.), 312-337-5440

■ An "intimate" and "inventive" American-Eclectic that's one of the most popular spots in River North owing to Steven Chiappetti's "robust and flavorful" menu and "spectacular presentations"; only a few gripes ("what's all the fuss about?") surface amid raves for an "absolute must" that may be "cramped" and "noisy, but worth it."

Mesón Sabika 🅂 26 | 25 | 23 | $28

(fka Emilio's Meson Sabika)

1025 Aurora Ave. (bet. Rte. 59 & Washington St.), Naperville, 630-983-3000

Northfield Village Ctr., 310 Happ Rd. (Willow Rd.), Northfield, 847-784-9300

■ Though Emilio Gervilla has left this Naperville Spaniard (he sold out to former partners), "the dining is still great", winning raves for "splendid tapas" and "wonderful sangria"; those with a taste for "elegant surroundings" particularly appreciate the setting – a "romantic", "old white mansion" with a "gorgeous patio in summer"; N.B. the Northfield branch is new and unrated.

Mia Francesca 🅂 24 | 16 | 19 | $26

3311 N. Clark St. (School St.), 773-281-3310

■ The restaurant that launched three sequels is a Wrigleyville phenomenon – a no-reservations Italian where patrons "gladly line up or dine at 5 PM" to secure a precious table; skeptics wonder what "makes it the Microsoft" of the Chicago scene, while pros praise "always delicious" and "affordable" food, especially the "superb pastas", and, of course, the "great people-watching."

Montparnasse 25 | 22 | 23 | $48

200 E. Fifth Ave. (east of Washington Blvd.), Naperville, 630-961-8203

■ "Special occasion restaurant" that some nominate as the "top French in the Western Suburbs"; "the area's prettiest room" features "absolutely outstanding food and service", leading loyalists to add that this gem "deserves more weekday patronage."

Morton's of Chicago 🅂 26 | 20 | 23 | $49

Newberry Plaza, 1050 N. State St., lower level (Maple St.), 312-266-4820

9525 W. Bryn Mawr Ave. (River Rd.), Rosemont, 847-678-5155

1 Westbrook Corporate Ctr. (22nd St. & Wolf Rd.), Westchester, 708-562-7000

■ Suveryors once again have voted Morton's the "best steakhouse in Chicago"; a "meat lover's paradise", it's built its reputation on "quality, aged steaks", plus "very attentive" service that some consider "the most consistent" around; there are those who feel the decor "needs an update", but why mess with success?

Nick's Fishmarket 24 | 23 | 24 | $48

1 First National Plaza, 79 W. Monroe St. (Clark St.), 312-621-0200

O'Hare International Ctr., 10275 W. Higgins Rd. (Mannheim Rd.), Rosemont, 847-298-8200 🅂

■ These Loop and airport-area, jacket-and-tie seafooders continue to be rated among the "tops in the city for fish" and "will wow you", even though they're "so expensive"; still, surveyors rationalize them as "anniversary restaurants" and "good for expense-account diners" looking for "swank" ambiance, "outstanding" service and "ahi that will send you into orbit"; N.B. post-*Survey*, when the Loop branch relocated in the same plaza, it added a more casual grill.

one sixtyblue S

F	D	S	C
–	–	–	E

160 N. Loomis St. (Randolph St.), 312-850-0303
The worst-kept secret in town is that this West Side Contemporary American (just blocks from the United Center) has Michael Jordan as a silent partner; but don't look for basketball memorabilia here – instead, there's Adam Tihany decor and dishes with culinary flash.

Park Avenue Cafe S

F	D	S	C
25	21	22	$46

Doubletree Guest Suites Hotel, 199 E. Walton Pl. (Mies van der Rohe Way), 312-944-4414
■ Fanciers of New American fare say Chicago's Streeterville sibling of this NYC original is an "oasis of class and service" with an "eclectic" menu served amid collectible Americana; the food is "exquisite", desserts are "too pretty to eat" and the "spectacular dim sum–style brunch" is a "fresh change"; for those who need extra convincing, it's all complemented by a "primo vino selection."

Pasteur Cafe S

F	D	S	C
24	23	19	$27

5525 N. Broadway (Bryn Mawr Ave.), 773-878-1061
■ Surveyors shout "welcome back!" to the top-rated Vietnamese in Chicago that's "better than ever" thanks to a "beautiful", more spacious new Edgewater location that's reminiscent of "old French Saigon"; look for "superb", "perfectly prepared" cuisine that's so popular that regulars advise going "late to avoid the noisy" crowds.

Printer's Row

F	D	S	C
25	21	23	$40

550 S. Dearborn St. (Congress Pkwy.), 312-461-0780
■ Reviewers have only "superlatives" for this "resilient" New American located south of the Loop and near the Auditorium Theater; it's "always a pleasure" to wade through Michael Foley's "innovative menu", especially for one of his "superb game dishes" ("best venison in the US"); an "attentive staff" contributes to an ambiance that's "perfect for pampering on that special occasion."

Rhapsody S

F	D	S	C
23	24	21	$35

CSO Symphony Ctr., 65 E. Adams St. (Wabash Ave.), 312-786-9911
■ Chef-partner Steven Chiappetti (Mango, Grapes) oversees this "innovative" American in the Loop's CSO Symphony Center, where you can expect "beautiful presentations that taste as good as they look" and are surprisingly affordable given the well-heeled, semi-captive audience; while only a corridor separates the dining room from the performance space, this "is more than just a pre-symphony locale"; indeed, given early-bird crowds, you can best appreciate it after the curtain goes up.

Ritz-Carlton Dining Room S

F	D	S	C
27	27	27	$59

Ritz-Carlton Hotel, 160 E. Pearson St. (Michigan Ave.), 312-573-5223
■ Chicago's highest-rated hotel restaurant showcases chef Sarah Stegner's "perfect" Contemporary French food and a cheese cart "so good it can't be legal"; factor in "outstanding service" that "makes you feel like a millionaire" and "classy yet unpretentious" decor, and it's no surprise that reviewers think dinner is akin to "a three-hour vacation"; P.S. Sunday brunch is "absolutely awesome."

Seasons S | 27 | 26 | 27 | $59

Four Seasons Hotel, 120 E. Delaware Pl., 7th fl. (bet. Michigan Ave. & Rush St.), 312-649-2349

■ "You feel you've arrived" when dining at this "lots of moolah" Michigan Avenue hotel room where "wonderful service", "beautiful decor" and Mark Baker's "delicious", "innovative" New American food add up to "first-class" dining; while it makes a "wonderful anniversary restaurant", surveyors say don't overlook the awe-inspiring brunch that's among "the best in Chicago."

Spago S | 24 | 22 | 22 | $42

520 N. Dearborn St. (Grand Ave.), 312-527-3700

◪ Chicagoans have embraced Wolfgang Puck's satellite and say it "deserves its hype", thanks to "puckishly delightful" (ouch) Cal cuisine and "excellent service with no attitude"; insiders advise "try the smoked salmon pizza" (it isn't always on the menu, but you can order it) and other "witty, wood-fired" pies, and check out the less pricey grill room; the main dining room is "beautiful" and a "great show", but "noisy."

Spiaggia S | 25 | 26 | 24 | $52

One Magnificent Mile Bldg., 980 N. Michigan Ave., 2nd fl. (Oak St.), 312-280-2750

■ Scores are as high as the prices at this luxury Italian that's "by far the city's best"; Paul Bartolotta's pastas are "phenomenal" ("the tortellini can make you cry"), but you "can't get a bad meal" regardless of what you order; the "romantic", "vibrant dining room" is "beautiful", as are its "spectacular views" of the lake and Michigan Avenue; add "exquisite service" that is "dedicated to detail" and you have "a great place to impress whomever you're with."

Spruce S | 23 | 23 | 23 | $49

230 E. Ontario St. (bet. Fairbanks & St. Clair Sts.), 312-642-3757

◪ The departure in mid-'98 of chef Keith Luce from this Streeterville New American leaves surveyors hoping the "innovative" and "artful" food will continue; the "gorgeous room" and remarkable wine list remain unchanged, of course, and the minority who found Luce's cooking "contrived" may be eager for a fresh face.

Tallgrass S | 28 | 23 | 26 | $58

1006 S. State St. (10th St.), Lockport, 815-838-5566

■ "Charming [Victorian] period decor" and "service so unobtrusive it's almost scary" are two highlights of this far-flung New French, the sophisticated sibling of Public Landing in historic Lockport; while it's a "long drive", Robert Burcenski's "outstanding" cooking is "creativity personified" and so, as "the suburban [restaurant equivalent of] Everest", it's "worth the trip."

302 West ▽ | 25 | 23 | 23 | $46

302 W. State St. (3rd St.), Geneva, 630-232-9302

■ Set in a "lovely" refurbished bank building, this "outstanding" Far West Suburban New American offers a "sophisticated menu" of "innovative cooking", a massive choice of desserts made on premises and an award-winning wine list; live music and the "watchful eye of hostess/co-owner Catherine Findlay" add to the atmosphere; overall, "bank on good food and an empty piggy bank."

	F	D	S	C
Topolobampo	27	24	25	$43

445 N. Clark St. (bet. Hubbard & Illinois Sts.), 312-661-1434

■ Rick Bayless' dressier, pricier sibling of the Frontera Grill (in the same River North building) is "reason enough to live in Chicago" say civic-boosting boasters who are proud to call this "best Mexican in the country" their own; a recent expansion has relieved the "cramped space" somewhat, but made it no easier to secure reservations for a "great experience" that "never disappoints" locals or their "out-of-town guests"; for those who "can't wait to go back", much of the menu changes bi-weekly.

	F	D	S	C
Trio S	27	25	27	$67

1625 Hinman Ave. (Davis St.), Evanston, 847-733-8746

■ This "amazing" North Shore Eclectic provides "one of the greatest culinary experiences you will ever have" thanks to "outstanding" service, "continually creative" cooking and artistic presentations so "visually striking" they look like "Cirque du Soleil on a plate"; a few claim that it's "fading from glory", but most think it's still a "winner" "for special occasions", and if you can handle the "expensive" tab, try the "to-die-for" degustation menu.

	F	D	S	C
Va Pensiero S	25	22	23	$39

Margarita Inn, 1566 Oak Ave. (Davis St.), Evanston, 847-475-7779

■ "Yesterday's ambiance, tomorrow's food" is one way of summing up Peggy Ryan's highly rated North Shore Italian, an "exquisite gem" serving "innovative, delicious" cuisine in an "understated" and "romantic" environment; the low-key location may explain why "it's the least famous of the top-tier restaurants, yet one of the best" – it's "the place to take people you want to impress."

	F	D	S	C
Zealous	24	18	22	$42

174 N. York Rd. (1 block south of North Ave.), Elmhurst, 630-834-9300

■ Acolytes say this New American "real find in the Western suburbs" is "aptly named", since chef-owner Michael Taus "keeps outperforming himself" with "innovative", "strongly flavored" food and "amazing presentations"; though there's "not much ambiance" in the "small" storefront setting, it's "the place to go if you think no one's doing anything new."

TOP 15 FOOD RANKING

	Restaurant	Cuisine Type
28	Maisonette	Classic French
27	Palace	New American
	Precinct	Steakhouse
	BonBonerie	Bakery/Tearoom
26	Phoenix	New American
25	Grand Finale	American/French
	Germano's	N/S Italian
	Morton's of Chicago	Steakhouse
	Orchids	Regional American
24	J's Fresh Seafood	Seafood
	Barresi's	N/S Italian
	Plaza 600	New American
	Boca	Eclectic/New American
	Primavista	N/S Italian
	La Petite France	Classic French

OTHER IMPORTANT PLACES

Chez Alphonse	Classic/New French
Dee Felice Cafe	Cajun/Creole
Iron Horse	New American
JoAn	Japanese
Montgomery Inn	BBQ
Mullane's	Eclectic
Nicola's	Northern Italian
Pacific Moon	Asian
Pomodori	Pizza
Scalea's	N/S Italian
Trio	New American

	F	D	S	C
Barresi's Italian Restaurant	24	19	22	$28

4111 Webster Ave. (Blue Ash Rd.), Deer Park, 513-793-2540

■ This family-run "cozy neighborhood Italian bistro" with "attentive service" and a "long-standing reputation" is one of the city's "best-kept secrets"; surveyors like its "terrific value", "authentic" menu and "homey but classy" feel – plus the chance to rub shoulders with some of Cincinnati's most prominent citizens.

	F	D	S	C
Boca S	24	18	17	$20

4034 Hamilton Ave. (Blue Rock Rd.), 513-542-2022

◪ Funky Northside is the perfect home for this "hip" Eclectic–New American; local Birkenstockers and foodies in search of "imaginative" fare pack the renovated storefront on weekends, unfazed by absentminded service and ear-splitting din; modest prices are another reason why it's a "promising newcomer."

	F	D	S	C
BonBonerie	27	17	20	$8

2030 Madison Rd. (O'Bryon St.), 513-321-3399

◪ Upscale neighbors stand in line Saturday mornings for the "best pastries in town" and "fabulous scones" at this tony O'Bryonville bakery-cum-tearoom with plebeian prices; it's "the perfect place to bring your mother or best friend" for a "ladies' lunch" or tea.

Chez Alphonse — | — | — | E

654 Highland Ave. (Grand Ave.), Fort Thomas, KY, 606-442-5488

Former Maisonette maitre d' Alphonse Kaelbel offers Classic and New French regional cuisine to a loyal following in the quiet KY suburb of Fort Thomas; formal service and a winning wine list strong on Alsatians offset the plain-Jane setting; dinner only.

Dee Felice Cafe S 23 | 20 | 20 | $21

529 Main St. (6th St.), Covington, KY, 606-261-2365

■ You'll think you're in New Orleans at this "crowded", "dark" and "smoky" cafe on the edge of the Covington Main Strasse district that can get every bit as raucous as Bourbon Street; "jumpin'" Dixieland jazz, "spicy" food and "super" service provide a true "Cajun feeling in Kentucky."

Germano's Restaurant 25 | 19 | 21 | $23

9415 Montgomery Rd. (bet. Cooper & Remington Rds.), Montgomery, 513-794-1155

■ "Carefully prepared, authentic Italian" fare is on the bill at this family-run suburban in the Montgomery shopping district; though waits can be "long" and some find it "way too pricey" (especially off-menu seafood specials), its sportswear-clad fans tout the "great" fish, desserts and "sidewalk action" visible from window tables, adding that its "nicer" new location makes it "even better."

Grand Finale S 25 | 24 | 23 | $22

3 E. Sharon Ave. (Congress Ave.), Glendale, 513-771-5925

■ An "always busy", antiques-filled "Victorian-style house" in stately Glendale boasting the "best brunch", "excellent crêpes", "incredible desserts" and other "high-quality" American-French food; though some complain about "uncomfortable chairs" and "long waits for tables", it's a Cincinnati "institution."

Iron Horse S — | — | — | M

40 Village Sq. (Sharon Rd.), Glendale, 513-771-4787

Hands-on owners (the Sawyer family) are much in evidence at this recently renovated and expanded historic tavern set trackside in charming Glendale Village Square; the competent, occasionally inventive American fare is cordially served in a setting livened by jazz on weekends, and by passing trains the rest of the week.

JoAn — | — | — | VE

3940 Olympic Blvd. (Mineola Pike), Erlanger, KY, 606-746-2634

A Toyota exec hungry for the tastes of home is behind this austere Japanese in the shadow of Erlanger's Toyota plant; the offerings go beyond the expected sushi and sashimi, with Kotaro Nakamura guiding novices through the many courses of a kaiseki meal including delicacies like *ankimo* (monkfish liver); the presentation is artful and the prices commensurate with the quality.

J's Fresh Seafood Restaurant S 24 | 21 | 22 | $26

Regency Condos, 2444 Madison Rd. (Dana Ave.), 513-871-2888

■ "Wonderful fresh seafood" and a "quiet atmosphere with excellent service" are hallmarks of this recently updated Hyde Park standby; though it can be "pricey", "mature" residents from the condos above consider it their private dining room, while others like to go midweek for the "terrific antipasti bar."

La Petite France 24 | 17 | 20 | $22
3177 Glendale-Milford Rd. (Reading Rd.), 513-733-8383
◪ The suburban strip mall location and theme park interior mask an "authentic French restaurant with real accents"; the "comfortable" ambiance of this "undiscovered gem" makes it a "good place to visit with old friends", but take note: this is "rich" cuisine.

Maisonette 28 | 28 | 28 | $48
114 E. Sixth St. (Main & Walnut Sts.), 513-721-2260
■ Chef Jean-Robert de Cavel's Mediterranean touch has brought this Downtown Classic French into the '90s and earned it the city's top food rating; "meticulous" cuisine, "formal" rooms and "proper" service prompt well-heeled patrons to rave "best in America – never fails"; though a few say "overrated", "a Midwestern dream of deluxe", to most it's the ultimate for "special occasions" at prices that, while high, should make both coasts envious.

Montgomery Inn S 23 | 19 | 21 | $20
9440 Montgomery Rd. (Cooper Rd.), Montgomery, 513-791-3482
Montgomery Inn Boathouse S
925 Eastern Ave. (Eggleston Ave.), 513-721-7427
◪ "World-class" ribs make up for "rushed" service and waits at these "crowd-pleasing" BBQ "meccas" that draw "people from miles around", especially to the Downtown Boathouse location with its river view; some find the sauce too sweet, but the fact that the ribs are shipped to fans nationwide says something.

Morton's of Chicago S 25 | 23 | 23 | $38
Tower Pl., 28 W. Fourth St. (Race St.), 513-241-4104
◪ "Portions are enormous and so is the bill" at this Downtown steakhouse with a "clubby", "very corporate" setting filled with high rollers and tourists; service is "prompt and sharp" and most have no beef with the beef in this "carnivore heaven"; critics want smaller servings with prices to match.

Mullane's ⊄ 23 | 18 | 19 | $15
723 Race St. (8th St.), 513-381-1331
■ The "hippest spot Downtown" produces "good", health-oriented Eclectic food in a "quirky, fun" setting populated by local residents, artists and grateful vegans; they're drawn by bargain prices, the "communal" ambiance and a "different" menu; the pace of service can be glacial, but you can have your palm read while you wait.

Nicola's Ristorante – | – | – | E
1420 Sycamore St. (Liberty St.), 513-721-6200
There's a Tuscan touch to this classy Over-the-Rhine Northern Italian with Uptown prices and polished service; just minutes by car from the Music Hall, it's a good choice for elegant dining before the opera or symphony and you can practice your Italian while supping on bruschetta, calamari, osso buco, panna cotta and more.

Orchids 25 | 27 | 24 | $35
Palm Court, Omni Netherland Plaza, 35 W. Fifth St. (Race St.), 513-421-9100
◪ "Elegant dining" with "unobtrusive service" in one of the city's "prettiest" rooms keeps expense-accounters returning to this Midwestern Regional in the soaring atrium of a "glamorous" "art deco masterpiece"; dissenters suggest the food and service aren't up to the decor, but a meal here "makes you feel important."

Pacific Moon S | 23 | 17 | 19 | $21

Market Place Complex, 8300 Market Place Ln. (Montgomery Rd.), Montgomery, 513-891-0091

■ "East meets West" at this suburban "gourmet Asian" serving the "best Pacific Rim" fare in town to an upscale following that likes the "interesting" food, "knowledgeable" service and "awesome presentation" backed by "good jazz" on weekends; why is it that some think Asian food this good still has to be cheap?

Palace, The S | 27 | 26 | 26 | $41

Cincinnatian Hotel, 601 Vine St. (6th St.), 513-381-6006

■ "Excellent, innovative" cuisine (Cincinnati's "best hotel food") and "ballet-like service" prompt return visits to this "intimate" New American in a restored Downtown landmark; it's a "favorite place to celebrate" or simply enjoy a very "elegant evening."

Phoenix, The Restaurant at the | 26 | 25 | 25 | $30

812 Race St. (9th St.), 513-721-8901

■ What many call Cincinnati's "best fine dining value" offers a "club" ambiance in a "beautiful old building" on Downtown's Garfield Place; this "imaginative" New American will "cater to vegetarians" and has "excellent" wines and "competent" service; despite a few "inconsistent" reports, it mostly does a "terrific" job.

Plaza 600 S | 24 | 21 | 22 | $27

600 Walnut St. (6th St.), 513-721-8600

■ This slick and "trendy" Downtown New American with International influences bustles on performance nights at the adjacent Aronoff Center; it's a "creative" "NY bistro right here in River City", offering "beautiful presentations" and lots of "après-theater" appeal; though some dislike the decibel level and smoke, "they get you to the show on time" and satisfied.

Pomodori Pizzeria and Trattoria S | 23 | 13 | 17 | $14

125 W. McMillan St. (Moerlein Ave.), 513-861-0080 ◐

7880 Remington Rd. (Main St.), Montgomery, 513-794-0080

◪ A popular campus hangout that makes the grade with "creative brick-oven pizzas" made in full view; the marginal neighborhood and occasionally erratic service are offset by "very reasonable prices" and the chance that "you'll see someone you know."; N.B. a second location in suburban Montgomery opened in early 1997.

Precinct, The S | 27 | 22 | 24 | $34

311 Delta Ave. (Columbia Pkwy.), 513-321-5454

■ "Meat rules" at this "hype"-heavy "jock hangout" in a former police station in historic Columbia-Tusculum; visiting celebs and wanna-bes overlook the "noisy", "crowded" rooms and sometimes "rushed" service to enjoy "melt-in-your-mouth" steak that many judge to be the "best this side of the Mississippi."

Primavista S | 24 | 25 | 22 | $28

Queens Tower, 810 Matson Pl. (bet. Price & W. 8th Aves.), 513-251-6467

■ "Attractive", tavernlike Italian in a Price Hill high-rise that's a top choice for "romantic meals" or entertaining visitors, mostly for its "magnificent view looking east to Downtown and the river"; opinion on the food runs from "pretty good" to "superb", but the point is "Cincy looks great from here."

Scalea's – | – | – | E

320 Greenup St., (Park Pl.), Covington, KY, 606-491-3334.
Foodies are flocking to Covington, KY, for this contemporary Italian with local celeb-chef Anita Cunningham in the kitchen and a slick crew in the dining room; the pricy pastas, risottos and more are complemented by the instructive all-Italian wine list, and the tony crowd looks good in the understated decor; word to the wise: the adjacent deli sells the best Italian sausage in town.

Trio S 23 | 18 | 21 | $17

Jos. A. Bank Plaza, 7565 Kenwood Rd., Kenwood, 513-984-1905
■ Seniors and families rule the early evenings at this newly renovated and expanded "classy, casual" New American bistro that's a frequent post-movie and shopping stop thanks to its Uptown decor, "interesting" food, "fresh fish" and extensive choice of wines by the glass; this may be the city's favorite midpriced table.

Cleveland

TOP 15 FOOD RANKING

	Restaurant	Cuisine Type
28	Johnny's Bar/Fulton	Continental/N. Italian
27	Sans Souci	Mediterranean
	Chez François	Classic French
	Hyde Park Grille	Steakhouse
	Baricelli Inn	French/Italian
	Parker's	New French
	Shuhei	Japanese
26	Classics	Continental
	Morton's of Chicago	Steakhouse
	Giovanni's	Northern Italian
	Hyde Park Chop House	Steakhouse
	Hyde Park Downtown	Steakhouse
	Riverview Room	New American
25	Luchita's	Mexican
	Sergio's	Brazilian

OTHER IMPORTANT PLACES

Restaurant	Cuisine Type
Fratello's	N/S Italian
Gavi	N/S Italian
Johnny's Downtown	Continental/N. Italian
Lockkeeper's Inn	Eclectic
Market Square Bistro	New American
Phnom Penh	Asian
Tutto a Posto	Eclectic

F | D | S | C

Baricelli Inn 27 | 27 | 26 | $43

2203 Cornell Rd. (Murray Hill Rd.), 216-791-6500

■ This "elegant", "romantic" old mansion in Little Italy has an "ambitious menu" of "sophisticated" French and Italian fare plus an extensive wine list; though "expensive", a much cheaper bistro menu was recently introduced for more casual patio dining in season; some find service "slow", but that gives diners more reason to linger, sometimes late enough to make use of the inn.

Chez François S 27 | 27 | 25 | $40

555 Main St. (Liberty Ave.), Vermilion, 440-967-0630

■ "Excellent" French food and a "lovely setting" on the river a stone's throw from Lake Erie make this "romantic" destination a "place to celebrate something special" and "worth the trip" from Cleveland or Toledo; book ahead because summer weekends are crowded and it closes from New Year's through early March.

Classics 26 | 28 | 27 | $43

Omni International, 2065 E. 96th St. (Carnegie Ave.), 216-791-1300

◪ Boasting one of the city's most "romantic" and "elegant" settings, with a harpist and violinists on selected evenings, this pricey "special occasion" hotel Continental is "very classic" indeed; a small faction finds it "stuffy" and says the food "doesn't match the decor", but to most it's simply "one of the best."

Fratello's | 25 | 18 | 22 | $21 |
32085 Electric Blvd. (Lear Rd.), Avon Lake, 440-871-3054
■ "Terrific", simply prepared Italian food explains the appeal of this casual "neighborhood" winner where sauces (and calamari) "are the best", portions are large and the wine list was recently expanded; the decor is unexciting and service can be slow, but most are too busy enjoying their meal to notice.

Gavi S | 23 | 25 | 22 | $32 |
38257 Glenn Ave., Willoughby, 440-942-8008
■ This "great new addition" to the far East Side is dishing up "big servings" of "excellent" Italian fare served by "friendly" staff in a renovated old Downtown powerhouse; remember to leave room for the divine desserts and bring bucks because it's considered "a bit pricey" for the locale.

Giovanni's Ristorante | 26 | 24 | 26 | $43 |
25550 Chagrin Blvd. (Richmond Rd.), Beachwood, 216-831-8625
◩ A very "elegant" and formal setting for "excellent" Northern Italian dining; fans don't mind paying stiff prices for "top-notch" food that includes innovative twists on old standards, but while some revel in the ultra-"fancy" service, others find it "too much of a good thing"; P.S. the "desserts are fabulous."

Hyde Park Chop House | 26 | 21 | 24 | $35 |
34205 Chagrin Blvd. (S.O.M. Center Rd.), 216-464-0688
■ Like its two siblings, this chophouse is always "busy" because it always provides "great steaks" that are a "good value" given free side dishes like the tasty Greek salad; some find it "noisy and crowded", but that's what you'd expect from a "hot local spot."

Hyde Park Downtown | 26 | 25 | 25 | $35 |
123 Prospect Ave. (W. 2nd St.), 216-344-2444
■ The newest branch of the local steakhouse chain moved in right next to Morton's Downtown but is holding its own with steaks that are "reason to never become a vegetarian", enhanced by a "powerhouse" (but pricey) wine list; as ratings attest, most feel it's "sure to be a winner."

Hyde Park Grille | 27 | 24 | 25 | $35 |
1823 Coventry Rd. (bet. Hampshire & Lancashire Rds.), Cleveland Heights, 216-321-6444
■ The original and, by most accounts, best of Cleveland's Hyde Park steakhouse trio, offering "consistently excellent food and service" in a "very New York City" atmosphere; the dark paneled bar is where many regulars prefer to eat.

Johnny's Bar on Fulton | 28 | 21 | 25 | $38 |
3164 Fulton Rd. (Trent Ave.), 216-281-0055
■ Rated No. 1 for Food in Cleveland, this "lively" Continental–Northern Italian has long earned raves for its "superb" food and wines and "nostalgic" art deco setting in a converted old tavern; it can be "quite expensive" but most rate it a "good buy" given the quality and unusually large portions; at lunch you can sample this "total class" act for a fraction of the dinner price.

Johnny's Downtown S

F	D	S	C
25	24	23	$38

1406 W. Sixth St. (bet. St. Clair & Superior Aves.), 216-623-0055
◪ It's tough living up to its big brother on Fulton, and while everyone agrees that the Downtown Johnny's has "well-prepared and presented" Northern Italian–Continental food, many rate it "one small step below" the original; still, its "cool, comfortable" marbled setting scores higher and it's a lot easier to get to.

Lockkeeper's Inn

F	D	S	C
24	20	22	$31

6190 Canal Rd. (Rockside Rd.), Valley View, 216-524-9404
■ The menu is typical upscale steakhouse fare, but the specials are "innovative" Franco-Californian cuisine at this Eclectic "up-and-comer" with an award-winning wine list; though "pricey", it's a pleasant "surprise" to find such "creative cuisine, warm ambiance and friendly service" in a "historic" setting in the southern suburbs.

Luchita's S

F	D	S	C
25	13	21	$15

3456 W. 117th St. (Governor St.), 216-252-1169
■ It looks like a "hole-in-the-wall" from outside, but the interior has been remodeled and locals think it has the "best", "most authentic" Mexican food in town: "the real McCoy", "great salsa", "good mole"; but it's "perhaps too real for the Chi-Chi's crowd."

Market Square Bistro S

F	D	S	C
25	20	21	$25

16725 Chillicothe Rd. (E. Washington St.), Bainbridge Twp., 440-543-5115
■ This American bistro has been drawing SRO crowds in a strip mall outside of Chagrin Falls, where patrons watch chefs in the open kitchen turning out big portions of "inventive", "healthier-style" pizzas, pastas, fish, beef and more; the atmosphere is bright and "lively" if a bit "too loud" for some.

Morton's of Chicago S

F	D	S	C
26	23	24	$40

The Avenue at Tower City Ctr., 1660 W. Second St. (Prospect Ave.), 216-621-6200
■ "Portions are too large" insist some (ditto prices), but admirers of this upscale chain steakhouse say "big works here" thanks to "perfectly prepared" meat, lobsters and side dishes served in a "classy" room by "attentive" staff; even if you "feel like a glutton", don't forget dessert: "the Grand Marnier soufflé is to die for."

Parker's S

F	D	S	C
27	23	24	$42

2801 Bridge Ave. (28th St.), Ohio City, 216-771-7130
■ Chef Parker Bosley's big following is pleased that he's opened the doors of his "sophisticated" Ohio City New French for weekday dinner (previously served weekends only); while it's slipped a tiny bit from its former No. 1 Food ranking, most praise "excellent", "imaginative" cuisine, made with mostly local ingredients, though a few balk at "small portions" for "very big prices"; this is one of the few places in town where jackets are still required.

Phnom Penh Restaurant S ≠

	F	D	S	C
▽	27	12	20	$16

13124 Lorain Ave. (W. 131st St.), 216-251-0210
■ Considered the best value around for quality Asian fare, with such a "wide variety" of "spicy" Cambodian, Thai and Vietnamese offerings that it's "hard to choose" – just about everything is "excellent" and served by a patient, helpful staff in "no-frills" surroundings; BYO and there's no corkage fee (or wine glasses).

Riverview Room S | 26 | 28 | 26 | $42

Ritz-Carlton, 1515 W. Third St. (bet. Huron Rd. & Prospect Ave.), 216-623-1300

■ One of the city's most "elegant" dining rooms draws raves for its "impressive views", "unobtrusive service" and "superior" Contemporary American fare that a new chef has made a bit more cutting-edge and eclectic; it's "first-class all the way" (price included) and Sunday brunch is widely considered the best around.

Sans Souci S | 27 | 27 | 26 | $35

Cleveland Renaissance Hotel, 24 Public Sq. (Superior Ave. & W. 3rd St.), 216-696-5600

■ Earning Cleveland's No. 2 Food rating, this Mediterranean hotel dining room is "not cheap, but is a great value" given its "superb", "imaginative" cuisine, "beautiful" atmosphere and "excellent" service; its annual two-month fall lobster menu is one of the most popular promotions in town.

Sergio's in University Circle | 25 | 19 | 22 | $32

1903 Ford Dr. (Bellflower Rd.), 216-231-1234

■ Chef Sergio Abramof, who spent 10 years cooking Italian at Giovanni's, is tantalizing diners with "unique Brazilian food" in this "small", bright, "noisy" University Circle space where diners go nuts for his "creative" fare; many consider it one of Cleveland's best.

Shuhei, The Restaurant of Japan S | 27 | 21 | 22 | $27

23360 Chagrin Blvd. (Green Rd.), Beachwood, 216-464-1720

■ Hiroshi Tsuji previously owned Shujiro, one of Cleveland's top-rated restaurants, and he's keeping up that tradition at this "stylish" Japanese serving "excellent sushi", seafood and "wonderful" traditional fare, all beautifully presented; be sure to book – most nights it's packed and "noisy."

Tutto a Posto S | 24 | 21 | 22 | $26

13114 Larchmere Blvd. (N. Moreland), 216-283-7529

■ Chef Michael Tsonton and his "excellent staff go overboard to please" at this "up-and-coming" Eclectic where "creative" fare including "great risotto" and the chef's seven-course 'whim dinner' are served in an "inviting" muraled setting; the all-European wine list is well-thought-out and features hard-to-find bottles.

Columbus

TOP 10 FOOD RANKING

	Restaurant	Cuisine Type
28	L'Antibes	Classic/New French
	Handke's	Eclectic/New American
27	Refectory	Classic French
	Rigsby's	Eclectic/Italian
26	Rotolo's Pizza	Pizza
	Lindey's	New American
	Hyde Park Grille	Steakhouse
	Restaurant Japan	Japanese
	Worthington Inn	Traditional American
	Morton's of Chicago	Steakhouse

OTHER IMPORTANT PLACES

Bexley's Monk	Eclectic
Bombay Grille	Indian
Cameron's	Regional American
Cap City Fine Diner	Traditional American
Crescendo Pastaria	N/S Italian
Figlio Wood-Fired Pizza	Pizza
Giuseppe's Ritrovo	N/S Italian
Harold's Cajun Glory	Cajun/Creole
Hunan Lion	Chinese
Latin Rooster	Latin American
Merlot	Continental/New Amer.
Sapporo Wind	Japanese
Shaw's	Traditional American
Taj Palace	Indian
Trattoria Roma	N/S Italian

F | D | S | C

Bexley's Monk S — 25 | 23 | 23 | $24

2232 E. Main St. (College Ave.), 614-239-6665

■ "Good seafood", "excellent pasta", "imaginative pizzas" – "it all comes together" at this inventive Eclectic that has "kept Bexley from starving for years"; apart from griping about service ("too friendly", "snooty") and a few claims that it's "overrated", most enjoy this "lively place" that "switch hits well for business or pleasure."

Bombay Grille S — – | – | – | M

6665 Dublin Village Ctr. (Saw Mill Rd.), Dublin, 614-336-2610

This Northwester is a leader in the local Indian sweepstakes, and while the setting is smoke-free, the menu offers all heat levels; big eaters will appreciate the upscale all-you-can-eat lunch buffet.

Cameron's S — 25 | 21 | 23 | $24

2894 E. Main St. (Enfield Rd.), Bexley, 614-235-3662

2185 W. Dublin-Granville Rd. (Linworth Rd.), Worthington, 614-885-3663

◪ The Regional American fare is "creative", service is "friendly" and the setting is full of "good energy" at this Bexley and Linworth duo; grumblers claim they're "small, crowded" and "noisy", but for most it's "worth" the din and high-ish prices for "innovative" dining.

Cap City Fine Diner & Bar S — 22 | 21 | 21 | $18

1299 Olentangy River Rd. (bet. 3rd & 5th Aves.), 614-291-3663
1301 Stoneridge Dr. (bet. Hamilton & Morse Rds.), Gahanna, 614-478-9999

◪ Even those who complain that this "trendy diner for the '90s" is "overpriced" and "overrated" grudgingly admit that they're "glad it's here" because the "food is tasty" and the variety's "good, from the meat loaf to the salmon"; there's also an "excellent raw bar" but "go early"; the Stoneridge Drive branch is newer.

Crescendo Pastaria — – | – | – | M

6860 Riverside Dr. (Rte. 161), Dublin, 614-761-3333

This one-time ugly duckling of a pizza joint/restaurant moved to different Northwest quarters and grew up into this full-service, tablecloth-equipped place; it now offers a moderately priced, monthly changing menu of regional Italian cuisine accompanied by arguably the best Italian wine list in town.

Figlio Wood-Fired Pizza — 25 | 20 | 22 | $17

1369 Grandview Ave. (bet. 3rd & 5th Aves.), 614-481-8850
3712 Riverside Dr. (Fishinger Rd.), 614-459-6560

■ It's "small", "noisy" and "always crowded", but the "great neighborhood atmosphere" and "yuppie pizza at its finest" keep pulling 'em in to Grandview despite the no-reserving policy (which is being relaxed weeknights) and because of the no-smoking policy; only the wines elicit pricing complaints; N.B. the Upper Arlington branch is newer and has a pleasant patio.

Giuseppe's Ritrovo Italian Café — – | – | – | M

2268 E. Main St. (Drexel Ave.), Bexley, 614-235-4300

A modest, family-run trattoria that's not generic Italian but a source of authentic Calabrian, Sicilian and other regional fare, where tomato, garlic and the olive reign and low prices are the rule; N.B. it now has a wine license, and the wines are priced-right too.

Handke's Cuisine — 28 | 25 | 25 | $33

520 S. Front St. (bet. Beck & Blenkner Sts.), 614-621-2500

■ "Masterfully done" Eclectic–New American food by a "certified master chef" wins raves at this Brewery District wine cellar, even if the subterranean "vaulted-ceiling" setting draws mixed reaction: "wonderful", "unique" vs. "dark, dingy"; some also cite "slow service" and "nouvelle cuisine portions", but it's deemed well "worth the effort" and cost to enjoy superlative "global cuisine."

Harold's Cajun Glory Café — – | – | – | M

1355 Bethel Rd. (Godown Rd.), 614-538-1822

Bringing a taste of the Big Easy to Columbus, this dinner-only cafe serves Cajun-Creole fare in the spiffed-up quarters of a former fast-food joint; moderate prices are a plus and there's no smoking.

Hunan Lion S — 24 | 22 | 23 | $17

2038 Crown Plaza Dr. (Reed Rd.), 614-459-3933

■ A "classical setting" for "high-class, first-rate Chinese" food in the Northwest; despite "white linen" ambiance, it's a "comfortable" place with "friendly, welcoming" service; some say it's even better with the "new wine list and menu."

Restaurant	F	D	S	C
Hyde Park Grille	26	21	24	$29

Hyde Park Grille
1615 Old Henderson Rd. (Larwell Dr.), 614-442-3310
◪ You can start with the "best martini" during the "best happy hour in town", which makes it easier to endure "long waits" for this Upper Arlington's "excellent steaks" in a "dark ambiance" that some find "elegant" and others "tired."

L'Antibes — 28 | 23 | 25 | $33
772 N. High St., Ste. 106 (Warren Ave.), 614-291-1666
■ This Near North Side "classical and classy" French is "quiet and intimate" (some say "almost too small"), with an atmosphere as "cozy as someone's house" and "superbly prepared" traditional and modern cuisine that garners the city's top food ratings; only Columbusites rate it "expensive."

Latin Rooster Rotisserie S — ▽ 21 | 12 | 19 | $12
Stoneridge Plaza, 389 Stoneridge Ln. (bet. Hamilton & Morse Rds.), Gahanna, 614-471-4567
■ "Finally, Latin American home cooking" wakes up Gahanna taste buds with this "friendly, family-owned gem" that offers an "unusual menu" including Peruvian specialties; surveyors enjoy the "new and interesting" dishes with "different" flavors so much that they wish the menu could be "expanded a bit."

Lindey's Restaurant S — 26 | 25 | 24 | $25
169 E. Beck St. (Mohawk St.), German Village, 614-228-4343
◪ Because it "has the best bistro atmosphere" in "trendy German Village", this "institution" is "always jammed" with "people-watchers" – of course, the "mouthwatering" New American fare is also a draw; some find it "too noisy" and "yup-oid" with "surly" service and "overrated" food, but they're vastly outnumbered by those for whom Lindey's is "ever in and ever worthy of it."

Merlot — 24 | 22 | 23 | $28
5252 Norwich St. (Columbia St.), Hilliard, 614-529-1995
◪ A "cute little house made into a restaurant", this Continental–New American "dining mecca in Hilliard" earns kudos for its "excellent, interesting" (if at times uneven) food and brickbats for wine that's "way overpriced"; for a "romantic" evening, reserve the "private room" with a single table.

Morton's of Chicago S — 26 | 24 | 25 | $38
2 Nationwide Plaza, Ste. 100 (Chestnut St.), 614-464-4442
◪ Even those who rave about "superb" beef, "some of the best service around" and the "pleasurable" ambiance of this "clubby" Downtown steakhouse find the portions "overwhelming", while more delicate appetites decry a "vulgar display of gluttony"; there's unanimity about the cost ("huge" – "make sure you're on an expense account") and a grumble or two about cigar smoke.

Refectory Restaurant — 27 | 26 | 26 | $35
1092 Bethel Rd. (near Rte. 315 at Kenny Rd.), 614-451-9774
■ The "professional staff", "romantic" setting in an "old church", "spectacular wine list" and "classic haute cuisine" leave surveyors searching for superlatives to describe this Northwest French: "world-class", "as close to perfection as we have", "nothing else comes close"; it's Columbus' Most Popular restaurant and a favorite "for that special evening."

Restaurant Japan S | 26 | 15 | 21 | $19

Kenny Ctr., 1173 Old Henderson Rd. (Kenny Rd.), 614-451-5411

■ It's no longer "always crowded" at the new location of this Northwest ethnic that serves what many reviewers rate as the "best Japanese" food in Columbus; if "no one speaks English", that could be taken as further proof that it's "really authentic."

Rigsby's Cuisine Volatile | 27 | 24 | 25 | $29

698 N. High St. (Lincoln Rd.), 614-461-7888

■ The "bustling" ambiance, live music and "stunning, artsy" setting in Columbus' Short North "bohemian art district" don't distract raters from Italian-Eclectic "bistro fare at its best"; everything – starting with the bread – is judged "excellent" at this lively (and often "noisy") "place to see and be seen."

Rotolo's Pizza S ⊄ | 26 | 9 | 22 | $9

1749 W. Fifth Ave. (Glenn Ave.), 614-488-7934

■ Whether you call it "the best", "great" or an all-time "favorite", pizza's the thing at this Grandview-area carryout with "friendly" service from a "hardworking family"; only the addition of "eat-in facilities could improve" on this kind of pizza "perfection."

Sapporo Wind S | 25 | 19 | 19 | $19

6188 Cleveland Ave. (south of I-270), 614-895-7575

■ A contender for "best Japanese", this "elegant" Northeaster earns raves for its "artistic, exquisite" food – "didn't think fish this fresh could get to Ohio"; apart from a few reports of "slow service", most find no fault with its "beautiful presentations" and flavors.

Shaw's Restaurant S | 24 | 23 | 23 | $20

123 N. Broad St. (Wheeling St.), Lancaster, 740-654-1842

■ "Worth the drive" to Lancaster, this country inn American with a changing menu offers "all the food trends plus steaks, chops" and "moderate wines" in an "elegant, old-world" setting; there's no faulting the "reasonable prices", but "slow service" can irritate.

Taj Palace S | – | – | – | M

3794 Fishinger Blvd. (Mill Run Shopping Ctr.), 614-771-3870

This reasonably priced, well-run Northwester turns out fine Indian cuisine; though it has the hottest tandoori ovens around, there's no smoke to compete with its fragrant aromas.

Trattoria Roma | 25 | 15 | 21 | $21

Woodward Park, 1270 Morse Rd. (Maize Rd.), 614-888-6686

■ "Don't be fooled" by the "cramped" setting in a Northeast strip mall – this spot wins votes as Columbus' "best Italian", offering "a wonderful dining experience" enhanced by "a good wine list" and "knowledgeable" service.

Worthington Inn S | 26 | 25 | 24 | $27

649 N. High St. (Rte. 161), Worthington, 614-885-2600

◪ Most find the atmosphere of this Worthington-area "historic" inn "quaint" and "charming", and the Traditional American menu "well done and presented", if "pricey"; contrarians don't get the mix of "celestial stars and moon with colonial decor" and call the food "uneven" and service "pompous", but they're outvoted.

TOP 20 FOOD RANKING

	Restaurant	Cuisine Type
29	French Room	Classic French
28	Riviera	French/Mediterranean
	Mansion on Turtle Creek	Southwestern
27	Pyramid Room	Continental/French
	Cafe Pacific	Seafood
	Laurels	Eclectic
	Bob's Steak & Chop House	Steakhouse
	Barclays	Modern British
	York Street	New American
26	Del Frisco's	Steakhouse
	Fogo de Chao	Brazilian/Steakhouse
	Nana Grill	New American
	Mediterraneo	Mediterranean
	Hôtel St. Germain	Continental/French
	Sea Grill	Seafood
	Grape	Eclectic
	Star Canyon	Southwestern
	Green Room	New American
	Chez Gerard	French Bistro
25	Morton's of Chicago	Steakhouse

OTHER IMPORTANT PLACES

Al Biernat's	Seafood/Steakhouse
Ali Baba Cafe	Middle Eastern
Anzu	Pacific Rim
AquaKnox	Seafood
Arc-En-Ciel	Chinese/Vietnamese
Bistro A	Mediterranean
Chamberlain's	Steakhouse
EatZi's	Eclectic
Fish	Seafood
Javier's	Mexican
Lavendou	French Bistro
Liberty	Asian
Lombardi Mare	Italian/Seafood
Mainstream Fish House	Seafood
Matt's No Place	Regional American
Mi Piaci Ristorante	Northern Italian
Sevy's Grill	New American
Sonny Bryan's	BBQ

	F	D	S	C
Al Biernat's S ▽	26	26	26	$50

4217 Oaklawn Ave. (bet. Herschel St. & Wycliff Ave.), 214-219-2201

■ Al Biernat, for many years the popular maitre d' of The Palm in Dallas, recently opened this eponymous surf 'n' turfer in the space that used to be the hip Joey's; his lobster salad is already a hit, as are his "awesome" sea bass and hefty cuts of beef, but the food doesn't come cheap.

Ali Baba Cafe 23 | 9 | 16 | $14

1905 Greenville Ave. (Oram St.), 214-823-8235

■ This "family-run" Middle Eastern "yuppie haven" is "casual and fun, except when overcrowded" – which it often is, given the many fans of its "delicious" chicken, "hummus to die for" and other "really good", "cheap" eats; Greenville locals also like its "easy access" to nearby nightclubs, but those sensitive to garlic say "don't expect to talk to anyone for three days!"

Anzu S 24 | 24 | 21 | $30

4620 McKinney Ave. (Knox St.), 214-526-7398

■ "Unique" describes both the food and decor at this fusion specialist where an "elegant, sleek" setting with hundreds of colorful origami cranes dangling from the ceiling sets the stage for "exquisite" Pacific Rim fare ranging from "wonderful sushi" to "excellent desserts" such as a chocolate mousse–filled giant fortune cookie; the only thing missing from the "great California feel" is "the Pacific outside."

AquaKnox S 25 | 26 | 23 | $48

3214 Knox St. (Cole Ave.), 214-219-2782

◪ "A must for seafood lovers" is the word on this "sophisticated" Knox/Henderson standout; while the "gorgeous" decor is "worth" seeing, what really draws the "chic clientele" is "impeccable", imaginative aquatic fare from Stephan (Star Canyon) Pyles' "real jewel" of a menu; still, it's "expensive" and some cite "tons of attitude" (from the staff and crowd).

Arc-En-Ciel S 21 | 9 | 16 | $14

3555 W. Walnut St. (Jupiter Rd.), Garland, 972-272-2188

■ This "huge" (1,600 seats), no-frills Garland Asian is "a true bargain", offering "possibly the best dim sum in town" ("get there early for the best variety") along with a "very wide menu" of other Chinese and Vietnamese fare; service is "average" and there's not much decor, but "even if you don't like Chinese food" it "makes you a believer"; call ahead to make sure it's not closed for a function.

Barclays S 27 | 24 | 26 | $42

2917 Fairmont St. (bet. Cedar Springs Rd. & Routh St.), 214-855-0700

■ "Queen Elizabeth wishes she had food this good" say fans of this "quaint" "Cotswald cottage" offering "consistently good" Modern British food in a "completely unpretentious", "romantic" ambiance; chef-owner Nick Barclay "greets each visitor as an honored guest in his home" – "he really cares and it shows", from the "interesting menu" to the "gracious service."

Bistro A S 24 | 23 | 22 | $32

6815 Snider Plaza (Hillcrest Rd. & Lovers Ln.), 214-373-9911

◪ "Off to a great start", this "nice addition to Snider Plaza" earns solid ratings for its "wonderful" Mediterranean fare and "sleek" yet "informal" setting, though some wonder how long ever-on-the-go Avner Samuel ("best chef in Dallas") will stick around; despite a few grumbles about "small portions" and service slips, it's very popular, so "make reservations."

Bob's Steak & Chop House | 27 | 22 | 24 | $38 |

4300 Lemmon Ave. (Wycliff Ave.), 214-528-9446

■ This "classic steakhouse" with the requisite "masculine, clubby" look serves some of "the best steak in town (best value too)" and is also lauded for its lamb chops and side dishes (it "wins the 'great carrot' prize" for its honey-glazed version); grumblers cite "tight quarters" and warn "don't breathe in the lounge – full of cigars", but others find it the "most intimate", comfy steakhouse around.

Cafe Pacific | 27 | 26 | 25 | $34 |

24 Highland Park Village (Mockingbird Ln. & Preston Rd.), 214-526-1170

■ "The best seafood in Dallas by far" rave fans of this "elegant" Highland Park bistro that wows surveyors with "salmon to die for", "noteworthy" seviche and the "best damn New England clam chowder west of Boston Harbor"; "old money, old wine, new food" sums it up, and if a few complain of snooty waiters "direct from France", more cite "polished service" and good "people-watching" courtesy of the "Chanel/Escada/Hermès set."

Chamberlain's S | 24 | 22 | 23 | $39 |

5330 Belt Line Rd. (bet. Montfort Dr. & Prestonwood Blvd.), 972-934-2467

■ Besides offering "some of the best" beef in town, owner-chef Richard Chamberlain is a "master of sauces and fish" and "makes a lovely event of eating" at this Far North Dallas steakhouse; with a "calm, cool" ambiance and "attentive" service, it's an "indulgent", "guilty pleasure", but you may have to endure a long wait, "even with reservations", to enjoy it.

Chez Gerard | 26 | 22 | 23 | $34 |

4444 McKinney Ave. (1 block south of Knox St.), 214-522-6865

■ For "traditional Country French" dining, this "intimate, upscale" bistro "still works every time", offering "outstanding" lamb, "terrific soufflés" and "great pommes frites" along with "excellent" (a few say "snobby") service; it's thoroughly Gallic, right "down to the boutique wine list", and admirers rate it "one of the best French for the price", but even they don't like waiting despite reservations.

Del Frisco's Double Eagle Steak House | 26 | 23 | 24 | $47 |

5251 Spring Valley Rd. (N. Dallas Tollway), 972-490-9000

◪ Legions of loyalists consider this "the best" steakhouse not just in Dallas but "in the country" – "if my husband could pick his last meal on earth, this would be the place" is typical praise; nitpickers fault "long" waits, sometimes "arrogant" service and "expense-account" prices ("everything à la carte"), but most think it's "worth the cost" to experience "steak heaven."

EatZi's S | 23 | 19 | 19 | $14 |

3403 Oak Lawn Ave. (Lemmon Ave.), 214-526-1515

■ "A lifesaver", "incredible takeout", "the best grocery store ever" typify reaction to this gourmet market/cafe, a "novel concept" offering a "fantastic selection of fresh, hard-to-get" provisions plus Eclectic prepared fare; it can be "chaotic" and "crowded", but fans say it's the "best thing to happen to Dallas since we found 'black gold'" – "wish there were more" (there are, but in other cities).

Fish S | 22 | 19 | 18 | $38

Paramount Hotel, 302 S. Houston St. (Jackson Rd.), 214-747-3474

◪ Though hailed by *Esquire* magazine as one of the country's best seafooders, this Downtowner draws mixed signals from surveyors; while admirers credit it with "fab fish", "beautifully presented" in a "sophisticated" setting with jazz piano, foes torpedo "haphazard" service and "inconsistent" food; both sides find it a bit "pricey."

Fogo de Chao S | 26 | 22 | 26 | $37

4300 Belt Line Rd. (Midway Rd.), Addison, 972-503-7300

■ "Wow!" – this "new and different" Brazilian steakhouse offers an unending parade of grilled meats and poultry presented on swords by gaucho-esque waiters; it's mostly a "meat lovers' haven", but there's also a "gorgeous" salad bar and it's hard to beat for "great value and atmosphere"; "go hungry", and even then you may feel "like a goose being force-fed for foie gras."

French Room, The | 29 | 29 | 28 | $61

Adolphus Hotel, 1321 Commerce St. (bet. Ackard & Field Sts.), 214-742-8200

■ Rated No. 1 for Food, Decor and Service in Dallas, this "flawless" Classic French combines "incredible" cuisine with a "beautiful, very formal" setting and "skilled service" to achieve the "ultimate dining experience" – this is "romance at its best" and, remarkably, most detect "no stuffy airs" ("I felt like a queen"); "*très cher*" it is, but such "very special" experiences rarely come cheap.

Grape, The S | 26 | 22 | 23 | $26

2808 Greenville Ave. (bet. Monticello Ave. & Vickery Blvd.), 214-828-1981

■ Aging "like fine wine" say admirers of this Eclectic bistro that's been going strong for over 25 years and remains "one of the most romantic restaurants around"; with its dark, "comfy, laid-back room", "nifty wine" list and blackboard menu featuring the likes of "terrific mushroom soup" and pâté, it's an "all-time favorite."

Green Room, The S | 26 | 20 | 21 | $32

2715 Elm St. (Crowdus St.), 214-748-7666

■ "Funky" and "eclectic" describe both the ambiance and the "creative food" at this "hip" Deep Ellum New American; Marc Cassel (ex Star Canyon) runs the kitchen and his nightly four-course 'Feed Me' prix fixe ($36 without wine, $56 with) is a popular "good deal"; the "wonderful open patio" is a plus on fine evenings.

Hôtel St. Germain | 26 | 27 | 26 | VE

Hôtel St. Germain, 2516 Maple Ave. (bet. Cedar Spring Rd. & McKinney Ave.), 214-871-2516

■ The "exceptional European" ambiance of this Victorian home, replete with antiques, sets the stage for French-Continental fare that most find "exquisite" and "a bargain" even at the prix fixe tab of $75; considered the "epitome of elegance", it's a "classy" place "for a tea" and also holds "great wine tastings."

Javier's S | 25 | 24 | 23 | $26

4912 Cole Ave. (Harvard Ave.), 214-521-4211

■ "Excellent", "real Mexico City" eats, including the "best mole in Dallas" and "awesome black bean soup", are served in an "upscale" yet "low-key" ambiance at this "favorite"; it's "crowded and noisy", but "if you can get in, you can't go wrong"; N.B. the goat entree ranks as one of Dallas' best forkfuls.

Laurels 27 | 27 | 23 | $49

Westin Park Central, 12720 Merit Dr. (I-635, Coit Rd. exit), 972-851-2021

■ Commanding an "excellent view" from atop the Westin Park Central, this 'global fusion' specialist offers what some call "the ultimate dining in Dallas"; acclaimed chef Danielle Custer has foodies exulting over her "exciting", "innovative" Eclectic menu ("trust her even though she's under 30"), which is served by a pro staff in an "elegant" ambiance – in sum, a "class operation."

Lavendou 24 | 24 | 21 | $31

19009 Preston Rd. (bet. Frankford Rd. & Plano Pkwy.), 972-248-1911

◪ A "great addition to Far North Dallas" say admirers of this Provençal bistro that conjures up the real thing with its "quaint" interior and "well-prepared" fare along the lines of onion soup, soufflés and niçoise salads; despite critics who cite "slow service" and feel it sometimes "misses the mark", most call it a "keeper."

Liberty S 22 | 18 | 19 | $21

5631 Alta Ave. (Greenville Ave.), 214-887-8795

◪ "Flavors fire up in every bowl" at this "fashionable" Lower Greenville Asian offering "funky fusion" fare including a "wonderful assortment of noodle dishes"; some say the menu could "be more risky" ("too sweet, no heat"), but the "happening atmosphere" and "reasonable prices" make it a most "welcome addition."

Lombardi Mare S 23 | 25 | 22 | $34

Village on the Parkway, 5100 Belt Line Rd. (Montfort Dr.), Addison, 972-503-1233

■ "The little black dress is alive and well" at this "chic", "very Uptown" Far North Italian seafooder praised for its "excellent", "fresh" (albeit "a bit pricey") aquatic fare and "attentive service"; it's "worth a trip just to see" the place, especially the bar scene ("better than a movie"), which unfolds beneath goldfish swimming in bowls suspended overhead.

Mainstream Fish House S 22 | 15 | 19 | $19

Preston Forest Shopping Village, 11661 Preston Rd. (Forest Ln.), 214-739-3474

■ Landlocked locals say this "surprise" in a North Dallas strip mall can be relied on for "good, plain seafood" that's the "freshest around" and served at "reasonable prices"; standouts include New England chowder served in a 'bread pot', the "best gumbo" in town, legendary lobster enchiladas and a killer Key lime pie.

Mansion on Turtle Creek S 28 | 28 | 27 | $56

Mansion on Turtle Creek, 2821 Turtle Creek Blvd. (Gillespie St.), 214-559-2100

■ "Top class in every way", Dallas' Most Popular restaurant showcases the "awesome" Southwestern fare of Dean Fearing, who "sets the standard" with dishes like lobster tacos, tortilla soup and crème brûlée; a "classy" setting and "knowledgeable" (a few say "stuffy") service are more reasons why it's "worth a splurge" – "when you hit the lottery, this is the place to celebrate!"

Matt's No Place ▽ 24 | 16 | 20 | $24

Lakewood Theater Plaza, 6326 La Vista Dr. (Gaston Ave.), 214-823-9077

■ "No other place like it" proclaim fans of this Lakewood Regional American with a "casual Texas theme" and a "club"-like feel (its phone number was unlisted until recently); followers appreciate its 'Texas prairie' fare with a "Mexican and chuck wagon" slant, including wild game, creek-bottom shrimp and smoked spuds.

Mediterraneo S | 26 | 25 | 24 | $38

Preston Frankford Crossing, 18111 Preston Rd. (Frankford Rd.), 972-447-0066

◪ "One of the first great ones in Far North Dallas" say fans of this Mediterranean with "imaginative food", "understated elegance" and "some of the best service in town"; on the downside, it can get "noisy", but it's a place "to be seen", not necessarily heard.

Mi Piaci Ristorante S | 24 | 24 | 21 | $32

14854 Montfort Rd. (Belt Line Rd.), Addison, 972-934-8424

■ This "elegant, sophisticated" Addison Northern Italian is "a great package", with a "romantic" setting, a "cozy wine cellar" and "excellent" fare; chef Kevin Ascolese's monthly cooking demos are a hit, as is the risotto "to die for" and homemade breadsticks, so perhaps it doesn't matter if a few grumble about service "attitude."

Morton's of Chicago S | 25 | 23 | 24 | $43

501 Elm St. (Houston St.), 214-741-2277

14831 Midway Rd. (1½ blocks south of Belt Line Rd.), Addison, 972-233-5858

■ For the last word in "excellent prime beef from the Midwest", old-school meat eaters turn to this Downtown and Addison steakhouse duo; they're "expensive", but the combination of "large portions", "attentive service" and elegant atmosphere (with muted lighting, dark wood and etched glass) is sure to "impress clients"; cigars and a selection of ports help make every meal an occasion.

Nana Grill S | 26 | 27 | 25 | $44

Wyndham Anatole Hotel, 2201 Stemmons Frwy., 27th fl. (I-35, Market Ctr. exit), 214-761-7470

■ With its "breathtaking" view of the Downtown skyline, this hotel New American offers some of the "most romantic" dining around; it's also an ideal place to "entertain" or celebrate, thanks to "excellent food", "terrific service", a "superb wine list" and popular holiday buffets, all of which justify the "expensive" tab.

Pyramid Room S | 27 | 27 | 27 | $51

Fairmont Hotel, 1717 N. Akard St. (Ross Ave.), 214-720-5249

■ This "well-kept secret" offers "everything you'd want" in French-Continental dining, i.e. "classy, quiet" ambiance and "outstanding" food and service; the prix fixe dinner ($48 for four courses, $64 with wines) is a "wonderful value", and celebrants proclaim this "the place for anniversaries, proposals, birthdays and clinching" deals.

Riviera, The S | 28 | 27 | 28 | $57

7709 Inwood Rd. (Lovers Ln.), 214-351-0094

◪ Some of "the best food in the city" (rated No. 2 in Dallas) gives this French-Med a strong start, and it goes the distance with a "suave" setting, "primo" wine list and a staff that treats each patron as a "pampered guest"; however, it stumbles a bit in the eyes of critics who find the prices and the noise level too high.

Sea Grill S | 26 | 18 | 23 | $28

2205 N. Central Expy. (Park Blvd.), Plano, 972-509-5542

■ "Great chef, wish he weren't so far out" say Dallas-based fans of Andy Tun and his Plano fish house; it's called "one of the best" seafooders in the Metroplex with "beautiful presentations" and "wonderful" fare with Asian touches; adding to the enjoyment: "good service", a quiet ambiance and reasonable prices.

Sevy's Grill S | 22 | 22 | 20 | $27

8201 Preston Rd. (Northwest Hwy. & Sherry Ln.), 214-265-7389

◪ This New American is a "solid performer" that's considered "outstanding in its price range", with a "tasty" menu (including recently added items like heavenly truffled mashed potatoes and a decadent butter pecan cheesecake) enhanced by "good wine selections"; "noise is a problem", but they're working on it, and the back room is ideal for groups in search of privacy.

Sonny Bryan's Smokehouse | 21 | 11 | 15 | $11

302 N. Market St. (Pacific Ave.), 214-744-1610 S

Galleria, 133-75 Dallas Pkwy., 3rd fl. (LBJ Frwy. & N. Dallas Tollway), 972-851-5131 S

Republic Towers, 325 N. St. Paul St. (bet. Bryan St. & Pacific Ave.), 214-979-0102

4701 Frankford Rd. (bet. Dallas Pkwy. & Pear Ridge Rd.), 972-447-0102 S

2202 Inwood Rd. (bet. Forest Park & Harry Hines Blvd.), 214-357-7120 S

■ Texas reveres its BBQ, and to loyalists this "legend" is simply "the best BBQ in Dallas since dirt", especially the Inwood original; "no out-of-town guest should depart the state before eating this good meat", nor before learning to "love those onion rings"; hard-core connoisseurs need no encouragement to "put on some old clothes and go wallow" in the 'cue – and they never fail to "take home some sauce."

Star Canyon S | 26 | 27 | 24 | $41

3102 Oak Lawn Ave. (Cedar Springs Rd.), 214-520-7827

■ Sure, it's "hard to get reservations" at this Texan-Southwestern, but that's because so many people think "Stephan Pyles does it best" when it comes to "interesting combinations of tastes and flavors" and "impeccable presentation" of dishes like the "best bone-in rib eye ever"; "amazing", "Texan elegant" decor and sharp service help make it a "true Texas feast" that's worth the expense and effort to get in.

York Street | 27 | 22 | 26 | $39

6047 Lewis St. (Live Oak & Skillman Sts.), 214-826-0968

■ This "cozy" "hidden gem" in Old East Dallas offers a "fabulous" New American menu enhanced by "personalized service" – there's "no friendlier staff in town than owner Felissa" Shaw and company; add a "romantic, intimate" setting and you have the ideal "date place" and "a real find."

Denver Area & Mountain Resorts

TOP 20 FOOD RANKING

	Restaurant	Cuisine Type
29	Piñons	New American
	Q's	New American
28	Papillon Cafe	New French
	Keystone Ranch	New American
	Highlands Garden Cafe	New American
27	Little Nell	New American
	Wildflower	New American
	Sushi Den	Japanese
	Sweet Basil	New American
	Morton's of Chicago	Steakhouse
	Flagstaff House	Continental
	Mirabelle	New French
	Tante Louise	Classic/New French
	Palace Arms	Continental/Trad. Amer.
	Charles Court	Eclectic/New American
26	European Cafe	Continental/New Amer.
	240 Union	New American
	Cafe Jordano	Southern Italian
	John's	Med./New American
	Tivoli Deer	Continental

OTHER IMPORTANT PLACES

Aubergine Cafe	Med./New American
Bang!	Traditional American
Barolo Grill	Northern Italian
Brasserie Z	Traditional American
Briarwood Inn	Continental
Campagna	Northern Italian
Campo di Fiori	N/S Italian
Dandelion	New American
Denver Chop House	Regional American
Domo	Japanese
Fourth Story	Regional American
Full Moon Grill	Italian/Mediterranean
India's	Indian
Jax Fish House	Seafood
Laudisio	N/S Italian
Potager	Mediterranean
Renaissance	Med./New American
Strings	New American
Vesta Dipping Grill	New American

	F	D	S	C
Aubergine Cafe S	25	21	24	$22

225 E. Seventh Ave. (bet. Grant & Sherman Sts.), Denver, 303-832-4778

■ Provence meets Sorrento at this "splendid", intimate Am-Med bistro south of Downtown; the "charming" decor is a hit, as is the "yummy" "menu that changes daily"; diners also tip their hats to the patio, "service that's a notch above" and the "good wine list."

Bang! — | — | — | I
3609 W. 32nd Ave. (bet. Lowell Blvd. & Meade St.), Denver, 303-455-1117
Aptly named, since it offers some truly rare bang-for-the-buck dining, this Traditional American in the Highlands is short on space but big on focus: cooks Jeff Oakley and Cissy Yin work from a limited menu of 10 entrees and a few salads and desserts, but such concentration allows each item to be pretty close to perfect; there's no liquor and patrons place orders at a counter, but that hasn't kept the crowds away.

Barolo Grill 25 | 25 | 23 | $30
3030 E. Sixth Ave. (Milwaukee Ave.), Denver, 303-393-1040
◪ This pricey East Denver super-Tuscan is as hip as Denver allows: "it's crowded but tolerable" to be among the throngs of with-it "wanna-bes", "stars like John Elway" and *molti trenditi*; "these people know their Italian" and the food's enhanced by good wines, but drawbacks are "noise" and service that can be "pompous."

Brasserie Z S — | — | — | M
815 17th St. (Stout St.), Denver, 303-293-2322
One of Denver's most visually striking restaurants takes up the entire high-vaulted lobby of the former Colorado Guaranty Bank Downtown; this gorgeous space delivers hearty, plainspoken American bistro eats and sports one of Denver's better-priced wine lists; not surprisingly, it's become a hot spot.

Briarwood Inn S 25 | 27 | 25 | $31
1630 Eighth St. (6th Ave.), Golden, 303-279-3121
■ A Golden destination for admirers aplenty, this Continental is "awash in béarnaise" yet an "oldie but goldie"; "wonderful" staff "makes a fuss" over prom dates and other romantics who enjoy its "lovely", traditional setting; if a few find the folderol "costly" and "overrated", more call it tops "for special occasions and holidays."

Cafe Jordano 26 | 16 | 23 | $14
11068 W. Jewell Ave. (Kipling St.), Lakewood, 303-988-6863
■ The Italian ambiance is espresso-thick at this neighborhoody Neapolitan storefront in South Lakewood, which fans say proves that "if they speak Italian, they must know how to cook it"; "small" and cozy, "it's like having dinner with the family" that runs the place, with "terrific" service and low prices to boot.

Campagna S ▽ 27 | 22 | 26 | $36
435 W. Pacific Ave. (bet. Aspen & Townsend Sts.), Telluride, 970-728-6190
■ Tuscany tumbled from the sky one day and landed in Telluride say savorers of this "romantic" little spot serving "Michelangelo's Italian cuisine – fresh, innovative and attractive"; "when she's good, she's very good", and as ratings show, that's often; there's a super, well-selected wine list too.

Campo di Fiori ▽ 25 | 22 | 22 | $34
205 S. Mill St. (Hopkins St.), Aspen, 970-920-7717
■ "It don't get no better" than this fancy Italian in Aspen – a "warm, welcoming" entry that draws "crowds" for its "excellent" eats; amici have only one complaint – "long lines during ski season."

Charles Court S | 27 | 28 | 27 | $38

Broadmoor Hotel, 1 Lake Ave., Colorado Springs, 719-634-7711
◪ The fine dining room of Colorado Springs' Broadmoor Resort, this Eclectic–New American boasts a fine view of Broadmoor Lake from an "elegant" English manor house–like setting; most rate the food often "great", "as long as budget doesn't matter"; however, some find it "overpriced" with occasionally "stuffy" service.

Dandelion S | 25 | 24 | 21 | $29

1011 Walnut St. (bet. 10th & 11th Sts.), Boulder, 303-443-6700
◪ This "hot" spot in Boulder draws fans with its "innovative" American menu, "superb service" and "atmosphere that can't be beat"; but detractors decry "tables six inches apart", food in "tiny quantities for the price" and "deafening noise"; "a welcome addition" that "likes itself a bit too much" is the word for now.

Denver Chop House S | 24 | 25 | 21 | $23

1735 19th St. (Wynkoop St.), Denver, 303-296-0800
◪ All aboard the chew-chew train at this popular LoDo "hot spot", a former railroad shed "so close to Coors Field you can catch foul balls", serving steak and Regional American fare; it draws cheers for pre- or post-theater eats and "people-watching", jeers for at-times "arrogant service", but it's so "in" you'd better reserve.

Domo | – | – | – | M

Nippon Kan Cultural Ctr., 1365 Osage St. (14th Ave.), 303-595-3666
Domo means 'thanks' in Japanese, and that's what you'll give after dining on the authentic, traditional dishes offered here; noodle bowls, teriyakis, vegetarian and curry dishes are served in a setting straight out of rural Japan.

European Cafe | 26 | 22 | 24 | $28

Arapahoe Village Ctr., 2460 Arapahoe Ave. (bet. 28th & Folsom Sts.), Boulder, 303-938-8250
◪ One of the first eateries in Colorado to take off in an international way, this "amazing hole-in-the-wall" in a Boulder mall delivers what well-heeled fans call "good food for special times"; its "superb quality", "beautifully arranged" American-Continental cuisine is backed up by near-"perfect" (a few say "rather snooty") service; cynics cite "pretentious", "stuck in a rut" cooking and say the mall location "undermines the food", but they're a minority.

Flagstaff House S | 27 | 28 | 26 | $42

1138 Flagstaff Rd. (on Flagstaff Mountain), Boulder, 303-442-4640
■ When "you want to be sure to make an impression", admirers say this Continental is the place thanks to "great food and a great view" over Boulder from Flagstaff Mountain; most rate it "one of the best", but a few die-hard dissenters contend that it's just a place "to spend a lot" for "overrated, outdated" food and "overbearing service"; the winning wine list is a decided plus.

Fourth Story Restaurant & Bar S | 18 | 24 | 19 | $19

2955 E. First Ave. (Milwaukee St.), Denver, 303-322-1824
■ Cherry Creek's Tattered Cover bookstore is home to this Regional American on (where else?) its fourth floor; the chef offers "cuisine stretching for excellence" complemented by an "extensive wine list" (250 by the bottle, 35 by the glass); you'll eat in a "lovely room" "surrounded by books" and a "trendy, yuppie clientele."

Full Moon Grill S — | — | — | M

Village Shopping Ctr., 2525 Arapahoe Ave. (Folsom Ave.), Boulder, 303-938-8800

Moonstruck fans of this Boulder Italian-Mediterranean wrote in to say that, despite its "modest location", "genius" chef Bradford Heap turns out a "creative" menu "with every single thing bursting with flavor"; an "innovative wine list" goes well with the "excellent" food, making for a highly "satisfying" experience.

Highlands Garden Cafe 28 | 26 | 25 | $24

3927 W. 32nd Ave. (Perry St.), Denver, 303-458-5920

■ The "charming Victorian" "gem" of a house that hosts this New American in North Denver is a fitting frame for its "sophisticated, bold and innovative" cooking; with "beautiful gardens" outdoors, "lovely wines" and prices that make it a "great value", it's a hit "for special occasions."

India's S 25 | 21 | 20 | $20

Tamarac Sq., 3333 S. Tamarac Dr. (Hampden Ave.), Denver, 303-755-4284

■ "Definitely the best in Denver" gush enthusiasts of this "elegant" Southeast Denver Indian and its "fabulous", "marvelous, exotic" fare including a "great pig-out lunch buffet" for $6.95; "service is a little slow, but the food is worth the wait" – "each dish is a delight."

Jax Fish House S 25 | 19 | 20 | $22

928 Pearl St. (9th St.), Boulder, 303-444-1811
1539 17th St. (Wazee St.), Denver, 303-292-5767

◪ Oceans of praise for the No. 1 seafooder in our *Colorado Survey*, a "great little place" in Boulder that reels in "yuppies with cellular phones" who are hooked on the "excellent", "innovative" fin fare, "hip, cool bar" and "California feel"; the noise level is "often intolerable", but that's the price you pay for popularity; N.B. the LoDo outpost opened post-*Survey*.

John's 26 | 22 | 25 | $33

2338 Pearl St. (23rd St.), Boulder, 303-444-5232

■ Most agree that this "old Boulder standby" in a "small house" delivers on "consistently fabulous and inventive" Mediterranean–New American cooking, with "ambiance, service and reliability" as other strong suits; a few feel it's "pricey" and "coasts on its history", but they're outvoted.

Keystone Ranch 28 | 28 | 27 | $43

Keystone Ranch Rd. (2½ mi. off Hwy. 6), Keystone, 970-496-4161

◪ A favorite for trekkers to the mountains, this prix fixe New American near the Keystone ski area receives raves for its "beautiful setting", "always reliable" cooking (game is a highlight) and "educated" servers; but it also provokes complaints of "long waits" and "expensive" pricing.

Laudisio S 25 | 20 | 22 | $27

Willow Springs Ctr., 2785 Iris Ave. (28th St.), Boulder, 303-442-1300

◪ Boulder's "best" Italian and "special occasion" "secret" earns raves for its "excellent food" and "extensive wine list", but it also gets whatsa-mattas for "cramped seating" in a strip mall site, "attitude problems [on the part of] both the waiters and patrons" and an "overrated and overpriced" menu; complainers are clearly a minority, however, because it's "always busy and bustling."

Little Nell Restaurant 🅂 | 27 | 26 | 27 | $40 |

The Little Nell Hotel, 675 Durant St. (base of Aspen Mountain), Aspen, 970-920-6330

■ "The best in Aspen" per enthusiasts, this New American dishes up "incredible presentations" of "imaginative food" in the "quiet elegance" of a "gorgeous room" in a Relais & Châteaux property; "attentive" staff and a "tremendous wine list" are icing on the cake.

Mirabelle | 27 | 27 | 25 | $43 |

Beaver Creek Resort, 55 Village Rd. (Hwy. 6), Avon, 970-949-7728

■ "Posh and expensive, but worth it" is the majority view on this Beaver Creek New French that serves chef Daniel Joly's "fine food" in a "cozy ", rustic mountain ranch house; the minority on the other side of the fence calls it "disappointing" and "overfancy."

Morton's of Chicago 🅂 | 27 | 24 | 25 | $43 |

1710 Wynkoop St. (17th St.), Denver, 303-825-3353

◪ This LoDo outpost of the national chain is a veritable "beef blizzard" that impresses with "superb steaks", "pro service" and a "wonderful cigar selection"; it also draws gibes about high prices ("bring a cash cow"), "snooty" service, "side dishes that leave a lot to be desired" and portions too big "for non–football players", but "they really know how to do steak."

Palace Arms 🅂 | 27 | 27 | 27 | $40 |

Brown Palace Hotel, 321 17th St. (Tremont Pl.), Denver, 303-297-3111

■ The crowning jewel of Downtown's century-old Brown Palace Hotel, this American-Continental gets the royal 'oui' for its "elegant" setting "dripping with atmosphere", "excellent" food and service that's "tops"; it offers "class at a price", and remember, gents, to don that coat and tie.

Papillon Cafe 🅂 | 28 | 24 | 24 | $29 |

250 Josephine St. (bet. 2nd & 3rd Aves.), Denver, 303-333-7166

■ "All his schooling in France paid off" for Radek Cerny, who is turning out "exquisite presentations" of modestly priced New French fare with Asian influences at this recent addition; "attentive service" and "a good wine list" add to the pleasure, and while the decor is no match for the food quality, this is "the place to be seen" in ever-busy Cherry Creek North; "valet parking is a plus."

Piñons 🅂 | 29 | 27 | 27 | $46 |

105 S. Mill St. (Main St.), Aspen, 970-920-2021

■ Most are willing to shell out for the "aggressively expensive but delicious" cooking at this Aspen New American, especially since it comes with "great ambiance", supermodern Western decor and first-rate service; there's a master sommelier on board and the wine list shows it, with special bottlings from around the world.

Potager | – | – | – | M |

1109 Ogden St. (bet. 11th & 12th Sts.), 303-832-5788

The owner swears 'to get the best that we can get' and that means seasonal ingredients go into a monthly changing menu emphasizing Pan-Med cooking sprinkled with some California curlicues; the wine list is simple, fairly priced and full of 'little guys' from around the world; N.B. don't miss the $20 tastings on Fridays.

Q's S 29 | 25 | 27 | $34

Hotel Boulderado, 2115 13th St. (Spruce St.), Boulder, 303-442-4880

■ This Boulder New American has a "romantic", "formal setting" in one long, beautiful room in the Hotel Boulderado ("the perfect place for an affair") and chef John Platt cooks "froufrou well done"; given the "outstanding, innovative" food, "attentive service" and "good wine list", it's no wonder most consider it a fair deal.

Renaissance S ▽ 28 | 24 | 26 | $50

304 E. Hopkins Ave. (Monarch Ave.), Aspen, 970-925-2402

■ One of the "best" in all Colorado for New American–Med dining in a lovely setting with a big (and expensive) wine list; it draws a few gibes for "attitude", "high prices" and "rich sauces", but in view of the quality those are just quibbles.

Strings S 25 | 23 | 23 | $29

1700 Humboldt St. (17th Ave.), Denver, 303-831-7310

◪ This Uptown New American, with high-end Italian touches, gets more votes than any other Colorado nonchain eatery: from praise such as "delicious food with something for everyone", "hip and happening", "best in all areas" to pans such as "I don't get the hype", "disappointing", "too trendy, too smug"; by most accounts, "it's a first stringer" for Denver dining.

Sushi Den S 27 | 24 | 20 | $24

1487 S. Pearl St. (Florida Ave.), Denver, 303-777-0826

◪ Everyone agrees that this "very chic", "way cool" Washington Park "Gen X headquarters" offers "Denver's best sushi by far"; but "get there by 4:30 PM or plan to wait" because the hip, modern setting is "always crowded" (and always "too loud to talk").

Sweet Basil S 27 | 23 | 24 | $32

193 E. Gore Creek Dr. (Bridge St.), Vail, 970-476-0125

■ Surveyors are wild about this Vail standout (some even call it "best in Colorado") for being "always great" and open year-round; chef Thomas Salamunovich's "truly creative" New American food is "good day in, day out" and enhanced by a "wonderful" setting overlooking Gore Creek, "stellar service" and a fine wine list; basically, "it's impossible to order a bad item" here.

Tante Louise 27 | 25 | 26 | $37

4900 E. Colfax Ave. (Eudora St.), Denver, 303-355-4488

■ Everyone's "favorite maiden aunt" has been "very good for a very long time", serving Classic and Contemporary French fare in a "romantic, elegant setting" comprised of two attached houses; the "special touches" provided by owner Corbin Douglass prompt fans to call him and his chef Michael Degenhart "the best team in Denver"; some tout the "best wine list" too.

Tivoli Deer S 26 | 25 | 24 | $32

26395 Hilltop Dr. (Hwy. 74), Kittredge, 303-670-0941

■ A definite albeit "different" destination in Kittredge, this "classy" Continental with a Scandinavian accent offers a prix fixe menu Saturdays (à la carte other days) that customers call "a great dining experience"; it's "romantic" and "beautiful" – "the place for a very special occasion"; P.S. "complimentary inclusive wine" means you'll need "a room or a designated driver after dining here."

240 Union S | 26 | 22 | 24 | $24 |

240 Union Blvd. (3 blocks south of 6th Ave. Frwy.), Lakewood, 303-989-3562

■ Raves go to the "close-to-perfect food and service" and "attractive" decor at this "California-style" New American "oasis" in the West suburbs that's "surprisingly casual for such a nice place"; surveyors applaud the "superb fish" and wine list but find the "noise" irritating.

Vesta Dipping Grill S | – | – | – | M |

1822 Blake St. (bet. 18th & 19th Sts.), Denver, 303-296-1970

Arguably the classiest, most delicious restaurant in LoDo, this New American specializes in skewers of meat or seafood grilled over an open flame and served with various salsas or dips; while that sounds simple, the restaurant itself is art: from the long, swirling bar and ghost-like wall sconces to the enormous, cone-shaped lights that descend to white crystal points.

Wildflower S | 27 | 26 | 26 | $40 |

The Lodge at Vail, 174 E. Gore Creek Dr. (base of Vail Mountain), Vail, 970-476-5011

■ Considered by many "Vail's best", this New American marries "intense flavors" with "a beautiful setting" featuring thousands of lifelike silk flowers that nay-say winter; with "excellent service" and noteworthy wines, it's "superb in every way", though "not cheap."

Detroit

TOP 10 FOOD RANKING

	Restaurant	Cuisine Type
28	Lark	Eclectic/French
27	Golden Mushroom	Continental
	Opus One	New American
26	Zingerman's Deli	Deli
	Cafe Bon Homme	New French
	Moro's Dining	N/S Italian
25	Pike Street	Traditional American
	Ritz-Carlton Grill	Traditional American
	Moveable Feast	Continental/New Amer.
	Morton's of Chicago	Steakhouse

OTHER IMPORTANT PLACES

Cousins Heritage Inn	New American
Earle	French/Italian
Five Lakes Grill	New American
Mon Jin Lau	Asian
Rattlesnake Club	New American
Ristorante di Modesta	Northern Italian
Rowe Inn	Regional American
Steve's Backroom	Middle Eastern
Tapawingo	New American
Too Chez	New American
Tribute	New American
Whitney	New American

F | D | S | C

Cafe Bon Homme 26 | 23 | 24 | $29

844 Penniman Ave. (bet. Harvey & Main Sts.), Plymouth, 734-453-6260

◪ The "lovely" country French ambiance of this Plymouth "special occasion" place is matched by classically based Contemporary French cooking that most judge "outstanding"; a few critics claim that the "polished" service can be "slightly precious" and the "fancy" food is not quite up to its rep, but as ratings attest, praise far outweighs grumbles.

Cousins Heritage Inn 25 | 23 | 24 | $30

7954 Ann Arbor Rd. (bet. Baker & Main Sts.), Dexter, 734-426-3020

■ "Year after year", this "beautiful" old house "in a quiet town" just west of Ann Arbor is favored for celebrations thanks to softly lit, "dignified" rooms and a short but "classic" New American menu featuring hard-to-find game and "seasonal vegetables"; it's what "one hopes to find" in a country restaurant, except that it's perhaps "a bit cramped."

Earle, The S 25 | 22 | 22 | $24

121 W. Washington St. (S. Ashley St.), Ann Arbor, 734-994-0211

◪ Take "someone you love" to this jazz-filled "hideaway" in Downtown Ann Arbor that provides an "intimate", candlelit setting for a "relaxing" meal of "first-rate" country French-Italian fare complemented by some of the region's best wines; on a simpler note, try its wine bar for drinks and a light dinner "without a large bill"; critics find the ambiance "gloomy" and food "heavy", but they're obviously outvoted.

Five Lakes Grill | – | – | – | M |
424 N. Main St. (Commerce Rd.), Milford, 248-684-7455
Brian Polcyn (ex Pike Street and Acadia), one of the most talented chefs around, is cooking in a 147-seat storefront in this tiny village an hour northwest of Detroit; locals and mobile food fans arrive for the likes of his signature roast duck with apple cider sauce, and there's a series of light offerings for the diet challenged.

Golden Mushroom | 27 | 23 | 25 | $32 |
18100 W. Ten Mile Rd. (Southfield Rd.), Southfield, 248-559-4230
■ Defining fine Continental dining in Detroit for nearly two decades, this "classic" has been a training ground for many of the area's best chefs; the "professional" supervision of semi-retired "master chef" Milos Cihelka (Derin Moore now serves as executive chef) consistently produces "premier" meals, focusing on mushrooms and game, matched by "excellent" wines; even if some find the decor "dated", most advise "save up" to enjoy "one of the best."

Lark, The | 28 | 27 | 28 | $50 |
6430 Farmington Rd. (north of Maple Rd.), W. Bloomfield, 248-661-4466
■ "World-class" Eclectic-French cooking (ranked No. 1 for Food in the Detroit area) combined with rustic Portuguese decor and the "hospitality" of Jim and Mary Lark earn this West Bloomfield boutique high ratings; it's "hip to bash it" and it takes a "big wallet and a big stomach" to do justice to its prix fixe menu, but its status as Michigan's Most Popular restaurant speaks for itself.

Mon Jin Lau ◐ S | 24 | 20 | 21 | $19 |
1515 E. Maple Rd. (Stephenson Hwy.), Troy, 248-689-2332
■ Not only does this "nouveau" Troy Asian boast "adventurous" cooking, but it also has "great wines", a "classy" setting and knows how to "mix a martini"; the menu blends Chinese, Thai and French influences, providing an "interesting twist on the old standbys" plus "unique" specials; no wonder it's "very crowded."

Moro's Dining S | 26 | 16 | 22 | $19 |
6535 Allen Rd. (Southfield Rd.), Allen Park, 313-382-7152
◪ A long-standing south suburb Italian "secret" for "outstanding scampi and veal", salad tossed tableside and flambéed desserts; "huge portions" and a lack of pretension have kept this Detroit old-timer busy for years; some find the atmosphere "romantic", but as decor ratings indicate, not everyone agrees.

Morton's of Chicago S | 25 | 23 | 24 | $34 |
1 Towne Sq. (N. Northwestern Hwy.), Southfield, 248-354-6006
◪ Top-quality "red meat" draws carnivores who like to "smoke cigars, listen to Frank Sinatra and enjoy their own wine" in the "men's club ambiance" of this classy chain steakhouse; some aren't into this kind of "beef feast" (too many "pinky rings and 'nieces' "); those who are say "go starving" and "bring money."

Moveable Feast, The | 25 | 24 | 22 | $31 |
326 W. Liberty (2nd St.), Ann Arbor, 734-663-3278
◪ It's "hard to go wrong" at what admirers call Ann Arbor's "best", a "high-toned", lace-edged Victorian with "beautifully presented" Continental-American fare; the ever-changing menu "can be very inventive", and if it "sometimes misses" (ditto the service), odds are you'll enjoy an "excellent" meal in a "quiet, refined" setting.

Opus One 27 | 26 | 26 | $36
565 E. Larned St. (Beaubien St.), 313-961-7766
■ "First class in every way", from the "elegant" etched glass, marble and mahogany decor interior and personal "pampering" to its "top-notch" New American menu and "sensational" desserts; though "pricey", it's "reliably impressive" and a byword for business entertaining for Detroit's Downtown power brokers.

Pike Street Restaurant 25 | 22 | 23 | $29
18 W. Pike. St. (bet. Saginaw St. & Wide Track Dr.), Pontiac, 248-334-7878
■ A "diamond in the rough" of Downtown Pontiac, this American standout remains "consistently good" and "cosmopolitan"; the "innovative" kitchen turns out "hearty, wholesome" fare that's beautifully presented in a turn-of-the-century wood-and-brick setting; most rate it "just plain excellent."

Rattlesnake Club 25 | 24 | 22 | $31
Stroh's River Pl., 300 River Pl., 313-567-4400
■ New American star-chef Jimmy Schmidt presides over this polished wood-and-marble, river-view dining room; its elegant "NYC" setting, culinary artistry and "outstanding quality" make "the snake" a premier "client" and "special events" spot; "excellent" wines are the icing on the cake.

Ristorante di Modesta S 25 | 21 | 22 | $27
29410 Northwestern Hwy. (12 Mile Rd.), Southfield, 248-358-0344
◪ It's usually a "scene" at this western suburban "media hangout", where "terrific" Northern Italian food is spiced by local celeb sightings; it's "trendy, tasty" and has great ambiance, but reports of "arrogance" suggest they need to "turn down the attitude."

Ritz-Carlton Grill S 25 | 27 | 26 | $33
Ritz-Carlton Hotel, Fairlane Plaza, 300 Town Ctr. Dr. (bet. Hubbard & Southfield Svc. Drs.), Dearborn, 734-441-2100
■ An ambiance of sheer "luxury" and an "unobtrusive", "well-trained staff" enhance the American menu of grilled meats and seafood at this "impressive" hotel dining room opposite Ford World HQ; it gets high marks all-around and is "extra special for special occasions"; "it's the Ritz" says it all.

Rowe Inn S 28 | 21 | 25 | $36
6303 County Rd. 48 (1 mi. east of city center), Ellsworth, 616-588-7351
■ "A great reason to go north", this "jewel" in Michigan's outstate resort area, with a "cozy" ambiance reminiscent of the French countryside, has long set a regional standard as a source for "outstanding and creative" Michigan cuisine paired with "one of the top wine lists in the US"; with a "classy", unpretentious wood-paneled setting, it competes with nearby Tapawingo, whose chef-owner started here, for top gourmet honors.

Steve's Backroom 25 | 17 | 20 | $12
19872 Kelly Rd. (bet. 7 & 8 Mile Rds.), Harper Woods, 313-527-7240
■ In a tiny, "very clean" BYO cafe in back of a well-run Middle Eastern market owned by a Lebanese couple, diners discover the "best grape leaves and kibbe" they've "ever tasted" and "never had anything I didn't like"; this Harper Woods hideout is "a real surprise for the unknowing."

Tapawingo ■S | 29 | 26 | 27 | $38

9502 Lake St. (County Rd. 48), Ellsworth, 616-588-7971

■ Judged by many the "best restaurant" around (others bestow this honor on the Rowe Inn), this "oasis of class" five hours north of Detroit in Michigan's resort area is set in a lovely old house on a private mini-lake surrounded by huge willows; "beautiful presentations" highlight "creative, flavorful" New American fare that emphasizes Michigan ingredients; aside from an occasional grumble over "snotty" staff, most say this "ultimate experience" is "worth the drive" and price.

Too Chez | 23 | 22 | 21 | $25

27155 Sheraton Dr. (I-96), Novi, 248-348-5555

◩ Snappy and "stylish", this "chic" New American (with Italian accents) is "a treat for the eyes" thanks to modern decor sparked by colorful art and a mosaic floor; most say it pleases the palate with "original" cooking (pizzas, pastas, house-smoked salmon), but critics judge the menu "hit-or-miss" and find the place "too trendy" and "loud"; in the NW suburbs next to a Sheraton and handy to I-96, it's popular for business lunch and lights up even more at dinner.

Tribute | – | – | – | VE

31425 W. 12 Mile Rd. (W. Orchard Lake Rd.), Farmington Hills, 248-848-9393

Opulent white-linen, check-your-wallet-at-the-door west suburban Contemporary American with sophisticated International accents that opened in 1996 amid great fanfare, including the news that it had lured away chef Takashi Yagihashi from Chicago's vaunted Ambria; after a few early teething pains, diners are now paying tribute to at least excellent and sometimes flawless meals and service, just as was intended; open Tuesday–Saturday.

Whitney, The ■S | 25 | 28 | 24 | $36

4421 Woodward Ave. (Canfield Rd.), 313-832-5700

◩ If you "want to impress, take them here" say fans of this stunning 1890 mansion built by lumber baron David Whitney on Detroit's threadbare main drag; it boasts the most "majestic" decor around (cut glass, carved wood, a sweeping staircase), and though some say the changing New American menu "could be better", most are satisfied by the hefty offerings; the "awesome" Sunday brunch gets a thumbs-up from surveyors, and there's a "terrific" bar with jazz on the third floor.

Zingerman's Deli ■S | 26 | 18 | 20 | $12

422 Detroit St. (Kingsley St.), Ann Arbor, 734-663-3354

■ Mavens debate whether "Ann Arbor's pride" is the "best deli in the Western Hemisphere" or merely "the Midwest"; "huge, wonderful corned beef sandwiches" and a long menu of "fabulous" combos on "heavenly breads" (they bake their own) mean it's always "crowded and noisy" despite taking over the building next door for more tables; it's also a "serious" "gourmet grocery" with coffees, meats, cheeses, smoked fish and other exotica.

Fort Lauderdale

TOP 10 FOOD RANKING

	Restaurant	Cuisine Type
28	Darrel & Oliver's Cafe	New World
27	Eduardo de San Angel	Mexican
	Primavera	Northern Italian
	Mark's Las Olas	New World
26	La Brochette Bistro	French Bistro
	Il Tartufo	Northern Italian
	Cafe Arugula	Italian/Mediterranean
25	By Word of Mouth	New American
	Rainbow Palace	Chinese
	Armadillo Cafe	Southwestern

OTHER IMPORTANT PLACES

Black Orchid Cafe	Continental/New Amer.
Brooks	American/Continental
Cafe Seville	Spanish
Casa D'Angelo	Northern Italian
Darrel & Oliver's/Grill	New World
Himmarshee Bar & Grille	New American
Hobo's Fish Joint	Seafood
Hot Chocolates	Eclectic
Ichiban	Japanese
Kasbah Moroccan	Moroccan
Maui Grille	Hawaiian
Reed's River House	Regional Amer./Southern
Sunfish Grill	Seafood

F | D | S | C

Armadillo Cafe S — 25 | 17 | 22 | $30

4630 SW 64th Ave. (bet. Davie & Griffin Rds.), Davie, 954-791-4866

■ In "an out-of-the-way" location in western Broward, this casual (you can "color on the tablecloths") Southwestern is "worth the drive" for its "creative menu", including "standout black-and-white bean soup", "great tenderloin tacos" and "the best roast lamb"; it's "expensive, but worth it" – "the closest you'll get to Santa Fe in South Florida."

Black Orchid Cafe S — – | – | – | VE

2985 N. Ocean Blvd. (1 block south of Oakland Park Blvd.), 954-561-9398

A roomful of orchids sets the stage for an inspired if pricey menu from chef George Telles, who offers exotica such as Canadian elk loin, tenderloin of buffalo and grilled ostrich along with more conventional Continental–New American fare; a fine, moderately priced wine list adds appeal.

Brooks S — 24 | 23 | 24 | $31

500 S. Federal Hwy. (south of Hillsboro Blvd.), Deerfield Beach, 954-427-9302

◪ "One of Broward's better restaurants" offers classic American-Continental cuisine in an "elegant" setting with a "Euro feel"; some don't like the "old, stuffy" ambiance or "heavy sauces", but "the blue-haired set loves it here" and, as ratings show, so do most; "utterly dependable" sums it up.

	F	D	S	C
By Word of Mouth	25	15	22	$30

3200 NE 12th Ave. (north of Oakland Park Blvd.), 954-564-3663
■ Despite its "off-the-beaten-path" location, this American "gourmet heaven" is "too good to pass up"; fans rave about the "excellent food and great desserts", and if the interior reminds some of "eating in a bus station", there's always takeout.

	F	D	S	C
Cafe Arugula S	26	22	24	$37

3150 N. Federal Hwy. (½ mi. south of Sample Rd.), Lighthouse Point, 954-785-7732
■ "A dedicated chef and his wife" have always been the keys to success for this "wonderful" New American eatery, and now Dick and Carolann Cingolani have returned to their roots with a new Med-Italian menu (instituted post-*Survey*); prices have been reduced, but it still offers excellent service and gracious dining.

	F	D	S	C
Cafe Seville	22	18	22	$25

2768 E. Oakland Park Blvd. (Bayview Dr.), 954-565-1148
■ This "romantic" Spanish in a shopping center offers "excellent paella" plus "nontraditional" Iberian cuisine "with a twist"; a few complaints of "inconsistent" quality are outnumbered by praise for the "very good" food, "warm ambiance" and "good service."

	F	D	S	C
Casa D'Angelo S	–	–	–	E

1201 N. Federal Hwy. (north of Sunrise Blvd.), 954-564-1234
After stints at several South Florida restaurants, Florence native Angelo Elia has returned to Fort Lauderdale as executive chef–partner at his eponymous Tuscan grill; the handsome room complements his high-end cuisine – oak-grilled items excel, creative pasta combos are beautifully executed and dessert standouts include a heavenly tiramisu.

	F	D	S	C
Darrel & Oliver's Cafe Maxx S	28	22	26	$38

2601 E. Atlantic Blvd. (26th Ave.), Pompano Beach, 954-782-0606
■ It's "crowded" and "loud" to the max, but it's "one of the best restaurants in the tri-county area"; from an open kitchen, chef/co-owner Oliver Saucy sends forth "innovative", "cutting-edge" New World cuisine enhanced by "superb" wines and "sharp service"; the decor may be "less exciting" than the fare, but even so it's a "winner" and ranked No. 1 for Food in Broward.

	F	D	S	C
Darrel & Oliver's East City Grill S	–	–	–	E

Riviera Hotel, 505 Atlantic Blvd. (Hwy. A1A), 954-565-5569
Giani Respinto is the new man in the kitchen at Darrel Broeck and Oliver Saucy's popular New World outpost which isn't just a copycat of their very successful Pompano Beach operation; here there's an oceanfront setting and the kitchen starts early and finishes late, turning out breakfast, lunch and dinner.

	F	D	S	C
Eduardo de San Angel	27	22	25	$33

2822 E. Commercial Blvd. (Bay Dr. & 28th Ave.), 954-772-4731
■ Founder Eduardo Pria has moved on, leaving this "small", award-winning storefront "gourmet" Mexican in the very capable hands of brothers Luis, Rafael and Jose; offering what many call "the best Nouvelle Mexican outside of Mexico City", it's rated No. 2 for Food in Broward County and offers "beautifully presented", innovative fare, "delightful" environs and "personal, prompt service"; "in a class by itself" sums it up.

Himmarshee Bar & Grille S | – | – | – | M |

210 SW Second St. (bet. 2nd & 3rd Aves.), 954-764-5154

Major new talents Peter Boulukos (chef/co-owner) and Tim Petrillo (co-owner) rehabbed a storefront in a burgeoning Downtown locale and are dazzling diners with locally conceived, grown or caught New American fare with a multicultural flair; prices are fair and you won't need an encyclopedia to decipher the ingredients.

Hobo's Fish Joint S | – | – | – | E |

Palm Springs Plaza, 10317 Royal Palm Blvd. (Coral Springs Dr.), Coral Springs, 954-346-5484

Even without a water view, this 'fish joint' from husband-and-wife team Steven LaBiner and Janet Ribera is easily one of South FL's finest seafooders, serving a dozen varieties of fresh, expertly cooked fish to a well-heeled crowd of knowledgeable suburbanites; an excellent wine list and pro service enhance the experience.

Hot Chocolates ◐ S | – | – | – | E |

Barnett Bank Bldg., 3101 N. Federal Hwy. (Oakland Park Blvd.), 954-564-5552

One of the finest restaurants to hit Fort Lauderdale in some time, with offbeat but elegant decor (best described as Erté meets *The Flintstones*) as a backdrop for an Eclectic menu featuring creative combos that work; though on the expensive side, it's a place to see and be seen by South Florida trendsetters who also know good food.

Ichiban S | – | – | – | M |

Shoppes of Arrowhead, 2441 S. University Dr., Davie, 954-370-0767

The name means 'number one', and this little Japanese retreat west of Fort Lauderdale lives up to its moniker; whether patrons opt for traditional floor-level tatami dining or the American tables and chairs, they are delighted with servings of delectable sushi and sashimi, perfectly executed tempura and other somewhat less-familiar but equally impeccable Nipponese fare.

Il Tartufo S | 26 | 19 | 21 | $35 |

2400 E. Las Olas Blvd. (west of the Intracoastal Bridge), 954-767-9190

■ "Excellent pasta" and other "well-prepared" fare earn high marks for this "storefront" Northern Italian with "attentive" service, a "romantic, old-world ambiance" and a kitchen that specializes in seafood and veal; considered "Broward's top Italian" by some, it's "expensive, but not overpriced" for the quality.

Kasbah Moroccan Restaurant S | – | – | – | M |

420 N. Federal Hwy. (2 blocks north of Atlantic Blvd.), Pompano Beach, 954-941-4277

Caftan-clad chef-owner Zakaria ('call me Zak') Tadlaoui's unique eatery is highly recommended for its authentic Moroccan food, gracious dining rituals and tent-like decor; the traditional five-course dinner allows first-timers to sample all the exotic flavors at one sitting, making for a memorable experience.

La Brochette Bistro S | 26 | 20 | 21 | $26 |

Embassy Lakes Shopping Ctr., 2635 N. Hiatus Rd. (Sheridan St.), Cooper City, 954-435-9090

◪ "Everything is served on a skewer" in this shopping center bistro, and those who "like this cooking style" call the chef "an artist" and the food "delicious"; apart from a few jabs at "indifferent" service, most say it's a "great find."

Mark's Las Olas S | 27 | 25 | 24 | $36

1032 E. Las Olas Blvd. (SE 10th Terr.), 954-463-1000

◪ Chef-owner Mark Militello "has done it again" with his second New World cuisine showcase; a "hot spot" on Las Olas Boulevard, it attracts crowds with an eclectic, daily-changing menu built around "unique" flavors and served in a "hip", albeit "noisy", ambiance; though some complain of "rude attitude" and high prices, that doesn't stop admirers from planning "far in advance" to get a reservation.

Maui Grille S | - | - | - | E

5022 N. Federal Hwy. (49th St.), Lighthouse Point, 954-571-7788

True to its name, this grill offers authentic Hawaiian cuisine prepared by Stuart Hirsch, using herbs, spices, salad greens, seafood and wine from Hawaii; the food is a virtual kaleidoscope of colors and flavors, the ambiance is decidedly tropical and the prices are right for this north Lauderdale neighborhood eatery.

Primavera S | 27 | 22 | 24 | $36

830 E. Oakland Park Blvd. (bet. Dixie Hwy. & NE 6th Ave.), 954-564-6363

■ For a "special night", it's hard to beat this "elegant" Northern Italian; with "lovely food", including "a fancy display of appetizers and desserts", it wins Broward's top ratings for Italian and also earns praise for its "caring staff, from the front of the house to the back of the kitchen", and handsome setting; as you'd expect, it's "pricey", but what's rather unexpected is its shopping center locale.

Rainbow Palace S | 25 | 23 | 24 | $31

2787 E. Oakland Park Blvd. (Bayview Dr.), 954-565-5652

■ "You'd never guess" from the plain exterior of this Chinese that inside is one of the most "beautiful" dining rooms; also impressive is the "innovative", "first-rate" gourmet fare ("great dumplings", "tasty orange beef") and "elegant service", making it a "true palace" that's "worth every cent."

Reed's River House S | - | - | - | E

301 SW Third Ave. (Broward Blvd.), 954-525-7661

Southern regional cuisine and decor exist in perfect harmony at this recently restored, early 20th-century mansion fronting the New River; serving a down-home mix of flavors from South Carolina's low country, the deep South and the Florida Keys, it draws local wheeler-dealers and others who enjoy gracious service in intimate, beautifully appointed rooms, many with fireplaces.

Sunfish Grill | - | - | - | M

2771 E. Atlantic Blvd. (28th Ave.), Pompano Beach, 954-788-2434

Owner–executive chef Tony Sindaco prepares excellent seafood at this informal, colorful 42-seat former Mexican luncheonette in Pompano Beach; both full-time residents and 'snowbirds' are drawn by its tantalizing aromas, fine desserts and varied, moderately priced wine list.

Fort Worth

TOP 10 FOOD RANKING

	Restaurant	Cuisine Type
28	Cacharel	New French
	Del Frisco's	Steakhouse
27	Saint-Emilion	French Bistro
26	Bistro Louise	Mediterranean
25	Railhead Smokehouse	BBQ
	Angeluna	New American
	Kincaid's	Hamburgers
	La Piazza	N/S Italian
24	Angelo's Barbeque	BBQ
23	Cafe Aspen	New American

OTHER IMPORTANT PLACES

Restaurant	Cuisine Type
Buffet at the Kimbell	New American
Grape Escape	Eclectic
Joe T. Garcia's	Mexican
On Broadway	N/S Italian
Randall's Gourmet	Eclectic
Reata	Southwestern
Reflections	New American

	F	D	S	C
Angelo's Barbeque ⊄	24	15	17	$11
Angeluna S	25	23	22	$29
Bistro Louise	26	25	22	$27
Buffet at the Kimbell Museum S	19	23	16	$12

Angelo's Barbeque ⊄ — 24 | 15 | 17 | $11

2533 White Settlement Rd. (University Dr.), 817-332-0357

■ The granddaddy of Fort Worth smoked meats is "a museum of BBQ" to fans who say this "dark and smoky" "golden oldie" dishes up "the best damn BBQ in the state", or maybe "the universe", along with the "coldest beer"; if a few doubters say "good but no longer the best", more consider this "the real deal."

Angeluna S — 25 | 23 | 22 | $29

215 E. Fourth St. (bet Calhoun & Commerce Sts.), 817-334-0080

◪ Some of "Fort Worth's most original food" can be found at this "trendy" Downtowner praised for its "nouveau" American fare and "light, airy" setting with a cloud-motif ceiling; though it also draws some complaints ("loud", "uneven", "all show"), it's a definite "hot spot" and a "great location for Bass Hall" concertgoers.

Bistro Louise — 26 | 25 | 22 | $27

Stonegate Commons, 2900 S. Hulen St. (Oak Park Ln.), 817-922-9244

■ With "lovely" decor that hints of Provence and the Riviera, Fort Worth's Most Popular restaurant is a "comfortable, elegant" retreat offering "fresh, innovative" Mediterranean fare that makes "excellent use of spices"; it's "perfect for a ladies' lunch" and enough of a "treat" to "drive from Dallas to eat here."

Buffet at the Kimbell Museum S — 19 | 23 | 16 | $12

Kimbell Art Museum, 3333 Camp Bowie Blvd. (1 block west of University Dr.), 817-332-8451

■ This lunch favorite in the acclaimed Kimbell Art Museum boasts (no surprise) "beautiful surroundings" plus "interesting" New American food that's "outstanding for a museum" – in fact, some go for "lunch first, then art"; regulars are especially happy now that chef "Shelby's back"; N.B. dinner served Fridays only.

Cacharel 28 | 25 | 26 | $40

2221 E. Lamar Blvd. (bet. Ballpark Way & Hwy. 360), Arlington, 817-640-9981

■ Rated No. 1 for Food in Fort Worth, this "exceptional", "elegant" New French set atop an office building is considered "*the* place for any important occasion"; offering "very consistent" food (including "soufflés to die for"), a "quiet" setting and "attentive service" with an eye for "detail", it's "expensive" but could show other restaurants "how it's done."

Cafe Aspen 23 | 20 | 22 | $26

Frost Bank Shopping Plaza, 6103 Camp Bowie Blvd. (Bryant Irvin Rd.), 817-738-0838

◪ A Fort Worth pioneer in New American cuisine that's still a "favorite" for "wonderful seasonal fare" served in a cozy, romantic setting by a "courteous" staff led by an owner "who's always there and concerned"; despite scattered reports of "disappointing" meals, the fact that it has a "steady loyal following" says a lot; P.S. "dinner in the bar is one of the best-kept secrets in town."

Del Frisco's Double Eagle Steak House 28 | 26 | 26 | $47

812 Main St. (8th St.), 817-877-3999

◪ The "classiest joint to get a steak and still wear your boots" describes this dark, clubby "meat lover's paradise" with beef "to die for" (rated No. 2 for Food in Fort Worth); "superb service" is a plus, and though some find "cigar smoke a turnoff" and call it "too noisy" and "expensive", most consider it "well worth" the tab.

Grape Escape, The S ▽ 21 | 21 | 22 | $22

500 Commerce St. (4th St.), 817-336-9463

◪ The city's first wine bar, in an ideal location facing Bass Performance Hall, is "a small, fun place" serving "surprisingly good" Eclectic nibbles in a stylish, "relaxed atmosphere"; though grumblers say it's hard to make "a full meal" out of the small plates and call it "pricey for what you get", most are happy to focus on the "great wine flights" served by an "extremely knowledgeable" staff.

Joe T. Garcia's S ⊭ 21 | 21 | 20 | $16

2201 N. Commerce St. (NW 22nd St.), 817-626-4356

◪ A Fort Worth "landmark" for over 60 years and "still going strong", thanks to some of "the best margaritas and Mexican food" around plus a "fantastic" patio ("sit by the pool") that makes "you feel you're really in Mexico"; not everyone agrees ("tourist-oriented", "bland food"), but to its "cult following" it's "unbeatable."

Kincaid's Hamburgers ⊭ 25 | 14 | 18 | $8

4901 Camp Bowie Blvd. (Eldridge St.), 817-732-2881.

■ "No decor, no service, who cares? – best burger ever" sums up this ancient grocery store beloved for its "good, old-fashioned, greasy burgers" made from "high-quality meat"; sit at a picnic table or follow the lead of regulars and eat standing at the counters.

La Piazza S 25 | 25 | 22 | $33

University Park Village, 1600 S. University Dr. (2 blocks south of I-30), 817-334-0000

◪ Easily the most elegant Italian nook in town ("great for a date"), with a "loyal following" for its "consistently first-rate food"; but it doesn't come cheap and may be served with a side of "attitude."

On Broadway Ristorante S ▽ 22 | 18 | 20 | $19
Hulen Point Shopping Ctr., 6306 Hulen Bend (Hulen St.), 817-346-8841
◪ A tradition in the shopping stretch of southwest Fort Worth, this "popular" Italian "keeps on keeping on" as an "always dependable, underrated sleeper" offering "good, middle-of-the-road" fare featuring "sauces full of flavor and garlic"; if some feel it benefits from "not much competition in the area", that doesn't faze fans who simply "love this place."

Railhead Smokehouse 25 | 18 | 19 | $12
2900 Montgomery St. (I-30), 817-738-9808
■ Rave reviews go to the "best all-around BBQ in Fort Worth", serving up "huge platters" of "superior" beef, ribs and chicken with "delectable sauces" that are "worth the pounds" gained; a "clean, safe location" also helps make it "hugely popular", and while that can mean long lines and noise, it also means "lots of interesting customers" and a "great patio scene."

Randall's Gourmet Cheesecake Co. ▽ 25 | 25 | 22 | $24
907 Houston St. (bet. 8th & 9th Sts.), 817-336-2253
■ "Don't let the name fool you" – this "quiet, intimate" Downtown Eclectic hideout offers a "great overall dining experience"; the menu is "limited" but "delicious", enhanced by a "good wine list" and ambiance that makes you "feel you're in NYC"; in sum, a "little jewel" – and yes, "save room" for the cheesecake.

Reata S 23 | 26 | 22 | $30
Bank One Bldg., 500 Throckmorton St., 35th fl. (bet. 4th & 5th Sts.), 817-336-1009
◪ Perched high atop a bank building, this nouveau Southwestern named for the ranch in *Giant* offers "cowboy cuisine with an upscale twist that works" in a matching setting that's rated No. 1 for Decor in Fort Worth; though some call it "overpriced" and wish the "food matched" the "beautiful view", most like its "unique" style and call it the ideal place to impress "a Yankee."

Reflections ▽ 26 | 25 | 26 | $43
Worthington Hotel, 200 Main St. (Houston St.), 817-882-1765
◪ "Excellence in fine dining" is what admirers find at this stunning hotel dining room offering artistic presentations of New American fare in an elegant, "romantic" ambiance; the less impressed say it "can be wonderful – or not so", but solid ratings across the board side with those who call it "a treat", albeit a pricey one.

Saint-Emilion S 27 | 24 | 25 | $36
3617 W. Seventh St. (Montgomery St.), 817-737-2781
■ A favorite for elegant Country French cuisine, this intimate winner is lovely for "an anniversary or special celebration" thanks to "always superb duck" and other "authentic", "high-quality" bistro fare enhanced by a "very good wine list", attentive service and "romantic" ambiance; a caring owner is another reason why it's considered "one of the best."

TOP 20 FOOD RANKING

	Restaurant	Cuisine Type
27	Alan Wong's	Regional Hawaiian
	La Mer	Classic French
	Roy's	Eurasian/Pacific Rim
25	Cliquo	Classic French
	Hoku's	International
	Hy's Steak House	Steakhouse/Trad. Amer.
	Orchids	Continental/Int'l
	Yohei Sushi	Japanese
	Azul	Mediterranean
	3660 on the Rise	Pacific Rim
	Ruth's Chris	Steakhouse
	Bali-by-the-Sea	Eurasian/Reg. Hawaiian
	Kyo-Ya	Japanese
	Cascada	Mediterranean
	Golden Dragon	Chinese
24	Ono Hawaiian Foods	Regional Hawaiian
	Prince Court	Pacific Rim
	Kacho	Japanese
	Legend Seafood	Chinese/Seafood
	Sam Choy's	Regional Hawaiian

OTHER IMPORTANT PLACES

A Pacific Cafe	Pacific Rim
Ciao Mein	Chinese/Italian
David Paul's Diamond Head	New American
Hau Tree Lanai	International/Seafood
Indigo	Eurasian
Mariposa	Regional American
Michel's	Classic French
Palomino	Mediterranean
Singha Thai	Thai

F | D | S | C

Alan Wong's S — 27 | 20 | 24 | $45

McCully Ct., 1857 S. King St., 5th fl. (bet. Hauoli & Pumehana Sts.), 808-949-2526

■ Fans of "culinary genius" Alan Wong and his "brilliant" Regional Hawaiian cuisine that "looks as good as it tastes" proliferated after Wong won the 1996 James Beard Best Chef of the Northwest award in his first full year in his own digs; it's now Oahu's Favorite Restaurant and for most, the "imaginative" fare and "cutting-edge wine list" are worth the "long wait" and "pricey" tab, even if some bemoan "plain decor" that "doesn't equal the food."

A Pacific Cafe S — 23 | 21 | 21 | $36

Ward Ctr., 1200 Ala Moana Blvd. (bet. Piikoi St. & Ward Ave.), 808-593-0035

◪ "Exquisite presentation" and a "lovely blend of flavors" have harnessed a steady luncheon trade, although evening reviewers find the "dinner menu a more worthy showcase" of Jean-Marie Josselin's latest "imaginative" Pacific Rim entry in Ward Centre; but the jury is out on the "Jules Verne meets Jacques Cousteau" decor and reactions to service range from "excellent" to "slow."

Azul 25 | 24 | 25 | $55

Ihilani Resort & Spa, 92-1001 Olani St., Kapolei, 808-679-0079

■ An "elegant, intimate" room with "classy decor", "impeccable Mediterranean cuisine", the "best wine list in town" and some of "the best service in Hawaii" nails this West Oahu resort's premier restaurant, tailored for expense-account guests and "special occasion" local dining; count on the freshest fish, "great" olive-crusted rack of lamb and a "wow" tab at this "fancy" "getaway."

Bali-by-the-Sea 25 | 27 | 25 | $46

Hilton Hawaiian Village, 2005 Kalia Rd. (Ala Moana Blvd.), 808-941-2254

■ "Elegant service" and "awesome" Eurasian fare with Hawaiian accents are just the beginning of the charms of this popular "class act" in Waikiki that also offers "romantic ambiance", "outstanding ocean scenery", "splendid service" and a "good wine cellar" enhanced by a "knowledgeable wine staff."

Cascada S 25 | 25 | 23 | $36

Royal Garden Hotel, 440 Olohana St. (bet. Alawai Blvd. & Kuhio Ave.), 808-945-0270

■ Thanks to Nick Sayada's "luscious" Mediterranean fare, this hotel hideaway has become a magnet that draws local culinary sophisticates to Waikiki; most reserve this "romantic", "serene", "garden" "oasis", complete with a waterfall and a "pool like a Roman castle", for a "special occasion" evening; however, midday service has returned thanks to demand from the ladies who lunch.

Ciao Mein S 23 | 23 | 22 | $32

Hyatt Regency Waikiki, 2424 Kalakaua Ave., 808-923-2426

■ A much-acclaimed Waikiki Chinese-Italian ("the best of both worlds"), producing "well-prepared", "clever" dishes served amidst "eclectic decor"; while some find it "expensive", others say it's one of the "few places that's worth what they charge."

Cliquo 25 | 19 | 23 | $40

Niu Valley Ctr., 5730 Kalanianaole Hwy. (bet. E. & W. Halemaumau Sts.), 808-377-8854

■ If you're tired of all the "Pacific Rim mishmash, this is the place to get back to French cuisine" say Francophiles high on this "hidden gem" in an "unlikely" strip mall location; expect "excellent" classic dishes, a "wonderful staff" and a "peaceful", "romantic" ambiance.

David Paul's Diamond Head Grill S – | – | – | VE

Colony Surf Hotel, 2885 Kalakaua Ave., 2nd fl. (opp. Kapiolani Park), 808-922-3734

David Paul Johnson, who has been a hit in Maui with his Lahaina Grill, brings his winning New American fare to Honolulu at this smashingly designed 226-seater at the foot of Diamond Head; tequila shrimp with firecracker rice, kalua duck and Kona coffee roast rack of lamb are among the signature dishes that are drawing locals who don't seem to mind the stiff tab; jazz most nights is a plus.

Golden Dragon S 25 | 25 | 22 | $34

Hilton Hawaiian Village, 2005 Kalia Rd. (Ala Moana Blvd.), 808-946-5336

◪ Reviewers rave about the "excellent food, decor and service" at this Waikiki hotel Chinese with a "beautiful beachside locale"; it's "expensive but tasty" and fans say "if you order just one dish, make it lobster curry with fried *haupia* [coconut]" – "it's God's gift to food."

Hau Tree Lanai S | 20 | 25 | 20 | $27

New Otani Kaimana Beach Hotel, 2863 Kalakaua Ave. (opp. Kapiolani Park), 808-921-7066

◪ This "magic" beachfront International seafooder is a "favorite Kaimana" spot for a "romantic old Hawaii dinner" under "the huge hau tree"; even those who say the "food isn't up to the setting" admit it's a "great place" for "breakfast in paradise."

Hoku's S | 25 | 26 | 25 | $47

Kahala Mandarin Oriental Hotel, 5000 Kahala Ave., 808-739-8779

■ "Find any excuse to go" to this "rising star" declare fans of the "memorable", "innovative" International cuisine from the open kitchen of chef Oliver Altherr; diners also applaud the "exceptional" service and "classy yet unpretentious" oceanview setting; many "would like to visit again" – "if [they] could afford it."

Hy's Steak House S | 25 | 24 | 24 | $39

Waikiki Park Heights Hotel, 2440 Kuhio Ave. (Uluniu Ave.), 808-922-5555

■ "Caring" service "spoils" diners at this "elegant", "clubby", steakhouse in Waikiki that's been lauded as the "absolute best in Honolulu" for 20 years ("so old, it's new again"); expect "top quality" from the "kiawe-grilled steaks that can't be beat" to the rack of lamb; all of it makes locals "feel like a million dollars", which is why "expensive" but "worth it" is the consensus.

Indigo | 23 | 23 | 21 | $28

1121 Nuuanu Ave. (Hotel St.), 808-521-2900

◪ A highly rated but controversial Downtown "Bali in Chinatown" Eurasian; boosters applaud the "exciting", "exotic" "grazing" dishes, "pleasant courtyard tables" ("if lucky"), weekend jazz and convenient location next to the Hawaii Theater; foes cite "teeny-weeny" portions and "flavors that do not always complement each other"; nightly valet parking weighs in on the plus side.

Kacho S | 24 | 22 | 22 | $37

Waikiki Parc Hotel, 2233 Helumoa Rd. (Kalia Rd.), 808-921-7272

■ Reviewers are enraptured by this "classy" Waikiki Japanese "gem" offering "elegant" Kyoto-style dishes that for "flavor and beauty can't be beat"; but one of the "best Japanese restaurants on Oahu" doesn't come cheap – "I'm glad someone else paid."

Kyo-Ya S | 25 | 25 | 23 | $39

2057 Kalakaua Ave., 808-947-3911

■ Reserve a tatami room and be "treated like a shogun" at this "peaceful" Waikiki Japanese where the artistic dishes are such "a feast for eyes and stomach" ("great butterfish misoyaki") that "you don't want to ruin them" by taking a bite; most agree it's "pricey but worth the money spent" – "somebody take me again."

La Mer S | 27 | 28 | 27 | $65

Halekulani Hotel, 2199 Kalia Rd. (beachfront at end of Lewers St.), 808-923-2311

■ To "pull out all the stops", this "romantic" open-air hotel dining room "right on the water" is "definitely worth the expense"; expect a "fabulous Diamond Head view", "the finest French cuisine" prepared by chef Yves Garnier, "impeccable service" and an atmosphere of "subdued elegance" – more than enough reason to "put on a jacket" (required) and spend "three hours on dinner."

Legend Seafood S | 24 | 14 | 15 | $20

Chinese Cultural Plaza, 100 N. Beretania St. (River St.), 808-532-1868

■ The specialty at this "busy as a bee" Chinatown "favorite" is "the absolute best dim sum in Honolulu", although the "great seafood dishes" served by a "friendly staff" get nods of approval too; surveyors say it's the "closest to real Hong Kong cuisine in Hawaii", so most don't mind that it's "without charm."

Mariposa S | – | – | – | E

Neiman Marcus, 1450 Ala Moana Blvd., 3rd fl., 808-951-3420

When the tony Texas store Neiman Marcus staged its Honolulu opening in '98, much of the spotlight was on its third-floor restaurant with views of Ala Moana Park and the ocean; exec chef Douglas Lum offers three regional cuisines: Texan (Red River ribs, brisket), Northwestern (salmon and other fresh fish daily) and Hawaiian–Pacific Rim; prices are about what you'd expect at Neiman Marcus.

Michel's S | 22 | 26 | 23 | $53

Colony Surf Hotel, 2895 Kalakaua Ave., 808-923-6552

◪ Fans feel this "reborn" Classic French on the toe of Diamond Head "has it all" – a "breathtaking view of the surf", "decor that matches the setting" and "excellent food and service"; but equally vocal foes write it off as "ridiculously overpriced" with "supercilious service" and "overrated food"; still, it remains a favorite for "romantic dinners" and "special occasions."

Ono Hawaiian Foods ⊭ | 24 | 9 | 16 | $13

726 Kapahulu Ave. (bet. Date & Winam Sts.), 808-737-2275

◪ "You'll never leave here hungry", but "be prepared to wait" at this "cramped", "hole-in-the-wall" "classic" on Waikiki's eastern boundary road that's cheered as "best in its class" for "cheap", "authentic Hawaiian" grub like the "biggest *laulaus* in town"; "the name says it all" at this "highly recommended local dive."

Orchids S | 25 | 27 | 25 | $41

Halekulani Hotel, 2199 Kalia Rd. (beachfront at end of Lewers St.), 808-923-2311

■ This oceanside International blooms in the "most beautiful open-air setting on the beach" – a "romantic" "spot to watch the sun set and the moon rise"; its "exquisite cuisine" and "gracious", "professional staff" make it a "favorite" "for a special occasion"; Sunday brunch is a "must not miss", even though it's "very pricey."

Palomino Euro Bistro S | 23 | 27 | 23 | $30

Harbor Sq:, 66 Queen St. (bet. Bethel & Nimitz Sts.), 808-528-2400

■ A "new hot spot" on the Downtown scene that earns a "gold medal" from fans for its "gorgeous bar, sophisticated ambiance" and Mediterranean menu; "smart and trendy", it's a "place to see and be seen", but surprisingly it's "very reasonably priced."

Prince Court Restaurant S | 24 | 22 | 22 | $36

Hawaii Prince Hotel Waikiki, 100 Holomoana St. (Ala Moana Blvd.), 808-944-4494

■ Chef Gary Strehl holds court here with "innovative Pacific Rim" cooking; his à la carte or buffet "lunches and dinners are terrific" and Sunday brunch is a serious contender for the "best in town"; "unbelievably courteous service" and "great views of the marina", especially at sunset, add to an "always pleasant experience."

Roy's S | 27 | 21 | 24 | $40

6600 Kalanianaole Hwy. (Keahole), Hawaii Kai, 808-396-7697

■ This "expensive", "imaginative" Eurasian "crackles with the creativity" of Roy Yamaguchi, the "grandfather of Pacific Rim cuisine" and "still the master" of "beautifully presented", "gold standard" "designer food", although it's "too noisy", "too crowded" and "too far from town" in Hawaii Kai; "try the bar downstairs for a quieter dine."

Ruth's Chris Steak House S | 25 | 19 | 22 | $38

Restaurant Row, 500 Ala Moana Blvd. (bet. Punchbowl & South Sts.), 808-599-3860

■ Whether it's lauded for serving some of the "best steaks in town", "in the state" or "in the world", the same adjectives apply to this Restaurant Row establishment: "thick", "tasty", "juicy" and "succulent"; beefeaters boast you "can't beat the porterhouse for two"; it's "expensive" but "worth it."

Sam Choy's Diamond Head S | 24 | 20 | 22 | $35

Hee Hing Plaza, 449 Kapahulu Ave., 2nd fl. (opp. Ala Wai Golf Course), 808-732-8645

◪ Sam's Hawaiian Regional "plate lunch has a college degree" cheer boosters of this "luxe", "local-style restaurant" on the fringe of Waikiki with "wonderful decor", "no pretensions" and "hard-to-get reservations"; "humongous portions" ("two meals in one") lift "leftovers to a new height" for some but offend many, and the "noise" and "erratic service" displease most.

Singha Thai S | 23 | 21 | 21 | $27

Canterbury Pl., 1910 Ala Moana Blvd. (Ena Rd.), 808-941-2898

■ "What a treat" agree acolytes of this "refined Thai" whose "elaborate food" and "excellent desserts" are "similar to gourmet restaurants in Bangkok"; having "exotic Royal Thai dancers" perform tableside is also a "nice touch"; it's all orchestrated by an "imaginative chef-owner" (Chai Chaowasaree) who "loves his work and it shows."

3660 on the Rise S | 25 | 19 | 22 | $37

Wilhelmina Rise, 3660 Waialae Ave., 808-737-1177

■ Chef-owner Russell Siu "pairs the unusual with spectacular results" – "from appetizer to dessert it's perfection" – at this Kaimuki Pacific Rimmer; while some carp that the "tuna-can seating" is "like eating on a crowded bus", most feel the "quality of the food rises above the cramped and noisy atmosphere."

Yohei Sushi | 25 | 17 | 20 | $28

Kokea Business Complex, 1111 Dillingham Blvd., 808-841-3773

■ Located near West Honolulu's airport/industrial area, this is a "low-key" "power lunch hangout" where the "most creative sushi chefs" produce "excellent" food that's the "epitome" of Japanese; fans don't even flinch at the "big prices" because of the "quality."

Houston

TOP 20 FOOD RANKING

	Restaurant	Cuisine Type
28	La Réserve	New American
27	Chez Nous	Classic French
	Ruggles Grill	Southwestern
	Cafe Annie	Southwestern
	Rotisserie for Beef & Bird	Traditional American
	Brennan's of Houston	Cajun/Creole
	DeVille	Eclectic
	Chez Georges	French Bistro
	Kelly's Del Frisco's	Seafood/Steakhouse
	Anthony's	Continental/New Amer.
26	Patisserie Descours	Desserts/Sandwiches
	Lynn's Steakhouse	Steakhouse
	Damian's	N/S Italian
	Empress	Chinese/Pacific Rim
	Riviera Grill	Mediterranean
	Tony's	N/S Italian
	Pappas Bros.	Steakhouse
	Brenner's	Steakhouse
	Churrascos	South Amer./Steakhouse
25	Clive's	Continental

OTHER IMPORTANT PLACES

Américas	Eclectic/New American
Golden Room	Chinese/Thai
Goode Co. Barbecue	BBQ
Hunan	Chinese
La Colombe d'Or	New French
La Griglia	N/S Italian
La Mora	Northern Italian
La Tour d'Argent	Continental/French
Mark's	New American
Nino's	N/S Italian
Pappasito's Cantina	Tex-Mex
Rainbow Lodge	Regional American
Redwood Grill	New American
Sierra Grill	Seafood/Southwestern
Simposio Ristorante	N/S Italian
Tasca	Eclectic

	F	D	S	C
Américas	24	25	22	$27

Saks Pavilion, 1800 Post Oak Blvd. (San Felipe), 713-961-1492

◪ The noise in both the upstairs dining room and downstairs bar is "ear-shattering" and the "decor looks like Dr. Seuss on drugs", but this Pan-American is the "coolest place in town"; head here for "great martinis" and "daring food" (i.e. tortilla with lamb cracklings), family-style sides and desserts like the house *tres leches* ("heaven on a plate"); penny-pinchers say "go for lunch – same food, half the price" or try the bar's tapas menu.

Anthony's
27 | 25 | 24 | $36

Highland Village, 4007 Westheimer (Drexel), 713-961-0552

■ This luxe Highland Village European-American may be "Tony's little brother" in age and price, yet many feel it's "the best of [Tony] Vallone's restaurants"; despite a few gripes ("sometimes snooty", "hasn't seated a reservation on time yet"), most say "this is what dining is all about"; specialties include "great duck pillows", "heavenly" osso buco and "Houston's best tiramisu, bar none"; "excellent in every way – take a client."

Brennan's of Houston S
27 | 27 | 26 | $32

3300 Smith (Stuart), 713-522-9711

■ A Houston landmark for 30 years, this "smoothly sophisticated" Texas-Creole is "all-around excellent", with an "ambitious, eclectic menu", "unbearably romantic" courtyard and terrific brunch; "even New Orleans doesn't have a better New Orleans restaurant" than this sibling to NO's famed Commander's Palace; insiders advise "reserve the kitchen table and let chef Carl [Walker] do his thing – you'll never forget."

Brenner's Steak House S
26 | 18 | 22 | $34

10911 Katy Frwy./I-10 W. (near Wilcrest), 713-465-2901

◪ The "menu and decor haven't changed in 30 years" at this much-liked steakhouse in a '50s-style ranch house on the interstate, where waitresses recite a menu that includes rib eyes and German fried potatoes, "yummy" blue cheese dressing and strudel; true, it's "not much to look at and the help can be surly", yet fans tout "the best steaks, bar none."

Cafe Annie
27 | 26 | 26 | $41

1728 Post Oak Blvd. (San Felipe), 713-840-1111

■ In a strip center in the shadow of The Galleria, this Southwestern is Houston's Most Popular restaurant and "encapsulates everything good about Texas and Gulf Coast food"; chef-owner Robert Del Grande's "innovative" cuisine features elegant, flavor-charged dishes such as beef filet with mole sauce and lobster enchiladas; for the majority this is "the benchmark for quality" dining.

Chez Georges
27 | 20 | 24 | $35

11920-G Westheimer (Kirkwood), 281-497-1122

■ Georges and Monique Guy's tiny "bona fide French" bistro is "intimate" and terribly romantic (Valentine's Day is always booked in advance); classically trained, Georges produces food that's beautifully presented, but "flavor is the goal here"; to inside-the-Loopers, the Far Westside location may seem "halfway to San Antonio", but it's "well worth seeking out", especially when the six-course prix fixe menu is offered.

Chez Nous
27 | 22 | 26 | $36

217 S. Ave. G (Staitti), Humble, 281-446-6717

■ Set in an old converted Pentecostal church in this tiny bedroom community, Gerard and Sandra Brach's French is a "Houston best-kept secret"; while a few note "Americanized dishes", most praise the "surprising quality" of the food, "attentive service" and "lovely atmosphere"; "in my Humble opinion", declare locals, you won't regret making the drive.

Churrascos 26 22 23 $24

9705 Westheimer (Gessner), 713-952-1988
Shepherd Sq., 2055 Westheimer (S. Shepherd), 713-527-8300

■ The "restaurant name equals the best dish" at these eclectic South American steakhouses – it's a marinated, grilled tenderloin with garlicky *chimichurri* sauce; besides "great beef", there's excellent fish, and most agree a meal here sure is "cheaper than flying to South America."

Clive's 25 24 24 $37

517 Louisiana (bet. Prairie & Texas), 713-224-4438

◪ With its cozy bar, dimly lit power-dining room and one of the few real belowground wine cellars in town, this quiet, classy Theater District Continental is "a touch of NYC in Houston"; under the direction of Clive Berkman, the kitchen turns out "elegant" plates of "well-prepared" fare complemented by "extraordinary" wines.

Damian's 26 23 24 $29

3011 Smith (near Elgin), 713-522-0439

■ What many judge "Houston's finest Italian", on the southern Downtown perimeter, is the scene for "business lunches deluxe"; the food is "excellent" and the creative kitchen under Luigi Ferre doesn't mind going off the menu; this "*bellissimo*" operation has "a real family" ambiance and the comfy dining room feels like it's been here forever; for a special meal, book the room in the kitchen.

DeVille S 27 27 27 $39

Four Seasons Hotel, 1300 Lamar (bet. Austin & Caroline), 713-650-1300

■ With a splendid view of the Convention Center, this "formal room with superior and often original" Eclectic cuisine "scores high on all accounts" and is "not as expensive as you expect"; "one of the few quiet places Downtown", it's "elegant" with fine service, making it a prime "place to entertain"; brunch rates a "wow."

Empress 26 23 24 $27

Champions Village, 5419-A FM 1960 W. (Champion Forest), 281-583-8021

■ "The best East-meets-West" cuisine in the city is turned out by this highly regarded fusion kitchen in Champions; under chef-owner Scott Chen, it's an unexpected find with ambitious cooking, an award-winning wine list, "discreet staff" and "beautiful" ambiance; though "pricey for Chinese", you get "white-glove" treatment.

Golden Room 23 19 21 $17

1209 Montrose (bet. W. Dallas & W. Gray), 713-524-9614

■ Like a jade jewel box, this tiny room is an "undiscovered gem" for Thai fans; most skip the Chinese half of the menu in favor of "adventurous, first-rate" Thai fare such as savory satays and sinus-clearing soups; owner Supatra Yooto is eager to please, but call ahead if you'd like an off-the-menu dish.

Goode Co. Barbecue S 23 18 18 $10

8911 Katy Frwy./I-10 W. (Campbell Rd. exit), 713-464-1901
5109 Kirby Dr. (Westpark), 713-522-2530

■ "You can smell the mesquite smoke a mile away", so you'll know you're near "Houston's best BBQ", which fans call "the food beer was invented for"; crammed with Texana ("the buffalo head on the wall scared my 12-month-old, but she loved the BBQ"), they're the place to "take out-of-towners" to see "a BBQ joint as it should be."

Hunan S
25 | 24 | 22 | $20

Saks Pavilion, 1800 Post Oak Blvd. (San Felipe), 713-965-0808

◪ "George Bush says it's great, and I can confirm it" reports one fan of this "stunning" Tanglewood-area Chinese with "excellent food" and "flawless service"; while some critics find it "too pricey" and "living on past glories and the largesse of tourists from Mexico City", the faithful "keep returning" for dishes like "always good" savory squab packages and scallops in black-bean sauce.

Kelly's Del Frisco's S
27 | 20 | 23 | $30

14641 Gladebrook (Stuebner-Airline), 281-893-3339

■ Resa Kelly's steakhouse/seafooder is a "beefeater's delight", a "classy, understated, grown-up place" that serves what some call the "best beef in town, perfectly cooked, with well-executed sides"; in a northern suburb about 25 minutes from Downtown, it blends a supper club feel ("the piano bar is a plus") with a business ambiance, making it a "great place to take customers"; dinner only.

La Colombe d'Or S
23 | 25 | 23 | $38

La Colombe d'Or Hotel, 3410 Montrose (Harold), 713-524-7999

◪ Once the baronial home of Exxon founder Walter Fondren, this "unique, elegant" "grand mansion" near the University of Saint Thomas impresses many with "outstanding decor", "terrific" Contemporary French food and "service like service ought to be"; but while fans consider it "Houston's finest" and "worth the big bucks", a few note that the "too European" staff "can leave one feeling like a peasant."

La Griglia S
25 | 24 | 23 | $25

River Oaks Ctr., 2002 W. Gray (McDuffie), 713-526-4700

◪ In the heart of River Oaks, this "upscale, lively" Italian is a "good place to start a night on the town", offering "atmosphere, aroma" and appetizing pastas and grills; the "fantastic" setting is a circus of bawdy murals and mosaics, and the "inventive" kitchen "gets better all the time"; though some are put off by the social scene and noise ("use sign language"), it's "primo for people-watching."

La Mora Cucina Toscana
25 | 23 | 23 | $25

912 Lovett Blvd. (bet. Montrose Blvd. & Westheimer), 713-522-7412

■ "Deceptive from the outside, delightful inside" sums up this Tuscan set in a made-over bungalow in a funky part of Montrose; chef-owner Lynette Hawkins Mandola has raised this pretty little eatery from its infancy, offering "excellent Italian" food, especially the grilled meats and bean dishes; while a few claim both kitchen and service are uneven, many more call it "an island of pleasure."

La Réserve
28 | 27 | 26 | $42

Omni Hotel, 4 Riverway (Woodway & S. Post Oak Ln.), 713-871-8181

■ Houston's highest food rating is testament that this hotel dining room is "a special place for a special meal"; executive chef Denis Xavier Meurgue's "innovative" menu is hard to pigeonhole, but can be summed up as great American products presented in French style; some find the formal setting "a little too elegant and stiff", but far more call it "romantic" and say "the best part of life is having dinner at this class act."

La Tour d'Argent — 24 | 26 | 23 | $34

2011 Ella Blvd. (T.C. Jester), 713-864-9864

◪ "Wonderful atmosphere" and "fine food" earn high ratings for this "pricey" "hideaway", a special occasion French-Continental just inside the North Loop with a "romantic" ambiance (complete with harpist) and log cabin decor that recalls "rural France"; but a vocal minority objects to "all those antlers" and finds the food "inconsistent"; still, "they make you feel very special, even if your name doesn't regularly appear on the society page."

Lynn's Steakhouse — 25 | 21 | 24 | $34

955 Dairy-Ashford Rd. (bet. Katy Frwy./I-10 W. & Memorial Dr.), 281-870-0807

■ Lynn Foreman's "West Side jewel", known for its steaks and award-winning wine list, is a "good place to impress someone"; the traditional dining room is cozy, even romantic, and the attentive staff has a knack for knowing what you want before you do; if some find the menu limited, others sigh "if I were rich, I'd eat there often."

Mark's American Cuisine S — – | – | – | E

1658 Westheimer (Dunlavy St.), 713-523-3800

Despite attempting a quiet debut, chef-owner Mark Cox, formerly of Tony's, couldn't keep hard-core fans from stampeding his new restaurant; look for lavish, eclectic American food in a charming setting that includes silver-star lights hung from a vaulted midnight-blue ceiling, bare wood floors and distressed walls.

Nino's Restaurant — 25 | 20 | 22 | $21

2817 W. Dallas (bet. S. Shepherd & Montrose), 713-522-5120

■ The Mandolas own many eateries, but fans say this is their "best"; slightly off the beaten track in a converted two-story house, dimly lit and fragrant with garlic, roast meats and spunky pasta sauce, it has "authentic" Italian food and a staff that makes you "feel you're at grandma's"; recommended dishes include rotisserie chicken, fettuccine Alfredo and "always-good daily specials."

Pappas Bros. Steakhouse — 26 | 26 | 24 | $36

5839 Westheimer (bet. Chimney Rock & Fountain View), 713-917-0090

■ Near The Galleria, this popular chophouse from the ubiquitous Pappas family is a "fun place for a steak and cigar, not a quiet, romantic" meal; all food is à la carte, which may "run the bill to expensive", but if you're on an expense account, try this "very elegant" "Chicago-style steakhouse that anyone from the Windy City would be proud to call their own"; "reservations are a must."

Pappasito's Cantina S — 23 | 20 | 21 | $15

10409 Katy Frwy./I-10 W. (Gessner), 713-468-1913
15280 North Frwy./I-45 N. (Airtex), 281-821-4500
6445 Richmond Ave. (Hillcroft), 713-784-5253
7050 FM 1960 W. (Willowbrook Mall), 281-893-5037
13070 Northwest Frwy./290 (Hollister), 713-462-0245
2515 S. Loop W. 610 (S. Main), 713-668-5756
11831 I-10 E. (Federal Rd.), 713-455-8378
10005 FM 1960 Bypass (Hwy. 59 N.), Humble, 281-540-9664
12000 Southwest Frwy./59 S. (Wilcrest & Murphy Rd. exit), Stafford, 281-240-0099

Pappasito's Cantina (Cont.)

20099 Gulf Frwy./I-45 S. (NASA Rd. 1), Webster, 281-338-2885

■ The Pappas family's cantinas are so cleverly hokey, they're like "stepping across the border, mariachis and all"; most love the "yuppie Tex-Mex food in linebacker quantities" (the sizzling fajita platter is famous) and applaud "good service" from a "clean-cut staff"; the noise is "oppressive" so "bring earplugs", but the sheer energy and "*muy bueno*" eats make this "a must-stop."

Patisserie Descours — 26 | 13 | 18 | $11

1330-B Wirt Rd. (Westview), 713-681-8894

◪ Pastry chef Marilyn Descours "is a perfectionist – everything she touches tastes and looks divine" rave fans of this tiny, bare-bones West Side dessert/sandwich shop; many of her pastries are served at other restaurants, but you can go to the source for a slice or the whole thing; a few suggest the staff "needs to smile."

Rainbow Lodge S — 23 | 27 | 22 | $30

1 Birdsall (Memorial Dr.), 713-861-8666

◪ The "lovely, romantic setting" and "multilevel dining room" with views at this rustic fishing lodge on the banks of Buffalo Bayou make it "a one-of-a-kind oasis" complete with "cute ducks and raccoons"; even though the "much improved" Regional American kitchen can still be "uneven", devotees say "there's no better place for a very special evening", and it's "fabulous for brunch" as well.

Redwood Grill S — 24 | 23 | 22 | $27

Chelsea Mkt., 4611 Montrose (south of Southwest Frwy./59 S.), 713-523-4611

■ The "urban chic gentry" have made this Museum District New American their playground for "fun martinis" and good grills; set in Chelsea Market, Manfred Jachmich's latest boasts "superb" food and snazzy decor; some feel it "needs a better wine" list, but most think it's a fine "addition to upper-end dining."

Riviera Grill — 26 | 14 | 20 | $27

10655 Katy Frwy./I-10 W. (Beltway 8), 713-974-4445

■ Relocated from its original "unattractive" strip center site (making the above decor rating obsolete), this Mediterranean draws raves from "local foodies" as "an incredible find" thanks to chef-owner John Sheely's "wonderful, innovative food" – roasted sea bass, lush pork chops, pastas and more.

Rotisserie for Beef & Bird — 27 | 24 | 26 | $34

2200 Wilcrest (north of Westheimer), 713-977-9524

■ "Joe Mannke has a first-class operation" in this Westside "colonial" country inn famed for wild game dishes (boar and elk are recommended), homemade potato chips that start every meal and a "super wine list"; the "owner cares and he shows it" by employing a "sweet staff" that pampers diners; in sum, this American is an "all-around excellent" choice and an "honest big-buck value."

Ruggles Grill S — 27 | 21 | 22 | $25

903 Westheimer (east of Montrose), 713-524-3839

◪ "Creative-looking food that tastes wonderful" and "decadent desserts" have earned Bruce and Susan Molzan's Southwestern grill Houston's No. 3 ranking for Food; however, critics knock the chronic waits ("an 8 PM reservation means 9 PM"), painful noise ("don't expect to converse") and tight quarters.

Sierra Grill S
23 | 20 | 20 | $23

4704 Montrose (south of Southwest Frwy./59), 713-942-7757

◪ Sparkling fresh seafood might make you guess that chef-owner "Charlie Watkins catches the fish after you order it"; if some think this progressive Southwestern chef is "overdoing trendy combos of ingredients" and find the wines "expensive", far more laud the "mind-bending" menu, "large portions" and handsome decor.

Simposio Ristorante Italiano
– | – | – | M

5591 Richmond Ave. (Chimney Rock), 713-532-0550

West of The Loop but east of Richmond's thriving singles scene, Simposio has a spare, confident dining room that practically glows, its gold-sponged walls set off by oversized, gilt-framed mirrors; Alberto Baffoni's classic Italian repertoire of seafood, meat, game and pastas is the perfect counterpoint to the stylish setting.

Tasca ◐
– | – | – | M

908 Congress St. (Travis St.), 713-225-9100

Originally billed as a tapas bar, this Downtown newcomer in a renovated historic building across from Market Square is far more than that: chef Charles Clark's food is a successful blend of cross-cultural influences: Mediterranean, Asian and even Southern (i.e. a fine cornmeal-crusted catfish); the setting, featuring whitewashed walls and wood trim, can be painfully noisy at night.

Tony's
26 | 27 | 26 | $46

1801 Post Oak Blvd. (south of San Felipe), 713-622-6778

◪ After a year's absence, Tony Vallone's "aristocratic" Italian "for the rich and famous" is back and, by most accounts, "better than ever"; though completely redone, the style remains unstintingly grand and it's again the "to-be-seen place"; critics say "overhyped, overpriced" and even some fans dislike the kitchen's new direction ("we want the old menu back"), but most salute a "welcome return" and ask "what would Houston do without it?"

TOP 15 FOOD RANKING

	Restaurant	Cuisine Type
27	Cafe Allegro	New American
	American Restaurant	New American
26	Bristol Bar & Grill	Seafood
	Peppercorn Duck Club	Traditional American
	Tatsu's	Classic French
	Plaza III	Steakhouse
	India Palace	Indian
	Metropolis	Eclectic/New American
25	La Mediterannee	Classic French
	Grille on Broadway	New American
	Woks	Chinese
	Mrs. Peter's	Traditional American
	Stroud's	Traditional American
	Paulo & Bill's	N/S Italian
	Vineyards	Continental/New Amer.

OTHER IMPORTANT PLACES

Bluebird at City Garden	Vegetarian
Grand St. Cafe	Eclectic
Houston's	Traditional American
Jack Fiorella's	BBQ
Japengo	Pacific Rim
J.J.'s	Steakhouse
Jun's	Japanese
Le Fou Frog	Classic French
Macaluso's	Continental/Italian
Savoy Grill	Seafood/Steakhouse
Starker's Reserve	Traditional American
Stephenson's	Traditional American
Stolen Grill	Eclectic/New American
Yia Yia's Eurobistro	Eclectic

	F	D	S	C
American Restaurant	27	28	27	$43

Crown Ctr., 200 E. 25th St., Ste. 490 (Grand Ave.), 816-426-1133

■ Surveyors stand up and cheer for this "stellar" Downtown New American that elevates "KC from a cow town to a cosmopolitan city"; "elegant" ambiance, a "spectacular view", "superb service" and "unusual offerings" from a "creative" kitchen explain why it's one of KC's most popular restaurants and lovely "for special occasions", though "it's so pricey" it may be a "once-a-year treat."

	F	D	S	C
Bluebird at City Garden S	24	20	19	$10

1700 Summit St. (17th St.), 816-221-7559

■ A Downtown "favorite" offering "imaginative Vegetarian" fare (much of it culled from "their own garden") that "makes meat and spuds folks forget they've eaten veggie"; loyalists like its "funky, friendly" "coffeehouse feel" and modest prices, so get there early or face a wait; the attached natural foods market is "delightful."

Bristol Bar & Grill S | 26 | 25 | 25 | $22

Town Center Plaza, 5400 W. 119th St. (Nall Ave.), Leawood, KS, 913-663-5777

■ This relocated, revered seafooder still draws raves; "Johnson County thanks the Plaza for giving us this gem" known for "top-quality" fish and "the best biscuits"; "lovely" decor makes it the place for an "occasion", but it may be a "pricey" one.

Cafe Allegro | 27 | 24 | 26 | $35

1815 W. 39th St. (State Line Rd.), 816-561-3663

■ Surveyors savor "quiet, sophisticated" dining at this Westport New American that's "run like a restaurant should be run"; KC's No. 1 for Food and Popularity, it's "top-drawer" all around with an "intimate", "romantic" setting, "good wine list", "helpful" staff and "imaginative menu" that's "always memorable, sometimes sublime"; the only persistent gripe: it "costs an arm and a legro."

Grand St. Cafe S | 24 | 24 | 23 | $20

4740 Grand St. (Brush Creek & Main St.), 816-561-8000

■ "Possibly the most urbane restaurant in the city" is this Plaza-area Eclectic where "a gourmet meal can be had for very low prices"; there's "always excitement in the air" at this "spot to see and be seen" while enjoying "unusual sandwiches", "creative specials" and "the best pork chop you'll ever have"; the "airy, refreshing" decor is another draw, so "expect to wait."

Grille on Broadway S | 25 | 18 | 25 | $24

3605 Broadway (bet. 36th & 37th Sts.), 816-531-0700

■ This tiny New American tucked between Downtown and Westport is a "hidden secret" offering "some of KC's best fish", a "good wine selection" and "personalized service"; it's "very cozy" (some say "cramped") but well "worth the wait and discomfort."

Houston's S | 23 | 21 | 22 | $16

Country Club Plaza, 4640 Wornall Rd. (bet. 47th & Main Sts.), 816-561-8542
7111 W. 95th St. (Metcalf Ave.), Overland Park, KS, 913-642-0630
2820 W. 53rd St. (Shawnee Mission Pkwy.), Shawnee, KS, 913-722-3524

■ An "excellent operation" with "something for everyone" sums up this upscale, "good value" American chain "noted for ribs" and "the best salads in the universe" plus good service; it's no surprise that they generate "outrageous waits": "please take reservations."

India Palace S | 26 | 14 | 20 | $14

9918 W. 87th St. (bet. Farley Rd. & Switzer Ave.), 913-381-1680

■ Admirers think this Johnson County storefront is "by far KC's best Indian", even though the "standard, boring decor" hardly lives up to the name; what folks like is the "very authentic" food, including a "great lunch buffet", and "very friendly owner"; a "good vegetarian selection" is another ingredient in its recipe for success.

Jack Fiorella's Smoke Stack of Martin City S | 25 | 18 | 19 | $14

13441 Holmes Rd. (W. 135th St.), 816-942-9141

■ Many consider this KC's "best overall BBQ" place thanks to "amazing" ribs, "killer" beans and a menu that "puts some thought into side dishes"; it earns extra points for specialties such as "smoked fish and lamb and beers from everywhere"; quality makes it "a better deal than most people realize", but the main gripes are "too crowded" and "should take reservations."

Japengo [S] — | — | — | E
600 Ward Pkwy. (Pennsylvania Ave.), 816-931-6600
Bold, bright Pacific Rim cuisine is drawing raves and crowds at this new Plaza restaurant that replaces Parkway 600; the Asian- and island-influenced menu features creative combinations and a wide array of choices, especially for seafood lovers, and diners get to do a good bit of sampling since dishes are served one at a time to encourage sharing.

J.J.'s [S] 24 | 22 | 23 | $24
910 W. 48th St. (Belleview St.), 816-561-7136
■ Upscale Plaza-area steak and wine specialist with "pizazz"; "the food lives up to the wine, and that's saying a lot" because "if someone stomps it, J.J.'s pours it", and the array of wines is "well matched to the food"; besides "really good" steaks, "nobody cooks fish better" gush fans.

Jun's Japanese 24 | 19 | 20 | $19
7660 State Line Rd. (76th St.), Shawnee, KS, 913-341-4924
■ To many, this longtime suburban fixture is the town's top Japanese, serving the "best sushi, hands down" – "gosh, this sure doesn't taste like Kansas"; critics complain of high prices and say the "sporadic" service "needs improvement", but they're solidly outvoted by those who call this "a real treat in KC."

La Mediterranee 25 | 22 | 24 | $30
9058 Metcalf Ave. (91st St.), Overland Park, KS, 913-341-9595
◪ "Beautifully prepared and presented food" wins applause at this "posh" Classic French whose move to Johnson County from the Plaza causes admirers to declare "the 'burbs have arrived"; its "authentic cooking" and "first-class" service represent "European quality at its best" for many, but critics contend it's "slipped", becoming "too expensive" and a bit "pretentious."

Le Fou Frog [S] — | — | — | E
400 E. Fifth St. (Oak St.), 816-474-6060
Classic French fare from chef-owner Mano Rafael, a Marseilles native, is offered at this casual bistro in the River Market area; duck confit, steak au poivre paired with perfect pommes frites, mussels steamed with white wine and an aromatic cassoulet stocked with fat sausages and chunks of lamb and duck are just some of the reasons why it has quickly become a magnet for food lovers.

Macaluso's 25 | 18 | 21 | $24
1403 W. 39th St. (Terrace St.), 816-561-0100
◪ Most diners enjoy the "carefully prepared food" and "casually elegant decor" at this Westport Continental-Italian; but while many also "love the personal touch" of owner Tom Macaluso, calling him "the perfect host", a few claim he "plays favorites"; "crowded", "noisy" conditions also draw fire, but that's the price of popularity.

Metropolis American Grill 26 | 23 | 24 | $25
303 Westport Rd. (Broadway & Main St.), 816-753-1550
■ "Still fresh" even though it's "become a classic", this Westport New American–Eclectic impresses with its "innovative" menu, "artistic presentations" and "upscale", "funky decor"; though "trendy" it's "consistently good", and if the small room is "too crowded" and "loud" for some, the bottom line is "everybody goes."

Mrs. Peter's S 25 | 21 | 23 | $11

4960 State Ave. (47th St.), Kansas City, KS, 913-287-7711

■ This longtime, family-style fried chicken specialist in Kansas City, KS, is a "Sunday afternoon American classic" with some of the "best fried chicken and biscuits" around plus other "hard-to-beat home cookin'" served in a "homey atmosphere" that's "cute to look at"; most "like the mood" and the food, even if there is "no booze."

Paulo & Bill's S 25 | 24 | 24 | $20

16501 Midland Dr. (I-435), Shawnee, KS, 913-962-9900

■ Johnson County hot spot offering an "American take on Italian food"; long-underserved Shawnee locals say "we need" a place like this, applauding its "wood-fired pizzas and Tuscan feel", "impeccable service" and "platters for sharing" that are "fun for the family"; in short, "another winner" from the PB&J group.

Peppercorn Duck Club S 26 | 26 | 26 | $32

Hyatt Regency Crown Ctr., 2345 McGee St. (Pershing Rd.), 816-435-4199

◪ By most accounts, this popular Downtown hotel American has its ducks neatly in a row, with "always superb" food (including "heavenly" duck and "a dream" of a chocolate dessert buffet), "romantic atmosphere" and "pampering" service; critics cry fowl over "pricey, predictable" fare and claim those desserts "need help", but as ratings attest, they're a much smaller flock.

Plaza III S 26 | 24 | 24 | $29

Country Club Plaza, 4749 Pennsylvania Ave. (Ward Pkwy.), 816-753-0000

■ The "gold standard" of KC steakhouses, this "Plaza landmark" is "a celebration of red meat" that's "first-rate" all around, from the "best cocktails" and steak soup starter ("worth the trip alone") to the top-notch beef and "wine steward who knows his business"; the "handsome", "dark wood and cigar smoke" setting "impresses clients", and though the tab is steep it merits "every penny."

Savoy Grill S 24 | 25 | 24 | $27

Hotel Savoy, 219 W. 9th St. (Central Ave.), 816-842-3890

◪ "A trip back in time", this Downtown surf 'n' turf "landmark" still "knows how to cook fish" as well as "steaks and lobsters the size of Honda Civics" ("so is the bill"); fans applaud the "unmatched elegance" of the setting and "waiters who don't miss a thing", and if a few find it "stuffy", more hope this KC "classic" goes on forever.

Starker's Reserve 28 | 27 | 27 | $38

201 W. 47th St. (Wyandotte St.), 816-753-3565

■ Formerly a "unique" private dining facility attached to the now-defunct Harry Starker's, this Traditional American with a wine country theme has been opened to the public; though the above ratings were earned before the change, surveyors who sampled its "outstanding food" and big wine list at private affairs hope it will be as much of a "treat" (albeit a pricey one) in its new role.

Stephenson's Old Apple Farm S 23 | 22 | 22 | $18

16401 E. 40 Hwy. (Lee's Summit Rd.), 816-373-5400

■ Over 50 years old and "still hard to beat", this "one of a kind" American offers "real country flavor" via "extremely good, simple food" – "go if you love chicken or brisket or apple dumplings" and "don't miss" the fruit daiquiris; with "huge" portions and "rustic" decor, it's a "great place to take the family" for "down-home" dining.

Stolen Grill – – – E

904 Westport Rd. (Southwest Tfwy.), 816-960-1450

This Westport American-Eclectic is easily KC's most exciting new fine dining establishment in years and is drawing crowds with a changing menu of cutting-edge cooking that's influenced by a number of cuisines but is uniquely its own; to experience it, patrons are willing to put up with cramped seating and a high noise level in a minimalist setting.

Stroud's S 25 17 21 $14

1015 E. 85th St. (Troost Ave.), 816-333-2132

5410 NE Oak Ridge Dr. (bet. I-35 & Vivion Rd.), 816-454-9600

■ These KC originals remain "the benchmark for home-choked fried chicken"; you might wait two hours for a table and "you can hear your arteries harden" as you eat, but "you don't care" given the best poultry "on the planet", "real mashed potatoes" and "food-of-the-gods gravy"; it's also "the best deal in town."

Tatsu's 26 22 23 $26

Summerset Plaza, 4603 W. 90th St. (Roe Ave.), Prairie Village, KS, 913-383-9801

◪ A "suburban surprise" in Johnson County serving "elegant, interesting" Classic French food that's "perfection on a plate", enhanced by "smooth sauces" and a "lovely atmosphere"; a few dissenters complain that the limited menu is "always the same" and the service "doesn't always measure up" to the cooking.

Vineyards, The S 25 21 21 $24

505 Spring St. (Rock St.), Weston, MO, 816-640-5588

■ "Classic cuisine" in a "cozy" antebellum home in Weston is "definitely worth the drive"; Continental techniques blended with American ingredients yield "very good, interesting" dishes, while the "wonderful service" and charmingly "quaint" candlelit setting make it "a special place for a special occasion"; "dining on the porch on a cool evening is heaven"; closed Tuesdays.

Woks, The S 25 20 22 $12

Westchester Sq., 8615 Hauser Dr. (87th St.), Lenexa, KS, 913-541-1777

■ "Beautifully prepared" food from a "varied menu" makes this Johnson County contemporary Chinese a "favorite" and arguably "KC's best Chinese"; besides "consistently good" cooking, it offers "great service" and "very good value."

Yia Yia's Eurobistro S 24 25 23 $21

Hawthorne Plaza, 4701 W. 119th St. (Roe Ave.), Overland Park, KS, 913-345-1111

■ This Johnson County European-Eclectic "hot spot" is "the best of the PB&J group" in many eyes; combine "ultrafriendly" staff, a "comfortable" setting and a kitchen that "takes creative risks that generally work" and you have "simply the best"; "everything clicks here" and it's both "unpretentious and classy – a rare mix."

Las Vegas

TOP 10 FOOD RANKING

	Restaurant	Cuisine Type
27	Emeril's New Orleans	Creole/Seafood
26	Sterling Brunch	Eclectic
	Andre's	Classic French
	Michael's	Continental
	Steak House (Circus Circus)	Steakhouse
	Spago	Californian
25	Morton's of Chicago	Steakhouse
	Piero's	Northern Italian
	Mayflower Cuisinier	Chinese
	Steakhouse (Binion's)	Steakhouse

OTHER IMPORTANT PLACES

Aqua	Seafood
Buccaneer Bay Club	Seafood/Steakhouse
Chin's	Chinese
Coyote Cafe	Southwestern
Drai's	Californian/Eclectic
Hugo's Cellar	American/Continental
Le Cirque/Osteria del Circo	Italian/New French
Le Montrachet	French Bistro
Madame Ching's	Asian
Monte Carlo	Continental/New French
Napa	Californian/Eclectic
Olives	Mediterranean
Palace Court	Continental/New French
Picasso	Eclectic
Prime	Steakhouse
Second Street Grill	Pacific Rim
Terrazza	N/S Italian
Tillerman	Seafood/Steakhouse
Tre Visi	N/S Italian

	F	D	S	C
Andre's French Restaurant S	26	24	25	$42

401 S. Sixth St. (Bridger Ave. & Las Vegas Blvd.), 702-385-5016
Monte Carlo Hotel, 3770 Las Vegas Blvd. S. (bet. Flamingo Rd. & Tropicana Ave.), 702-730-7777

■ "A perennial favorite" in a "lovely old restored house" in Historic Downtown; the chef-owner "never fails" to produce the "best French food in town", enhanced by the "great wine list, impeccable service" and "superb dessert soufflés"; a few critics sniff that it's "very pricey" and "stuffy service" could improve, but for most it's an "LV must"; N.B. the Monte Carlo location opened post-*Survey.*

	F	D	S	C
Aqua S	–	–	–	VE

Bellagio, 3600 Las Vegas Blvd. S. (Flamingo Rd.), 702-693-7223
San Francisco chef Michael Mina has transplanted his successful Aqua concept to the Bellagio's splendid Conservatory; elegant yet relaxed, it offers contemporary seafood with French and California touches, either à la carte or via tasting menus.

Buccaneer Bay Club S — – – M

Treasure Island, 3300 Las Vegas Blvd. S. (bet. Flamingo & Spring Mountain Rds.), 702-894-7350
In a handsome dining room filled with "booty" (and scenes of the namesake bay where the British navy and pirates once did battle), the somewhat pricey but satisfying menu combines surf 'n' turf dishes with some Continental specialties; Treasure Island guests get preference, so others are advised to reserve ahead.

Chin's S — 23 21 21 $24

Fashion Show Mall, 3200 Las Vegas Blvd. S. (Spring Mountain Rd.), 702-733-8899
■ "Elegant all the way" with cooking "elevated to the highest level" (and, some say, the prices as well), this "upscale" Cantonese in the Fashion Show Mall on the Strip is a lunchtime "hangout" for "high-profile locals" and "doctors' wives"; its original strawberry chicken and tossed chicken salad are now standards imitated elsewhere; but despite good ratings, the "slow service" irks some and naysayers ask "what's the big deal?"; the answers range from "dim sum – yum yum" to "very hip" and "always top-notch."

Coyote Cafe S — 23 22 20 $25

MGM Grand, 3799 Las Vegas Blvd. S. (Tropicana Ave.), 702-891-7349
■ "Innovative" Southwestern fare – a "Santa Fe import" courtesy of celeb chef Mark Miller – has the "people-watching" and "noise level" both up a notch at the MGM Grand; a casual patio cafe and stylish grill room for dinner offer a choice of menus and prices; though a few "unimpressed" phobes label the fare "Santa Fake", they are overruled by the majority who rate this "a taste sensation."

Drai's S — – – E

Barbary Coast Hotel, 3595 Las Vegas Blvd. S. (Flamingo Rd.), 702-737-0555
There's a terrific California-Eclectic menu with the best calf's liver ever and a good selection of fresh fish and seafood, but you have to be a 'special customer' to get the langoustine that's not on the menu; the chic, comfortable decor, congenial staff and owner (Victor Drai) and good, fairly priced wine list are luring locals back to the Strip; have coffee and dessert in the appealing, library-like lounge, which is open only to Drai's diners.

Emeril's New Orleans Fish House S — 27 25 23 $42

MGM Grand, 3799 Las Vegas Blvd. S. (Tropicana Ave.), 702-891-7374
■ The prices and food (top-rated in Las Vegas) are equally "breathtaking" at this Creole-style restaurant in the MGM Grand; a "terrific menu" featuring "excellent seafood" is "comparable" to that at celeb chef Emeril Lagasse's namesake New Orleans hot spot; occasional "inconsistencies" and "inattentive" service can "disappoint", but don't deter those who know "delicious" when they taste it; N.B. the oyster bar and cafe are good values.

Hugo's Cellar S — 25 23 25 $31

Four Queens Hotel, 202 E. Fremont St. (3rd St.), 702-385-4011
■ "Improbable gourmet Downtown" in the Four Queens Hotel that's been "good for many years", this "very nice, very expensive" American-Continental is "great for an intimate rendezvous"; with a "wonderful wine list and sommelier", it's also a "special event" favorite, though "for these prices there should be tablecloths"; however, the "roses for the ladies" are winners.

Le Cirque ◐ S | – | – | – | VE |
Bellagio, 3600 Las Vegas Blvd. S. (Flamingo Rd.), 702-693-8100

Osteria del Circo ◐ S | – | – | – | E |
Bellagio, 3600 Las Vegas Blvd. S. (Flamingo Rd.), 702-693-8150
Side-by-side in the Bellagio sit Sirio Maccioni's LV versions of his popular NYC restaurants; Adam Tihany's circus-inspired decor sets the stage for French fare with contemporary touches at Le Cirque (where jackets and ties are required) and Tuscan fare at Circo (more relaxed but still elegant); run by Maccioni's sons Mario, Mauro and Marco, both offer views of the hotel's fountain-filled lake.

Le Montrachet Bistro S | 23 | 25 | 23 | $48 |
Las Vegas Hilton, 3000 Paradise Rd. (bet. Desert Inn Rd. & Karen Ave.), 702-732-5651
■ "Divine food" and "lovely service" in an "elegant" setting make this long-running French restaurant in the Las Vegas Hilton one of the "top hotel gourmet rooms" in town; while a few report "some snooty staff", there's also a "wonderful wine list" to enhance the "delicious" fare, another reason why "parking can be a problem."

Madame Ching's S | – | – | – | E |
Treasure Island, 3300 Las Vegas Blvd. S. (Spring Mountain Rd.), 702-894-7111
Elegance and Asian cuisine come together in an upscale theme eatery in Treasure Island on the Strip; named for China's legendary woman pirate, who had a penchant for fine things, this art-filled dining room and the prettily presented cuisine would please her.

Mayflower Cuisinier | 25 | 22 | 22 | $27 |
Sahara Pavilion North, 4750 W. Sahara Ave. (Decatur Blvd.), 702-870-8432
■ "Breathtakingly beautiful and delicious" "designer Chinese food with French flair" scores high at this "elegant" "place to be seen" in the Sahara Pavilion on the West Side; while the "super menu" strikes a few as "bizarre" and only "ok for an occasional meal", the main plaint is "slow" if "pleasant" service; but loyalists don't mind the wait for food that, while "expensive", is "as good as it gets."

Michael's S | 26 | 25 | 26 | $47 |
Barbary Coast Hotel, 3595 Las Vegas Blvd. S. (Flamingo Rd.), 702-737-7111
■ "Elegant, expensive" Continental dining room in the Barbary Coast on the Strip that's "a historical classic" with "red velvet flocked wallpaper" and "four waiters per table"; the "illuminated shrimp cocktails are a hoot" and "huge, delicious portions" of "the finest food" range from "great Dover sole" to "Châteaubriand and rack of lamb – none better" to cherries jubilee; it's a "favorite high roller's bistro", so despite high cost, reservations are at a premium.

Monte Carlo S | 24 | 24 | 24 | $45 |
Sheraton Desert Inn, 3145 Las Vegas Blvd. S. (Spring Mountain Rd.), 702-733-4524
■ "Romantic" Contemporary French–Continental dining room (an "old reliable" that was "once La Vie En Rose") in the Sheraton Desert Inn that's "expensive" and worth it; the "excellent food and presentation", "attentive service" and "sophisticated atmosphere" are "tough to beat"; it's favored by locals and visitors, who "like to go here" because it's the "fanciest overall in Vegas."

Morton's of Chicago S | 25 | 24 | 24 | $41

Fashion Show Mall, 3200 Las Vegas Blvd. S. (Spring Mountain Rd.), 702-893-0703

◪ "Expensive carnivore's paradise" in the Fashion Show Mall with "top-of-the-line steaks" and "a good wine list"; regulars like having personal "wine lockers" and savor the "manly decor", but the menu presentation of "raw food wrapped in plastic" turns off some; given "cigar smoke", some cite a "need for a nonsmoking area."

Napa S | – | – | – | E

Rio Hotel, 3700 W. Flamingo Rd. (off I-95), 702-252-7777

Formerly of DC's Jean-Louis at the Watergate, Jean-Louis Palladin has migrated to the posh restaurant in the Rio Hotel's Masquerade Village; working in an open kitchen, the chef creates outstanding Cal-Eclectic cuisine like truffled scallops, as well as seasonal dinner specials; if the more than 200 wines available by the glass aren't enough for you, tour the magnificent wine cellar downstairs.

Olives ◐S | – | – | – | E

Bellagio, 3600 Las Vegas Blvd. S. (Flamingo Rd.), 702-693-7223

Chef-owner Todd English's Boston favorite, Olives, now has a home in LV, where simple ingredients are turned into irresistible, earthy cuisine billed as 'interpretive Mediterranean' fare – most would just call it delicious; dine inside or on the patio by the hotel's lake.

Palace Court S | 24 | 26 | 25 | $52

Caesars Palace, 3570 Las Vegas Blvd. S. (Flamingo Rd.), 702-731-7110

■ "Glitzy and gaudy", there's "ambiance beyond compare" at this "expensive" Continental-French at Caesars Palace; the "always terrific experience" includes "wonderful wines, the finest caviar" and the "best cheesecake in LV"; foes say "worth it only if you're comped" and "the menu and room need updating", but most wax poetic over the "superb cuisine" and the "romantic pampering."

Picasso S | – | – | – | VE

Bellagio, 3600 Las Vegas Blvd. S. (Flamingo Rd.), 702-693-7223

Steve Wynn lured acclaimed chef Julian Serrano from SF's Masa to this stylish Eclectic, where Serrano's cooking (with Spanish and Southern French accents) is as original as the Picasso artwork and ceramics adorning the flower-filled room; prices are lofty, but the view of the hotel's lake is as superb as the food.

Piero's Restaurant S | 25 | 23 | 24 | $38

355 Convention Center Dr. (Paradise Rd.), 702-369-2305

■ "A favorite of well-heeled locals" and celebs, this "classic", "upscale" Northern Italian just east of the Strip is "a LV legend"; the "Runyonesque", "philanthropic owner" and service that can be "impeccable" and "rude" in the same night add to the "show"; fans "never had a bad meal here" and there's "bar action" too.

Prime S | – | – | – | E

Bellagio, 3600 Las Vegas Blvd. S. (Flamingo Rd.), 702-693-7223

Perhaps the most beautiful steakhouse anywhere, this new venture from Jean-Georges Vongerichten (of NYC's Jean Georges fame) has, as you'd expect, exceptional steaks and seafood, but what you might not expect is the powder blue marble floors, stunning bar and view of the hotel's lake; a romantic steakhouse? – yes!

Second Street Grill S 23 22 22 $22

Fremont Hotel, 200 E. Fremont St. (Casino Center Blvd.), 702-385-6277

■ "Surprisingly good, island-themed restaurant" in the Downtown Fremont Hotel that pleases with "superb food", "good value" and "Polynesian atmosphere"; this "tucked-away delight" provides stylish "creative Pacific Rim dining" (Hawaiian chef Jean-Marie Josselin consults) in a "small", "laid-back but colorful" setting; "it's an appealing, affordable concept."

Spago S 26 24 23 $32

Forum Shops at Caesars, 3500 Las Vegas Blvd. S. (Flamingo Rd.), 702-369-6300

■ "Everything it's cracked up to be", this "hyped" and "happening" Californian at Caesars offers "quintessential Wolfgang Puck" food and style in "exciting surroundings"; "where Puck goes good things follow" say devotees of the superchef who saved them from "food purgatory" and "revolutionized local dining"; it can be "noisy", "pricey" and a "bit too Puckish" for skeptics, but legions praise the "caring service", "inventive" food and stargazing.

Steakhouse, The S 25 22 23 $25

Binion's Horseshoe Hotel, 128 E. Fremont St., 24th fl. (Odgen Ave.), 702-382-1600

■ "An unbeatable view" makes this "best-value steakhouse" Downtown atop Binion's Horseshoe "a must for visitors to Vegas"; what's more, the "beef from Binion's ranch" is "outstanding", so patrons with hearty appetites overlook the sometimes "poor service" while they work on a "massive" 25-ounce porterhouse.

Steak House, The ◐S 26 23 24 $28

Circus Circus, 2880 Las Vegas Blvd. S. (bet. Sahara Ave. & Spring Mountain Rd.), 702-734-0410

■ "Grand, traditional steakhouse" with "old wood decor" in Circus Circus that is the highest-rated beef palace in Las Vegas and one of the category's "best bargains" as well; perhaps the setting needs some "updating", but with "great aged meat", "perfect lobster", "excellent service" and moderate prices, it can be "hard to get in", so reserve in advance unless staying at the hotel.

Sterling Brunch S 26 24 25 $50

Bally's Las Vegas, 3645 Las Vegas Blvd. S. (Flamingo Rd.), 702-739-4651

■ This "pricey" Sunday brunchery in Bally's on the Strip is an "excellent splurge" that's "worth every penny" and just might be "the most extravagant buffet ever"; "the boys love it", offering mock complaints about "too much fine food and champagne" and "how do you eat [$49.95] worth of breakfast?"

Terrazza – – – M

Caesars Palace, 3570 Las Vegas Blvd. S. (Flamingo Rd), 702-731-7110

In the smashing new Palace Tower in Caesars Palace on the Strip, this Italian offers lunch and dinner in its rustic dining room, cafe and outdoor dining patio that faces the grand new swimming pool; an adjacent lounge serves pizzas and assorted focaccia breads.

Tillerman, The S | 24 | 23 | 23 | $29

2245 E. Flamingo Rd. (Channel 10 Dr.), 702-731-4036

"Classic surf 'n' turf, a great wine list and service to match" are reasons why there's "always a wait at this fabulous place" on the East Side; the "steaks are as good as the seafood" and neither "can be beat if money doesn't count"; some complain about "snooty waiters" and say the style of "decor went out with bell-bottoms", but most find it "romantic" – the "best first-date place, if you want a second."

Tre Visi ◐S | ▽ 17 | 19 | 16 | $31

MGM Grand, 3799 Las Vegas Blvd. S. (Tropicana Ave.), 702-891-7331

Regional Italian specialities are served in a variety of settings in the MGM Grand; the 'three faces' include the "gourmet room" (La Scala), a patio cafe for dining and a bar; an "imaginative wine list" completes a picture that admirers consider "*très chic.*"

Los Angeles

TOP 25 FOOD RANKING

	Restaurant	Cuisine Type
28	Patina	Californian/New French
	Matsuhisa	Japanese/Seafood
	Sushi Nozawa	Japanese
	Chinois on Main	Asian/French
	Shiro	Asian/Cal./Seafood
27	Valentino	N/S Italian
	L'Orangerie	Classic French
	Belvedere, The	Asian/Cal./French
	Joe's	Californian
	Bel-Air Hotel	Californian/New French
26	Water Grill	Seafood
	Jozu	Pacific New Wave
	Campanile	Cal./Mediterranean
	R-23	Japanese
	Cafe Bizou	French Bistro
	La Cachette	New French
	Spago Beverly Hills	Californian
	Citrus	Californian/New French
	Pinot Bistro	French Bistro
	Ruth's Chris	Steakhouse
	Diaghilev	French/Russian
	Bernard's	Continental
	Hirosuke	Japanese
	Lawry's The Prime Rib	Steakhouse
	Bistro 45	Californian/French Bistro

OTHER IMPORTANT PLACES

Brent's Deli	Deli
Café Blanc	Japanese/New French
Chaya Brasserie	French Bistro/Italian
Chez Melange	Californian/Eclectic
Depot	Eclectic
Grill, The	Steakhouse/Trad. Amer.
JiRaffe	Californian
Lavande	New French
Locanda Veneta	Northern Italian
Michael's	Californian
Mimosa	French Bistro
Ocean Star	Chinese/Dim Sum/Seafood
Palm, The	Steakhouse
Parkway Grill	Californian
Yujean Kang's	Californian/Chinese

Bel-Air Hotel S | 27 | 29 | 27 | $51

Bel-Air Hotel, 701 Stone Canyon Rd. (north of Sunset Blvd.), Bel Air, 310-472-1211

■ Consistently rated SoCal's most beautiful room, this "stunning" Nouvelle Cal-French is reached by crossing an "enchanted" bridge over a swan-filled stream and heading down a flowered path into a "star-studded" room where the food is "perfect", the service "top-notch" and the fireplace always lit; for the "quintessential" "special occasion", try the private Table One in the kitchen.

Belvedere, The S | 27 | 28 | 28 | $52

Peninsula Beverly Hills Hotel, 9882 Little Santa Monica Blvd. (Wilshire Blvd.), Beverly Hills, 310-788-2306

■ Moving into first place for hotel dining in LA and ranked No. 1 for its "discreet service", this "incredible" Cal-French/Cal-Asian is an "elegant" "gathering place of the Louis XVIth crowd" as well as a "perfect" power breakfast and lunch feeding station for industry sharks from nearby CAA and William Morris; "it's superb in every way", but some say if you want a good table, "do be somebody."

Bernard's S | 26 | 27 | 26 | $50

Regal Biltmore Hotel, 506 S. Grand Ave. (bet. 5th & 6th Sts.), Downtown LA, 213-612-1580

■ The posh Contemporary Continental of choice for those who need to impress in the Downtown area, this "old great room" exuding "old money and old style" is a "refined" "throwback to an elegant era" where gentlemen are not out of place in tuxedos nor women in gowns, and harp music adds to the ambiance; to make an evening of it, there's limo service to the nearby Music Center.

Bistro 45 S | 26 | 23 | 24 | $40

45 S. Mentor Ave. (bet. Colorado Blvd. & Green St.), Pasadena, 626-795-2478

■ With ratings that keep rising, this art deco Cal-French bistro on a quiet side street is hailed not only as the "best restaurant in Pasadena" but as "better than most on the Westside as well", an "elegant yet innovative" "favorite" that's ideal "for wine lovers" ("get on their mailing list for winemaker dinners"); most agree this one "has it all – romance, class, great food, wonderful atmosphere."

Brent's Deli S | 25 | 14 | 20 | $13

19565 Parthenia Ave. (Tampa Ave.), Northridge, 818-886-5679

■ Despite sniffs from Westside snobs who can't believe that the area's best deli could be in a suburban Northridge shopping mall, local mavens agree that LA's No. 1 deli for six years running is the "best west of NYC", with a "killer menu" of "tasty" soups, "mmm pastrami" and "excellent Reubens", all in "huge portions"; "out of the way, but worth it", it even boasts the "friendliest service."

Cafe Bizou S | 26 | 19 | 23 | $25

14016 Ventura Blvd. (east of Hazeltine Ave.), Sherman Oaks, 818-788-3536

■ Like pilgrims in search of the Holy Grail, foodies travel long distances to dine at LA's second Most Popular restaurant, a Valley French "treasure" that some call the "best value in town", made sweeter by a $2 corkage fee that encourages diners to BYO; while the "decor could be better", acolytes swear the food is "as good as French gets" at this "real bistro", so reserve "a month in advance."

Café Blanc 25 | 15 | 22 | $40

9777 Little Santa Monica Blvd. (Wilshire Blvd.), Beverly Hills, 310-888-0108

■ One of the truest practitioners of the fine art of Cal-Asian cooking, Tommy Harase, is behind the stove at this "little jewel", offering a fixed price menu that "makes a statement without arrogance", blending "Japanese kaiseki and light French" fare with "artistry"; despite a few gripes about "sparse" portions and decor, devotees say this "humble chef" "deserves more of a following."

Campanile S 26 | 25 | 23 | $40

624 S. La Brea Ave. (bet. 6th St. & Wilshire Blvd.), LA, 323-938-1447

■ "Arguably the best" Cal-Med in town, this "cool LA hangout", adjacent to co-owner Nancy Silverton's La Brea Bakery, is where "gorgeous architecture meets food to die for", with chef Mark Peel grilling "consistently good", "earthy" fare in his open kitchen; don't miss the "excellent rack of lamb", fab bread or the family-style meals on Mondays – it's a taste of Southern France on La Brea.

Chaya Brasserie S 25 | 23 | 22 | $38

8741 Alden Dr. (bet. Beverly Blvd. & 3rd St., east of Robertson Blvd.), LA, 310-859-8833

■ "Gorgeous people, gorgeous food, gorgeous restaurant" sums up this "happening" French-Italian bistro with Asian touches that's "surprisingly good" given the "trendiness of the crowd" – a "very LA" mix of "Hollywood" types, decorators from the Pacific Design Center and "celeb doctors" from Cedars-Sinai; its "noisy, jumpin' bar" and "jazzy environs" are not for everyone, but those who like "the scene" say it's "still one of the finest after all these years."

Chez Melange S 25 | 20 | 24 | $31

Palos Verdes Inn, 1716 PCH (bet. Palos Verdes Blvd. & Prospect Ave.), Redondo Beach, 310-540-1222

■ In many ways the restaurant that put the beach-intensive South Bay "on the dining map", this "cheesy on the outside, delicious on the inside" upscale motel Cal-Eclectic (Italian, French, Japanese, Cajun, Chinese, Hawaiian – you name it) with a vodka and caviar bar offers "awesome food in an unlikely setting"; regulars swear you'll "never feel you've wasted your money" at this "quirky" "fave" where owners "Michael Franks and Robert Bell do it right."

Chinois on Main S 28 | 23 | 23 | $45

2709 Main St. (bet. Ocean Park Blvd. & Rose Ave.), Santa Monica, 310-392-9025

■ Consistently the top-rated of Wolfgang Puck's SoCal empire, this Franco-Asian "adventure in decor and dining" "excites the eyes and palate" with an "innovative", if "deafening", high-energy setting (designed by wife Barbara Lazaroff) showcasing Wolf's cutting-edge "Puckerized Chinese" cuisine; "whoever thought catfish could taste so good?" – "as Arnold might say, 'I'll be back.'"

Citrus S 26 | 23 | 23 | $45

6703 Melrose Ave. (1 block west of Highland Ave.), LA, 323-857-0034

■ Both Michel and Alain are gone, but this Cal-French with a "magic touch" remains "year in and year out a winner" for its "creative menu" of "classic food" ("love the crab cakes", the "best baby salmon", "memorable desserts") turned out from the glass-fronted kitchen; but a few cite a lack of "warmth" and note that with Hollywood types vying for tables, "seating depends on your juice."

Depot | 25 | 23 | 24 | $31
1250 Cabrillo Ave. (Torrance Blvd.), Torrance, 310-787-7501
■ Closed for months after a kitchen fire, this "unexpected gem in Torrance" is back and better than ever, with "imaginative" Eclectic (mostly Cal-Asian) food prepared by a "fast-rising star", chef-owner Michael Shafer; the "outstanding service" and "lovely" room in a former train station are more reasons this Chez Melange spin-off was missed; P.S. "cooking classes with chef Shafer are hilarious."

Diaghilev | 26 | 28 | 27 | $57
Wyndham Bel Age Hotel, 1020 N. San Vicente Blvd. (Sunset Blvd.), W. Hollywood, 310-854-1111
■ They may be lining up for bread in Russia, but here in LA the "caviar and flavored vodkas" are flowing at this "romantic" Franco-Russian retreat where "Dimitri is the ultimate maitre d'" and "you'll be treated like royalty no matter who you are"; "book a room in the hotel so you can totally indulge" at this "special occasion place if there ever was one" – then settle in for some "marvelous" beluga and you'll feel "like you're dining with the czar."

Grill, The S | 25 | 22 | 24 | $39
9560 Dayton Way (Wilshire Blvd.), Beverly Hills, 310-276-0615
■ "If you're serious about red meat", head for this classic "haven for power brokers" where "power plays and power food are the standard"; a virtual "men's club at lunch" (though women are always welcome), it's a world of "solid steaks and chops", "dark wood, polished brass" and "great bartenders" – in other words, it's "old-fashioned and New Yorkish . . . and we like it that way."

Hirosuke S | 26 | 19 | 23 | $24
17237 Ventura Blvd. (Louise Ave.), Encino, 818-788-7548
■ "Hiro does very special things with very fresh fish" at this wildly popular SF Valley Japanese, according to a loyal following that insists it's "the best sushi bar in town . . . period!"; although it's "friendly and welcoming" and the service is "excellent", this shopping mall eatery gets "crowded" so "be prepared to wait for a table" – then "try the Volcano."

JiRaffe S | 25 | 21 | 22 | $38
502 Santa Monica Blvd. (5th St.), Santa Monica, 310-917-6671
■ "Consistently good food and service" are the hallmarks of this "pleasantly elegant" (if rather understated) Californian, an "upscale find in Santa Monica" run by the dynamic duo of Josiah Citrin and Raphael Lunetta; although even fans cite noise and "close seating", the crowd is here for good reason: "clean flavors" that "couldn't be better" – "these guys have their feet on the ground."

Joe's S | 27 | 18 | 23 | $35
1023 Abbot Kinney Blvd. (bet. Main St. & Westminster Ave.), Venice, 310-399-5811
■ Call it "a synonym for heaven", this "casual", "cozy" Californian with "minimalist" decor in a rambling Venice storefront transcends its setting thanks to affable-yet-shy Joe Miller, a regular Joe who happens to be a "master chef", turning out "tasty" home cooking at prices that have locals singing "what a deal!"; the restaurant by which some "judge all others", it ranks in LA's Top 10 for both Food and Popularity, so be sure to "call ahead."

Jozu S | 26 | 24 | 25 | $41

8360 Melrose Ave. (4 blocks east of La Cienega Blvd.), W. Hollywood, 323-655-5600

■ Immune to the sophomore jinx, this Pacific New Waver improved its ratings as tout le monde discovered its "already legendary food and service"; expect owner Andy Nakano to greet you with a "complimentary glass of sake, a nice touch", followed by food "prepared to absolute perfection": "Chilean sea bass that's just heaven", "I can still taste the mussels in coconut milk", "great eggplant in miso"; "three cheers for chef Suzanne Tracht" at this "sublime, subtle" "Zen experience."

La Cachette S | 26 | 25 | 24 | $43

10506 Little Santa Monica Blvd. (bet. Beverly Glen Blvd. & Overland Ave.), Century City, 310-470-4992

■ "Superb presentation" is a hallmark of this "très unique", "cozy" Modern French where cinematically handsome chef Jean François Meteigner "pays attention to the room as well as the kitchen" while earning raves for his "French food without the heavy cream", such as "fabulous" tuna tartare; a "serene" and "wonderful restaurant that understands health-conscious eating habits", it's "slightly stuffy, but that's ok."

Lavande ▽ | 26 | 24 | 25 | $45

Loews Santa Monica Beach Hotel, 1700 Ocean Ave. (bet. Colorado Ave. & Pico Blvd.), Santa Monica, 310-576-3181

■ After leaving Citrus, Alain Giraud headed west for the beach, opening this Provençal French "winner with a drop-dead view of the Pacific" in the Loews Santa Monica Beach Hotel and garnering stellar surveyor reviews: "gorgeous, grand, gourmet", "brilliant", "creative" and "friendly", with the "best soupe de poisson" and "exquisite lavender ice cream" for dessert; "Santa Monica ain't St. Tropez, but you might think otherwise" after a meal at this newcomer with a "promising future."

Lawry's The Prime Rib S | 26 | 24 | 25 | $34

100 N. La Cienega Blvd. (½ block north of Wilshire Blvd.), Beverly Hills, 310-652-2827

■ To call this classic a "classic" is to understate the importance of this "LA original", a 60-year-old "throne room of red meat" where generations have gathered to celebrate every manner of "special occasion" in an "old-fashioned" setting where "you know what to expect": "unbeatable" "melt-in-your-mouth" prime rib "served from a rolling cart"; major carnivores should consider the "Diamond Jim Brady cut, as big as a *Flintstones* brontosaurus burger."

Locanda Veneta | 25 | 17 | 21 | $35

8638 W. Third St. (bet. Robertson & San Vicente Blvds.), LA, 310-274-1893

■ The first of the current wave of regional Italians to appear on the LA dining scene, this "very small" Venetian "makes up in taste what it lacks in size", offering "great food in what looks like a converted toolshed"; the menu of "great gnocchi", "divine mushroom risotto" and other "home-cooked" specialties, created by the ubiquitous team of Jean-Louis De Mori and Antonio Tomassi, includes dishes "handed down from Antonio's grandmother" – "they still do it right and make it feel new."

L'Orangerie S 27 28 26 $62

903 N. La Cienega Blvd. (bet. Melrose Ave. & Santa Monica Blvd.), W. Hollywood, 310-652-9770

■ Last of the French Classicists (RIP L'Ermitage, Le Restaurant, La Chaumière, L'Escoffier), and the priciest European restaurant in town, this "special occasion" Gallic earns high ratings and rapturous praise ("words fail") for its "fabulous food" in what some call "the best formal room in town" with the "most spectacular flowers"; it's a "trip to Paris by way of La Cienega."

Matsuhisa S 28 18 23 $52

129 N. La Cienega Blvd. (north of Wilshire Blvd.), Beverly Hills, 310-659-9639

■ The annual tag-match between Matsuhisa and Patina continues, with Patina this year edging out Nobu Matsuhisa's "astonishing" Japanese seafooder; despite a growing empire of Nobus, the original remains "sushi heaven" and, just as importantly, the place for "exceptional", "innovative" cooked seafood from the 40-page Japanese-Peruvian-French fusion menu: miso-flavored black cod and so forth; "even the Little Mermaid would eat seafood" here.

Michael's 26 26 23 $48

1147 Third St. (north of Wilshire Blvd.), Santa Monica, 310-451-0843

■ "Still original" after all these years, Michael McCarty's "upscale" Californian with the "loveliest garden" is a "class act all the way" that makes "special occasions always more special"; if Michael is in town (he has a branch in NYC), he'll "treat you like royalty" while you dine on dishes that admirers rate among the "best in town"; memo to those who admire McCarty's *GQ* style: "be like Mike."

Mimosa 24 19 20 $37

8009 Beverly Blvd. (2 blocks east of Crescent Hts. Blvd.), LA, 323-655-8895

■ For many, this is LA's "great French bistro", an "adorable" room that "transports you to Paris" thanks to the presence of Jean-Pierre Bosc in the kitchen and Silvio De Mori out front; "outstanding in all respects", with "authentic" chow such as a "wonderful" charcuterie plate with cornichons pickled and olives cured in-house, this "trendy eatery" "takes bistro food to a new level."

Ocean Star S 24 16 16 $21

145 N. Atlantic Blvd. (bet. Emerson & Garvey Aves.), Monterey Park, 626-308-2128

■ Despite the influx of Hong Kong–style Chinese restaurants into the San Gabriel Valley, this seafood palace remains the Prince of Prawns, a massive series of rooms serving "amazing dim sum" at lunchtime and "awesome seafood" in the evening, with a whole edible aquarium living in tanks built into the walls; "save the $3,000 airfare" – this banquet hall is "as authentic as it gets."

Palm, The S 25 19 20 $46

9001 Santa Monica Blvd. (bet. Doheny Dr. & Robertson Blvd.), W. Hollywood, 310-550-8811

■ Outsiders (i.e. most everybody) who are herded to "the back room, aka Siberia" call this a place for "those with more money than they know what to do with", but for such fortunates, this "cholesterol temple" offers "fab steaks" and lobsters, a bar that knows the semiotics of martinis and waiters who've seen much and forgotten little; here's proof that the "biggest slabs of beef aren't strolling Santa Monica Boulevard", but "do be prepared to pay up."

Parkway Grill S | 26 | 24 | 24 | $34

510 S. Arroyo Pkwy. (bet. California & Del Mar Blvds.), Pasadena, 626-795-1001

■ Founding chef Hugo Molina has gone off to a restaurant of his own, but regulars report the "food is still fine" at this casually elegant Californian, a "place for festive feasting" that's turned into an "institution", with an organic garden, "some of the best wines by the glass" and a kitchen that "keeps reinventing itself"; the Spago of Pasadena, it's "hip, noisy, the place to be."

Patina S | 28 | 24 | 26 | $55

5955 Melrose Ave. (bet. Highland Ave. & Vine St.), LA, 323-467-1108

■ Last year Patina wound up half a heartbeat behind Matsuhisa, and this year it's half a heartbeat ahead, making Joachim Splichal's "creative" flagship No. 1 for Food in LA, while remaining the city's Most Popular restaurant; an "icon of interesting and scrumptious" Contemporary Cal-French food with German-Austrian accents, it's the "top of the top" and a "favorite in every way"; biggest worry – "don't spread the empire too thin."

Pinot Bistro S | 26 | 24 | 24 | $40

12969 Ventura Blvd. (½ block west of Coldwater Canyon Ave.), Studio City, 818-990-0500

■ Where Patina is Splichal Serious, Pinot is Splichal as Homeboy, getting loose and down with "casual elegance" that works for special occasions and regular nights on the town; the original Valley "oasis" is "worth the trip" to experience "what a French cafe should be", with "outstanding food" and a "very refined", "light, airy" setting that isn't so much Pinot Noir as it is Pinot Blanc.

R-23 | 26 | 21 | 21 | $33

923 E. Third St. (bet. Alameda St. & Santa Fe Ave.), Downtown LA, 213-687-7178

■ Over the years some have given up on finding this "cool, Zen-like" sushi bar hidden down an alleyway in an oddly artsy, seemingly "abandoned" section of Downtown, where "serene sushi" is consumed in a "minimalist" warehouse room by "the young and rich" perched on "interesting cardboard chairs"; the "beautifully presented" fish could hardly be fresher or better, so while you may need to "watch your back . . . it's well worth it."

Ruth's Chris Steak House S | 26 | 21 | 23 | $40

224 S. Beverly Dr. (bet. Olympic & Wilshire Blvds.), Beverly Hills, 310-859-8744

■ It may be a chain, but that doesn't stop this Beverly Hills branch of the N'Awlins meatery from serving the top beef in town, "huge portions" of "fab prime steaks" that are "soft as butter" and, in fact, "served sizzling in butter" – a "cardiologist's nightmare" but a meat eater's dream; "excellent creamed spinach" is among the sides at this "decadent" dining experience where the food is "sooo goood!"

Shiro S | 28 | 19 | 25 | $40

1505 Mission St. (Fair Oaks Ave.), S. Pasadena, 626-799-4774

■ Though there's a modest-sized menu at this bento box of a Cal-Asian seafooder in South Pasadena, most know it for "the catfish! nothing more need be said"; an "exquisite masterpiece" of a dish, flavored with ginger slices and ponzu sauce, it's so popular that "whole tankfuls of catfish go to heaven" daily, although a few independent sorts report "every dish is a masterpiece."

Spago Beverly Hills S | 26 | 26 | 23 | $50

176 N. Cañon Dr. (½ block north of Wilshire Blvd.), Beverly Hills, 310-385-0880

■ Chinois on Main may rank higher, but Spago is the crown jewel in the Puckian universe, and Spago Beverly Hills is the Spago against which all other Spagos are judged, a "celebrity hangout" offering "all that you expect in imaginative food" ("no one makes a smoked salmon pizza like Puck") in a "jumping", "pretty room" where wife Barbara Lazaroff has outdone herself in terms of new wave decor; it's "high marks all around" for this "hot spot", although, not surprisingly, reservations are "tough."

Sushi Nozawa | 28 | 9 | 18 | $37

11288 Ventura Blvd. (2 blocks west of Vineland Ave.), Studio City, 818-508-7017

■ The cuisine at this "thimble-sized" Japanese storefront is sushi and sushi only, served by a "master chef" who insists you do it his way or not do it at all; "nobody takes more care in the purchasing of fish", making for an "amazing experience" as long as you "don't question Nozawa San", who reminds people of "that soup guy on Seinfeld"; "trust him" and you'll be rewarded with "superb fish" prepared with an "artist's eye."

Valentino | 27 | 24 | 26 | $54

3115 Pico Blvd. (bet. 31st & 32nd Sts.), Santa Monica, 310-829-4313

■ Consistently the top-rated Italian in SoCal, Piero Selvaggio's "superb restaurant with class" is responsible for moving LA from a land of lasagna to a suburb of Tuscany, complete with one of the world's great wine lists (a cellar of 130,000 bottles); "after 25 years, it just keeps getting better" thanks to an obsessive commitment to "top-quality" ingredients, including the best white truffles, olive oils and prosciutto – all "pricey but worth it"; lunch, served Fridays only, is a "wonderful", "quiet" experience.

Water Grill S | 26 | 25 | 24 | $38

544 S. Grand Ave. (bet. 5th & 6th Sts.), Downtown LA, 213-891-0900

■ Year after year, this University Restaurant Group "seafood paradise" ranks as the top fish house in LA, a "Downtown watering hole" with "lots of variety", including a "delightful" oyster bar displaying a constantly changing selection of bivalves; the "luxurious" but "comfortable" surroundings make it "great for entertaining clients" and "excellent for pre-theater" dining, although many note that the "prices reflect" the high quality.

Yujean Kang's S | 25 | 21 | 22 | $35

67 N. Raymond Ave. (bet. Colorado Blvd. & Walnut St.), Pasadena, 626-585-0855

8826 Melrose Ave. (1 block west of Robertson Blvd.), W. Hollywood, 310-288-0806

■ Kang is king thanks to his branches in Old Town Pasadena and West Hollywood, where he creates a sort of Cal-Chinese amalgam that's "delicate beyond belief", listed on menus that are "creative masterpieces" of wit and whimsy; some describe the food as Modern Chinese, but most are content to refer to it as Kangian cuisine, the "ultimate" "Chinese fusion" "with a twist" – in other words, cooking unlike anything you've tried before.

Miami/Miami Beach

TOP 10 FOOD RANKING

	Restaurant	Cuisine Type
27	Chef Allen's	New World
26	Palm	Steakhouse
	Hy-Vong	Vietnamese
	Joe's Stone Crab	Seafood
25	Giacosa	Northern Italian
	Tropical Chinese	Chinese/Dim Sum
	Le Festival	Classic French
	Caffe Abbracci	N/S Italian
	Christy's	Steakhouse
	Osteria del Teatro	Northern Italian

OTHER IMPORTANT PLACES

Astor Place B&G	Floridian
Blue Door	Brazilian/New French
Brasserie Les Halles	French Bistro/Steakhouse
Carpaccio	Northern Italian
China Grill	Asian/Eclectic
Chrysanthemum	Chinese
El Manara	Middle Eastern
Escopazzo	Northern Italian
Forge	American/Continental
Heights	Asian/Southwestern
Nemo	New American
Norman's	New World
Pacific Time	Pacific Rim
Red Fish Grill	Seafood
S & S Restaurant	Diner/Trad. American
Smith & Wollensky	Steakhouse
Versailles	American/Cuban
Wolfie Cohen's	Deli
Yuca	Cuban

F	D	S	C

Astor Place Bar & Grill S — | – | – | – | E |

Astor Hotel, 956 Washington Ave. (10th St.), Miami Beach, 305-672-7217
Housed in a hip boutique hotel, this hot spot has evolved into one of the very best restaurants on the beach; chef Johnny Vinczencz, aka the Caribbean Cowboy, turns out imaginative Floridian fusion dishes like corn-crusted yellowtail snapper with lemon boniato mash and a decadent lobster pot pie for a young, sophisticated set that happily piles in three-deep at the sleek lobby bar while waiting for tables on weekends.

Blue Door S — | – | – | – | VE |

Delano Hotel, 1685 Collins Ave. (17th St.), Miami Beach, 305-674-6400
Finally, after a half-dozen others failed to create food worthy of this hip hotel's drop-dead gorgeous Philippe Starck decor with towering white curtains and plump circular banquettes, chef Claude Troisgros has done it with a dramatic menu featuring French and tropical accents; inefficient service and towering prices don't deter the beautiful people from coming in droves.

Brasserie Les Halles ◐ S | – | – | – | M

2415 Ponce de Leon Blvd. (bet. Andalusia St. & Miracle Mile), Coral Gables, 305-461-1099

An oh-so-French bistro known especially for fine steaks, this very welcome addition to the Coral Gables dining scene became popular as soon as it opened in '97 and has continued to do a brisk business despite sluggish service and cramped quarters; fair prices, dynamic salads and an impressive wine list help make up for any flaws.

Caffe Abbracci S | 25 | 22 | 23 | $31

318 Aragon Ave. (bet. Le Jeune Rd. & Miracle Mile), Coral Gables, 305-441-0700

■ "You've never been hugged until you've dined" at this "never disappointing" Italian that lives up to its name (*abbracci* means hugs) with "impeccable, personal" service and a "warm" owner, Nino Pernetti; "ambitiously delicious" dishes, including top-notch tiramisu, make it "one of Miami's best", if you can stand the "noise."

Carpaccio S | – | – | – | E

Bal Harbour Shops, 9700 Collins Ave (96th St.), Bal Harbour, 305-867-7777

A darling of the couture set, this Northern Italian in Miami's ritziest shopping mall packs them in for elegant pastas, pizzas and, of course, carpaccio in a dozen variations; friendly waiters and a lively ambiance are more reasons why its chic patrons sometimes deign to wait in line on the sidewalk for a table – imagine!

Chef Allen's S | 27 | 24 | 25 | $39

19088 NE 29th Ave. (bet. Biscayne Blvd. & 191st St.), Aventura, 305-935-2900

■ "Always one of the city's top meals" is the consensus on chef Allen Susser's "innovative" New World cuisine; "sleek", modern decor and fine service complement the "artfully prepared" dishes that have won top ratings and international accolades; with an open kitchen that lets diners watch chef Allen "make wonders from appetizers to desserts", it's "a must for visitors and locals."

China Grill ◐ S | – | – | – | VE

404 Washington Ave. (5th St.), Miami Beach, 305-534-2211

Imported from NYC, this glitzy, neon-infused Eclectic quickly became a South Beach hot spot when it opened in '95; more of a lounge than a restaurant, it still attracts well-dressed swells who come for plates of Asian-inspired food big enough for a sumo wrestler (with prices that are equally intimidating).

Christy's S | 25 | 21 | 25 | $31

3101 Ponce de Leon Blvd. (Malaga Ave.), Coral Gables, 305-446-1400

◪ Popular for "power lunches" and family dinners, this contender for "Miami's best steakhouse" draws carnivores in quest of "awesome" beef and mighty Caesars, all served in huge portions by an "efficient" staff; critics deem the food "overrated" and find the setting "stuffy", but most say "if you love meat, this is it."

Chrysanthemum S | 23 | 17 | 19 | $26

1248 Washington Ave. (13th St.), Miami Beach, 305-531-5656

■ "A South Beach anomaly" that "takes Chinese cuisine to a higher level" with "wildly creative" dishes marked by "intense flavors"; while aesthetes suggest that "a few flowers would help" the decor, most toss bouquets at food that's "worth every penny", including "unique" fried spinach that alone is "worth the visit."

El Manara 24 | 15 | 20 | $18

5811 Sunset Dr. (bet. Red Rd. & US 1), S. Miami, 305-665-3374

■ Surveyors laud this Lebanese-Syrian storefront for its Paul Bunyon–size portions of "the best Middle Eastern food"; it's deemed "as good as it gets" for hummus, baklava and the like, which is why it's "popular" (hence "crowded").

Escopazzo ◐ S – | – | – | E

1311 Washington Ave. (13 St.), Miami Beach, 305-674-9450

This South Beach Northern Italian sleeper with fewer than a dozen tables is always booked in advance by cognoscenti who come for some of the finest risotto, pasta and wild game in town; plans for 1999 include an expanded dining room, which should help those without connections score a weekend table at this cozy winner.

Forge, The ◐ S 24 | 26 | 23 | $36

432 Arthur Godfrey Rd. (41st St.), Miami Beach, 305-538-8533

◪ This Miami Beach "classic" offers an "exotic", "rococo" setting for "romantic" meals featuring "excellent" Continental-American cuisine and a world-famous, "mind-boggling" wine list; to most it's a "feast for the eyes as well as the palate", but critics wish "the food were as good as the art" and all agree it's "expensive."

Giacosa S 25 | 22 | 23 | $36

394 Giralda Ave. (Le Jeune Rd.), Coral Gables, 305-445-5858

■ An "elegant" Coral Gables Italian that ranks as one of the area's standouts thanks to a "chef-owner who shows pride and skill" in his "beautifully prepared dishes"; diners enjoy "the best Northern Italian food this side of Tuscany", including "superb risotto", served by an "attentive" staff; though "pricey" it's "hard to beat", especially with the addition of live weekend music in a new annex.

Heights, The – | – | – | E

2530 Ponce de Leon Blvd. (Valencia St.), Coral Gables, 305-461-1774

The pairing of Asian and Southwestern cuisines makes a fine match at this intriguing hybrid in upscale Coral Gables where gorgeous decor and a handsome staff add eye appeal; though once under the same ownership as South Beach's wildly successful Pacific Time, this is no ugly stepchild – its food and service rank among the area's best, which helps justify the price.

Hy-Vong S ⌀ 26 | 10 | 14 | $17

3458 SW Eighth St. (bet. 34th & 35th Aves.), Miami, 305-446-3674

■ It helps to "have patience", but the "wait on the sidewalk" for a table and "slow service" are "worth it" for "spicy Vietnamese" fare that's as authentic as it gets; even though the original chef went out on her own in 1998, this still may be the "best hole-in-the-wall in Miami" and it's a "buy" too.

Joe's Stone Crab S 26 | 18 | 21 | $33

227 Biscayne St. (bet. Collins & Washington Aves.), Miami Beach, 305-673-0365

■ "Everyone who comes to South Florida eats at Joe's", a "shrine" that draws locals, tourists and celebs; epicureans wait "hours" (no reservations accepted) to enjoy its legendary specialties: "the best stone crabs, hash browns and Key lime pie"; a $5 million redo more than doubled the space in 1997, but savvy diners still come at 5 PM or for lunch, when waits are shorter; closed mid-May–mid-October.

	F	D	S	C
Le Festival	25	23	25	$33

2120 Salzedo St. (Alcazar Ave.), Coral Gables, 305-442-8545
■ Long recognized as "the best traditional French spot in Coral Gables", this "wonderful classic" never falters in delivering "impeccable food and service"; if it strikes some as a bit "heavy" and "stuffy", more are charmed by the "beautiful atmosphere" and "gracious" service at this landmark: "count on it to be excellent."

	F	D	S	C
Nemo ◐ S	–	–	–	M

100 Collins Ave. (1st St.), Miami Beach, 305-532-4550
In South Beach's up-and-coming sector south of Fifth Street, this pioneer has won loyalists who return for creative New American fare with multicultural accents served in a superchic (but at times loud) setting; helping to distinguish it are personable, intelligent service and a new raw bar featuring oysters, clams and caviar from around the world.

	F	D	S	C
Norman's	–	–	–	E

21 Almeria Ave. (bet. Douglas Rd. & Ponce de Leon Blvd.), Coral Gables, 305-446-6767
Norman Van Aken, award-winning chef, cookbook author and one of the originators of what has become known as New World cuisine, has created a national sensation with his elegant Asian- and Caribbean-inspired food served in this subdued Coral Gables space centered around an open kitchen that turns out wildly inventive (and delicious) concoctions like his signature rum and pepper painted grouper; it's one of Miami's very best.

	F	D	S	C
Osteria del Teatro	25	19	23	$34

1443 Washington Ave. (Española Way), Miami Beach, 305-538-7850
■ Exemplifying "Northern Italian at its finest", this little, "upbeat" corner restaurant attracts a loyal South Beach clientele with "superb pastas, desserts" and other "zesty" dishes that are expensive but "never disappoint"; it's "warm, friendly" and "great for people-watching", though some diners feel that "too many tables packed into a small place" makes it a bit "noisy."

	F	D	S	C
Pacific Time S	24	20	20	$35

915 Lincoln Rd. (bet. Jefferson & Michigan Aves.), Miami Beach, 305-534-5979
■ "Clever, innovative fare" lures "beautiful people" to this Pacific Rim–influenced spot on trendy Lincoln Road; chef-owner (and erstwhile model) Jonathan Eismann draws raves for his tuna tartare and other "exciting" dishes with "Asian flair"; the "noise may deafen" and portions are tiny, but many call it "one of the best" in Miami; N.B. for a lunch bargain, try the new cafe next door where the same quality food goes for a fraction of the cost.

	F	D	S	C
Palm Restaurant S	26	18	23	$39

9650 E. Bay Harbor Dr. (bet. 96th & 97th Sts.), Bay Harbor Island, 305-868-7256
■ "All that's missing is Al Capone" at this "old-style chophouse" that's sister to The Palm in NYC; even with numerous new steak chains recently opened, many still think that this "pricey" "meat eater's paradise" has "the best steaks in town" served by a polite, professional staff that "treats you royally" (if they know you).

Red Fish Grill S — | — | — | M

Matheson Hammock Park, 9610 Old Cutler Rd. (Kendall Dr.), Coral Gables, 305-668-8788

On the water's edge, this fish house in Matheson Hammock Park is a favorite of the South Miami/Dade crowd who come by boat, bike and car for a seat with a spectacular view and good food from a seafood-centric menu; moderate prices boost its appeal.

S & S Restaurant 23 | 14 | 20 | $10

1757 NE Second Ave. (bet. 17th & 18th Sts.), Miami, 305-373-4291

■ A "counter-place" diner near Downtown Miami that looks like the model for Edward Hopper's Night Hawks; attorneys and mechanics alike wait patiently for an available stool to enjoy the "old-time home cooking" and daily specials at this "hole-in-the-wall heaven", which was recently sold to a new owner who insists that 'the same cooks and waitresses who have been there for almost 40 years' are still doing their thing.

Smith & Wollensky ◐ S — | — | — | VE

1 Washington Ave. (S. Pointe Park), Miami Beach, 305-673-2800

Though it opened on the heels of many other steakhouses in Miami, this quintessential NYC import stands out from the pack with its burnished wood decor, first-rate service, monstrous portions and spectacular waterfront view; valets leave the Rolls-Royces near the entrance and charge for the favor.

Tropical Chinese Restaurant S 25 | 19 | 22 | $24

7991 SW 40th St. (bet. Bird Rd. & 79th Ave.), Miami, 305-262-7576

■ Popular on weekends for "superb dim sum", this suburban outpost serves food that fans claim "rivals Hong Kong and NYC's Chinatown;" there's "never a bad meal here" and "elegant service" adds to the appeal; most say it's "as good as Chinese gets."

Versailles ◐ S 18 | 13 | 17 | $14

3555 SW Eighth St. (36th Ave.), Miami, 305-444-0240

■ An old standby in Little Havana that serves as the meeting place for Cuban power brokers, families and out-of-towners, this "Eighth Street icon" is a glorified diner that sparkles with chandeliers, murals and mirrors meant to evoke the French palace; but there's nothing fancy (or French) about the "hearty" Cuban-American good eats served by a personable but English-challenged staff.

Wolfie Cohen's Rascal House ◐ S 22 | 11 | 17 | $14

17190 Collins Ave. (172nd St.), N. Miami Beach, 305-947-4581

■ "The busiest place in town" is "part of Miami's history" serving deli fare that's "the closest thing to real NYC"; there's always "a line around the block to get in", but it's "worth" the wait and "every penny" for "the best" "big sandwiches and desserts" at this "last bastion where cholesterol is a virtue."

Yuca S 24 | 21 | 21 | $35

501 Lincoln Rd. (Drexel Ave.), Miami Beach, 305-532-9822

■ The name is an acronym for 'young upwardly mobile Cuban Americans', and that's who you'll find enjoying the "nouvelle Cuban cuisine" at this "cosmopolitan" South Beach standby with a view of the passing parade and sizzling weekend entertainment in the upstairs lounge; prices are *muy caro* but that doesn't stop crowds from pouring in for exciting "upscale" dining.

TOP 10 FOOD RANKING

	Restaurant	Cuisine Type
28	Goodfellow's	Regional American
27	Ristorante Luci	Northern Italian
	D'Amico Cucina	Northern Italian
	Manny's	Steakhouse
26	St. Paul Grill	Regional American
25	Schumacher's	Central European
	Kincaid's	American/Seafood
	Gardens of Salonica	Greek
	Origami	Japanese
	Morton's of Chicago	Steakhouse

OTHER IMPORTANT PLACES

Bar Abilene	Southwestern
Bayport Amer. Cookery	Regional American
Buca di Beppo	Southern Italian
Cafe Havana	Cuban
Dakota Bar & Grill	Regional American
Giorgio	Northern Italian
La Belle Vie	Mediterranean
Local	Irish
Loring Cafe & Bar	New American
Palomino	Californian/Italian
Table Of Contents	New American

F | D | S | C

Bar Abilene ◐ S — | — | — | M

1300 Lagoon Ave. (bet. Fremont & Hennepen Aves.), Minneapolis, 612-825-2525

From the folks who brought you Goodfellow's, here's the tongue-in-chic answer to 'yee-haw!', with 20 margaritas, even more tequilas, old black-and-white cowboy movies on (mercifully) silent monitors and grub that would make a cowpoke think he'd died and gone to Dallas (instead, it's trendy Uptown); don't miss the huitlacoche quesadillas or salmon with mango-habañero sauce.

Bayport American Cookery S 24 | 19 | 22 | $30

328 5th Ave. N. (Hwy. 95), Bayport, 612-430-1066

◪ Having only a single, "wonderfully creative prix fixe menu that changes weekly" involves a "risk" that the New Midwestern cuisine at this "small, lovely" storefront near the St. Croix can be "inconsistent", ranging from "inspired" to "poor"; a few critics also bay at "pretentious servers", but most consider it "very special" and "worth the drive" (25 miles) to this "small-town oasis."

Buca di Beppo S 20 | 21 | 21 | $16

1204 Harmon Pl. (12th St.), Minneapolis, 612-638-2225
2728 Gannon Rd. (Shepard Rd.), St. Paul, 612-772-4388
7711 Mitchell Rd. (Hwy. 5), Eden Prairie, 612-724-7266

■ It's "time to loosen the belt" when faced with "too much food" at these "Italian family spots"; they're "kitschy", but the "gusto in the decor and the use of garlic" "make me wish I was Italian"; "bring hungry friends" who can handle noise and a no-reserving policy, which means "prepare to wait"; "a triumph" of "a lot for a little."

Cafe Havana – | – | – | M

119 Washington Ave. N. (2nd Ave.), Minneapolis, 612-338-8484

Of course there are cigars (the bar is blue with smoke) as well as dissolute cocktails and over-the-top, '50s Havana decor at this Cuban hot spot, now in Downtown Warehouse District quarters; there's also a menu that rhumbas from seviche, empanadas and black bean soup to snapper breaded in plantains, all devised by the mom of this mom-and-son-run place to see and be seen.

Dakota Bar and Grill S 23 | 21 | 21 | $24

Bandana Sq., 1021 Bandana Blvd. E. (Energy Park Dr.), St. Paul, 612-642-1442

■ On the outskirts of St. Paul, chef Ken Goff's "inspired menu" of "innovative" Regional Midwestern fare and "lots of good California wines" are smartly served in "pleasant", contemporary digs in a former railroad roundhouse; the bar has a special menu and "the best jazz in the Twin Cities" – "go for the food, stay for the music."

D'Amico Cucina S 27 | 26 | 25 | $35

Butler Sq., 100 N. Sixth St., Minneapolis, 612-338-2401

■ A "classy, modern Northern Italian" in the Warehouse District that's a "second home to Twin Cities power brokers" and the "star of the restaurant scene"; the polished, "accommodating" staff draws almost as much praise as the kitchen's "creative" fare and the "superb all-Italian wine list"; even those who complain it's *molto* "expensive" join the chorus of "*bella, bella.*"

Gardens of Salonica 25 | 18 | 14 | $9

19 Fifth St. NE (Hennepin Ave.), Minneapolis, 612-378-0611

■ This "tiny", family-run, "well-kept Greek secret" near Downtown serves "authentic" "fresh food" that's just like what some have "experienced in Greece"; it's "no-frills", "cheap" and "fabulous", driving fans to swear "I'd brush my teeth with their garlic spread."

Giorgio S 24 | 16 | 19 | $19

2451 Hennepin Ave. (24th St.), Minneapolis, 612-374-5131

■ "*Bene*" croon the hordes who canonize this "tiny", "crowded" Uptown storefront for its "fantastic", "authentic", "flavor-forward" Tuscan fare; never mind the staff with "an attitude" and "tables too close", go for "the best risotto in town"; aka "garlic lovers' heaven."

Goodfellow's 28 | 25 | 26 | $36

City Ctr., 40 S. Seventh St. (bet. Hennepin Ave. & Nicollet Mall), Minneapolis, 612-332-4800

■ For an "amazing" "variety of flavors" showcasing Regional American fare at its "best", plus a "wine list extraordinaire", "do not miss" this "sublime experience"; even the few who find the modern design of this room atop a Downtown shopping complex to be "cold" have warm words for a staff that "goes the extra mile"; "if you're going to drop a lot of dough, this is *the* place."

Kincaid's S 25 | 24 | 24 | $27

8400 Normandale Lake Blvd. (84th St.), Bloomington, 612-921-2255

◪ A "Midwest classic" that serves "fresh NW seafood" and "quality chops and steaks" in a suburban Bloomington office tower; "high ratings" go to a "solid menu" and "the best service in town" – a "great spot for business meals"; while a few detractors insist that a "snobby staff" and "no-character" decor make it a "boring" "suburbanite's dream", the faithful say it's "always a delight."

La Belle Vie Ⓢ — | — | — | E

312 S. Main St., Stillwater, 612-430-3545

The area's newest destination-dining darling lives up to its name, offering the imaginative Mediterranean-inspired menu of chef Tim McKee, who left D'Amico Cucina to open his own cafe in this vintage Stillwater storefront (about 25 miles from Minneapolis); those who recall the D'Amicos' much-mourned Azur can revel in déjà vu as well as *la belle vie* here as they dig into such delights as Tim's signature coppa-crusted rabbit loin.

Local, The ◐Ⓢ — | — | — | E

931 Nicollett Mall (10th St.), Minneapolis, 612-904-1000

A taste o' Ireland, but filtered through the palate of a chef who's gone upmarket with Irish cooking, offering the likes of fish 'n' chips with olive-caper tartar sauce in the pub and house-smoked salmon in the elegant, faux Victorian dining room; you'll find aspiring attorneys sipping single-malts everywhere (unless they're smart enough to spy the great wine finds).

Loring Cafe and Bar Ⓢ 20 | 22 | 14 | $19

1624 Harmon Pl. (Hennepin Ave.), Minneapolis, 612-332-1617

◪ Regulars say that the "bohemian", prop-shop "ambiance is magic", the "dust and wear and tear are part of the 'cool' decor" and the "sublime" "alley patio" with "rooftop sax" player is *the* place for "excellent" New American food; but foes say it could use some spiffing up and cite "rude" service; post-*Survey*, a new dining room offers a more formal (and costly, but still good-value) option to the funky bar, and servers' manners seem improved.

Manny's Steakhouse Ⓢ 27 | 21 | 25 | $33

Hyatt Regency Hotel, 1300 Nicollet Mall (Nicollet Ave. & 13th St.), Minneapolis, 612-339-9900

■ "They go berserk" with "monster slabs of beef" at this "heaven for meat lovers" in the Downtown Minneapolis Hyatt; a lippy, New Yorker–wanna-be staff provides a "macho experience" in a "cigars- and-scotch" "clubby atmosphere" for "red-meat fans on expense accounts" – "if I were a steer, this is where I'd want to end up"; the veal chops, lobsters and wine list are also "faves."

Morton's of Chicago Ⓢ 25 | 23 | 24 | $35

555 Nicollet Mall (6th St.), Minneapolis, 612-673-9700

■ You "feel naughty eating" in this "classic beef lovers'" spot, a "dark" "men's restaurant" that's a "perfect place to have an affair" or stage a "power dinner"; although some also find the setting "claustrophobic", "cramped" and "noisy", "you can't go wrong" with the "enormous" and "very expensive" portions of "serious steak and fish", even if they're "nothing you can't cook yourself."

Origami Ⓢ 25 | 20 | 20 | $19

30 N. First St. (1st Ave.), Minneapolis, 612-333-8430

■ A vintage Warehouse District storefront with a handsome, modern face-lift that serves "imaginatively prepared Japanese food"; this "really excellent, back-alley sushi bar" can be "kind of a tight fit" when crowded and "a bit pricey" for "small portions", but the "staff is helpful" and there's a "great sake selection."

Palomino S | 24 | 25 | 23 | $24 |

825 Hennepin Ave. (9th St.), Minneapolis, 612-339-3800

■ This "high-energy", "glitzy Cal-Italian" Downtown bistro serves "excellent" roasted meats, pizza and pasta to a "value-conscious yuppie clientele" that likes the "ambiance of a wood-burning oven and hanging herbs"; it's "great for pre-theater dining" or "power lunches", but it's tough to get in – "just tell everyone you're a producer" and you can "impress visitors with how hip you are."

Ristorante Luci S | 27 | 15 | 23 | $23 |

470 Cleveland Ave. S. (Randolph Ave.), St. Paul, 612-699-8258

■ "Reservations take weeks and they're worth planning for" at this "very noisy, very small" Highland Park trattoria where the Regional Italian fare is "wonderful", but "too many tables in too small a space" makes it "like eating in one lane of a bowling alley"; regardless, the "exquisitely prepared" meals and "personal service by the owners" make this "the closest we have to Italy."

Schumacher's New Prague Inn S | 25 | 26 | 23 | $26 |

Schumacher's Inn, 212 W. Main St. (Columbia St.), New Prague, 612-758-2133

■ It's "worth the drive" to this "charming", "romantic" inn in a small Czech town in southern Minnesota; the "owners are a delight" and "service is excellent", so the "old-world setting", replete with folk art and antiques, proves "a good place to be pampered" with "heavy, filling" (albeit "pricey") Mittel-Europa food; "take a big appetite and don't count calories" or "fill up on kolachke" sweet buns.

St. Paul Grill ◐ S | 26 | 26 | 24 | $26 |

St. Paul Hotel, 350 Market St. (bet. 4th & 5th Sts.), St. Paul, 612-224-7455

◪ "Fantastic" window seats with a "beautiful view of Rice Park" and "classic, high-back booths" make this "hard-to-get-into" hotel grill an "elegant" place for a "power lunch" or to "meet the cast of the Ordway" theater "after a show"; "impeccable service" delivers the "finest" steaks, salads and "excellent" "nouvelle Midwest" fare; though a few find it "dull and heavy", most agree there's "no contest – it's St. Paul's best" and "never disappoints."

Table Of Contents S | 23 | 16 | 19 | $20 |

1648 Grand Ave. (Snelling Ave.), St. Paul, 612-699-6595
1310 Hennepin Ave. (13th St.), Minneapolis, 612-339-1133

◪ "Stellar food at earthy prices" in a "classy" "bookstore setting" on Grand Avenue persuades many that this New American "should be declared a city treasure"; the "limited menu of top-quality" fare rates high, but a few say it's "sometimes straining for originality" and that "portions are small."

TOP 10 FOOD RANKING

	Restaurant	Cuisine Type
28	Saddle River Inn	French/New American
	Sagami	Japanese
	Ryland Inn	New French
27	Chez Madeleine	French Bistro
	Scalini Fedeli	Northern Italian
	Fromagerie	New French
	Cafe Panache	New French
26	28	New American
	Ruga	New American
	Frog & the Peach	Eclectic/New American

OTHER IMPORTANT PLACES

Dining Room	Continental/New Amer.
Doris & Ed's	Seafood
Green Gables	New American
Highlawn Pavilion	Continental/New Amer.
Manor	Continental/Trad. Amer.

F | D | S | C

Cafe Panache 27 | 20 | 24 | $41

130 E. Main St. (Lake St.), Ramsey, 201-934-0031

■ "New Jersey's beautiful people" pack chef-owner Kevin Kohler's Bergen County BYO Contemporary French for its "innovative, cutting-edge" cuisine (including "the best liver and duck on the planet"), "calm California feel" and "polished, friendly service"; it just may be the "best storefront restaurant in New Jersey."

Chez Madeleine 27 | 17 | 24 | $42

4 Bedford Ave. (Washington Ave.), Bergenfield, 201-384-7637

■ The "charming, elegant Madeleine" "oversees every detail" in front and her Swiss-born husband Gaspard Caloz (a "rare genius") mans the stoves of this Bergen County BYO French, producing such "gustatory pleasures" as "the best rack of lamb" and dessert soufflés so "delicious" that "you'll forget" there's "no ambiance", the seating is "too tight" and the place "too damn crowded."

Dining Room, The 26 | 27 | 26 | $55

Hilton at Short Hills, 41 JFK Pkwy., Short Hills, 973-379-0100

■ High marks go to this "civilized retreat" in the Short Hills Hilton, where "creative" New American–Continental food, a "romantic" ambiance (there's a harpist) and "unsurpassed service" add up to an "exceptional" experience that's "worth" the "ton of money" that they charge; only a few note a "small slide in food" recently.

Doris & Ed's S 26 | 20 | 22 | $42

348 Shore Dr. (Waterwich Ave.), Highlands, 732-872-1565

■ "If a fish decided to be eaten, this would be the place it would want to be cooked" insist regulars of this "simple" yet "elegant" seafooder offering "lovely" views of Sandy Hook Bay; toss in a "great wine list" and "caring" service and you can see why to get a seat on a summer weekend you have to "get there by 5 PM."

Frog and the Peach, The S 26 23 24 $47

29 Dennis St. (Hiram Sq.), New Brunswick, 732-846-3216

■ "Always tops" say those who've come to expect "artistically presented", "refreshingly different" "wild combinations" of New American–Eclectic cuisine (that may taste best with a vintage "expense account") presented by a "cordial" "attentive" staff in a "light, airy" "special occasion" setting; those on the prowl add that "it's a great place to meet a doctor on a Friday night" and the separate bar menu is a cheaper way to sample the fare.

Fromagerie S 27 25 25 $48

26 Ridge Rd. (Ave. of Two Rivers), Rumson, 732-842-8088

■ Gastronomes say "it gets better and better" every year at this "classy", "romantic", "charming" Monmouth County New French where the "foie gras melts in your mouth"; some of "the best food in NJ", "a great wine list", "lovely decor" and a "knowledgeable staff" add up to an experience that's "superb in every way"; start saving though because it's "expensive but worth it."

Green Gables S 26 23 24 $47

Green Gables Inn, 212 Center St. (bet. Bay & Beach Aves.), Beach Haven, 609-492-3553

■ Since there's no set menu, there's a "surprise every time" (and "you'd better like what the chef makes") at this "quiet", "romantic" Long Beach Island New American with Italian and French touches set in a 110-year-old Victorian; "if you have an experimental nature" and "if you can afford the price", this "rare dining experience" is "well worth trying."

Highlawn Pavilion S 22 28 23 $42

Eagle Rock Reservation (Eagle Rock & Prospect Aves.), West Orange, 973-731-3463

◪ There's an "unforgettable view" of the NYC skyline marred only by "cigaret smoke galore" at this Essex County New American–Continental; for many, the "fantastic food", "beautiful atmosphere" and "exemplary service" make it "tops for entertaining VIPs" or for "romance"; but others find the ambiance "noisy" and the fare "disappointing" for such "highfalutin prices", conceding only that it's "good for saying you're sorry" or when "someone else pays."

Manor, The S 24 26 24 $46

111 Prospect Ave. (Eagle Rock Ave.), West Orange, 973-731-2360

◪ For devotees of this "legendary" American-Continental in West Orange, the "incredible seafood buffet", "gorgeous grounds" and "outstanding service" add up to an "all-time favorite" for "special occasions" and "a reason to get married"; yet others divorce themselves from "dinosaur food", "pretentious service", "gaudy, gaudy" decor and decree that "nothing succeeds like excess."

Ruga 26 21 23 $39

4 Barbara Ln. (Rte. 287), Oakland, 201-337-0813

■ The "best in western Bergen County", this "sophisticated" New American receives raves for its "creative", "outstanding" fare, "excellent wine list", "intelligent" service and "beautiful setting surrounded by Edward Ruga's art"; "noise" and "waits" are the rule on weekends, but on weekdays the atmosphere is "great."

Ryland Inn, The 🅂 | 28 | 27 | 26 | $59 |

The Ryland Inn, Rte. 22W, Whitehouse, 908-534-4011

■ "Words cannot describe dining" at this "crème de la crème" of Jersey restaurants where "every detail is thought out"; located in a "charming inn" on "beautiful grounds" in Hunterdon County, it serves "exquisite" New French fare that's "perfect for special occasions (even if you have to make one up)"; an "extremely knowledgeable staff" ensures that even at these prices "it's worth the trip."

Saddle River Inn | 28 | 26 | 26 | $48 |

2 Barnstable Ct. (W. Saddle River Rd.), Saddle River, 201-825-4016

■ Chef-owner Hans Egg's "grande dame" New American–French "has no peer" enthuse admirers of this "romantic", "impeccably tasteful old barn" with the No. 1 Food rating in our *NJ Survey* and "professional service"; "the BYO policy is a real plus" and "lunch is a bargain"; "call now for dinner reservations next month."

Sagami 🅂 | 28 | 17 | 22 | $26 |

37 Crescent Blvd. (bet. Haddon Ave. & Collingswood Circle), Collingswood, 609-854-9773

■ There's definitely "no fish from the Delaware" at the No. 1 Japanese in our *NJ Survey* where chef-owner Shigeru Fukuyoshi's "heavenly" fare is "the absolute last word in sushi and sashimi" and "better than any in NYC, LA or SF"; you can also expect "wonderful" service from waitresses in "traditional garb" – another reason no one minds if it's "cramped" and "needs a redo."

Scalini Fedeli | 27 | 27 | 25 | $51 |

63 Main St., Chatham, 973-701-9200

■ "Bravo" – "at last we don't have to go to NYC" applaud admirers of chef Michael Cetrulo's "posh" Morris County Northern Italian BYO "brimming with excitement and vitality" since it "exploded onto the scene"; surveyors say it's "well worth the three-month wait" to sample the No. 1 Italian in our *NJ Survey* and savor the 1700s setting with "vaulted ceilings" and "great lighting."

28 🅂 | 26 | 19 | 20 | $34 |

28 Church St. (behind Claridge movie theater), Montclair, 973-744-9263

■ "If you want haute cuisine but don't feel like dealing with NYC, 28 is it" according to supporters of this "imaginative", "innovative" and "excellent" New American BYO that draws a "sophisticated" crowd; just "be prepared for noise" and service that can be "indifferent" or "slow"; the "no-reserving policy means bring an extra bottle for the wait."

New Orleans

TOP 20 FOOD RANKING

	Restaurant	Cuisine Type
28	Grill Room	Eclectic
	Peristyle	Contemporary Louisiana
27	Gabrielle	Contemporary Louisiana
	Brigtsen's	Cajun
	Ruth's Chris	Steakhouse
	Emeril's	Contemporary Louisiana
	Bayona	International/New Amer.
	Commander's Palace	Cajun/Creole
	Lafitte's Landing	Cajun/Creole
	La Provence	Classic French
	Le Parvenu	Creole/New American
26	Galatoire's	Classic French/Creole
	Ninja's	Japanese
	Crozier's	Classic French
	Young's	Seafood/Steakhouse
	Gautreau's	American/New French
	Bistro at Maison de Ville	French Bistro
	Kim Son	Vietnamese
	Dakota	Contemporary Louisiana
	Louis XVI	Classic French

OTHER IMPORTANT PLACES

Antoine's	Creole/French
Arnaud's	Creole/French
Brennan's	Creole
Christian's	Classic French/Creole
Clancy's	Creole/Eclectic
Delmonico	Creole
Irene's Cuisine	N/S Italian
La Riviera	N/S Italian
Lemon Grass Cafe	Vietnamese
Metro Bistro	French Bistro
Mike's on the Avenue	Eclectic/New American
Mr. B's Bistro	Creole
Nine Roses	Vietnamese
NOLA	Contemporary Louisiana
Pelican Club	Contemporary Louisiana
Rib Room	American/Continental
Upperline	Eclectic

	F	D	S	C
Antoine's	24	25	25	$44

713 St. Louis St. (bet. Bourbon & Royal Sts.), 504-581-4422

◪ This "special occasion" French-Creole "grande dame" may be "past its prime" and a bit "faded", but it still has a devoted following that believes "some things never go out of style", namely "classic elegance" and "charm"; insiders say the "appetizers are fantastic" and note that having "a great waiter really helps" to enjoy this "quintessential New Orleans restaurant."

Arnaud's S | 23 | 25 | 24 | $41

813 Bienville St. (bet. Bourbon & Dauphine Sts.), 504-523-5433

◪ "Lovely atmosphere" makes this elegant, 19th-century French Quarter classic one of "the great old New Orleans restaurants", even if opinions on the French-Creole fare range from "excellent" ("shrimp rémoulade alone is worth the trip") to "average food in a beautiful restaurant"; but all agree Sunday brunch is a standout.

Bayona | 27 | 26 | 25 | $39

430 Dauphine St. (bet. Conti & St. Louis Sts.), 504-525-4455

■ "Consistently great year after year" is the verdict on this "beautiful" French Quarter New American–International spot; chef Susan Spicer "works magic" for most diners, turning out "very creative" food that's usually "right on target", and though a few wish she would offer "more new dishes more often", most never tire of this "gem" that "continues to dazzle."

Bistro at Maison de Ville S | 26 | 24 | 24 | $38

Maison de Ville, 727 Toulouse St. (bet. Bourbon & Royal Sts.), 504-528-9206

■ Chef Greg Picolo is following in some big footsteps at this "tiny" (a few say "cramped"), "charming" French bistro, which has produced some superb New Orleans chefs, including Susan Spicer and the late John Neal; admirers say Picolo's doing a "great" job turning out "sophisticated fare" that's served in one of the French Quarter's coziest "hidden treasures"; it's always crowded, so reservations are strongly recommended.

Brennan's S | 25 | 27 | 25 | $44

417 Royal St. (bet. Conti & St. Louis Sts.), 504-525-9711

◪ "Still good after all these years" say admirers of this "romantic" Haute Creole French Quarter "landmark" with "the most lavish courtyard in the city"; all agree that "breakfast is spectacular" (albeit "expensive" and touristy), and even detractors concede it has "great ambiance", saying you "gotta go", "at least once."

Brigtsen's | 27 | 21 | 25 | $35

723 Dante St. (bet. Maple St. & River Rd.), 504-861-7610

■ "Wonderful food" that's "truly memorable" is what most diners find at this family-run Cajun that's ranked in New Orleans' top five for cuisine and set in a "quaint house" in the Riverbend area; it can be "too crowded", but that's because it attracts locals and tourists alike looking for "an exquisite meal" in an "intimate setting" with "personal service"; it's "a winner all-around" – "reserve early."

Christian's | 25 | 24 | 23 | $33

3835 Iberville St. (S. Scott St.), 504-482-4924

■ "Amen" exclaim converts to this Mid-City stalwart serving superb Classic French–Creole food in the "elegant ambiance" of an old converted church; "don't tell the tourists about this one" plead admirers whose main complaint is "cramped tables."

Clancy's | 26 | 21 | 23 | $33

6100 Annunciation St. (Webster St.), 504-895-1111

■ "Clubby Uptown hangout" "away from tourists" that enjoys a "strong local following" for its "first-rate" Creole-Eclectic fare and "lively", "see and be seen" ambiance; this "diamond in the rough" may be "noisy" and somewhat "overpriced", but it's an "always enjoyable", "classic" New Orleans neighborhood place.

Commander's Palace S | 27 | 28 | 27 | $43

1403 Washington Ave. (Coliseum St.), 504-899-8221

■ "The pinnacle of Creole food" say the myriad fans of the Brennan family's "New Orleans classic", the city's Most Popular restaurant; set in the heart of the Garden District, it's "pricey" but provides a "rarely matched experience", complete with "beautiful rooms" and "incredible service"; don't forget the "best jazz brunch."

Crozier's | 26 | 21 | 23 | $34

Petite Esplanade, 3216 W. Esplanade Ave. N. (bet. Causeway Blvd. & Severn Ave.), Metairie, 504-833-8108

■ "Classic French cuisine" that may be the "best food in Metairie", especially the "divine steak au poivre", can be had at this "often-overlooked jewel"; nothing avant-garde here, just "authentic", well-presented fare, "unhurried" service and pleasant decor, making for dining "so wonderful you forget you're in a shopping center."

Dakota, The S | 26 | 23 | 23 | $32

629 N. Hwy. 190 (1/4 mi. off I-12), Covington, 504-892-3712

■ "Duck spring rolls, a great wine list and cool art" help explain why fans say this North Shore "class act" serving Louisiana-accented American fare is "worth the 40-minute drive"; "excellent" food (try the "superb crab and Brie soup") and nicely appointed decor cause many to call it "best of the North Shore places."

Delmonico S | – | – | – | VE

1300 St. Charles Ave. (Erato St.), 504-525-4937

An instant success, Emeril Lagasse's latest venture, set in a historic building in the Lower Garden District with elegant, muted decor, is drawing crowds with 'grand Creole cuisine' featuring classic New Orleans dishes; it's very 'in', upscale and pricey, with welcome valet parking; N.B. if unable to climb stairs, request first-floor seating.

Emeril's | 27 | 22 | 25 | $43

800 Tchoupitoulas St. (Julia St.), 504-528-9393

■ A "must-go experience" say the legions of admirers dazzled by Emeril Lagasse's "vibrant" culinary flagship in the Warehouse District; while his Contemporary Louisiana cuisine is "pricey", it's "consistently excellent" and service is "fantastic", but it may be the "noisiest place in town"; even so, it's a "special occasion treat."

Gabrielle | 27 | 21 | 25 | $36

3201 Esplanade Ave. (bet. Broad St. & Carrollton Ave.), 504-948-6233

■ "It may be small, but it's superb" is the consensus on this "intimate", "friendly" Contemporary Lousiana cafe with Creole accents that's ranked in the top five for Food and is near the New Orleans Museum of Art; "great adaptations of local ingredients" result in "ab fab" cooking, but while many enjoy the "cozy" room, others find it "cramped" (enclosing the patio has added 20 seats).

Galatoire's S | 26 | 24 | 26 | $37

209 Bourbon St. (Iberville St.), 504-525-2021

■ "Don't ever change" plead locals who love this French Quarter "tradition"; the city's No. 2 favorite restaurant, it's a "classic" French–Haute Creole serving the likes of "the best trout meunière" in "elegant", turn-of-the-century surroundings; those "in the know" say "it's the place to be" for Friday lunch; N.B. the no-reserving policy has been eased for parties of eight Tuesdays–Thursdays.

Gautreau's 26 | 23 | 24 | $36
1728 Soniat St. (Danneel St.), 504-899-7397
◪ This Uptown "gem" serves "fine" New French–American fare in a "cozy", converted drugstore with original tin ceiling; the food is "innovative" (a few call it "uneven") and the ambiance is "low-key elegant", but most agree the "acoustics are horrible."

Grill Room S 28 | 29 | 27 | $50
Windsor Court Hotel, 300 Gravier St. (bet. S. Peters & Tchoupitoulas Sts.), 504-522-1992
■ "Tops in all categories" rave surveyors who rate this "superior" Eclectic No. 1 for Food, Decor and Service in New Orleans; located in the posh Windsor Court Hotel, it offers the city's "swankiest gourmet experience", complete with "superb" cuisine, "excellent" staff and "impeccable surroundings"; sure you pay for it, but this is "undoubtedly the best in town."

Irene's Cuisine S 25 | 21 | 22 | $29
539 St. Philip St. (Chartres St.), 504-529-8811
■ "Long waits" and no-reserving are "a turnoff" for some, but a "cozy" interior welcomes those who finally get inside this "find" serving "true Italian" food (plus some Gallic dishes) in a "romantic" Quarter setting; "Irene's rosemary chicken is the best" and prices are "affordable" – no wonder "word has spread."

Kim Son 26 | 15 | 20 | $17
349 Whitney Ave. (W. Bank Expy.), Gretna, 504-366-2489
■ The somewhat spartan decor is nothing to brag about at this West Bank Vietnamese, but who cares given such moderate prices for such "imaginative" food, including "subtle" clay pot meals and salt-baked seafood to "make your taste buds dance"; no question, it's so "delicious and cheap that it's habit-forming."

Lafitte's Landing S 27 | 24 | 23 | $33
10275 Hwy. 70, Sunshine Bridge Access Rd. (Hwy. 18), Donaldsonville, 504-473-1232
■ "Wonderful local cuisine" based on classic Cajun-Creole recipes with French flair describes the food at this elegant country inn, called "a must" by admirers of chef John Folse and his "beautiful presentations"; all agree it's "well worth the [one-hour] drive" from the French Quarter, and if you're looking for the perfect end to a day of plantation touring, "this is it."

La Provence S 27 | 26 | 24 | $40
25020 Hwy. 190 E. (bet. Lacombe & Mandeville), Lacombe, 504-626-7662
■ For "luxurious food in a cozy provincial setting" nothing beats this North Shore Country French inn, which is a 40-minute drive across Lake Pontchartrain; "chef Chris [Kerageorgiou] keeps going and going and his food is fabulous" say believers on both sides of the lake; it's "superb", especially in winter by the fire.

La Riviera 24 | 20 | 22 | $30
4506 Shores Dr. (bet. N. Clearview Pkwy. & W. Esplanade Ave.), Metairie, 504-888-6238
■ Fans extol "the best" fried calamari and osso buco in town plus "excellent veal and fish dishes" at this Metairie Italian "that's still good after many years"; it may be "loud", but "the crabmeat ravioli is worth the trip alone."

Lemon Grass Cafe | 23 | 16 | 20 | $23 |

216 N. Carrollton Ave. (bet. Bienville & Canal Sts.), 504-488-8335

A "superb, nouvelle Vietnamese" Mid-City addition serving "different", "very innovative" food in a "small", white-tablecloth setting; the decor strikes some as "uninspired" and "service can be slow", but few mind given "elegant", French-influenced Saigon fare.

Le Parvenu S | 27 | 23 | 24 | $29 |

509 Williams Blvd. (bet. Airline Hwy. & Jefferson Ave.), Kenner, 504-471-0534

Upscale decor in a "charming" house along with American-Creole fare that's "delicious" and "different" explain why fans applaud this "outstanding newcomer" in Kenner; while the folks in the 'burbs are lavish in their praise of this "delightful" addition, some cite service that's "too laid-back."

Louis XVI S | 26 | 26 | 25 | $49 |

St. Louis Hotel, 730 Bienville St. (bet. Bourbon & Royal Sts.), 504-581-7000

This "impressive" Quarter "classic" serves "real" French cuisine that's "elegant and refined" amidst "gorgeous surroundings"; though faulted by some for being "very expensive" with "waiters who hover too much", it remains a "special occasion" rendezvous.

Metro Bistro S | – | – | – | VE |

200 Magazine St. (Common St.), 504-529-1900

The latest from the Charley G's folks, this good-looking CBD French bistro is turning out highly touted fare from mussels to cassoulet; a redesigned interior (formerly Graham's) has made it more comfy and quiet, so it's already a big hit with the Downtown crowd.

Mike's on the Avenue S | 23 | 25 | 23 | $35 |

Lafayette Hotel, 628 St. Charles Ave. (bet. Girod & Poydras Sts.), 504-523-1709

"Asian-Southwestern-Creole may sound strange, but it's wonderful" say admirers of this "classy, upscale" New American–Eclectic, a CBD power-dining spot and "place to be seen"; while some think it's "lost a little of the magic since chef Mike [Fennelly] went to San Francisco", new chef Scott Serpas is winning fans.

Mr. B's Bistro S | 25 | 24 | 24 | $31 |

201 Royal St. (bet. Bienville & Iberville Sts.), 504-523-2078

"Superb food in the Brennan family tradition" is what you get at this Haute Creole run by Ralph Brennan and sister Cindy of the Commander's Palace clan; "one of the best" in the Quarter, it's "crowded", with good reason – i.e. "creative" food ("gumbo ya-ya is a must"), "service supreme" and a "vibrant, casual" ambiance.

Nine Roses S | 25 | 17 | 20 | $15 |

1100 Stephen St. (Stumpf Blvd.), Gretna, 504-366-7665

"Memorable" and "terrific" typify the glowing comments about this West Bank Vietnamese; it's an affordable, white-tablecloth place that's "wonderful for families" and a "great discovery" for fans of Asian food who say it transports them "back to old Saigon."

Ninja's | 26 | 14 | 19 | $19 |

8115 Jeanette St. (S. Carrollton Ave.), 504-866-1119

Even those who say this Carrollton Japanese has "the best sushi in town" admit that it's a "bit slow"; it's also low on decor, but this tiny, converted house is staffed by "friendly people" and offers a wide variety of affordable dishes and "very good" box sushi.

NOLA S 25 | 23 | 23 | $34

534 Rue St. Louis St. (bet. Chartres & Decatur Sts.), 504-522-6652

■ Trendy celeb chef Emeril Lagasse's "casual" Quarter "in-spot" earns high marks for its "innovative, excellent" Contemporary Louisiana cuisine, good service and "with-it atmosphere"; "noisy" and "crowded", it may not be relaxing, but it's a "feel-good place" and "more user-friendly" than Emeril's pricier flagship.

Pelican Club S 25 | 24 | 23 | $37

312 Exchange Alley (Bienville St.), 504-523-1504

◪ A "best-kept secret" in a tiny French Quarter alley offering "excellent" Contemporary Louisiana dishes with "Asian touches"; the "comfortable" setting may be plagued by "bad acoustics", but most find it a "happy" experience even if it's a bit "overpriced."

Peristyle 28 | 23 | 25 | $36

1041 Dumaine St. (bet. Burgundy & N. Rampart Sts.), 504-593-9535

■ Raves abound for this French Quarter "jewel", a "tiny but exquisite" Contemporary Louisiana–New American rated No. 2 for Food in the city; "wonderful, innovative", "fit for the gods" typify praise for chef-owner Anne Kearney's "exciting" fare, made all the better by valet parking and "personable service."

Rib Room S 25 | 25 | 23 | $37

Omni Royal Orleans Hotel, 621 St. Louis St. (bet. Chartres & Royal Sts.), 504-529-7046

■ An "elegant" French Quarter American-Continental that's been "a winner for years", serving the likes of "excellent prime rib" and the "best crab bisque on earth"; "clubby" and "consistent", it's a "power lunch place" providing prime people-watching.

Ruth's Chris Steak House S 27 | 21 | 25 | $39

711 N. Broad St. (Orleans Ave.), 504-486-0810
3633 Veterans Memorial Blvd. (Causeway Blvd.), Metairie, 504-888-3600

■ "Incomparable", "consistently great", "fantastic" – and so the praise goes for the "institution" that launched the nationwide steakhouse chain and is rated in New Orleans' top five for Food; its trademark is mouthwatering meat "sizzling" in butter plus divine sides such as creamed spinach and shoestring potatoes; the Broad Street original is a real power scene, especially at Friday lunch when it's a "politico heaven."

Upperline S 24 | 22 | 23 | $32

1413 Upperline St. (bet. Prytania St. & St. Charles Ave.), 504-891-9822

■ At this "consistently good" Uptown "neighborhood" Eclectic, "a bohemian interpretation of Cajun-Creole fare served with wit and style" awaits diners; "great food, great artwork, great service" and "moderately elegant" decor add up to "enjoyable" dining; all agree that owner JoAnn Clevenger is the "best hostess in town."

Young's 26 | 16 | 19 | $24

850 Robert Blvd. (Gause Blvd.), Slidell, 504-643-9331

◪ "Spectacular steaks with all the trimmings" can be yours at this simple North Shore steakhouse, if you can find it – there's still no sign outside; the fish is terrific too, and while there's not much charm in the setting, it's neat, clean and inexpensive – a winning combo that brings in crowds; be prepared for a "long wait."

New York City

TOP 20 FOOD RANKING

	Restaurant	Cuisine Type
28	Le Bernardin	New French/Seafood
	Daniel	Classic French
	Lespinasse	New French
	Chanterelle	New French
	Nobu	Japanese
	Aureole	New American
	Peter Luger	Steakhouse
27	Jean Georges	New French
	La Grenouille	Classic French
	Union Square Cafe	Eclectic/New American
	Les Célébrités	Classic French
	Il Mulino	Northern Italian
	Gotham Bar/Grill	New American
	Gramercy Tavern	New American
	La Côte Basque	Classic French
	Montrachet	New French
	Four Seasons	Continental
26	La Caravelle	Classic French
	Bouley Bakery	New French
	Oceana	Seafood

OTHER IMPORTANT PLACES

Aquavit	Scandinavian
Babbo	N/S Italian
Balthazar	French Bistro
Café des Artistes	Classic French
Carnegie Deli	Deli
Cena	New American
Eleven Madison Park	New American
FireBird	Russian
Le Cirque 2000	Classic French
Lutèce	New French
Manhattan Ocean Club	Seafood
March	New American
Mercer Kitchen	Eclectic/New French
Milos	Greek/Seafood
Oyster Bar	Seafood
Palm	Steakhouse
Park Avenue Cafe	New American
Patría	Nuevo Latino
Periyali	Greek
Picholine	Mediterranean
Rainbow Room	Eclectic/New American
Rao's	Southern Italian
River Cafe	New American
Shun Lee Palace	Chinese
Smith & Wollensky	Steakhouse
Sushisay	Japanese
Sylvia's	Soul Food/Southern
Tavern on the Green	New American
'21' Club	Traditional American
Union Pacific	New American
Windows on the World	New American

Aquavit S | 25 | 25 | 24 | $53
13 W. 54th St. (bet. 5th & 6th Aves.), 212-307-7311
■ In a "spectacular" waterfall and birch tree–decorated atrium that defines "Nordic chic", chef Marcus Samuelsson dazzles diners with "exquisite", "stylish" Scandinavian cuisine, including salmon and herring "as fresh as an Arctic breeze"; add "impeccable service" and you have "a really civilized experience"; if money is an object, eat at the more informal, less pricey upstairs cafe.

Aureole | 28 | 26 | 26 | $67
34 E. 61st St. (bet. Madison & Park Aves.), 212-319-1660
■ Consistently "one of NYC's best", Charlie Palmer's chart-topping East Side New American nears "perfection" with "wonderfully orchestrated meals" capped off by "spectacular" "Picasso-esque" desserts and "exceptional service"; add the floral displays and "elegant" townhouse setting-cum-garden and it's enough to "make you swoon"; so may the bill, but prix fixe lunch is "a great bargain."

Babbo ◐ S | – | – | – | E
110 Waverly Pl. (bet. MacDougal St. & 6th Ave.), 212-777-0303
One of the year's hottest newcomers, this "beautifully designed" duplex Village Italian marries the talents of restaurateurs Joe Bastianich (Becco, Frico Bar) and Mario Batali (Pó); look for the latter's trademark pasta tasting menu and a well-heeled foodie crowd; if you can reach them, reserve well in advance.

Balthazar ◐ S | 22 | 23 | 18 | $45
80 Spring St. (bet. B'way & Crosby St.), 212-965-1414
■ The occasionally grudging consensus is that "the hype is well deserved" at this "happening", "see and be seen" SoHo brasserie serving "surprisingly good" "French comfort food"; it's "as close to Paris as you can get" without flying, yet "so NY" in "rubbernecking" appeal; while the wait to get a reservation is "insane", once you get inside the staff is "friendly and professional."

Bouley Bakery ◐ S | 26 | 21 | 23 | $53
120 W. Broadway (Duane St.), 212-964-2525
■ If "not the old Bouley", most call David Bouley's "downsized", less formal TriBeCa sequel "another winner"; it's an intimate bakery-cum-restaurant with the "most amazing" breads and other "truly innovative", "gold standard" New French fare; though "you'll need a lot of bread" to pay, fans say "Bouley + food = greatness."

Café des Artistes ◐ S | 24 | 27 | 23 | $53
1 W. 67th St. (bet. Columbus Ave. & CPW), 212-877-3500
■ Splurging sybaritic surveyors sigh that George and Jenifer Lang's "dreamy" French "classic" is "a must" setting "for that one special occasion" – "propose", "seduce", "impress" or "apologize" – amid "flowers galore" and murals of nymphs cavorting immodestly; after being closed by a fire, it's back "better than ever" like "a phoenix."

Carnegie Deli ◐ S ≠ | 21 | 9 | 12 | $21
854 Seventh Ave. (55th St.), 212-757-2245
■ Maybe this renowned Midtown deli does "move 'em in, move 'em out", but you don't get *Rawhide*, you get "the best pastrami on the planet"; despite the elbow to elbow, communal-table decor and "brusque" staff, "you gotta love" the "mile-high sandwiches", cheesecake and other "high-cholesterol" eats at this "NYC must."

Cena ◐ S | – | – | – | VE |

12 E. 22nd St. (bet. B'way & Park Ave. S.), 212-505-1222
Thalia and Stephen Loffredo of Zoë launched this "sleek, polished" Flatiron New American this past summer; in back it offers high-end cuisine from Montreal-based chef Normand Laprise plus an up front option of casual, less costly dining; early reports suggest that the Loffredos have a fine chef, but need to beef up service.

Chanterelle | 28 | 26 | 27 | VE |

2 Harrison St. (Hudson St.), 212-966-6960
■ One of the defining restaurants of 1980s NY, David and Karen Waltuck's "elegant", "ethereal" French TriBeCan this year celebrates two decades of serving "artful" fare to a discriminating crowd, and there are no signs of slippage in the "austerely wonderful decor", "impeccable service" or "sophisticated cooking"; though "expensive" (dinner is $75 prix fixe only), check out the "best prix fixe lunch in town."

Daniel ◐ | 28 | – | 26 | $71 |

60 E. 65th St. (bet. Madison & Park Aves.), 212-288-0033
■ Daniel Boulud's French "crown jewel" is currently in the midst of moving to this new East Side location that formerly housed Le Cirque; thanks to his "sublime" culinary talents, the entire A-list food world is lining up for reservations in December to see what the new digs look like when this "just plain great" restaurant reopens.

Eleven Madison Park S | – | – | – | E |

11 Madison Ave. (24th St.), 212-889-0905
Just opening at press time, Danny Meyer's (Union Square Cafe, Gramercy Tavern) breathtaking newcomer overlooking Madison Square Park celebrates old NY hospitality in a grand art deco setting with chef Kerry Heffernan's (ex Bouley, Mondrian, The Polo) modern American take on Gallic fare; based on track records and a pre-opening visit, one can predict that this will certainly be one of the most important new restaurants to open this year, or any year; N.B. don't miss the private dining rooms with views of the soon-to-be-rejuvenated park.

FireBird S | 21 | 27 | 22 | $50 |

365 W. 46th St. (bet. 8th & 9th Aves.), 212-586-0244

FireBird Cafe S | 19 | 24 | 21 | $47 |

363 W. 46th St. (bet. 8th & 9th Aves.), 212-586-0244
■ The "opulent", "Fabergé-egg" decor and "splendid", "authentic" food at this duplex Theater District Russian befit "royalty", or at least those who miss the Russian Tea Room; the vodkas, caviar and blinis are also "tastefully over the top" and the $19.98 pre-theater dinner draws all *das*; there's a cafe-cum-cabaret next door.

Four Seasons | 27 | 27 | 26 | $65 |

99 E. 52nd St. (bet. Lexington & Park Aves.), 212-754-9494
■ "Still one of the best", this "quintessential NY institution" offers "unbelievably good", "creative" Continental food in "breathtaking", "dignified" and "ageless" Philip Johnson–designed rooms; touted for "power lunch" in the Grill Room and "special occasions" in the Pool Room, it makes you "feel like a player just by walking in"; "what's not to like?" – the easily outvoted minority considers it "cold", "stuffy", "clubby" and "absurdly overpriced."

Gotham Bar & Grill S | 27 | 25 | 25 | $56

12 E. 12th St. (bet. 5th Ave. & University Pl.), 212-620-4020

■ Perennially ranking among NY's Most Popular restaurants (No. 4 this year), this Village New American is deemed by many "the perfect NY restaurant"; not surprisingly, it gets raves on all fronts: for chef Alfred Portale's "amazing architectural" food, for its "lovely", "grand" setting, "impeccable" service", "terrific wine selection" and even for its "smart, stylish" crowd; on top of everything else, the $19.99 prix fixe lunch and accompanying $19.99 wine menu are "the best bargains in the city."

Gramercy Tavern S | 27 | 26 | 26 | $58

42 E. 20th St. (bet. B'way & Park Ave. S.), 212-477-0777

■ "It doesn't get any better": "you'll never want to leave" the "warm", "rustic elegance" of Danny Meyer's "top-drawer" American retro tavern, which ranks No. 3 for overall popularity in this year's *NYC Survey*, starting with chef Tom Colicchio's "delicious food", "everything works like a well-orchestrated production" that's "worth every penny"; and in case you're strapped for cash, bear in mind that the front room is "more affordable" and "takes walk-ins."

Il Mulino ◐ | 27 | 20 | 23 | $57

86 W. Third St. (bet. Sullivan & Thompson Sts.), 212-673-3783

■ "Can't be beat" applies to both the quality and quantity at this "dimly lit", "crowded", "authentic", "garlicky" Villager that's perennially and easily voted NYC's No. 1 Italian by our surveyors; "don't eat all day" because "everything is divine" and the "portions are enough to feed a small country"; since there's "always a wait, even with reservations" and the space is often "mobbed", many "prefer the quiet of lunch."

Jean Georges | 27 | 25 | 26 | $75

Trump Int'l Hotel, 1 Central Park West (bet. 60th & 61st Sts.), 212-299-3900

■ "Just one word: wow" say diners dazzled by "the jewel in the crown" of Jean-Georges Vongerichten and Phil Suarez's empire, a "cool, modernist" New French off Columbus Circle where "mind-blowing" "masterworks" ("brilliant", "off the charts", "NY's most exciting food") are "impeccably served" in a formal dining room, more casual cafe or outdoor terrace; the "spare" Adam Tihany decor is "ethereal" to some, "clinical" to others, but for most this yearling is a "total class act."

La Caravelle | 26 | 26 | 26 | $65

Shoreham Hotel, 33 W. 55th St. (bet. 5th & 6th Aves.), 212-586-4252

■ "Such beauty! such comfort! such food!" is the consensus at this Midtown "paragon" where diners rhapsodize over chef Cyril Renaud's "exquisite", "classic" but "innovative French cooking" and "gracious hosts" André and Rita Jammet who "really make you feel welcome"; it's "*très élégant, très* pricey, *très* worth it" – "not to be missed."

La Côte Basque S | 27 | 26 | 26 | $66

60 W. 55th St. (bet. 5th & 6th Aves.), 212-688-6525

■ "Elegant to the max", this "formal" Midtown "perennial favorite" "lives up to its legendary reputation"; chef Jean-Jacques Rachou's "timeless" Classic French fare, "stunning decor" (featuring murals of the Basque coast) and "exquisite service" add up to a "magical" meal; at $34, "lunch is a superb value" (dinner is $62 prix fixe only).

La Grenouille ◐ 27 | 28 | 27 | VE

3 E. 52nd St. (bet. 5th & Madison Aves.), 212-752-1495

■ "Almost nirvana", the Masson family's "classic" Midtown "stunner" seduces "sophisticated", style-setting Francophiles (we're talking "real celebrities") with "divine food" that's "as perfect as haute cuisine can be" and "well worth" the high prix fixe tab ($45 lunch, $80 dinner); add "tactful", "impeccable" black-tie service "amidst a bower of flowers" in "the most romantic room in NY" and you come up with "an exquisite dining experience"; P.S. the charming upstairs artist's studio is an ideal private party venue.

Le Bernardin 28 | 27 | 27 | $72

155 W. 51st St. (bet. 6th & 7th Aves.), 212-489-1515

■ "Long reign the king of the seas": surfacing at the top of NY's food rankings this year, Maguy LeCoze's "exquisite" French "temple to seafood" inspires a tidal wave of praise from over 2,400 surveyors; from the "unrivaled piscatorial pleasures" provided by chef Eric Ripert, to the "handsome" decor and "impeccable service", it's "as good as it gets, and keeps getting better", making it "worth every [prix fixe] penny" ($42 lunch, $70 dinner).

Le Cirque 2000 S 26 | 25 | 25 | $72

NY Palace Hotel, 455 Madison Ave. (bet. 50th & 51st Sts.), 212-303-7788

◪ Though some old clients lament "it's a long way from the Le Cirque we loved" and "a real assembly line for tourists", others say "updating gave a whole new life" to Sirio Maccioni's NY legend, now in Midtown's Villard Houses; most agree that longtime chef Sottha Khunn's French food and Jacques Torres' desserts remain "superb", and, while Adam Tihany's "dizzying" Disneyesque decor "still jars" many, even more find it a "whimsical, elegant" backdrop for world-class "people-watching" that's "the best show in town."

Les Célébrités 27 | 28 | 27 | $76

Essex House, 155 W. 58th St. (bet. 6th & 7th Aves.), 212-484-5113

■ "They go all out and succeed" at this "consummately elegant" French Classic, which once again garners sky-high ratings across the board; it may be a "super splurge", but surveyors tout it for a "special celebration" or pure "indulgence", reporting that the "scrumptious cuisine", "sumptuous" "Fabergé egg" room, "gracious service" and the "sheer theatrics" "never disappoint"; N.B. longtime chef Christian Delouvrier has recently moved to Lespinasse but his replacement, Luc Dimnet, has a good reputation.

Lespinasse 28 | 28 | 27 | $77

St. Regis Hotel, 2 E. 55th St. (bet. 5th & Madison Aves.), 212-339-6719

■ "And on the eighth day He created . . ."; anyone interested in fine dining, especially the swooning surveyors who describe a meal at this "baroque" Midtowner as "a life-changing experience", will be curious to see how this Asian-accented French "pinnacle" will survive its own life-changing experience following the departure of acclaimed chef Gray Kunz; fortunately, his replacement, Christian Delouvrier (ex Les Célébrités), also comes with high marks and there's no reason to suspect that the "impeccable service" and "breathtaking" decor will not stand up.

Lutèce 26 | 25 | 25 | $69

249 E. 50th St. (bet. 2nd & 3rd Aves.), 212-752-2225

■ Tampering with people's idea of perfection is risky, but this East Midtown haute French standard-bearer has met the challenge in the "après–André Soltner" era; despite nostalgia over the fabled chef's retirement, most agree that new chef Eberhard Mueller has presided over "a brilliant rebirth of a traditional restaurant with lighter, still wonderful food"; prix fixe only: lunch $38, dinner $65.

Manhattan Ocean Club ◐ S 25 | 22 | 22 | $56

57 W. 58th St. (bet. 5th & 6th Aves.), 212-371-7777

■ Dining at this Midtowner serving some of "the best seafood in the city" feels "like being at the captain's table" on a "Picasso-laden cruise ship"; "it'll cost you a lotta clams", but with its "wonderful" choice of "beautifully prepared" fish and "attractive" decor, most think you'd "have to work hard not to enjoy it."

March ◐ S 26 | 25 | 26 | $71

405 E. 58th St. (bet. 1st Ave. & Sutton Pl.), 212-754-6272

■ "Melt [someone's] heart" with a meal at this "very romantic", "tiny and tony" East Side brownstone with an "ethereal garden" out back; chef Wayne Nish's "exquisite" prix fixe menu of small New American dishes combined with "warm", "attentive" service leaves surveyors swooning; "it's hard to imagine a better experience."

Mercer Kitchen, The ◐ S – | – | – | E

Mercer Hotel, 99 Prince St. (Mercer St.), 212-966-5454

Jean-Georges Vongerichten's stylish SoHo newcomer downstairs in the Mercer Hotel has become an instant mecca for fashionable foodies and food-loving fashion plates, offering Provençal-Eclectic fare and mod pizzas from an open kitchen; communal tables, an upstairs tea bar and cafe complete one of 1998's hottest arrivals.

Milos, Estiatorio ◐ S 25 | 24 | 21 | $60

125 W. 55th St. (bet. 6th & 7th Aves.), 212-245-7400

■ At this "dazzling" Midtown Greek, the fish "could only be fresher if they swam to your plate", service is "first-rate" and the "soaring" space is the "handsomest" around; but per-pound pricing makes it "costlier than Harry Winston", so bring your "expense account" or stick to appetizers for an "affordable" taste of piscatory "paradise."

Montrachet 27 | 21 | 25 | $59

239 W. Broadway (bet. Walker & White Sts.), 212-219-2777

■ "Still one of NYC's finest", "even with the new chef" (Remi Lauvand, ex Le Cirque), Drew Nieporent's "splendid" TriBeCa bistro is "worth every cent" for "exquisite" French fare, "a wine list to die for" and "elegant" service; the decor may be a bit "minimalist", but there's "no better bargain" than Friday's $19.99 prix fixe lunch.

Nobu S 28 | 24 | 24 | $62

105 Hudson St. (Franklin St.), 212-219-0500

■ "Words can't describe how good" Nobu Matsuhisa's "unique" TriBeCa Nouvelle Japanese is, but surveyors try: "astonishing", "sublime", "masterful", "banzai"; with "handsomely simple" David Rockwell decor, bicoastal "celeb sightings" aplenty and a "staff that knows its stuff", it's "in a league of its own" and "must be experienced", preferably on an "expense account" (though prix fixe lunch is "a steal"); there's "one problem – can't get in."

Oceana 26 | 24 | 24 | VE

55 E. 54th St. (bet. Madison & Park Aves.), 212-759-5941

■ "Like dining first-class on the Titanic without that sinking feeling", this Midtown "goddess of seafood" wows diners with "exquisite" food, "bend-over-backwards" service and "gorgeous" "nautical" decor; of course, it's expensive (prix fixe only, $40 lunch, $62 dinner).

Oyster Bar 22 | 16 | 16 | $39

Grand Central, lower level (42nd St. & Vanderbilt Ave.), 212-490-6650

■ "Back and better than ever" after a fire, this "cavernous" "old NY" "landmark" in Grand Central induces "bivalve bliss" with its "phenomenally fresh" shellfish plus other "reliably good" seafood snappily served with "the right wines"; it's a quintessential "noisy" NY experience – "sit at the counter for a shucking good time."

Palm ◐ 25 | 15 | 19 | $53

837 Second Ave. (bet. 44th & 45th Sts.), 212-687-2953

Palm Too S

840 Second Ave. (bet. 44th & 45th Sts.), 212-697-5198

◪ These basic, sawdust-splashed East Side temples of carnivores, crustaceans and cholesterol continue to crowd in customers who praise their "delectable" steaks, "lobsters from Three Mile Island" and scrumptious sides; critics knock "gruff" waiters, "seedy" environs and the lack of a sign "reading 'men only' in the doorway."

Park Avenue Cafe S 25 | 23 | 23 | $55

100 E. 63rd St. (bet. Lexington & Park Aves.), 212-644-1900

■ Celebrated chef David Burke "never disappoints" at his "classy", "creative" East Side New American where meals are "amazing from the bread basket to the last bite" ("leave room for dessert – lots"); "warm" decor with an American folk art motif and "first-class service" are also why the well-heeled crowd easily digests "high prices"; P.S. reserve the kitchen room for a "unique" meal.

Patría S 25 | 22 | 21 | $50

250 Park Ave. S. (20th St.), 212-777-6211

■ "*Estupendo*" sums up this "upbeat, snazzy" Flatiron Nuevo Latino where Douglas Rodriguez whips up some of NY's "most exciting" food – "every bite is an explosion" of flavors from dishes presented "with flair"; though a few knock the "noisy", "festive" ambiance and "pricey" new dinner prix fixe formula, most say "don't miss it."

Periyali 25 | 21 | 23 | $47

35 W. 20th St. (bet. 5th & 6th Aves.), 212-463-7890

■ The Mount Olympus of Greek restaurants serves rarefied dishes "worthy of Zeus" in a "sophisticated" but "bucolic" Flatiron District room that "combines informality with elegance"; seafood stands out, e.g. the grilled octopus, and while it's "expensive", devotees eagerly return for an experience that's "simply wonderful."

Peter Luger Steak House S ⊅ 28 | 15 | 20 | $53

178 Broadway (Driggs Ave.), Brooklyn, 718-387-7400

■ "Cow heaven", this Williamsburg "institution" does "one thing perfectly" – porterhouse steak that's "in a class by itself", the "benchmark" for beef "in the USA, and possibly the world"; despite "crusty" waiters and German beer hall–style dining rooms devoid of more than "gruff" charm, over 3,400 surveyors vote Luger "NY's No. 1 steakhouse" – for the 15th year in a row.

Picholine ◐ S | 26 | 23 | 23 | $58

35 W. 64th St. (bet. B'way & CPW), 212-724-8585

■ Chef-owner Terrance Brennan's Mediterranean "original" near Lincoln Center continues to solidify its reputation as "one of NY's best"; with "smooth" service, "spacious" seating and a "splendid", "well-conceived" menu, "memorable" wines and cheeses, it's putting the West Side on NY's culinary map; N.B. lunch is the best value and the six-seat wine room is ideal for a private party.

Rainbow Room ◐ S | 21 | 28 | 23 | $65

GE Bldg., 30 Rockefeller Plaza, 65th fl. (bet. 49th & 50th Sts.), 212-632-5000

■ "It doesn't get any more NY" than this "ne plus ultra" 65-year-old, 65th-floor Rockefeller Center "art deco heaven" where star chef Waldy Malouf's American food, "breathtaking views" and a "dance with your honey" will transport you to "another era"; new Cipriani management takes over in December and has announced that the main room will only be open Friday night and for Sunday brunch, and the Promenade Bar will become Harry's Bar.

Rao's ⊄ | 25 | 16 | 22 | $52

455 E. 114th St. (Pleasant Ave.), 212-722-6709

■ "How do you join this club?" is the key question about this "always fun, atmospheric" century-old East Harlem Italian "tomato sauce classic" whose eight tables seem to be "booked through the year 3,000" with a mix of enthusiastic locals and VIPs; once you're in, "sing along" with Sinatra "on the jukebox" and, if you want to return in this lifetime, be sure to "be nice to Frankie."

River Cafe ◐ S | 24 | 27 | 23 | VE

1 Water St. (Brooklyn Bridge), Brooklyn, 718-522-5200

■ Compared to the unrivaled view of Downtown Manhattan, even star chef Rick Laakkonen's "excellent" New American food "becomes an added attraction" at this "consistent pleaser" under the Brooklyn Bridge; it's famed for "special occasions" ("win your lover's heart", "the place has 'I do' written all over it"), but you'll be treated well "whatever the occasion"; dinner is $68 prix fixe only.

Shun Lee Palace ◐ S | 24 | 22 | 22 | $45

155 E. 55th St. (bet. Lexington & 3rd Aves.), 212-371-8844

■ Surveyors are "emo–Shun Lee attached" to the "extraordinary flavors", "gold standard" service, "beautiful" Adam Tihany decor and "lavish" presentation at Michael Tong's East Midtown Chinese flagship; most "feel like royalty" and don't mind paying extra for "NY's best Chinese"; P.S. there's a "fabulous $19.99 prix fixe lunch."

Smith & Wollensky ◐ S | 23 | 17 | 19 | $52

797 Third Ave. (49th St.), 212-753-1530

■ "When you want a good steak", "they do it right" at this two-story "old boys' club" in East Midtown; not for the fainthearted, it's so popular it can get as "noisy" as "Times Square on New Year's Eve", but the way they pour fine wine no one's complaining.

Sushisay | 26 | 19 | 21 | $49

38 E. 51st St. (bet. Madison & Park Aves.), 212-755-1780

■ "Sophisticated" and "authentic", this Midtown Japanese gets high marks for its "swimmingly fresh" sushi, "outstanding" service and spare, clean setting; though "Tokyo prices" raise eyebrows, connoisseurs insist the "best sushi" is "worth every penny."

Sylvia's S 18 12 16 $27

328 Lenox Ave. (bet. 126th & 127th Sts.), 212-996-0660

■ A "NY classic", this Harlem Soul Fooder is renowned for its "stick to the ribs", "Southern homestyle cooking", "friendly" service and "homey" divey digs presided over by "charming" hostess-owner Sylvia Woods; though there's a risk of being run over by a tour bus crowd or having a heart attack from "your monthly fat quota" at one meal, every NYer should go – how about Sunday gospel brunch?

Tavern on the Green S 16 25 18 $49

Central Park West (bet. 66th & 67th Sts.), 212-873-3200

◩ "Like walking into a fairy tale", Warner LeRoy's "glittering" Central Park "landmark" is a "must-go" if only for the "sheer spectacle" of its "flamboyant" decor and "incomparable" setting; it may be a "tourist mecca" and snipers dub it "tacky on the green", but the New American food can be "surprisingly good" if kept simple and it "hardly matters what you eat" when seated in the "magical" garden or Crystal Room; also popular for private parties, "it's what NY is all about."

'21' Club 22 23 22 $56

21 W. 52nd St. (bet. 5th & 6th Aves.), 212-582-7200

■ "Better all the time", this "quintessentially NY" Midtown American "classic" has embraced chef Erik Blauberg's "greatly improved" menu, including updates of the beloved '21' burger and chicken hash; it remains a "glamorous" "institution" for CEO "power lunching", "people-watching" and impressing clients amidst "handsome", historic decor or in the private party rooms.

Union Pacific 25 25 23 $59

111 E. 22nd St. (bet. Lexington Ave. & Park Ave. S.), 212-995-8500

■ "A remarkable newcomer"; "star" chef Rocco DiSpirito "gives fusion a good name" at this "beautiful", "tranquil" Gramercy American with a global twist; surveyors report "one of the most interesting", "exciting" – albeit expensive – menus in town accompanied by a "great wine list" and "attitude-free service"; in sum, "a must-try."

Union Square Cafe S 27 24 26 $54

21 E. 16th St. (bet. 5th Ave. & Union Sq. W.), 212-243-4020

■ Voted NY's Most Popular restaurant for the third year in a row and offering "proof that consistent excellence is possible", Danny Meyer's "casual", "unpretentious" Union Square "icon continues to dazzle", thanks to Michael Romano's "always excellent" American-Eclectic cooking, a "warm", "caring" staff that's the "paradigm of service" and modest prices given the quality; "you can't help liking them even when you're denied a reservation."

Windows on the World S 20 27 22 $57

1 World Trade Ctr., 107th fl. (West St., bet. Liberty & Vesey Sts.), 212-524-7000

■ "Incomparable views" make this "once in a lifetime" American aerie "a must" for out-of-towners; however, even sophisticated NYers, who miss the recently closed Cellar in the Sky (which will be replaced by Wild Blue in early '99), tout chef Michael Lomonaco's "much improved" menu in the main dining room and the "best wine list in town."

TOP 10 FOOD RANKING

	Restaurant	Cuisine Type
28	Troquet	Californian/New French
27	Ritz	Continental
	Pascal	Classic French
26	Pavilion	Cal./Mediterranean
	Gustaf Anders	Continental/Swedish
	Morton's of Chicago	Steakhouse
	Ritz-Carlton	Classic French/Med.
	Five Feet	Asian/Californian
	Zov's Bistro/Bakery	Mediterranean
25	Cellar	Classic French

OTHER IMPORTANT PLACES

Antonello	Northern Italian
Aubergine	New French
Bistango	New American
Five Crowns	Continental
Golden Truffle	Eclectic
Mr. Stox	New/Trad. American
Pinot Provence	French Bistro

F | D | S | C

Antonello 25 | 24 | 25 | $41

S. Coast Plaza Village, 1611 Sunflower Ave. (Plaza Dr.), Santa Ana, 714-751-7153

■ This "perennially excellent" choice for "classic", "five-star" Northern Italian fare is "still the power restaurant of OC", attracting execs, politicos and expense-accounters who relish its "flawless" cuisine, "impeccable service" and "romantic" villa decor; for something truly "spectacular", dine "off the menu", but no matter how you order, expect a "special night out."

Aubergine – | – | – | E

508 29th St. (Newport Blvd.), Newport Beach, 714-723-4150

Surveyors can't wait for the late '98 reopening of this "gourmet oasis", which has been shuttered while chef-owners Tim and Liza Goodell expanded the space (and opened sibling Troquet in Costa Mesa); it's likely to lure back loyalists who previously praised it for some of "the best French cuisine" around with a "modern" twist.

Bistango S 24 | 23 | 22 | $34

19100 Von Karman Ave. (north of Campus Dr.), Irvine, 949-752-5222

■ For "sophisticated", "upbeat" dining favored by the executive elite, it's hard to top this "dramatic" atrium gallery that earns as much praise for its "exquisite artwork" as for its "colorful, imaginative" New American fare and "ever-changing" menu (try the "prix fixe for great value"); one of the "few OC spots with live music and dancing", the lounge is a "fun place to meet" and watch an "adult crowd" do their own brand of clubbing.

Cellar, The 25 | 23 | 25 | $44

Villa del Sol, 305 N. Harbor Blvd. (Wilshire Blvd.), Fullerton, 714-525-5682

■ "The best in Fullerton by far", this "old classic" presents "surprisingly good", time-honored French fare and an "extensive wine list"; it's "pricey", and some say "the menu needs a face-lift", but regulars like its "great basement space" where the "ambiance is tops" and say it's "excellent" "for celebrations"; dinner only.

Five Crowns S 24 | 24 | 24 | $36

3801 E. PCH (Poppy St.), Corona del Mar, 949-760-0331

◪ This "gem of an old-timer" offers "hearty" Continental fare including "the ultimate prime rib", "wonderfully served" in a "charming English inn" that's especially festive at Christmas when it's outfitted with holiday "decorations and carolers"; it may be "predictable" (a few say "tired") and some find it "overpriced", but most call it "living proof that some things age with class", even if the waitresses' lusty costumes do provoke a few gasps.

Five Feet S 26 | 19 | 21 | $37

328 Glenneyre St. (bet. Forest Ave. & Mermaid St.), Laguna Beach, 949-497-4955

◪ Fans claim Cal-Asian cuisine is "defined by" this Laguna hot spot featuring "quirky" creations that most credit with a touch of "genius"; the offbeat room is "crowded" with "too many thin people" who would "kill for the catfish", and though critics call it "consistently loud and inconsistently inspired", most say it's worth "a special trip" to "OC's version of Chinois on Main."

Golden Truffle 24 | 16 | 21 | $37

1767 Newport Blvd. (bet. 17th & 18th Sts.), Costa Mesa, 949-645-9858

■ Maverick chef-owner Alan Greeley "loves to play in the kitchen and it shows" say fans of this Eclectic, where "exotic, extremely good" fare makes it easy to overlook the "strip mall location" and "not much" decor; veterans say "let him surprise you with his choices" and advise "don't miss theme weeks" featuring menus revolving around truffles, lobster, blue crab and the like.

Gustaf Anders S 26 | 23 | 24 | $43

S. Coast Plaza Village, 1651 Sunflower Ave. (Bear St. side), Santa Ana, 714-668-1737

■ "As cool as a cruise through the fjords", this "treat for foodies" beguiles its "classy clientele" with "exceptional" Continental-Swedish fare including "beautiful fish", "unreal breads" and "the best gravlax and herring"; if some find the ambiance "too aloof", others say you can "actually converse" here and most agree that this "five-star" experience is well worth the drive and cost; P.S. its fabled holiday buffets "put smorgasbords on a whole new level."

Morton's of Chicago S 26 | 21 | 23 | $45

S. Coast Plaza Village, 1661 Sunflower Ave. (bet. Bear & Bristol Sts.), Santa Ana, 714-444-4834

◪ "Bring your dad and an appetite" to this highly rated source of "terrific protein" in the form of "huge", "perfect" steaks served in a "crisp" retro room that feels "so grown-up" (though the "megadecibel" noise level "detracts from the experience"); quibblers find the "show and tell" menu recitation "silly" and bemoan "exaggerated prices" ("everything is à la carte"), but plenty more deem it an "always reliable" "first-rate" choice.

Mr. Stox S
24 | 21 | 23 | $35

1105 E. Katella Ave. (bet. Lewis St. & State College Rd.), Anaheim, 714-634-2994

■ This "consistently outstanding" Anaheim "old favorite" endures by offering "superb" Traditional and New American fare (including "great homemade breads") accompanied by one of "the best wine lists in the county"; its "quiet", "cozy" setting retains a touch of "1960s ambiance", but that makes it all the more popular for "business meals", "older relatives" and "special holidays."

Pascal
27 | 22 | 24 | $43

1000 N. Bristol St. (Jamboree Rd.), Newport Beach, 949-752-0107

■ "Still superb" say loyalists who laud chef-owner Pascal Olhats' "marvelous" "bit of Provence near John Wayne Airport", where the menu is "classic", the cooking is "serious" and the result is "maybe the best French in SoCal"; though it's "in a shopping center", once inside, "oodles of roses", a canny wine list and "fine service" make it "even better than dining in France"; P.S. the adjoining Epicerie offers tempting (if pricey) take-home goodies for those on the run.

Pavilion S
26 | 27 | 27 | $45

Four Seasons Hotel, 690 Newport Ctr. Dr. (Santa Cruz Dr.), Newport Beach, 949-760-4920

■ A "very classy" room that "defines excellent hotel dining", this "ritzy" choice for "surprisingly inventive" Cal-Mediterranean fare earns lofty marks for its "spectacular food", "great wine list", "good spacing between tables" and premium Four Seasons service that all comes together for a truly "elegant experience"; if that's not enough, "the prix fixe specials are hard to beat."

Pinot Provence S
– | – | – | E

Westin South Coast Plaza, 686 Anton Blvd. (bet. Bristol St. & Town Ctr. Dr.), Costa Mesa, 714-444-5900

Joachim Splichal finally extends his golden Pinot dynasty to the Orange Coast with the debut of this instant hot spot with a palpable South-of-France character; the early word is that the cuisine served in this earthy, restful space will ably compete with any of the county's Gallic favorites, though the menu offers enough new flourishes to keep the buzz among foodies lively for months.

Ritz, The S
27 | 27 | 27 | $44

Newport Fashion Island, 880 Newport Ctr. Dr. (Santa Barbara Ave.), Newport Beach, 949-720-1800

■ "Always head and shoulders above the rest", this "posh", pricey Continental archetype, OC's Most Popular restaurant, "never disappoints" and "still lives up to its name", offering "outstanding" food and "old-style" service that's deemed "as good as it gets"; the setting may be a bit "masculine", but the "lovely" new Garden Room is "terrific"; in sum, "worth the cost and ride from LA."

Ritz-Carlton Laguna Niguel
26 | 28 | 26 | $50

Ritz-Carlton Laguna Niguel, 1 Ritz-Carlton Dr. (PCH), Dana Point, 949-240-5008

■ "Beyond elegant" say those enchanted by this "heavenly" "piece of the Garden of Eden" overlooking the Pacific; admirers call it "a dream" from "beginning to end" with "world-class" French-Med fare, "impeccable" service and lovely decor that's top-rated in OC; though "insanely overpriced", it's easy to "feel really special" here, even for just "a drink or dessert in the Library."

Troquet 28 | 24 | 25 | $44

S. Coast Plaza, 3333 Bristol St. (Town Ctr. Dr.), Costa Mesa, 714-708-6865

■ "The most interesting OC restaurant in a long time" might be an understatement: this "ascending star" has rocketed to the top of OC's food rankings in less than a year; "engaging" chef-owners Tim and Liza Goodell (of Aubergine fame) lure foodies to their "classy" South Coast Plaza bistro with "astounding" Cal-French fare like sweetbread sandwiches, "heavenly foie gras" and an unrivaled degustation menu; though "preposterously small portions" and the mega-mall location turn off a few, the smitten majority declares "you couldn't do better in Paris."

Zov's Bistro and Bakery Cafe 26 | 20 | 21 | $26

Enderle Ctr., 17440 E. 17th St. (Yorba St.), Tustin, 714-838-8855

■ Foodies flock to Tustin's much-adored, ever-expanding eatery for "consistently great", Mediterranean-accented cuisine that's "delicious, dynamic" and "full of passion and flavor", with "interesting salads", "great rack of lamb" and "baked goods to die for" earning special praise; owner Zov Karamardian ("she's a gem") shares her skills in a series of "wonderful" Monday night cooking classes, many featuring star chefs.

TOP 10 FOOD RANKING

	Restaurant	Cuisine Type
28	Victoria & Albert's	Traditional American
	La Coquina	New World
	Del Frisco's	Steakhouse
	Le Coq au Vin	French Bistro
27	California Grill	Californian
	Flying Fish Cafe	Seafood
26	Chatham's Place	Continental
	Manuel's on the 28th	Eclectic/New American
	Morton's of Chicago	Steakhouse
	Artist Point	Northwestern

OTHER IMPORTANT PLACES

Antonio's La Fiamma	N/S Italian
Bahama Breeze	Caribbean
Chez Vincent	Classic French
Citricos	Mediterranean
Enzo's on the Lake	Northern Italian
Fulton's Crab House	Seafood
Harvey's Bistro	French Bistro/New Amer.
Johnny River's	BBQ
La Grille	New French
Le Provence	New French
Maison et Jardin	Continental
Pebbles	Cal./New American
Peter Scott's	Continental
Rolando's	Cuban
Sergio's	N/S Italian
Winnie's Oriental Garden	Chinese

	F	D	S	C
Antonio's La Fiamma S	25	22	22	$26

611 S. Orlando Ave. (Maitland Ave.), Maitland, 407-645-1035

■ Expect "an evening of pampering" from this immensely popular Maitland Italian with "an excellent deli downstairs and fine dining upstairs"; the "authentic" cuisine is served "with an emphasis on keeping the customers happy" by a "knowledgeable staff" in a "lovely" albeit "painfully noisy" setting; some say the wine list is reason enough to go.

	F	D	S	C
Artist Point S	26	26	24	$30

Disney's Wilderness Lodge, 901 Timberline Dr. (World Dr.), Lake Buena Vista, 407-824-1081

■ "Deliciously unique Pacific Northwest food" is the specialty of this rustic, "breathtaking" room at Disney's Wilderness Lodge that's "like eating at Frank Lloyd Wright's house"; "still undiscovered by the crowds", it draws kudos for its "great salmon, wild game" and extensive regional wine list; for those seeking a "dining adventure, not a quick meal", this is a "hands-down favorite."

Bahama Breeze ◐ S | 22 | 24 | 20 | $17

8849 International Dr. (1 mi. south of Sand Lake Rd.), Orlando, 407-248-2499
499 E. Altamonte Dr. (Palm Springs Blvd. & State Rd. 436), Altamonte Springs, 407-831-2929

■ From the folks who brought you Red Lobster and The Olive Garden comes this "peppy" Caribbean-flavored chain acclaimed for its "creative", inexpensive food and "islandish" "party" feel; though a few say it "reeks of franchise" and can be "too much", it's nonetheless "crowded", so "go early or wait forever" to get in.

California Grill S | 27 | 27 | 25 | $36

Disney's Contemporary Resort, 4600 N. World Dr., Lake Buena Vista, 407-824-1576

■ One of Disney's "finest", this "superb" Californian atop the Contemporary Resort has it all: an "adventuresome" menu by chef Clifford Pleau, an "exciting wine program" with many by-the-glass choices and an "awesome" view, all of which come together so well that it's voted Central Florida's Most Popular restaurant; no surprise, it "can be difficult to get into", so reserve far in advance and "time your dinner for the Magic Kingdom fireworks."

Chatham's Place S | 26 | 22 | 25 | $33

Phillips Pl., 7575 Dr. Phillips Blvd. (Sand Lake Rd.), 407-345-2992

■ Though the Chatham family no longer owns it, this Continental remains a favorite (despite its proximity to touristy International Drive) for a "really delightful evening"; admirers like the fact that you can "dress up or down" and that everyone "is treated with the same attention as frequent guests"; regulars recommend the signature pecan-crusted grouper, calling it "world-class."

Chez Vincent | 24 | 21 | 21 | $28

533 W. New England Ave. (Park Ave.), Winter Park, 407-599-2929

◪ "Sharp, sophisticated and intimate", chef Vincent Gagliano's Classic French in Winter Park's redeveloped West End might be on the "wrong side of the tracks", but many call this "perfect little bistro" a "great addition" (though a few hedge that the "food is *almost* there"); while the "slaphappy" service takes some blows, the consensus is "trying hard and should get even better."

Citricos S | 25 | 26 | 26 | $40

Disney's Grand Floridian Resort & Spa, 4401 Grand Floridian Way, Lake Buena Vista, 407-939-3463

■ "Chef Roland Muller's innovative food" draws applause at this Disney Mediterranean at the Grand Floridian Resort, where the "stunning", "eclectic decor" and "very attentive service" also impress; though it might be a bit "noisy" and "a little pricey", the word on the boardwalk is that it's a "great new restaurant to try"; N.B. the wine pairings – for $20 more – come highly recommended.

Del Frisco's Steakhouse | 28 | 22 | 24 | $37

729 Lee Rd. (1½ blocks west of I-4), 407-645-4443

■ "Steaks are the signature", but "everything from appetizers to desserts is exquisite" say the many supporters of this "very special" Lee Road "guy place" with "dark wood" decor and a "clubby atmosphere" (the guys think it's "a great place to close a deal"); the few who "wish there were more nonbeef items" seem to miss the point: it's aimed at carnivores who "don't care about prices" given "humongous portions" of "excellent food."

Enzo's on the Lake
26 | 24 | 23 | $33

1130 S. Hwy. 17-92 (State Rd. 434), Longwood, 407-834-9872

■ "Enzo Perlini is hands-on" at his eponymous, "high-end" Longwood restaurant that some say is the "closest thing to an Italian trattoria in North America"; young lovers sigh it's a "first-rate first date place" as "there's passion in the food and staff", even if others claim nonregulars are "treated like you crashed a party"; most concur, however, "you'd swear you're in Italy having a meal in the country" thanks to its "beautiful location" on Lake Fairy.

Flying Fish Cafe S
27 | 26 | 25 | $34

Walt Disney World Boardwalk Resort, 1300 Epcot Resorts Blvd. (Buena Vista Dr.), Lake Buena Vista, 407-939-2359

■ "Disney outdid itself" at this Boardwalk seafooder, where "cutting-edge cuisine" served amid "fantastic decor" makes it "too good to pass up"; especially notable is the open kitchen view ("get a seat at the bar and watch them in action") and a "not-to-be-missed" chocolate volcano cake that will "knock your socks off."

Fulton's Crab House S
21 | 21 | 20 | $27

Downtown Disney, Pleasure Island, Lake Buena Vista, 407-934-2628

◪ "Terrific oysters without the fear" can be found at this Downtown Disney seafooder that prides itself on freshness and "good variety"; a few nonbelievers say "leave it to the tourists" and everyone warns "hold onto your wallet" as the tab can be "ridiculous", yet the "stunning" location (it's housed on an old paddle wheeler) and knowledgeable staff sway many.

Harvey's Bistro
24 | 23 | 22 | $23

Barnett Bank Bldg., 390 N. Orange Ave. (Livingston St.), 407-246-6560

■ It might be the "office building location", but this Downtown New American–French bistro has a "big city feel" that's "unlike Orlando" and helps make it popular "after work" or "before a basketball game" or the theater; the "inventive menu" utilizing fresh seasonal ingredients also earns respect, as does the "great ambiance and service"; the only complaint (which really is a compliment): "they close too early during the week."

Johnny River's Smokehouse S
– | – | – | M

5370 W. Colonial Dr. (Kirkman Rd.), 407-293-5803

Owner Johnny Rivers has converted an abandoned Red Lobster into an upscale barbecuerie in West Orlando and is packing in locals who come to sample a creative menu that includes turkey shank, BBQ ribs and pulled pork; make sure to save room for the Hershey bar bread pudding.

La Coquina S
28 | 27 | 27 | $41

Hyatt Regency Grand Cypress, 1 Grand Cypress Blvd. (State Rd. 535), 407-239-1234

■ "A class act that's hard to follow", this "very elegant" New World restaurant in the Grand Cypress Resort delivers a "romantic, special experience" in a "fairy-tale setting for grown-ups"; its "artistically presented" food, "top-shelf" service and "pretty" decor make it arguably "the most wonderful" dining adventure in Orlando; P.S. don't miss the "best Sunday brunch on Planet Earth."

La Grille S 25 24 25 $40

Mercado Village, 8445 International Dr. (1 mi. south of Sand Lake Rd.), 407-345-0883

■ Though touristy International Drive isn't known for serious food, this French entry proves there can be "great dining where you least expect it"; chef Marc Barnett's "well-thought-out", "inventive" menu uses "seasonal products", service is "outstanding" and the atmosphere "sweet", making this a "welcome addition" and maybe "the only reason to go to International Drive."

Le Coq au Vin S 28 22 25 $29

4800 S. Orange Ave. (Holden Ave.), 407-851-6980

■ Chef-owner Louis Perrotte's "tried-and-true" South Orlando bistro is "where Orlando's chefs dine" on their nights off, and with good reason: its Country French cuisine is so "affordable and unpretentious" and the setting so "warm" that you'll "hate to leave"; some fanatics go "just for the crème brûlée" or the "must-have soufflés", but everyone concurs "do not miss this" – "it's very popular, so make reservations."

Le Provence 26 23 23 $33

50 E. Pine St. (bet. Magnolia & Orange Aves.), 407-843-1320

■ "The food gets better every year" claim devotees of this Downtown Contemporary French that's called "consistently delightful", with "attentive service" and "stylishly updated" cuisine presented with "real flair" in an "intimate and serene" atmosphere; for a "romantic evening", "*c'est si bon.*"

Maison et Jardin S 26 27 26 $37

430 S. Wymore Rd. (½ mi. south of I-4 & State Rd. 436), Altamonte Springs, 407-862-4410

■ This "romantic", "special occasion" Altamonte Springs Continental in an "older house" with a "lovely garden setting" is "of another time and place", serving flaming desserts and "beef Wellington that dreams are made of"; "impeccable service" and an "exciting wine list" complement the "wonderful" though "pricey" menu, and while a tad "stuffy" for some (jackets requested), most say dining at the 'Mason Jar' (as it's locally known) is a "don't miss" experience.

Manuel's on the 28th 26 28 27 $49

Barnett Bank Bldg., 390 N. Orange Ave. (Livingston St.), 407-246-6580

■ Considered by some "the top restaurant in Florida" (and not just because of its 28th-floor location in Downtown Orlando), this "sophisticated" Eclectic–New American serves "world-quality" cuisine and "creative specials" in a "stunning" yet "intimate" room with a "view so good you'll forget the prices"; "attentive" "service teams" are the final touch that make it "spectacular all the way around" – this is "Orlando at its best."

Morton's of Chicago S 26 23 24 $45

7600 Dr. Phillips Blvd. (Sand Lake Rd.), 407-248-3485

◪ This "top-notch" chain steakhouse near Universal Studios serves beef that's "as close to perfect as you can get", topped off by the likes of a "Godiva hot chocolate cake to die for"; a "classy place for local execs", it exudes "a big city feeling" (i.e. it's "noisy" and filled with "cigar smoke") and can be "very expensive", thus some advise "go if you're not paying."

Pebbles S 24 22 22 $20

17 W. Church St. (Orange Ave.), 407-839-0892
Crossroads Plaza, 12551 State Rd. 535 (I-4), Lake Buena Vista, 407-827-1111
2110 W. State Rd. 434 (Douglas Ave.), Longwood, 407-774-7111
2516 Aloma Ave. (State Rd. 436), Winter Park, 407-678-7001

■ "A touch of California cuisine in a town of Disney dining", this New American chain offers what some call the "best total package for the money" thanks to its "gourmet-on-the-cheap" philosophy; fans rave about its "unusual", "always changing" menu, "great wine list" and "creative" salads (ask for the zucchini dressing); throw "reasonable prices" and good service into the mix and you have the "best 'every night' restaurant" in town.

Peter Scott's 25 25 24 $41

Longwood Village, 1811 W. State Rd. 434 (I-4), Longwood, 407-834-4477

■ An "elegant dinner club with entertainment, dancing" and "a '40s flair", this Longwood "lovers' retreat" is the "perfect place to propose" almost anything; Dover sole and venison osso buco are favorites on a Continental menu that pleases an "older crowd" at this "expensive" (some say "overpriced") "special occasion spot."

Rolando's S 24 11 20 $13

870 E. State Rd. 436 (Red Bug Lake Rd.), Casselberry, 407-767-9677

■ Some of the "best Cuban food north of Havana" is served at this Casselberry "local favorite", a "wonderful, family-operated restaurant" with "homestyle" cooking in a "neighborhood cafe atmosphere"; though the room could use brightening ("what decor?"), you'll feel like "part of the family" as it's so "friendly."

Sergio's S 25 24 23 $31

355 N. Orange Ave. (Robinson St.), 407-428-6162

■ "When you first walk into" this Downtown Italian, "you get the feeling this is a class act" thanks to its "charming" ambiance, "beautiful bar" and sophisticated touches like "roses for the ladies"; though some say "service could be more attentive", the "delicious food" and "great wine" maintain the "upscale" tone of this "special occasion", "NY-style" place.

Victoria & Albert's S 28 29 29 VE

Disney's Grand Floridian Resort & Spa, 4401 Grand Floridian Way, Lake Buena Vista, 407-824-2591

■ This American "crown jewel of fine dining" in Disney's Grand Floridian takes Metro Orlando's triple crown, placing No. 1 for Food, Decor and Service; the "best dress-up place in town", it offers "pure luxury" in the form of chef Scott Hunnel's "flawless" seven-course feast that includes "your own personalized menu" and "a rose for milady"; to savor this treat you must "book way in advance" (especially for the coveted chef's table in the kitchen) and though "you'll be treated like royalty, it costs a king's ransom."

Winnie's Oriental Garden 23 22 21 $19

1346 Orange Ave. (Hwy. 17-92), Winter Park, 407-629-2111

■ The "most upscale, fine dining" Chinese around is how fans describe this Winter Park yearling serving "exquisite, jewel-like food" that's evidence of a "delicate touch in the kitchen"; add "gracious hosting" and "stark, clean decor" to the mix and you have one of the "classiest" dining experiences in town; P.S. "check out the sink in the bathrooms."

Palm Beach

TOP 10 FOOD RANKING

	Restaurant	Cuisine Type
26	Cafe Chardonnay	New American
	La Vieille Maison	New French
	Auberge Le Grillon	Continental
	Kathy's Gazebo	Classic French
	Chef Reto's	New World
25	Cafe L'Europe	Continental/French
	La Tre	Vietnamese
	La Petite Maison	French Bistro
24	La Finestra	Northern Italian
	Tom's Place	BBQ

OTHER IMPORTANT PLACES

Acquario	Italian/Mediterranean
Aquaterra	New American
Boulevard Grill	New American
Citrus	New American
Craig's	Regional American
I&J Station House	Seafood
Janeiro	French/Mediterranean
Masquerade Cafe	Eclectic/New American
Max's Grille	New American
Morton's of Chicago	Steakhouse
Palm Beach Tavern	New American
Restaurant/Four Seasons	Floridian/French
Spoto's Oyster Bar	Seafood
32 East	New American

F | D | S | C

Acquario — | — | — | VE

The Esplanade, 150 Worth Ave. (bet. S. County Rd. & S. Ocean Blvd.), Palm Beach, 561-655-9999

Superior Italian-Mediterranean food from owner-chef Theo Schoenegger (ex NYC's San Domenico) makes for stylish dining in this warm, upscale locale; his tasting menu is a steal at $39.50, risotto is wonderful and desserts are a welcome exercise in overindulgence; N.B. check out the saltwater aquarium.

Aquaterra S — | — | — | VE

230 Sunrise Ave. (bet. Coconut Row & S. County Rd.), Palm Beach, 561-366-4000

Star chef Charlie Palmer (of NYC's Aureole fame) takes on Palm Beach with this noisy, modernistic (some would say cold) space that's something of a departure from the usual local style; expect New American fare with a modern (and sometimes confusing) twist – sea bass with caramelized fennel, for example.

Auberge Le Grillon S 26 | 23 | 25 | $35

6900 N. Federal Hwy. (1 mi. north of Yamato Rd.), Boca Raton, 561-997-6888

■ The "excellent" Continental-European food at this "tiny gem" is "worth mortgaging your house for"; "first-rate on all counts", it offers a "wonderful" (if "rich") menu, a "romantic" setting and "owners who care"; though a bit "cramped" (some say "cozy"), it's "absolutely charming"; N.B. the summer prix fixe is a great deal.

Boulevard Grill S — | — | — | E

514 Via de Palmas (Federal Hwy. & Mizner Blvd. SE), Boca Raton, 561-391-7734

The owners of the former Mon Petit Chou have expanded and brought in chef Andrew Swersky, who won raves during his stint at the Morada Grill; the result: an exciting and somewhat pricey New American that's won a following for such rich offerings as pasta stuffed with Maytag blue cheese and caviar, pizza with duck ham and Swersky's signature Morada duck done several ways.

Cafe Chardonnay S 26 | 22 | 25 | $32

Garden Square Shoppes, 4533 PGA Blvd. (Military Trail), Palm Beach Gardens, 561-627-2662

■ "A real star", this "trendy" New American in Palm Beach Gardens takes top food ratings in Palm Beach County with its "up-to-date" menu that manages to be "exciting" and "consistently good"; "excellent", unrushed service and "attractive" quarters enhance what is "always a worthwhile experience"; as you'd expect from the name, this "find" also has a "great wine list."

Cafe L'Europe S 25 | 26 | 24 | $39

331 S. County Rd. (Brazilian Ave.), Palm Beach, 561-655-4020

■ Offering "classic", "upper-crust dining in typical Palm Beach elegance", this award-winning French-Continental is "ideal for a special occasion" thanks to "fine food", "professional service" and a "beautiful" setting (post-*Survey*, it moved to South County Road); it's "pricey", but this "charming fave" is "a consistent winner."

Chef Reto's Restaurant S 26 | 22 | 25 | $37

41 E. Palmetto Park Rd. (Federal Hwy.), Boca Raton, 561-395-0633

■ The "talented" chef-owner "can really cook" at this small New World outpost in Boca Raton; with an ever-changing menu of "refreshing" fare, it specializes in "festivals that celebrate the cuisines of the world"; though still something of "a hidden secret", this "unique" place is judged one of South Florida's "best."

Citrus S — | — | — | VE

4400 N. Federal Hwy. (bet. Spanish River & Yamato Blvds.), Boca Raton, 561-394-0007

This whimsically appointed cafe serves seasonal New American cuisine with an innovative flair in an ambiance that recalls NYC's SoHo; you'll also find the likes of antelope, ostrich, venison and buffalo steak in season.

Craig's S — | — | — | E

2419 S. Dixie Hwy. (Okeechobee Hwy.), West Palm Beach, 561-655-2100

Craig Miller and Gary Boileau do wonders for Regional American fare (with nods to the Pacific Rim) at their NY brownstone–style storefront bistro; it's a place to rediscover pot roast and other richly flavored, attractively presented fare served in generous portions.

I&J Station House S — | — | — | M

233 W. Lantana Rd. (east of I-95), Lantana, 561-547-9487

The seafood is fresh and well-prepared at Steve Jankun and Tom Isola's handsomely refurbished old railroad station, but the main attraction is a 3,000-gallon lobster tank with a never-ending supply of Maine lobsters in all sizes; steamed clams, roasted garlic mashed potatoes and sinfully rich desserts also excel.

Janeiro 🅂 – – – E

191 Bradley Pl. (Seminole Ave.), Palm Beach, 561-659-5223

Gerard Reuther, who trained with Paul Bocuse and was personal chef to Charles de Gaulle, is now ensconced in this elegant French-Mediterranean; his sophisticated blending of classical and contemporary elements has patrons marveling as they dine stylishly on Versace-designed Rosenthal china and sip from crystal stemware; in case you're curious, the restaurant is named for Rio de Janeiro, one of owner Tom Youchak's favorite places.

Kathy's Gazebo Cafe 26 22 21 $38

(fka Gazebo Cafe)

Hyde Park Plaza, 4199 N. Federal Hwy. (bet. Yamato Rd. & Spanish River Blvd.), Boca Raton, 561-395-6033

■ "It's super fun to watch the chefs" as they "work their wonders" in the open kitchen of this "expensive, but excellent" French; however, mixed in with praise for the "fabulous" food are repeated complaints that "reservations are not honored"; aside from that "big minus", the consensus is "wonderful in every way."

La Finestra 🅂 24 21 22 $32

171 E. Palmetto Park Rd. (Mizner Blvd.), Boca Raton, 561-392-1838

■ The ambiance is "formal" at this "small and intimate" Northern Italian, so dress accordingly and enjoy a "first-rate" evening that includes "heavenly" food served in a "lovely" setting with music; insiders advise "if the menu offers wild mushrooms, get them."

La Petite Maison 25 23 24 $29

366 E. Palmetto Park Rd. (east of Federal Hwy.), Boca Raton, 561-750-7483

■ An "exceptional value", this "small", "mom-and-pop" bistro is applauded for its "well-prepared" French food and "personal attention"; it's a "delightful" experience topped by "super desserts."

La Tre 🅂 25 18 21 $29

(fka La Truc)

249 E. Palmetto Park Rd. (Federal Hwy.), Boca Raton, 561-392-4568

■ Now in new digs (outdating our decor rating), "the best-kept secret in Boca" offers some of the "best food in town" via a French-accented Vietnamese menu that's "innovative" and "authentic", served by a staff that's always gracious and professional despite an occasional "language problem."

La Vieille Maison 🅂 26 28 26 $44

770 E. Palmetto Park Rd. (2½ mi. east of I-95), Boca Raton, 561-391-6701

◪ "Royalty would be at home" in this restored, Mizner era–inspired home filled with European antiques; not only is it "beautiful in every way", it's also an "epicurean" delight thanks to "excellent" New French cuisine enhanced by first-class service; a few foes think it's "getting a little too vieille" and needs a "shake-up", but to most this is "as good as it gets" and "absolutely worth the trip."

Masquerade Cafe – – – E

640 E. Atlantic Ave. (bet. SE 6th & 7th Aves.), Delray Beach, 561-279-0229

Set in an attractive European-style passageway off the main drag, this intimate American-Eclectic cafe with playful masquerade-themed decor offers superior food accented by Asian-Med flavors and marked by beautiful presentations; the 'foot-long shrimp' (jumbo size and stuffed with spinach) is a delicious original.

Max's Grille S 23 | 22 | 21 | $28
Mizner Park, 404 Plaza Real (bet. Glades & Palmetto Pk. Rds.), Boca Raton, 561-368-0080
■ "Everyone comes" to Dennis Max's casual grill for "creative" New American fare, including "great meat loaf", served in a "lively" setting with an "open kitchen"; "long lines" and "noise" aside, "there's no better place to meet friends" and enjoy "delicious" food and "people-watching."

Morton's of Chicago S – | – | – | E
Phillip's Point Bldg., 777 S. Flagler St., West Palm Beach, 561-835-9664
The clubby atmosphere of this for-real steakhouse and the quality of its kitchen make this Downtown West Palm Beach branch of the national chain a winner; there's more than meat and potatoes here, but it's the prime rib and sirloin that keep this place a prime destination for the 'where's the beef' crowd.

Palm Beach Tavern – | – | – | M
251 Royal Palm Way, Palm Beach, 561-832-0385
As much as any dining room in Palm Beach, this fashionable American epitomizes the wealthy enclave's perceived image; here, for lunch and dinner, the elite meet to eat; they come for the handsome decor, personalized service and familiar but first-rate fare that includes vichyssoise, seafood and salads.

Restaurant at the Four Seasons Palm Beach Hotel S – | – | – | E
Four Seasons Palm Beach Hotel, 2800 S. Ocean Blvd. (Lake Worth Bridge), Palm Beach, 561-582-2800
With the arrival of "talented" chef Hubert de Marais, this once-typical hotel dining room has become one of the state's best; with a creative touch, Marais blends French and Florida styles into a unique nouvelle cuisine that has won many accolades.

Spoto's Oyster Bar ◐ S – | – | – | M
125 Datura St. (Flagler Dr.), West Palm Beach, 561-835-1828
Arguably the best that Downtown West Palm Beach has to offer, this seafooder offers perfectly cooked aquatic fare prepared by Bill Flatley (who grew up on his father's oyster boat), plus a raw bar and superior desserts; seating is tight and beware the noise level.

32 East S – | – | – | E
32 E. Atlantic Ave. (bet. 1st & Swinton Aves.), Delray Beach, 561-276-7868
Formerly a run-down antiques shop and bookie joint, now a smart New American with San Francisco accents offering chef Wayne Alcaide's eclectic menu that changes daily and features seasonal ingredients and garnishes; though expensive, everything from the homemade breads to the desserts and even the coffee is special.

Tom's Place 24 | 14 | 18 | $17
7251 N. Federal Hwy. (bet. Linton Blvd. & Yamato Rd.), Boca Raton, 561-997-0920
■ "Even Yankees have to love" the BBQ that's made this "noisy", "hectic" joint a Boca institution; the room gives new meaning to the word plain, but the "ribs are the best" "in America", and the "sauce is made with soul"; this is "real, down-home", "authentic Southern" eating at its best.

Philadelphia

TOP 20 FOOD RANKING

	Restaurant	Cuisine Type
29	Le Bec-Fin	Classic French
	Fountain	Continental/New French
	Le Bar Lyonnais	French Bistro
27	Sagami	Japanese
	Brasserie Perrier	New French
	Susanna Foo	Asian/New French
	Deux Cheminées	Classic French
	Mainland Inn	New American
	Isabella's	Italian/New French
	Swann Lounge	American/Continental
	Jake's	New American
	Mademoiselle de Paris	Desserts/French
	Dmitri's	Med./Seafood
	Dilworthtown Inn	Amer./Classic French
26	Ciboulette	New French
	Striped Bass	Seafood
	Coventry Forge Inn	Classic French
	Morton's of Chicago	Steakhouse
	Tacconelli's Pizza	Pizza
	Overtures	Mediterranean

OTHER IMPORTANT PLACES

Arroyo Grille	Southwestern
Audrey Claire	Mediterranean
Bistro St. Tropez	French Bistro
Buddakan	Pan-Asian
Fork	New American
La Veranda	Italian/Seafood
Monte Carlo Living Rm.	N/S Italian
Moshulu	International
Nan	New French/Thai
Opus 251	New/Regional American
Prime Rib	Steakhouse
Ristorante Di Palma	N/S Italian
Ritz-Carlton Grill	Med./New American
Rococo	New American
Rouge 98	New American
Venus & the Cowboy	Mediterranean
White Dog Cafe	New American

	F	D	S	C
Arroyo Grille S	15	20	16	$25

Leverington & Main Sts., 215-487-1400

This "supertrendy" Southwestern yuppeteria on its own little island in Manayunk is prized for its "attractive" clientele, "funky", "colorful" interior, "great deck" and "spacious parking lot"; a seriously high decibel level, "mediocre" food and "slow service" from the "young and the careless" only slightly diminish its appeal, especially for "good margaritas" "on a sultry summer night."

	F	D	S	C
Audrey Claire S ≠	22	17	20	$26

276 S. 20th St. (Spruce St.), 215-731-1222
■ "Spartan", "light and breezy" atmospherics, "innovative" Mediterranean cooking and a "young and hip" Center City crowd ("it feels like the TV show *Friends*") make this BYO the "new in-spot"; no reserving and "long waits" mean "get there early."

	F	D	S	C
Bistro St. Tropez	24	20	20	$31

2400 Market St., 4th fl. (23rd St.), 215-569-9269
■ An "artsy", "offbeat" location in the Marketplace Design Center sets the stage for this "authentic" French bistro, a "hip" place for "excellent food" at "reasonable prices for the quality"; toss in "great views" overlooking the Schuylkill, "cute waiters whose suggestions you should always take" and jazz on Thursday nights and it all adds up to a "hidden jewel."

	F	D	S	C
Brasserie Perrier S	27	27	25	$50

1619 Walnut St. (bet. 16th & 17th Sts.), 215-568-3000
■ "Another Georges Perrier masterpiece" rave legions of admirers blown away by this "suave", "art deco" Contemporary French, a "great new addition" to Restaurant Row at "more reasonable prices" than its older sibling, Le Bec-Fin; expect "wonderful presentations" and "complex tastes" from chef Francesco Martorella and a "superbly trained" staff; a few scoff at the 'brasserie' tag and "pricey wine", but overall – "believe the hype."

	F	D	S	C
Buddakan S	–	–	–	E

325 Chestnut St. (4th St.), 215-574-9440
Stunning decor (with a waterfall and 10-foot Buddha) serves as the backdrop for outstanding Pan-Asian cuisine at this noisy Old City newcomer from Stephen Starr, creator of the nearby Continental; it offers surprisingly professional service from a white-clad staff as well as a hot bar scene that draws moneyed folks of all ages.

	F	D	S	C
Ciboulette S	26	24	24	$52

Bellevue Bldg., 200 S. Broad St. (Walnut St.), 215-790-1210
■ Acolytes gush that Bruce Lim's "heavenly" New French in a "lovely" room in the Bellevue "lives up to its reputation"; and while his "appetizer portion" concept "adds up quickly", it also "allows for a taste of many wonderful selections" including "foie gras to quack about"; save room for the "fabulous dessert cart."

	F	D	S	C
Coventry Forge Inn	26	25	24	$45

3360 Coventryville Rd. (1½ mi. west of Rte. 100), Pottstown, 610-469-6222
■ Even after 44 years, the Callahans' "long-standing favorite" in Pottstown "hasn't lost its touch" for "excellent", "traditional" French fare in a "warm", "serene" country setting that even city folk don't mind driving to; "attentive" servers have "all the right moves" and the Saturday night prix fixe is an "excellent value."

	F	D	S	C
Deux Cheminées	27	28	26	$65

1221 Locust St. (bet. 12th & 13th Sts.), 215-790-0200
■ If you "forgot what it was like to have your senses exhilarated", Fritz Blank's "romantic" Classic French in an "elegant" Center City townhouse will remind you; "rich" dishes are "so amazing you'd swear they came from heaven" and service is "unobtrusive", though a few raise an eyebrow at the prices: "I want to eat on Limoges, not buy it."

Dilworthtown Inn, The S | 27 | 27 | 26 | $44

1390 Old Wilmington Pike (Brinton Bridge Rd.), West Chester, 610-399-1390

■ "What a romantic treat" sigh fans of this West Chester inn ("the prettiest of them all") that has "come back strong" after a fire; at the "Le Bec-Fin of the 'burbs", expect "wonderful" Classic French–American fare, "outstanding" wines, "impeccable" service and "incredible attention to detail" – the "goblets and silver glisten."

Dmitri's S ≠ | 27 | 13 | 19 | $23

795 S. Third St. (Catharine St.), 215-625-0556

■ It may be a "claustrophobe's nightmare", but this Mediterranean BYO in Queen Village is an "all-time favorite" for seafood ("the best octopus on the planet"); regulars recommend you "arrive at 5 PM" (with cash) or be prepared to "camp out for the evening"; P.S. "sit at the counter" to watch how "two cooks feed 40 people."

Fork S | 24 | 25 | 22 | $31

306 Market St. (bet. 3rd & 4th Sts.), 215-625-9425

■ "My new favorite" sums up reactions to this "casual" New American in Old City that oozes style, from its "cool chandeliers", "way hip" plates and "imaginative cutlery" to diners "as well-dressed as the decor"; toss in "fabulous food" and "so far, so good."

Fountain Restaurant S | 29 | 29 | 28 | $60

Four Seasons Hotel, 1 Logan Sq. (Benjamin Franklin Pkwy. & 18th St.), 215-963-1500

■ For "the most sophisticated dining in Philadelphia", it would be hard to top Jean-Marie Lacroix and company (and their ratings) at this "fabulous" Continental-French in the Four Seasons Hotel; businesspeople tout it as a "super meeting place" for a power lunch, and the brunch-and-dinner crowd says it's a "wow" for "imaginative", "sublime" food and "flawless" service in a room that's "elegance personified"; it "keeps Le Bec-Fin on its toes."

Isabella's S | 27 | 19 | 23 | $35

6516 Castor Ave. (bet. Hellerman & Magee Sts.), 215-533-0356

■ A French-Italian "find" on a "dull" Northeast strip ("foie gras on Castor Avenue – wow"); "excellent" food from "superchef" Ben McNamara is presented "beautifully", the service is "friendly" and while the interior is "cramped", that's a small price to pay since "if it were in Center City we would never get a reservation"; N.B. the food rating has risen three points since our last *Philadelphia Survey.*

Jake's S | 27 | 22 | 24 | $42

4365 Main St. (bet. Grape & Levering Sts.), 215-483-0444

■ Bruce Cooper's "first-class" New American is "Manayunk's bright star", an "understated" "wonder" with "knowledgeable" servers, an "outstanding" wine list and the "best nouvelle cuisine around", though when it's crowded you can "feel like a sardine."

La Veranda S | 23 | 21 | 19 | $41

Penn's Landing, Pier 3, Columbus Blvd. (bet. Arch & Market Sts.), 215-351-1898

■ A "hangout" for "politicos" and other "well-connected" types, this Penn's Landing Italian seafooder serves "superb" food in "generous portions" and offers "great waterfront views"; however, even admirers admit "unless you're somebody, service is slow" and "snooty", and the "wait is bad even with reservations."

Restaurant	F	D	S	C
Le Bar Lyonnais	29	24	25	$42

Le Bar Lyonnais

1523 Walnut St. (15th St.), 215-567-1000

■ "Why pay Le Bec-Fin prices with Le Bar downstairs?"; this "cozy" "gathering place" beneath Georges Perrier's older, "pomp and circumstance" shrine features a "sophisticated" French bistro menu and is a "romantic spot for drinks and dessert"; it may be "cramped" and "smoky", but "it's where those who really know great food at great prices go."

Restaurant	F	D	S	C
Le Bec-Fin	29	29	29	VE

Le Bec-Fin

1523 Walnut St. (bet. 15th & 16th Sts.), 215-567-1000

■ It's No. 1 across the board for Food, Decor and Service in Philadelphia and "everything they say about" Georges Perrier's "world-class" Classic French on Restaurant Row "is true": "exquisite, perfect" cuisine, "gorgeous" decor and "impeccable" yet "unintimidating" service; while wallet-watchers warn it's "expensive" (the prix fixe dinner is $118), devotees dub the $36 lunch a "bargain" because "if you die and go to 'food heaven', Le Bec-Fin will be the name over the door."

Restaurant	F	D	S	C
Mademoiselle de Paris	27	20	19	$12

Mademoiselle de Paris

122 S. 18th St. (Sansom St.), 215-751-0670

■ "Let *me* eat cake" swoon fans of this "civilized", "exquisite pâtisserie" off Rittenhouse Square where "beautiful" creations are "so good you need a cigaret afterward"; decor is "a little ooh-la-la over the top" and the "snotty service" is "right from Paris", but all agree "the search for perfection is over."

Restaurant	F	D	S	C
Mainland Inn	27	25	26	$42

Mainland Inn S

17 Main St. (Sumneytown Pike), Mainland, 215-256-8500

■ This "hard to beat" New American in an "idyllic pastoral setting" near Lansdale might be the "best-kept secret" in rural Montco; the "sophisticated menu", "excellent food" and "lap of luxury" atmosphere are lovingly maintained by "owners and a staff with a passion that makes for a great restaurant"; acolytes urge "if you haven't been there yet, go."

Restaurant	F	D	S	C
Monte Carlo Living Room	26	24	24	$51

Monte Carlo Living Room S

150 South St. (2nd St.), 215-925-2220

■ An "elegant" Italian with "warm" service that's a "romantic" retreat from South Street; chef Nunzio Patruno "has hands of gold", and the "decadent" disco upstairs is the place to work off the calories; it's pricey, but a "wonderful special event experience."

Restaurant	F	D	S	C
Morton's of Chicago	26	21	23	$49

Morton's of Chicago S

1 Logan Sq. (19th St., bet. Benjamin Franklin Pkwy. & Cherry St.), 215-557-0724

■ The Logan Square location of this "decadent" steakhouse chain is "always reliable" for "huge portions" of "top-quality" steaks, with a side of cigars; it's "especially good for expense accounts", pulling in "power people" who are there to "chew the fat."

Restaurant	F	D	S	C
Moshulu	17	25	18	$38

Moshulu S

735 S. Columbus Blvd. (South St.), 215-923-2500

◪ "Sailors never had it like this" on a "beautifully appointed" ship berthed on the southern edge of Penn's Landing; while some call it a "pleasant" place to "entertain out-of-towners" because it "harbors tasty" International fare, others pan "ho-hum food" and "steerage-class" "attitude."

Nan — | — | — | M

4000 Chestnut St. (40th St.), 215-382-0818
A French-Thai BYO in University City with sublime food from the chef of the late, great Alouette, and a restful, inviting atmosphere; it's certainly one of the better newcomers.

Opus 251 S 23 | 23 | 22 | $41

Philadelphia Art Alliance, 251 S. 18th St. (Rittenhouse Sq.), 215-735-6787
■ "An outstanding newcomer", this "innovative" country American with Asian accents in the Art Alliance off Rittenhouse Square serves "exquisitely prepared food" in an "elegant" ambiance with a "Euro feel" and "attentive service"; "patio lunch is wonderful."

Overtures S 26 | 24 | 23 | $36

609-611 Passyunk Ave. (bet. Bainbridge & South Sts.), 215-627-3455
■ Insiders insist this Mediterranean BYO "hideaway" off South Street is the "city's best value"; "astonishingly" "sophisticated" cuisine, "European service at its most professional" and "romantic atmosphere" add up to a "great date" place for making overtures.

Prime Rib S — | — | — | E

Warwick Hotel, 1701 Locust St. (17th St.), 215-772-1701
The showy DC and Baltimore steakhouse chain has swanked up a smashing space in the Warwick, with plush, leopard-print carpet, onyx walls and a baby grand, all to attract an older crowd hungry for the old days; huge portions of excellent, traditional food (the signature prime rib can feed an army) are served impeccably.

Ristorante Di Palma — | — | — | VE

114 Market St. (bet. Front & 2nd Sts.), 215-733-0545
This posh, sedate Old City Italian boasts a serious wine list and modern Italian cuisine from a strong kitchen fronted by Salvatore Di Palma, a well-traveled young South Philadelphian who earned good ratings in previous stints at other Philly kitchens.

Ritz-Carlton Grill S 24 | 24 | 25 | $44

Ritz-Carlton, Chestnut & 17th Sts. (Liberty Pl.), 215-563-1600
◪ The Ritz-Carlton's "elegant" New American–Mediterranean is a "businessman's hangout" ideal for entertaining "important clients" on an expense account with "delicious", "creative" food and "inspired wine dinners"; the "great tables and chairs" are perfect "when in the mood for the *Lifestyles of the Rich and Famous*."

Rococo S 22 | 26 | 19 | $38

123 Chestnut St. (2nd St.), 215-629-1100
■ This "hip", "NY-like" New American is "the place to see and be seen" in Old City; expect everything to be "beautiful", from the "fantastic" "nouvelle" fare to the people ("wear black, be thin") to the "breathtaking room", "sexy cigar" lounge and "happening bar"; but it can get "so loud that it's difficult to hold a conversation."

Rouge 98 ◐ S — | — | — | M

Rittenhouse Claridge Apt. Bldg., 205 S. 18th St. (bet. Locust & Walnut Sts.), 215-732-6622
Neil Stein, of Striped Bass fame, has turned the wine shop in the Rittenhouse Claridge into a sexy, '20s-style Paris salon with a comfy bar; delicious Euro-American food from chef Peter Dunmire keeps the crowd around into the wee hours.

Sagami S 27 | 17 | 21 | $29

37 Crescent Blvd. (1 block north of Collingswood Circle), Collingswood, NJ, 609-854-9773

■ Hordes "happily make the trek" to Collingswood to put up with "long waits", a "basement setting" and seating that's "as tight as a phone booth" for "impeccably fresh" "sublime" sushi served by a "helpful", "efficient" staff; it's "the best Japanese restaurant in the area" ("by a large stretch") and No. 1 in the *Philadelphia Survey*.

Striped Bass S 26 | 28 | 24 | $56

1500 Walnut St. (15th St.), 215-732-4444

■ Ratings haven't budged at Neil Stein's "power heavy" seafooder in the heart of Center City's Restaurant Row; Allyson Thurber's "superb" food is still "tops" and the old bank vault decor is still a "knockout"; though the usually "stellar" service can occasionally be "snotty" and you might holler "holy mackerel!" when the check arrives, this place is "never dull" and remains a Philly favorite.

Susanna Foo ◐ S 27 | 26 | 25 | $49

1512 Walnut St. (bet. 15th & 16th Sts.), 215-545-2666

■ "The blending of Asian and French cuisines is a marriage made in heaven" at this Restaurant Row favorite, where the "smashing", "understated" "new decor" (up four notches from the last *Philadelphia Survey*) now lives up to the "sublime", "sparkling" creations and "fine", "attentive" service; there's still some quibbling over the "skimpy potions" but overall, it's easily No. 1 in its genre.

Swann Lounge & Cafe ◐ S 27 | 27 | 26 | $38

Four Seasons Hotel, 1 Logan Sq. (bet. Benjamin Franklin Pkwy. & 18th St.), 215-963-1500

■ A "civilized" American-Continental in the Four Seasons, singled out for its "lovely" flowers, lunch buffet, "best afternoon tea", Saturday night dessert bar and Sunday brunch; since it's "almost as good as the Fountain", it's (even at these prices) "a best value."

Tacconelli's Pizza S ⊄ 26 | 8 | 15 | $15

2604 E. Somerset St. (bet. Almond & Thompson Sts.), 215-425-4983

■ Where else but this incredibly popular, 50-year-old, cash-only Port Richmond parlor would patrons be required to reserve their dough in advance to get a piece of the "best pizza in the world" ("especially the white" version); but remember, since it's just pizza, period, you may want to "bring your own salad" and wine; P.S. it's dethroned DeLorenzo's as Philly's No. 1 pizzeria.

Venus & the Cowboy - | - | - | E

1700 Benjamin Franklin Pkwy. (17th St.), 215-568-3770

A well-executed (if almost precious) Mediterranean menu and calm feel mark the Center City solo debut of chef Alison Barshak (ex Striped Bass); service is sharp and the bar scene is lawyer-heavy.

White Dog Cafe S 24 | 21 | 20 | $32

3420 Sansom St. (34th St.), 215-386-9224

■ Even if you "don't like her politics" (what some call a "politically correct atmosphere"), "your tail won't stop wagging" after sampling Judy Wicks' "consistently creative" and "delish" New American food; the dog-themed, "eclectic" Penn campus setting has "cozy little rooms" that get "noisy" and "crowded", but everyone agrees this is a "unique Philadelphia restaurant."

Phoenix/Scottsdale

TOP 10 FOOD RANKING

	Restaurant	Cuisine Type
29	Pizzeria Bianco	Pizza
28	Vincent Guerithault	Southwestern
27	Mary Elaine's	Eclectic
	Los Dos Molinos	Mexican
	Ruth's Chris	Steakhouse
	Marquesa	Spanish
	Morton's of Chicago	Steakhouse
26	Chaparral	Continental
	Golden Swan	Southwestern
	RoxSand	International

OTHER IMPORTANT PLACES

Arizona Kitchen	Southwestern
Bistro 24	Classic French
Eddie's Grill	Eclectic/New American
Latilla Room	Regional American
Lon's at the Hermosa	Eclectic
Michael's at the Citadel	New American
Palm Court	Continental
Roaring Fork	Southwestern
Tarbell's	New American
T. Cook's	Italian/Spanish
Terrace Dining Room	N/S Italian
Windows on the Green	Southwestern
Wright's	New American

F | D | S | C

Arizona Kitchen ▽ 24 | 23 | 25 | $30

Wigwam Resort, 300 E. Indian School Rd. (bet. Litchfield & Dysart Rds.), Litchfield Park, 602-935-3811

■ "Excellent", "imaginative Southwestern dishes" using regional ingredients combined with a "charming" ambiance of whitewashed stucco, beamed ceilings and brick floors make the trip "off the beaten path" to the "grand old" Wigwam Resort on the far Westside well worthwhile.

Bistro 24 S — | — | — | E

Ritz-Carlton Hotel, 2401 E. Camelback Rd. (24th St.), Phoenix, 602-468-0700

An early-morning to late-night bistro (formerly the tony Ritz-Carlton Restaurant/Grill) offering interesting variations on traditional French (steak au poivre, croque monsieur and mussels marinière) in a more casual and less expensive (whew!) setting than its predecessor; "*quelle surprise*", you can even eat at the bar.

Chaparral S 26 | 26 | 26 | $37

Marriott's Camelback Inn, 5402 E. Lincoln Dr. (Tatum Blvd.), Scottsdale, 602-948-6644

■ The "warm, cozy, elegant" setting of this "top-notch" resort restaurant may seem like an "upscale time warp" to some, but it is nonetheless the place to go for "traditional" Continental food "from the '60s" served by a staff adept at giving the "royal treatment"; reviewers report that it's a good choice "for holidays or special occasions", and even the lovely coffee service is "memorable."

Eddie's Grill S | 23 | 22 | 21 | $26

Valley Commerce Ctr., 4747 N. Seventh St. (Camelback Rd.), Phoenix, 602-241-1188

◪ "Chichi" patrons "love" popular chef Eddie Matney as much as they love his neon-lit "trendy" Midtown Eclectic–New American serving "creative, hip, flavorful" food with Mediterranean and Asian accents, enhanced by "great" drinks and people-watching overlooking the koi pond; a "big following" agrees it's "one of the best", but a few gripes about "sketchy service" have some suggesting the "cutting edge needs sharpening."

Golden Swan S | 26 | 27 | 26 | $34

Hyatt Regency Scottsdale, 7500 E. Doubletree Ranch Rd. (Scottsdale Rd.), Scottsdale, 602-991-3388

■ A "breathtaking" setting and "amazing" food are the hallmarks of this two-tiered Southwestern with an "exquisite" patio and "romantic" dining gazebos set in a "lovely" koi-filled lagoon; diners enjoy "first-class service and food" including the "best BBQ salmon" and "most interesting Sunday brunch around"; "if you can afford it, go."

Latilla Room S | ▽ 26 | 28 | 25 | $44

Boulders Resort, 34631 N. Tom Darlington Dr. (Carefree Hwy.), Carefree, 602-488-9009

■ "One of the best resort dining rooms", this "elegant" American Regional with a seafood emphasis "is as good as it gets" according to delighted surveyors (and although voting was light, sky-high ratings back up the claim); a very few balk at "stuffy" service, but others find it "sophisticated."

Lon's at the Hermosa Inn S | 23 | 26 | 19 | $30

Hermosa Inn, 5532 N. Palo Cristi Rd. (Stanford Dr.), Paradise Valley, 602-955-7878

◪ This "rustic" redo of a "delightful" historic ranch house makes for what admirers call a "feel-good" "getaway place", with "fabulous" Eclectic fare combining French bistro, Italian cafe and SW tastes (plus a "great" brunch); but reports of "spotty" service and "inconsistent" food have "faded" the charm for a few.

Los Dos Molinos | 27 | 18 | 20 | $13

260 S. Alma School Rd. (bet. Main St. & Broadway Rd.), Mesa, 602-835-5356 ⊄

8646 S. Central Ave. (south of Baseline Rd.), Phoenix, 602-243-9113 S

■ "Not for the fainthearted", these "funky", friendly, no-frills siblings are "a fire-eater's paradise" for "truly great", "Santa Fe–style" Mexican food that "doesn't get any better"; there's no reserving, but the blue corn tortillas, near-flammable salsas (featuring Hatch, New Mexico chiles) and "exceptional carne adovada" make the "too-long waits" well "worth it."

Marquesa S | 27 | 28 | 26 | $38

Scottsdale Princess Resort, 7575 E. Princess Dr. (Scottsdale Rd., north of Bell Rd.), Scottsdale, 602-585-4848

■ Fans laud this "regional treasure" with "bright, authentic" Spanish colonial decor, "superb service", "excellent paella" and other "outstanding" dishes that pay homage to Cataluña and the Basque region; it's "elegant and relaxing", with a Spanish market–style brunch on the garden patio and a tasty tapas menu.

Mary Elaine's 27 | 28 | 26 | $45

Phoenician Resort, 6000 E. Camelback Rd. (60th St.), Scottsdale, 602-423-2530

■ This "magnificent", "elegant" rooftop restaurant is a top "posh" spot for making "monumental memories", especially while viewing a "beautiful sunset"; but it offers more than romance – namely, "creative" Eclectic cuisine, a premier wine list, "sparkling service" and a "great jazz vocalist"; in sum, it's "perfect, but a little pricey."

Michael's at the Citadel S – | – | – | E

The Citadel, 8700 E. Pinnacle Peak Rd. (Pima Rd.), N. Scottsdale, 602-515-2575

This casually elegant dining room in The Citadel offers chef Michael DeMaria's interesting take on New American fare; it's been winning accolades as one of the area's best since opening a year ago, thanks to its excellent food and personable service.

Morton's of Chicago S 27 | 26 | 26 | $47

Esplanade Complex, 2501 E. Camelback Rd. (24th St.), Phoenix, 602-955-9577

◪ "Big beef" and "upscale" mahogany surroundings in the Valley make what admirers call the "best steak in town" a "sybaritic experience"; but it's "pricey", as you'd expect, and the "cigar smoke" is "too much" for some.

Palm Court S 24 | 25 | 24 | $35

Scottsdale Conference Resort, 7700 E. McCormick Pkwy. (bet. Scottsdale & Hayden Rds.), Scottsdale, 602-991-9000 x522

■ "Quiet elegance", "fine" Continental cuisine and "outstanding tableside" preparation make this "wonderful hotel restaurant" a "favorite celebration" destination as well as a place for "serious dinners" anytime; but what's a "delightful experience" to most is too "expensive" and "stuffy" to a few casual types, who object to "the dress code in the summer heat"; N.B. be sure to check out the "excellent" Sunday brunch.

Pizzeria Bianco S 29 | 17 | 21 | $17

623 E. Adams St. (7th St.), Phoenix, 602-258-8300

■ This relocated but still "too small" pizzeria specializes in "outstanding" "Neapolitan-style" pizza made from scratch by an Italian master; the pies are baked in a brick oven and topped with homemade mozzarella and other "top-quality ingredients" that also go into the "terrific salads" and sandwiches; the No. 1 Food rating in Arizona – and "long waits" – speak volumes; N.B. the decor score doesn't reflect the location change.

Roaring Fork – | – | – | M

7243 E. Camelback Rd. (N. Scottsdale Rd.), Scottsdale, 602-947-0795

Acclaimed chef Robert McGrath, who won many fans and high ratings during his previous stint at Windows on the Green at the Phoenician, is now dishing up his scintillating 'American Western Cuisine' at this copper-and-brick, dinner-only Scottsdale outpost; it's making a name for itself as one of the area's best.

RoxSand S 26 | 24 | 23 | $31

Biltmore Fashion Park, 2594 E. Camelback Rd. (26th St.), Phoenix, 602-381-0444

■ "Electric" describes this "place to be seen" with "stunning" decor and "new taste sensations" switched on by a "master" of transcontinental "fusion cooking" ("save room" for the "fabulous desserts"); it's also "excellent" for "quiet" meals on the balcony.

Ruth's Chris Steak House S 27 | 23 | 24 | $36

2201 E. Camelback Rd. (22nd St.), Phoenix, 602-957-9600
7001 N. Scottsdale Rd. (Indian Bend Rd.), Scottsdale, 602-991-5988

Many beef lovers hope there's "a Ruth's Chris in heaven" – here on earth, they go to these "friendly", "dark", "opulent rooms" for "large" hunks of the "best steak imaginable", though at these prices they should "throw in a potato"; they also love the "excellent fish", yet some could do without the sizzling "mess" of butter on which the steaks are served ("ruined too many ties").

Tarbell's S 24 | 24 | 23 | $31

3213 E. Camelback Rd. (32nd St.), Phoenix, 602-955-8100

Clean, contemporary decor and an open kitchen turning out "exciting" New American cuisine cause diners to proclaim this an "excellent" addition that "fits like a glove"; not everyone agrees ("pretentious", "inconsistent") and even admirers find it "pricey", but "good wines" and "solid service" help win over the majority.

T. Cook's S – | – | – | M

Royal Palms Inn, 5200 E. Camelback Rd. (Arcadia St.), Phoenix, 602-808-0766

Featuring Tuscan, Spanish and Mediterranean fare cooked on an open-hearth grill, this restaurant in the renovated Royal Palms Inn offers delectables that pique the palate; you can look forward to being served such dishes as loin of lamb with wild mushrooms and couscous or rotisserie-roasted chicken by a casual yet precise staff; N.B. don't miss the 250-year-old Mexican fountain.

Terrace Dining Room S 25 | 27 | 24 | $34

Phoenician Resort, 6000 E. Camelback Rd. (60th St.), Scottsdale, 602-423-2530

The "least-known jewel" among this "plush" resort's dining options is "exquisite in every detail", done in marble and rich pastels, with a patio overlooking lush gardens and pools; Italian fare is served in style, with live music and an "incredible" brunch.

Vincent Guerithault on Camelback S 28 | 25 | 26 | $42

3930 E. Camelback Rd. (40th St.), Phoenix, 602-224-0225

At this "national treasure" (Phoenix/Scottsdale's Most Popular restaurant), classic French cooking techniques are combined with SW ingredients by chef Guerithault, yielding "superb" food many rate "best in the area", enhanced by exceptional wines and "irresistible desserts"; though a few claim that the menu "needs re-energizing", for most this "romantic", "*très élégant*" "event" is "worth every penny" – tops "for special occasions."

Windows on the Green S 24 | 26 | 24 | $31

Phoenician Resort, 6000 E. Camelback Rd. (60th St.), Scottsdale, 602-941-8200

Above the resort's manicured course, golf scores are forgotten in this elegant but "casual" setting where a "pampering" staff serves "surprisingly classy" SW food accented by tastes from the Old South and the Caribbean; some say it's best for "leisurely lunch."

Wright's S ▽ 25 | 27 | 25 | $37

Arizona Biltmore, 2400 E. Missouri St. (24th St.), Phoenix, 602-955-6600

Named for the architect who inspired the original resort, this room's "unique" lines, "comfortable" grace and "private patios" all echo the Frank Lloyd Wright style – as does the light, direct, "superb" New American fare; admirers think this one "has it all."

Portland

TOP 10 FOOD RANKING

	Restaurant	Cuisine Type
28	Cafe des Amis	French Bistro
	Genoa	Northern Italian
27	Wildwood	Northwestern
	Heathman	French/Northwestern
	Zefiro	Eclectic
26	Assaggio	N/S Italian
	Paley's Place	Northwestern
	3 Doors Down Café	Med./New American
	Nick's Italian Cafe	Northern Italian
25	L'Auberge	Eclectic/New French

OTHER IMPORTANT PLACES

Atwater's	Northwestern
Cafe Azul	Mexican
Caffè Mingo	N/S Italian
Couvron	New French
Esparza's	Tex-Mex
Higgins	Northwestern
Saucebox	Asian
Tapeo	Spanish
Typhoon!	Thai

	F	D	S	C
Assaggio	26	22	22	$19

7742 SE 13th Ave. (Lambert St.), 503-232-6151

■ "Excellent" Italian food, "very reasonable prices and friendly staff" keep this "cozy" Sellwood spot "crowded"; with "great pasta" and "superior appetizers and desserts", many consider it "Portland's best Italian"; popularity (and no reserving for less than six) can mean a wait, best spent at the adjoining wine bar, Enoteca.

	F	D	S	C
Atwater's S	24	27	24	$34

U.S. Bancorp Tower, 111 SW Fifth Ave., 30th fl. (W. Burnside St.), 503-275-3600

■ On the 30th floor of a Downtown bank tower, with a "beautiful" view, "classy" decor and a "great bar" with jazz, is one of the city's top "special occasion" places; most find the "excellent" NW cuisine a match for the setting, and the presence of chef Joe Nouhan may win over doubters who deem it "overrated."

	F	D	S	C
Cafe Azul	–	–	–	E

112 NW Ninth Ave. (bet. Couch & David Sts.), 503-525-4422

Sophisticated and complex, this colorful Pearl District Mexican is a recent transplant from McMinnville; from top-shelf margaritas to exquisite moles, tortillas, braised meats and tamales, it raises Mexican to a higher level, but some might find prices a bit high too.

	F	D	S	C
Cafe des Amis	28	24	27	$32

1987 NW Kearney St. (20th Ave.), 503-295-6487

■ "Reliably solid", this "authentic French bistro" (rated No. 1 for Food in Portland) set in a converted house in the NW district is a "blessedly calm place for special occasions" and oozes "wall-to-wall charm"; dishes such as the "filet in port garlic sauce" are "to die for" and "the duck in blackberry sauce is the best."

Caffè Mingo S ▽ 24 | 21 | 22 | $21

807 NW 21st Ave. (bet. Johnson & Kearney Sts.), 503-226-4646

■ "A pleasant surprise – we welcome it to the area" crow NW district locals over this "perfect, cheap Italian" with "well-prepared food" from a limited menu; not surprisingly, this small cafe is "crowded" (a few gripe "too long a wait"), but for the majority enthusiasm is strong: "Mingo, bingo! I like a lot!"

Couvron ▽ 30 | 26 | 28 | $46

1126 SW 18th Ave. (Madison St.), 503-225-1844

■ "Wow" sums up response to this "creative" Westside New French serving architecturally "haute cuisine – it's literally piled on the plate, a revelation for eye" and palate; service ranges from "tops" to "very slow", the small room can seem "close" and prices are as high as the presentations, but it's worth it for "food as art"; try the tasting menu, a succession of "outstanding" dishes.

Esparza's Tex Mex Cafe 23 | 20 | 19 | $14

2725 SE Ankeny St. (28th Ave.), 503-234-7909

■ What some call the "only worthwhile Tex-Mex in the NW" offers "home-smoked meats", "great guacamole" and other "authentic" food in a "busy, fun" setting; standouts include fried cactus and "fab brisket", and be sure to "try the specials" in this "'50s soda shop gone wild"; there's no reserving but it's "worth the wait and hubbub" to taste something from Joe's little smoker.

Genoa 28 | 23 | 27 | $45

2832 SE Belmont St. (29th Ave.), 503-238-1464

◪ Expect "superb service" along with some of "the most authentic Italian food in town" at this "beautiful" place with prix fixe menus that roam the Italian landscape; you may get "too much food", but you'll enjoy a leisurely, gracious meal that's "worth" the steep tab; a very few find it "overrated", but far more call it an "all-time favorite."

Heathman, The S 27 | 25 | 25 | $36

Heathman Hotel, 1001 SW Broadway (Salmon St.), 503-241-4100

■ Surveyors heap high praise on "one of the last great experiences in fine dining and service" at this hotel restaurant; French chef Philippe Boulot crafts "very good, innovative tastes" by melding "NW game" and other fresh, local ingredients with "solidly French" techniques; the results are served in "just about as perfect a room as you can get", making any meal here simply "splendid."

Higgins Restaurant & Bar S 25 | 22 | 23 | $33

1239 SW Broadway (Jefferson St.), 503-222-9070

◪ This "romantic, special occasion place" with "yummy eats, flattering lighting" and an attractive bi-level setting is a "total delight" say fans of the "wonderful fresh dishes and great smells" produced by Greg Higgins' Alsatian-influenced NW cooking; the many who call it a "class act" and "one of Portland's best" are countered by some who find the food "too far over the edge."

L'Auberge S 25 | 24 | 24 | $35

2601 NW Vaughn St. (bet. 26th & 27th Aves.), 503-223-3302

◪ "Consistently good" New French fare with eclectic accents is served in a "classy", "charming setting" at this "old faithful", where fans even praise "low-key food like burgers and ribs"; N.B. only the bistro, not the main dining room, is open Sundays.

Nick's Italian Cafe S | 26 | 16 | 22 | $29

521 NE Third St. (bet. Evans & Ford Sts.), McMinnville, 503-434-4471

◪ This original Wine Country hangout is still "worth the drive" for "top-notch" Northern Italian food that's "not to miss" on a tour of the area; it's especially good "now that one can order à la carte weeknights" so the meal doesn't have to be "tediously lengthy", but light eaters wish they'd "reduce the portions."

Paley's Place | 26 | 20 | 25 | $35

1204 NW 21st Ave. (Northrup St.), 503-243-2403

■ Dining at this NW district turn-of-the-century home is "like being invited to your best friend's for a gourmet dinner"; one of the warmest spots in town, it offers "surprisingly good" NW fare from a creative, French-inspired chef, plus "personable" service; a post-*Survey* remodeling expanded the space and added a bar.

Saucebox Cafe & Bar | – | – | – | M

214 SW Broadway (Burnside St.), 503-241-3393

East meets West at this swank Downtown Pan-Asian that's as well known for its cocktail-sipping crowd as for its Vietnamese salad rolls, roasted Javanese salmon and other fare; but to enjoy these exotic flavors may mean dealing with noise and attitude.

Tapeo | – | – | – | M

2764 NW Thurman St. (28th Ave.), 503-226-0409

Modeled after a Spanish tapas bar, this festive NW district spot serves zesty fare and Spanish wines in an intimate setting; expect a wait, especially on weekends, when there's also a flamenco guitar.

3 Doors Down Café | 26 | 20 | 24 | $22

1429 SE 37th Ave. (Hawthorne Blvd.), 503-236-6886

■ "The kind of hole-in-the-wall you're always looking for", offering "good" Med-American fare and "great attention to detail" in a "cozy" setting; "no reservations and no place to wait" doesn't bother fans who exclaim over the "things they do with pasta."

Typhoon! S | ▽ 22 | 18 | 20 | $18

2310 NW Everett St. (23rd Ave.), 503-243-7557

Typhoon! on Broadway S | – | – | – | M

Imperial Hotel, 400 SW Broadway (Stark St.), 503-224-8285

■ Bo Kline's "creative cooking dispels the myth of boring Thai food" at this NW district eatery with "flavor that isn't compromised by spiciness"; the "food is great to look at and to eat" and signature appetizers venture into new territory with stunning success; N.B. a spacious new branch has just blown into the Imperial Hotel.

Wildwood S | 27 | 24 | 24 | $32

1221 NW 21st Ave. (Overton St.), 503-248-9663

◪ You can chart the seasons by creative chef Cory Schreiber's use of "exceptionally fresh" ingredients at this NW-themed, blond wood–adorned space; tables are "cramped", "noise" can annoy and some find the place "too trendy", but with an "exciting menu" including "great mussels", it's considered "one of Portland's best."

Zefiro | 27 | 22 | 24 | $33

500 NW 21st Ave. (Glisan St.), 503-226-3394

◪ "An outstanding kitchen" turns out "excellent" Eclectic fare at this "hip" hot spot with "artsy" decor; though "everyone is busy impressing everyone" else, they also enjoy the Asian-Med accents; some would prefer lower prices, but to most it's "worth the money."

Salt Lake City & Mountain Resorts

TOP 10 FOOD RANKING

	Restaurant	Cuisine Type
28	Mariposa	New American
	New Yorker Club	Continental/Trad. Amer.
27	Fresco Italian Cafe	Northern Italian
	Chez Betty	Eclectic
26	Metropolitan	Eclectic
	Glitretind	New American
25	Ichiban Sushi	Japanese
	Red Iguana	Mexican
	Pomodoro	Californian/Italian
	Mandarin	Chinese

OTHER IMPORTANT PLACES

Baci Trattoria	N/S Italian
Capitol Cafe	Eclectic
Chimayo	Southwestern
Cucina	Deli
Grapevine	Continental
Grappa	N/S Italian
La Caille	Eclectic
Lakota	Regional American
Log Haven	Eclectic
Market St. Broiler/Grill	Seafood
Riverhorse Cafe	New American
Sundance Tree Room	Regional American
Tuscany	Northern Italian

F | D | S | C

Baci Trattoria 22 | 24 | 21 | $22

134 W. Pierpont Ave. (off W. Temple St., bet. 200 & 300 South), Salt Lake City, 801-328-1500

◪ "Cosmopolitan" Downtown Italian that earns praise for its "arty" decor (30-foot stained-glass murals), but mixed reviews for its service and food: "fantastic", "best Italian in SLC" vs. "assembly line"; but a "young crowd" finds it a "fun place to meet friends."

Capitol Cafe S – | – | – | M

54 W. 200 South (W. Temple St.), Salt Lake City, 801-532-7000

An innovative chef and owners with years of local experience are behind this success, a cozy Eclectic with a window-walled bright setting, "superior service" and "excellent" "bistro chic" food including brick-oven pizzas, savory sandwiches and delicately seasoned soups; it's handy for Downtown dining and a "worthy" choice for the theater crowd, so book ahead, especially weekends.

Chez Betty S 27 | 21 | 25 | $36

Copper Bottom Inn, Deer Valley Dr. (Short Line Rd.), Park City, 435-649-8181

■ Some of "Utah's best food" is made even "better by the warm atmosphere" at this "charming" Park City Eclectic; with "delicious" fare and a "great staff", it's a "favorite" in the eyes of fans; dinner only, closed Tuesdays (and Wednesdays off-season); N.B. a post-*Survey* change in owners hasn't changed the kitchen or the menu.

Chimayo S

-	-	-	E

368 Main St., Park City, 435-649-6222

Related to the highly rated Grappa by management only, this Park City Southwestern in the former Barking Frog site on Main Street offers authentic regional tastes including fresh and dried chiles, beans and mesquite-grilled game accented by homemade ice creams, sorbets and pastries; call ahead for reservations.

Cucina S

23	23	19	$12

1026 E. Second Ave. (bet. Q & R Sts.), Salt Lake City, 801-322-3055

■ This Downtown deli/gourmet grocery (the top-rated deli in our *Utah Survey*) stands out in the Avenues neighborhood with a "comfortable atmosphere" and "fresh", "pleasantly presented" edibles, including "delicious olive bread" and "incredible scones made on the premises", to take out or not; it's "wonderful for lunch" but can be "very expensive for what you get" according to a few frugal patrons.

Fresco Italian Cafe S

27	23	25	$27

1513 S. 1500 East (bet. Emerson & Kensington Aves.), Salt Lake City, 801-486-1300

■ Expect a "truly pleasant experience" at this "small, charming" Northern Italian (the No. 1 Italian in our *Utah Survey*) in a quiet, residential Eastside neighborhood; admirers call it a "romantic jewel" with "superb", "creative" food and "perfect ambiance", including a summer patio that "can't be beat"; while a few find it "too formal" and unaffordable, most appreciate the "special care taken with each meal"; N.B. dinner only.

Glitretind S

26	26	25	$42

Stein Eriksen Lodge, 7700 Stein Way (Royal St.), Deer Valley, 435-649-3700

◪ "Go and be pampered" in a "lovely ski resort setting" with a "classic, old-money feel" and "great summer deck dining"; though "expensive", devotees deem it "worth every penny" to enjoy "superb" New American fare prepared by "one of the state's best chefs" (returning after a season's sabbatical); doubters say it's low on value, high on "snob appeal", but that's always been part of Deer Valley's cachet.

Grapevine, The

▽

25	23	24	$25

129 N. 100 East (bet. 100 & 200 North), Logan, 435-752-1977

■ The "Café des Artistes of Northern Utah" dispenses Continental cuisine in a restored Victorian home with several charming dining rooms; loyalists laud it as "first-class" and a "great find" with "great food"; dinner only, Wednesday–Saturday; call to reserve.

Grappa S

25	28	21	$38

151 Main St., Park City, 435-645-0636

◪ "Stunning decor" and "fabulous" Italian food made with "fresh, high-quality ingredients" explain why most don't mind if service can seem "a little inattentive" given the tab at this Park City standout; a few sniff that success "went to their heads" and now they're "overbooked and overpriced", but ratings side with those who say it's one of "the best in Utah."

Ichiban Sushi & Japanese Cuisine S 25 | – | 22 | $23

336 S. 400 East, Salt Lake City, 801-532-7522

Newly relocated from Park City to bigger space in a historic 100-year-old church in Downtown SLC, this Japanese standout still features the work of the "talented" female sushi pro whose 22 years of experience (and an apprenticeship in Japan) help explain why surveyors voted it Utah's No. 1 Japanese in its previous home; tempura and sukiyaki round out the menu, and regulars can still store their personalized chopsticks on-site.

La Caille S 21 | 29 | 23 | $42

9565 S. Wasatch Blvd. (3500 East), Little Cottonwood Canyon, 801-942-1751

You "can't beat" the "wonderful farmhouse atmosphere" at this "beautiful" Eclectic that looks like it belongs in château country but is actually in Sandy, where "wildlife can be a nuisance" ("be ready to share your meal with the ducks"); while some call the food "superb", others maintain it's "average" and "expensive"; even so, it's a "great place to take out-of-towners."

Lakota S – | – | – | M

389 W. 200 South (400 West), Salt Lake City, 801-519-8300
The Caledonian, 751 Main St., Park City, 435-658-3400

New to Downtown and Park City, this exciting duo with classy Cal-inspired decor (but starkly contrasting views: ski lifts vs. the city homeless shelter) offers Regional American fare ranging from the bayou to the heartland; extensive wine choices and comfy bars make them welcome respites, especially after an event at the Delta Center or a day on the slopes.

Log Haven S 22 | 27 | 21 | $29

3800 South (Wasatch Blvd., 4 mi. up Millcreek Canyon), Salt Lake City, 801-272-8255

The "food has improved considerably" at this Eastside Eclectic where a California-trained chef now offers Southwestern- and French-influenced food that finally competes with the "beautiful canyon setting" with waterfalls, ponds and streams; though our food rating has yet to catch up, post-*Survey* diners have been lauding it as one of the tops in the state.

Mandarin Restaurant 25 | 19 | 20 | $15

348 E. 900 North, Bountiful, 801-298-2406

"And you thought China" was overcrowded – wait until you visit the top-rated Chinese in our *Utah Survey* where "parties of 12 are not uncommon" and no reserving means there's "always a line" (which "begins at 5 PM"); regulars say it serves "by far Utah's finest Chinese food", enhanced by attractive decor, good service and "moderate prices"; in sum, worth the trip to Bountiful.

Mariposa, The S 28 | 26 | 25 | $39

Silver Lake Lodge, 7600 Royal St., Deer Valley, 435-645-6715

"What you would expect at Deer Valley": this "romantic", ski season–only New American in a mountaintop resort lodge is where "the rich dine", but most agree it's "worth" the high-altitude prices thanks to "superb cuisine", fine service and an atmosphere of "understated elegance"; foes insist it's "stuffy" and "not as outstanding" as its rep, but as ratings attest, they're solidly outvoted.

	F	D	S	C
Market Street Broiler S	23	21	21	$20

260 S. 1300 East (300 South), Salt Lake City, 801-583-8808

Market Street Grill S

54 Market St. (off Main St., bet. 300 & 400 South), Salt Lake City, 801-322-4668

The "best fresh seafood between Seattle and Boston" at "moderate" prices explains why these Downtown fish houses (also serving ribs, steaks and pastas) are considered "consistent winners" and an "excellent value" by most surveyors; though a few say they're "overrated" and carp about "hit-or-miss" service, the fact that they're "often crowded" says a lot.

	F	D	S	C
Metropolitan, The	26	28	24	$52

173 W. Broadway (bet. 200 & 300 West), Salt Lake City, 801-364-3472

Though it draws swipes like "great place to go when your home equity loan comes through – to celebrate and because you'll need it", this "posh" Downtown Eclectic is one of the "brightest stars" on the scene and "great for impressing clients", offering "outstanding food" (though in sometimes small portions) and sharp service in a "great room"; still, revolving chefs and mile-high tabs cause some to say it's "not worth" it unless someone else pays.

	F	D	S	C
New Yorker Club	28	26	26	$37

60 W. Market St. (off Main St., bet. 300 & 400 South), Salt Lake City, 801-363-0166

A "Downtown sanctuary with staying power" and "big-city elegance" sums up "Utah's premier fine-dining spot" and the Most Popular place in our *Utah Survey*; a nearly 20-year-veteran "creative chef" turns out "outstanding" American-Continental fare, and it's "still the place to meet the in-crowd"; a few say it's "pricey" with a "stuffy" private club air, but to most this basement space is tops; N.B. there's a nightly shuttle to concerts and the theater.

	F	D	S	C
Pomodoro S	25	17	23	$24

Hillside Plaza, 2440 E. Fort Union Blvd., Sandy, 801-944-1895

Don't let the "unlikely" Sandy strip mall locale deter you; diners agree that this "innovative" Cal-Italian offers "excellent" food in a "big open room" with "friendly" service; the "garlic mashed potatoes are to die for" and "fantastic wines" add to the pleasure, as do involved owners who "show they care"; closed Mondays.

	F	D	S	C
Red Iguana S	25	12	17	$13

736 W. North Temple St. (bet. 700 & 800 West), 801-322-1489

The No. 1 Mexican in our *Utah Survey* pays little heed to decor, with a '40s functional look spiffed up by a Joe Montana cardboard cut-out; but nobody notices the surroundings given "killer Mexican food" that's arguably "best in the West"; try the "specialty moles" (10 kinds) and "great chile verdes"; N.B. the crowding has eased a bit with the opening of a center-city sibling, Blue Iguana.

	F	D	S	C
Riverhorse Cafe S	25	23	22	$32

540 Main St., Park City, 435-649-3536

There's some "very good" New American cuisine served at this second-story site where regulars advise "avoid the big", "noisy" main room in favor of "the deck in summer" or the airy atrium space; though it's pricey and some report "inconsistent quality", it still wins praise for "beautiful" presentations and "good variety", and it's a great spot to "watch the tourists."

Sundance Tree Room 🅂 | 24 | 25 | 22 | $28 |

Six miles up Provo Canyon, North Fork Canyon Rd., Sundance, 801-223-4200

■ "Look for Robert Redford" at this "delightful" Regional American where "interesting combos" of "fresh ingredients", an "excellent Sunday brunch" and a "pleasant, rustic setting" combine to create "one of Utah County's best" restaurants; a few spoilers suggest the movie star "is a better environmentalist than a restaurateur", but they're outvoted by fans who feel "Redford did it right", especially with the recent addition of a James Beard–honored chef.

Tuscany 🅂 | 23 | 28 | 22 | $27 |

2832 E. 6200 South (I-215, exit 6), Salt Lake City, 801-277-9919

◪ A "beautiful renovation" turned the Heather Restaurant into this Northern Italian that boasts former Utah Jazz center Mark Eaton as a partner; though a handful tag the food "mediocre", most praise such "excellent" fare as savory pastas, unusual salads and more; a cigar lounge (hard to find in Utah) is just one reason to plan ahead or risk a "four-week wait for weekend reservations."

San Diego

TOP 10 FOOD RANKING

	Restaurant	Cuisine Type
28	El Bizcocho	Classic/New French
27	WineSellar & Brasserie	New French
	Sushi Ota	Japanese
	Mille Fleurs	New French
	Azzura Point	Cal./Mediterranean
	Pamplemousse Grille	Californian/New French
26	Rancho Valencia	Californian/Continental
	George's at the Cove	New American
	Belgian Lion	Belgian/Classic French
	Laurel	New French

OTHER IMPORTANT PLACES

Anthony's Star of the Sea	Seafood
Cafe Japengo	Asian/Eclectic
Cafe Pacifica	Seafood
Delicias	Californian
Mixx	Eclectic
Morton's of Chicago	Steakhouse
Rainwater's	Steakhouse
Salvatore's	Northern Italian
Taka	Asian/Eclectic
Tapenade	French Bistro
Thee Bungalow	Classic French
Vignola	New French
Vivace	Northern Italian

	F	D	S	C
Anthony's Star of the Sea S	23	22	23	$39

1360 N. Harbor Dr. (Ash St.), 619-232-7408

◪ A "classic" place to "impress out-of-towners" on the Downtown waterfront, this "pricey", 30-year-old seafooder has a "formal" mood and jacket-suggested policy that help retain the favor of a well-heeled crowd; while some miss "the old menu", others find the food "improved" since the arrival of a Ritz-Carlton chef, and a redo set for early '99 should please those who cite "'60s" decor.

	F	D	S	C
Azzura Point S	27	26	25	$45

Loews Coronado Bay Resort, 4000 Coronado Bay Rd. (Silver Strand Blvd.), Coronado, 619-424-4477

■ This airy room on the second floor of the view-endowed Loews Coronado Bay Resort is where "serious" foodies join hotel guests for chef James Boyce's "innovative" Cal-Med fare as well as some "great sunsets"; it's a "special occasion vacation in our hometown" that's even more appealing now with "smashing new decor."

	F	D	S	C
Belgian Lion, The	26	21	23	$36

2265 Bacon St. (W. Point Loma Blvd.), 619-223-2700

◪ "Expensive but very good" Belgian-French in Ocean Beach that reminds some of "grandma's parlor" with its lace doily–strewn decor, but most ignore the setting and enjoy "wonderful cassoulet" and other "hearty" fare; if some claim service isn't always doting, fans revel in "personal attention" and find this Coulon family veteran "still great"; open Thursday–Saturday, dinner only.

Cafe Japengo S | 25 | 24 | 20 | $29

Hyatt Regency La Jolla, 8960 University Ctr. Ln. (bet. La Jolla Village & Lebon Drs.), 619-450-3355

◪ Emphatically "too noisy", this "yuppie heaven" at the epicenter of the Golden Triangle offers "excellent", "artistic sushi" and other Asian-inspired food in an "elegant Japanese setting" that's such a "place to be seen" for singles that those over 30 head to quieter tables in back; while staffers are "great for viewing", they can be "slow", which fuels critics who say "overrated."

Cafe Pacifica S | 25 | 22 | 22 | $31

2414 San Diego Ave. (Old Town Ave.), 619-291-6666

■ "Tremendous seafood" with an "innovative" edge is the specialty of this "consistently strong" performer on the border of historic Old Town, which "never disappoints" the knowledgeable locals and tourists who come here for "great sunsets" and a well-priced menu that draws on solid California cuisine traditions; while undeniably "charming", it "could use more space around the tables."

Delicias | 25 | 26 | 24 | $36

6106 Paseo Delicias (La Granada), Rancho Santa Fe, 619-756-8000

■ "Fresh flowers" and "beautiful" country French decor serve as the backdrop for an equally good-looking crowd at this "cozy", "comfortable" Californian in the heart of wealthy Rancho Santa Fe; while the "warm, intimate" ambiance attracts the most comments, high ratings also go to the "excellent" food and "careful" service; in sum, "worth a visit", especially for lunch.

El Bizcocho S | 28 | 26 | 26 | $44

Rancho Bernardo Inn, 17550 Bernardo Oaks Dr. (Rancho Bernardo Rd.), Rancho Bernardo 619-675-8550

■ The last bastion of black-tie service in San Diego, this grand hotel dining room may be "far, far" from Downtown in Rancho Bernardo, but it takes top honors for its "world-class" Classic and Contemporary French food; the "sublime" service and "elegant decor" add to the appeal, and while it's "pretty pricey" (especially the wine list), most agree the raves are "well deserved"; P.S. don't overlook the "best brunch" in town.

George's at the Cove S | 26 | 26 | 25 | $37

1250 Prospect St. (bet. Cave & Ivanhoe Sts.), La Jolla, 619-454-4244

■ This "real La Jolla tradition" is again voted San Diego's Most Popular restaurant thanks to "impressive" New American fare from chef Scott Meskan and a triple-tiered setting offering "romantic", "less expensive" dining "on the roof under a full moon", a pricier ground-floor main room that "can't miss for business" meals, and a bar in between; if "hospitable" host George is around, it's even easier to see why this place is "consistently on top."

Laurel Restaurant & Bar S | 26 | 26 | 22 | $38

505 Laurel St. (5th Ave.), 619-239-2222

◪ "The place to take guests who think SD is a hick town" say admirers of this "sleek, sexy", dinner-only eatery near Balboa Park, with a "big city feel" that gives an extra edge to Douglas Organ's "superb", midpriced New French cuisine; it's "great before the theater" and, as you'd expect from the younger sister of WineSellar & Brasserie, there's an "excellent wine list", so even if some find it noisy, with uneven service, more "wish they were open for lunch."

F	D	S	C

Mille Fleurs S | 27 | 27 | 26 | $54 |

Country Squire Courtyard, 6009 Paseo Delicias (Avenida de Acacias), Rancho Santa Fe, 619-756-3085

◪ Set in a blissfully beautiful Mediterranean-style villa in rural Rancho Santa Fe, this "big bucks" Contemporary French "for the horsey set" features "wonderful" food served in a "romantic" (a few say "stuffy") setting that "looks like France"; if some find the service "pompous" and the "small portions" "grossly overpriced", a majority considers owner Bertrand Hug's discreet retreat "the ideal special occasion restaurant."

Mixx S | 23 | 20 | 21 | $28 |

3671 Fifth Ave. (Pennsylvania Ave.), 619-299-6499

◪ "Innovative food" 'without boundaries' wins 'em over at this "reasonably priced" Eclectic in "trendy" Hillcrest that's quietly decorated to show off the youngish, "see and be seen" crowd; the only points of contention are over service that "could be better" and weekend blues and jazz, which some would nix and others savor; otherwise, it's "one of the best newer restaurants."

Morton's of Chicago S | 26 | 24 | 25 | $48 |

285 J St. (bet. 2nd & 3rd Aves.), 619-696-3369

■ Meat lovers would gladly "take out a second mortgage" to finance a trip to this "dark", "woody", casually elegant Downtown steak palace serving notoriously "huge portions" of the "best beef this side of Chicago"; of course, cost isn't an issue for the expense-account crowd that heads here for "first-class" food and service, and though a few find the raw meat menu cart shtick too much, most aren't cowed by it.

Pamplemousse Grille S | 27 | 24 | 25 | $43 |

514 Via de la Valle (opp. Del Mar Racetrack, bet. Jimmy Durante Blvd. & S. Coast Hwy. 101), Solana Beach, 619-792-9090

■ "Beautiful people" and horse racing types (in season) jockey for a table at this "noisy", art-filled, understatedly elegant Cal-French in an office building near the sea, where former NYer Jeffrey Strauss brings "imagination and talent" to an "exceptional, exciting" menu that's "always a treat", right down to "the best tarte Tatin in San Diego"; still, some label it "overpriced."

Rainwater's ◐ S | 25 | 22 | 24 | $38 |

1202 Kettner Blvd. (B St.), 619-233-5757

◪ "Our version of Morton's, but better" say some San Diegans of this homegrown steakhouse, a spacious, clubby "power location" "for a business lunch" on the second floor of a restored building near the Downtown waterfront; it pleases expense-account "big shots" with "delicious beef", "tempting" (if "pricey") wines and a "wine room for parties", but foes find it "stuffy" and "overrated."

Rancho Valencia S | 26 | 29 | 25 | $44 |

Rancho Valencia Resort, 5921 Valencia Circle (Rancho Diegueno Rd.), Rancho Sante Fe, 619-759-6216

■ Surveyors say "you can't beat the ambiance" at this smashingly "beautiful" room, part of the ever-so-"exclusive" Rancho Valencia Resort near Rancho Santa Fe; besides generally "superb" Cal-Continental fare with Pacific Rim accents, it boasts a "great view", "leisurely service" and the "prettiest patio" on which to "lose the day" ("feels like you're on vacation"); in sum, well "worth the drive."

Salvatore's S

25 | 23 | 23 | $34

750 Front St. (G St.), 619-544-1865

■ This long-running, "classy" favorite at the base of Downtown's most exclusive condominium tower produces "good, old-fashioned Northern Italian" fare in a "sophisticated", handsomely "rococo" setting; the "high-quality" kitchen is overseen by Raffaella Gangale while "charming" husband Salvatore plays host – so successfully that some think he "makes the experience."

Sushi Ota S

27 | 13 | 17 | $26

4529 Mission Bay Dr. (Balboa Ave.), 619-270-5670

■ Despite an "odd location" near the freeway at the backside of Pacific Beach, this Japanese shrine is "always crowded" because the chef is an "artist with a knife", turning out "creative" sushi that's "the best in San Diego"; the food is so good that "visitors from Tokyo specifically request" a visit here, and it more than makes up for "lunch counter decor" and "inconsistent service"; N.B. reservations are strongly recommended.

Taka S

26 | 19 | 21 | $29

555 Fifth Ave. (Market St.), 619-338-0555

■ The "trendy" young things who populate the Gaslamp Quarter agree that Taka is the "best" and "hippest" Downtown sushi bar, and its Asian fusion menu offers a "superb" alternative to the Italian fare that dominates the neighborhood; while the claim that "beautiful folks" get top treatment is open to debate, there's no denying the "long lines", so hunker down.

Tapenade S

– | – | – | E

7612 Fay Ave. (bet. Kline & Pearl Sts.), La Jolla, 619-551-7500

Jean-Michel and Sylvie Diot left behind successful restaurants in New York to raise their family in sunny La Jolla, and their new venture, which opened in the Downtown area in summer '98, has drawn early raves from fans who call it the "best new French" and predict it "will be big"; offering a seafood-heavy bistro menu in a breezy, South of France–like setting, it's fairly "pricey", but the well-heeled clientele doesn't seem to mind.

Thee Bungalow S

25 | 19 | 23 | $34

4996 W. Point Loma Blvd. (Bacon St.), Ocean Beach, 619-224-2884

◪ For more than a decade, chef Edmund Moore has followed a successful recipe blending generous portions, hearty French cuisine and reasonable prices at this "excellent standby" in an "old Ocean Beach house"; the older "regular crowd" sings the praises of the "best roast duck", "bargain" early-bird menu and "fantastic" value wine list, drowning out the few who think the food's too "heavy" and the decor "needs updating."

Vignola S

▽ 26 | 20 | 24 | $34

St. James Hotel, 828 Sixth Ave. (bet. E & F Sts.), 619-231-1111

■ Though too new to be widely known by surveyors, this simply but pleasantly decorated newcomer, which opened on the fringe of Downtown's sizzling Gaslamp Quarter in spring '98, is earning early praise for its "awesome foie gras" and other "innovative French fare" from "hot" chef Fabrice Poigin, who is warmly remembered from previous stints around town; "reasonable prices" and a smoothly trained young staff are pluses.

Vivace S

22 | 25 | 21 | $41

Four Seasons Resort Aviara, 7100 Four Seasons Pt. (bet. Aviara Pkwy. & Poinsettia Ln.), Carlsbad, 760-603-6999

This "beautiful" Northern Italian in Carlsbad's new, striving-for-five-stars Four Seasons Resort Aviara earns a warm reception as a "welcome addition" to the North County scene; though the well-heeled suburbanites who flock to this "elegant" enclave express some reservations ("needs to work harder on the food", "pricey"), the more lenient note that it's "still new" and improving.

WineSellar & Brasserie S

27 | 20 | 25 | $42

9550 Waples St. (bet. Mira Mesa Blvd. & Steadman St.), 619-450-9557

Douglas Organ is too old now to be the enfant terrible of San Diego chefs, but his casually chic, New French "hidden gem" in Sorrento Mesa remains a true "original" that's "worth a trip to the warehouse district", offering "the best marriage of food and wine" as well as "attentive service"; some find it "too expensive for the decor", but with 3,000 wines to choose from and a six-variety tasting every Saturday (lunch optional), it's "heaven" for oenophiles.

San Francisco Bay Area

TOP 20 FOOD RANKING

	Restaurant	Cuisine Type
29	French Laundry	American/French
28	La Folie	New French
	Masa's	New French
	Ritz-Carlton Din. Rm.	New French
	Chez Panisse	Californian
	Terra	American/Continental
27	Fleur de Lys	New French
	Sent Sovi	American/French
	Chez Panisse Cafe	Californian
	Aqua	Cal-French/Seafood
	Erna's Elderberry	Californian/New French
	Pacific's Edge	Californian
26	Campton Place	New American
	Boulevard	New American
	Fringale	French Bistro
	Postrio	Californian
	Roy's at Pebble Beach	PacificRim
	Hawthorne Lane	New American
	231 Ellsworth	Classic/New French
	Acquerello	Northern Italian

OTHER IMPORTANT PLACES

Bistro Jeanty	French Bistro
Charles Nob Hill	New French
Chez Michel	New French
Cypress Club	Californian/New French
Domaine Chandon	Californian/New French
Eos	Eclectic/Euro-Asian
Farallon	Californian/Seafood
Globe	New American
Grand Cafe	Californian/New French
House	Asian/New American
Jardiniere	New French
Lark Creek Inn	Traditional American
mc^2	Californian/New French
Meetinghouse	New American
MoMo's	New American
Moose's	Californian
Oliveto	Italian/Med.
Park Grill	Continental
PlumpJack Cafe	Mediterranean
Rose Pistola	Northern Italian
Rubicon	Californian/New French
Scala's Bistro	French/Italian
Shanghai 1930	Chinese
Slanted Door	Vietnamese
Spago Palo Alto	Californian
Tommy Toy's	Chinese
Tra Vigne	N/S Italian
Viognier	Cal./Mediterranean
Vivande	N/S Italian
Wente Vineyards	Californian/Italian

Acquerello | 26 | 22 | 25 | $50

1722 Sacramento St. (bet. Polk St. & Van Ness Ave.), 415-567-5432

■ The white truffle pasta is "worth every scent" at this "romantic", "blissfully subdued" and "costly" Van Ness/Polk "haute Italian"; a few dissenters say "its appeal eludes me", but "suave" waiters, a "fabulous wine list" and "truly elegant" decor have most thinking they've "dined and gone to Tuscany."

Aqua | 27 | 26 | 24 | $54

252 California St. (bet. Battery & Front Sts.), 415-956-9662

■ "Still-stellar", "top-end" Downtown Cal-French that's "heaven for the ichthyophagous" (i.e. a fish eater's paradise), dazzling diners with "enthralling seafood" in a "beautiful, classy and sophisticated" setting; despite quibbles over "tiny portions" and a staff that, while "extremely attentive", strikes some as "just shy of pretentious", most sigh "superb from the minute you walk in the door."

Bistro Jeanty S | – | – | – | M

6510 Washington St. (east of Hwy. 29), Yountville, 707-944-0103

Restaurant-goers like what they taste at this "very authentic" French in Yountville, run by popular Napa Valley chef Philippe Jeanty (ex Domaine Chandon); presenting "excellent Jeanty fare" that sticks to proven bistro classics like rabbit and cassoulet, it's "already a big hit" with foodies who are bored with fuss and fusion.

Boulevard S | 26 | 26 | 24 | $47

1 Mission St. (Steuart St.), 415-543-6084

■ "Still fabulous after all these years", Nancy Oakes' SOMA art nouveau–style New American has become for many the "standard by which SF should be judged"; if cynics decry "gussied-up comfort food", most praise the "flat-out scrumptious" fare and "pampering" by a "top-of-the-line" staff; in short, "Nancy walks the walk" and Boulevard is once again voted SF's Most Popular restaurant.

Campton Place S | 26 | 26 | 25 | $52

Campton Place Hotel, 340 Stockton St. (bet. Post & Sutter Sts.), 415-955-5555

■ "Everything works" say fans of this Downtown New American: "breakfast, lunch or dinner – they're all winners", due to chef Todd Humphries' "delicious, unusual cuisine", plus the "impeccable service" and "serene" ambiance ("like eating in a bank vault"); a few concede that while the "amazing flavors" are "always a delight", they "long for larger portions at these prices."

Charles Nob Hill S | 25 | 25 | 25 | $58

1250 Jones St. (Clay St.), 415-771-5400

◪ "A secret" waiting to be discovered, this "elegant" Nob Hill New French in an "intimate" flower-filled setting that feels like "Europe of 100 years ago" showcases "chef-to-watch" Ron Siegel's "superb" menu (laced with "surprise treats") and "gracious", "polished" service; yes, it's "expensive", but . . . "wow."

Chez Michel S | 25 | 23 | 22 | $51

804 N. Point St. (Hyde St.), 415-775-7036

◪ "Take your French friends" and "prepare to be schmoozed" by host-owner Michel Elkaim (whose "loquacious" approach draws mixed reactions) at this pricey "society hangout"; its "outstanding" New French menu, "sophisticated" ambiance and "impeccable service" make it an "oasis of civility" near Fisherman's Wharf.

Chez Panisse
28 | 24 | 26 | $61

1517 Shattuck Ave. (bet. Cedar & Vine Sts.), Berkeley, 510-548-5525

■ "Why pay to fly to Provence?" – Alice Waters' "temple of Californian cuisine" is a "joy" that "can't be beaten", set in a "lovely" Arts and Crafts house in North Berkeley; "each course is a revelation", explained by "intelligent" servers, and though a few who refuse to genuflect snap "don't teach me how to eat at these prices", most consider this "the quintessence of great dining"; N.B. there is a set menu and reservations are essential.

Chez Panisse Cafe
27 | 22 | 23 | $37

1517 Shattuck Ave. (bet. Cedar & Vine Sts.), Berkeley, 510-548-5049

■ Alice Waters "sets the standard" with this "uncompromisingly good" cafe upstairs from her fabled Berkeley restaurant, where "incredible" Californian cuisine is served with "great spirit" and "seasonal changes keep it interesting"; no-rezzies means you "could grow old waiting", but most "wouldn't mind" in pursuit of what may be the "best informal dinner in America."

Cypress Club S
21 | 25 | 20 | $45

500 Jackson St. (bet. Columbus Ave. & Montgomery St.), 415-296-8555

◪ "Straight out of *Alice in Wonderland*" "on acid", this North Beach Cal–New French supper club, "emphatically" decorated with "impressive breast-shaped light fixtures", is a "loud, wild, great place to party" with sometimes "surprisingly excellent" food, "divine" desserts and a stellar wine list; a few naysayers claim the "party's over" (the kitchen "sometimes misses" and "service needs help"), but it's still a "fun-timer" for most.

Domaine Chandon S
25 | 25 | 24 | $49

1 California Dr. (Hwy. 29), Yountville, 707-944-2892

■ "What's not to like?" – this New French–Californian at the Domaine Chandon winery covers all bets with "superb food", "elegant" indoor/outdoor ambiance, the "nicest staff in the Valley", "world-class" desserts and a great wine list; concern over the departure of longtime chef Philippe Jeanty (see Bistro Jeanty) has been dispelled by the "quality and style" of Robert Curry's new regime; prices are "out of sight", but "to eat better you'll have to fly to France."

Eos Restaurant & Wine Bar S
25 | 20 | 21 | $38

901 Cole St. (Carl St.), 415-566-3063

■ "Innovator" Arnold Eric Wong achieves an "impeccable fusion" of East and West at his "stylish" Cole Valley bistro where the "flavorful" fare and "architecturally stunning presentations" pair beautifully with the "amazing wine list" from the adjacent "warm and casual wine bar"; a few critics cite "too much hype" and claim "prices are soaring with success", but to those who have long asked "when will they get valet parking?" – they finally have.

Erna's Elderberry House S
27 | 27 | 27 | $67

48688 Victoria Ln. (Hwy. 41), Oakhurst, 209-683-6800

■ Take a "worthwhile trip" to this "exquisite" gourmet destination near Yosemite National Park, where the "château ambiance" and "imaginative menus" (Cal-French with Austrian accents) contribute to the sense of "luxurious" "event" dining; most feel it's "absolutely outstanding" – "simply one of the best restaurants in America."

Farallon S 24 | 27 | 23 | $52

450 Post St. (bet. Mason & Powell Sts.), 415-956-6969

■ Plunge into an "undersea adventure of the most appetizing kind" at this lavish Downtown Californian seafooder dressed in the "best Pat Kuleto design yet", complete with jellyfish lamps; but "don't let the whimsical decor fool you – this is serious food", prepared by Mark Franz and served by an "attentive" staff; a few critics call it an "overpriced trip to SeaWorld" but fish lovers find it "fabulous."

Fleur de Lys 27 | 27 | 26 | $67

777 Sutter St. (bet. Jones & Taylor Sts.), 415-673-7779

■ Gourmands are "still in love with chef Hubert Keller" and most find "not a flaw" at his "endlessly satisfying" Downtown New French with "smooth-as-silk" service, a "stunningly beautiful", newly redecorated room and cuisine that's "a celebration for the taste buds"; "Hubert cares about food and his guests", and though a few find the ambiance slightly "stuffy", this "dazzling" (and costly) gem is just about "perfect" in nearly everyone's book.

French Laundry S 29 | 27 | 28 | $74

6640 Washington St. (Creek St.), Yountville, 707-944-2380

■ "Words can't describe it", but everyone tries: chef Thomas Keller puts "artistry and thought" into each dish at this Napa French-American, earning it SF's No. 1 Food rating; "indefatigable service" keeps the plates flowing with "clockwork precision" while diners bask in the "epitome of class and refinement"; it's arguably the "most exciting place to eat in America", but prices are "amazing" too and since everyone wants a taste of "pure heaven", reserve far in advance.

Fringale 26 | 19 | 22 | $38

570 Fourth St. (bet. Brannan & Bryant Sts.), 415-543-0573

■ Francophiles get a "frisson of delight" at this "outstanding" SOMA French where chef Gerald Hirigoyen executes "creative and exceptional" "contemporary" bistro cuisine accented with Basque influences; though it's "cramped" and "service can be erratic", a "lively", "happy atmosphere" pervades the "intimate" room and most agree they're "never disappointed" here; P.S. "reserve way ahead" – but still expect to "wait."

Globe ◐ 21 | 18 | 19 | $36

290 Pacific Ave. (bet. Battery & Front Sts.), 415-391-4132

◪ This "hip", "hot" Downtown "late-night" "scene" projects a "NYC ambiance" with "cramped" seating and a "noisy", "diverse" crowd that appreciates ex-Spago chef Joseph Manzare's "truly astonishing" New American fare (this is "where the other chefs in town eat") and a front of the house that "always makes you feel welcome"; doubters who complain about the "hype" wonder "what's the big deal?"

Grand Cafe S 21 | 26 | 21 | $35

Hotel Monaco, 501 Geary St. (Taylor St.), 415-292-0101

◪ Evocative of "Paris in the '30s", the "dramatic", "stylish" and "elegant" beaux arts setting is the main draw at this Downtown New French–Californian; although the food is "vastly improved" (the signature polenta soufflé is "heavenly" and desserts are "astonishing"), many diners still wish it would "live up to the room"; nevertheless, it's one of the "best choices in the Theater District."

Hawthorne Lane 🅂 | 26 | 25 | 24 | $49 |

22 Hawthorne St. (bet. 2nd & 3rd Sts.), 415-777-9779

■ "The big hitters gather" at Anne and David Gingrass' "highly regarded" Downtown Cal–New American to indulge in "superb food" (from "amazing appetizers" to "desserts that are works of art") served by a staff that attends to "every little detail" in an "elegant setting"; a few critics quibble about "bird-sized" portions and think the cavernous space lacks "soul", but most who've walked down this Lane find it "everything a restaurant should be."

House | 23 | 17 | 20 | $29 |

1230 Grant Ave. (bet. Columbus Ave. & Vallejo St.), 415-986-8612
1269 Ninth Ave. (bet. Irving St. & Lincoln Way), 415-682-3898 🅂

■ These "lively", "surprisingly affordable" North Beach and Inner Sunset Asian–New American siblings with "minimalist decor" have surveyors "hankering" for the "big tastes and big portions" of their "always interesting and delicious" delights like "must-try sea bass" and "wonderful noodles"; they can be "noisy, noisy" and while a few grumblers claim "this fusion stuff can be overrated", to most they're "hip joints with good food" that "never disappoints."

Jardiniere 🅂 | 25 | 26 | 22 | $51 |

300 Grove St. (Franklin St.), 415-861-5555

■ "Traci does it again" – Traci des Jardins' "flashy" and "fabulous" Civic Center supper club designed by Pat Kuleto features a "snazzy" central bar and packs "more glitz than a Hollywood premiere", making it a true "occasion restaurant"; even those who cringe at "obscene prices" and small portions ("bring tweezers") admit that the "stunning" New French food can induce "love at first bite" and applaud "smashing service"; in sum, "*extraordinaire*."

La Folie | 28 | 23 | 25 | $62 |

2316 Polk St. (bet. Green & Union Sts.), 415-776-5577

■ Roland Passot's "close to perfect" Van Ness/Polk New French is "at the very top" of its class – the "true craftsmanship in the kitchen" is abetted by "wonderful presentation" and "impeccable service"; throw in a "breathtaking room" and "superb wine list" and it rates as the "best super splurge in town", so "bring your armored car" and treat yourself.

Lark Creek Inn 🅂 | 24 | 25 | 23 | $41 |

234 Magnolia Ave. (Tamalpais Dr.), Larkspur, 415-924-7766

◪ "After a few flat notes", this Lark is "singing" again; the kitchen at Brad Ogden's Larkspur American is producing "some superb cooking" and a "terrific brunch", enhanced by "gracious" service; the lavish decor ("Martha Stewart's dream come true") is balanced by a redwood garden where you can dine in "your hiking clothes."

Masa's | 28 | 25 | 27 | $78 |

Hotel Vintage Court, 648 Bush St. (bet. Powell & Stockton Sts.), 415-989-7154

■ "Words can't describe" dining at this "simply superb" Downtown French, and though revered chef Julian ("what can you say about brilliance?") Serrano has packed his bags for Las Vegas (putting a question mark next to the above food rating), no changes are planned for the "astonishing" menu as new chef Chad Callahan takes over; since the same formal decor, "subdued" ambiance and "flawless service" should prevail, it's likely to remain "sublime."

mc² ◐ S | – | – | – | E

470 Pacific Ave. (Montgomery St.), 415-956-0666

Check out your sense of relativity at this pricey, style-conscious new Downtown Cal-French in the landmark Barbary Coast Building whose design is light-years ahead of the competition thanks to Mark Cavagnero, the co-architect responsible for the redo of the California Palace of the Legion of Honor; in the kitchen, Yoshi Kojima creates stunning, refined cuisine with Japanese overtones.

Meetinghouse, The | 24 | 21 | 23 | $39

1701 Octavia St. (Bush St.), 415-922-6733

■ Most predict this "upscale", "fine-tuned" Pacific Heights New American offering "uncomplicated yet innovative selections" from a "limited but well-prepared menu" is "destined for the long run"; the Shaker-inspired decor is "simple, clean and homey", service is "friendly and professional" and the all-American wine list is choice.

MoMo's S.F. Grill S | – | – | – | E

760 Second St. (Embarcadero), 415-227-8660

This lavishly designed SOMA New American hit the South Beach area with a splash in summer '98, gearing up early for the crowds-to-come from nearby PacBell Park; in the classic grill-style dining room, the oversized, play-ball menu features Tricia Tracy's (ex Roti) fabulous comfort food, and there's also a cheery alfresco patio and happening bar scene.

Moose's S | 21 | 21 | 20 | $36

1652 Stockton St. (bet. Filbert & Union Sts.), 415-989-7800

■ Ed Moose's "upbeat" Californian on Washington Square is a "movers and shakers hangout" exuding "class, style" and "SF energy"; patrons laud chef Brian Whitmer's "professional food", as well as the "knowledgeable" staff; since "Moose runs a good show", this is one hot spot that "never disappoints."

Oliveto Cafe & Restaurant S | 24 | 21 | 20 | $41

5655 College Ave. (Shafter Ave.), Oakland, 510-547-5356

◪ Ex Chez Panisse chef Paul Bertoli's "cutting-edge Mediterranean fare" at this "scintillating" East Bay Italian includes "melt-in-your-mouth pasta", gnocchi "like little clouds" and "great roasted game"; a few naysayers argue that its "reputation exceeds reality" and report "unenthusiastic service", but most agree this place "seems to improve with age" and rate it "Oakland's finest."

Pacific's Edge S | 27 | 28 | 24 | $57

Highlands Inn, Hwy. 1 (Highland Dr.), Carmel, 831-622-5445

■ "Believe all the hype": this wallet-whomping Carmel Californian is "one of the best in the West", with "fine cuisine", a "superb wine list", "savvy servers" and "stark interiors" designed to enhance the "out-of-this-world view"; most think it edges close to "absolute perfection" and suggest "take someone you love."

Park Grill S | 24 | 21 | 22 | $38

Park Hyatt Hotel, 333 Battery St. (Clay St.), 415-296-2933

■ For "power eating" in "beautiful surroundings", this "gem" in the Park Hyatt offers "splendid" Continental fare, "wonderful service" and a "clubby atmosphere"; it's the "perfect business lunch" or dinner choice and rates as one of the "best hotel restaurants in the city", but a few find it "a little stuffy for pleasure dining."

PlumpJack Cafe | 25 | 22 | 23 | $42 |

3127 Fillmore St. (bet. Filbert & Greenwich Sts.), 415-563-4755

■ This "intimate" Union Street Mediterranean is the "apotheosis of yuppie chic" and attracts a "clubby" society clientele, but it's "not as pretentious as it appears"; chef Maria Helm's "wonderful food", a "high-caliber" retail-priced wine list and "unfussy", "very informed servers" make it "just swell" in nearly everyone's book; the new Tahoe location shares similar assets.

Postrio S | 26 | 26 | 24 | $50 |

Prescott Hotel, 545 Post St. (bet. Mason & Taylor Sts.), 415-776-7825

■ "It's all been said before and it's all true": Wolfgang Puck's "visually impressive" SF outpost on Post is a high-ticket "power spot" where "stellar" Cal cuisine courtesy of chefs Mitchell and Steven Rosenthal is matched with "impeccable service"; surveyors confirm the high standards at this "continuing classic" – "yes, they are as good as they think they are"; P.S. it's "great for breakfast" too.

Ritz-Carlton Dining Room | 28 | 28 | 28 | $63 |

Ritz-Carlton Hotel, 600 Stockton St. (bet. California & Pine Sts.), 415-296-7465

■ The "last word in pampered elegance", this "benchmark" New French in the Ritz-Carlton Hotel continues to "live up to its reputation"; challenge your overdraft protection and settle into "opulent" surroundings for "above and beyond" service and chef Sylvain Portay's "impeccable food", which includes "generous amounts" of truffles and caviar; "if you're going to spend a bundle, do it here."

Rose Pistola ◐S | 22 | 20 | 18 | $36 |

532 Columbus Ave. (bet. Green & Union Sts.), 415-399-0499

◪ Reed Hearon's premium "see and be seen" Italian creates "a lot of buzz" with its stylish, "inviting room" and family-style servings of "rustic" but "expertly executed" Ligurian dishes "whose flavors sing"; some suspect a case of "overhype", reporting "snobby attitude" and "almost intolerable noise", but most say it "deserves every laudatory comment" and call it "tops in North Beach."

Roy's at Pebble Beach S | 26 | 26 | 24 | $44 |

The Inn at Spanish Bay, 2700 17 Mile Dr. (Congress Rd.), Pebble Beach, 408-647-7423

■ With its "breathtaking setting" overlooking Pebble Beach, Roy Yamaguchi's "celebration place" on 17 Mile Drive is designed to spare diners a "trip to Honolulu"; the "inspired" Pacific Rim cuisine draws on Eastern and Western influences to weave a "culinary dream", and the "extremely friendly, warm" ambiance bids aloha; this one's "not to be missed" for the island vibes.

Rubicon | 23 | 20 | 21 | $47 |

558 Sacramento St. (bet. Montgomery & Sansome Sts.), 415-434-4100

◪ A "button-down crowd" soaks up the "clubby ambiance" at this expensive Downtown New French–Californian backed by investors Robert De Niro, Francis Ford Coppola, Robin Williams and NYC restaurateur Drew Nieporent; though a few say it "looks great but has no soul", many do cross this Rubicon for chef Scott Newman's "really creative" menu and the "outrageous" desserts, while some feel that sommelier Larry Stone and his "extremely sophisticated wine list" "are the hit here."

Scala's Bistro ◐ S | 23 | 23 | 21 | $36 |

Sir Francis Drake Hotel, 432 Powell St. (bet. Post & Sutter Sts.), 415-395-8555
■ You "can't go wrong" at this "hip" Union Square bistro where a "zesty energy infuses the whole experience", from the "interesting, varied" French-Italian menu to the "warm, happy atmosphere" and "superfriendly waiters"; though it might be "too hectic" at times and "a bit busy for intimate conversation", this "tough reservation is worth it" and night owls gloat that "the kitchen is open late."

Sent Sovi S | 27 | 21 | 24 | $51 |

14583 Big Basin Way (5th St.), Saratoga, 408-867-3110
◪ "Genius" David Kinch is the talent behind the "enormously satisfying" cuisine at this "fabulous" top-dollar French-American in Saratoga; foes who call it "pompous" are badly outnumbered by devotees who dub the service "elegant" and wish the restaurant were "closer to home."

Shanghai 1930 S | 19 | 23 | 17 | $38 |

133 Steuart St. (bet. Howard & Mission Sts.), 415-896-5600
◪ George Chen's popular SOMA Chinese offers "innovative Asian dishes" in a "distinguished" ambiance that's "like being transported to an era of elegance"; if a few feel "shanghaied" by "overpriced", "small portions", most maintain this "exciting newcomer" is a place to "bask in luxury"; P.S. there's "super jazz" Tuesday–Saturday.

Slanted Door S | 25 | 19 | 18 | $28 |

584 Valencia St. (17th St.), 415-861-8032
■ At this "dynamite" Mission "nouveau Vietnamese", "eating is an art form" thanks to an "inspired" menu ("believe the hype"); it might be in a "dicey" locale and "too noisy", but its "knowledgeable staff" and "sexy" ambiance ("dress hip") make some call it "one of the city's best"; P.S. "take a cab" as "parking is nonexistent."

Spago Palo Alto S | 25 | 23 | 23 | $52 |

265 Lytton Ave. (Bryant St.), Palo Alto, 650-833-1000
■ Stargazers report there are "no celebrities" at the pricey Peninsula version of Wolfgang Puck's signature Californian, but the food puts on a "spectacular" show of its own ("wow"); the "lively ambiance" and "unbelievably good" service add to the sparkle; now "Silicon Valley movers and shakers" have a Puck installation to themselves – "it's about time, Wolf!"

Terra S | 28 | 25 | 26 | $51 |

1345 Railroad Ave. (bet. Adams & Hunt Sts.), St. Helena, 707-963-8931
■ "Hiro is heroic!": Hiro Sone's highly rated and "way understated" St. Helena destination is a fave for "serious dining" on "exquisite" cuisine that melds American and Continental influences; prices are extraterrestrial, but the "staff takes care of you" and the ambiance is "cozy and welcoming", making it "fabulous from start to finish."

Tommy Toy's Cuisine Chinoise S | 25 | 25 | 24 | $50 |

655 Montgomery St. (Washington St.), 415-397-4888
■ Tommy Toy's "simply marvelous" Downtown Chinese is a "ritzy", "gorgeous venue" with "seductive", French-tinged cuisine, if sometimes "overwhelming service" (some claim they may try to "talk you into the high-end prix fixe"); yes, it's "expensive", but "if you want to be spoiled", this is the place.

Tra Vigne S 25 25 22 $39

1050 Charter Oak Ave. (Hwy. 29), St. Helena, 707-963-4444

■ St. Helena Italian hot spot with a "villa setting" and a patio amid the vineyards that's "pure escapism"; the kitchen follows through with consistently "excellent" cuisine and service gets good marks too; a few skeptics say it's "overrated", but the majority is enchanted: "you could be in Tuscany."

231 Ellsworth 26 20 25 $45

231 S. Ellsworth Ave. (bet. 2nd & 3rd Aves.), San Mateo, 650-347-7231

■ "Still tops in the 'burbs" on many scorecards, this "excellent" San Mateo French delivers "beautifully presented food" and "extremely attentive service"; it may be "a little dark" and due for "remodeling", but it's a "Peninsula standby" and partisans say "it still knocks me out"; P.S. the prix fixe lunch is a "gourmet bargain."

Viognier S 24 21 20 $43

Draeger's Mkt., 222 E. Fourth Ave. (bet. B St. & Ellsworth Ave.), San Mateo, 650-685-3727

■ "Perfectly executed cooking" courtesy of chef Gary Danko (ex Ritz-Carlton Dining Room) is the calling card of this San Mateo Cal-Mediterranean; aficionados claim "one can taste the essence" of the ingredients and deem it "heaven for discriminating palates", though some say "Danko needs a staff to match" his ambition.

Vivande Ristorante S 21 22 20 $39

Opera Plaza, 670 Golden Gate Ave. (bet. Franklin St. & Van Ness Ave.), 415-673-9245

◪ "When you want to be civilized", admirers recommend the "beautiful setting" and "grand style" of Carlo Middione's showcase Civic Center Italian, with a Sicilian-inspired menu that's also deemed an "elegant treat"; the less enthused find the food "expensive for what you get" and say it "doesn't live up to the decor", yet it remains a "destination" for many who rate it "lick-the-plate good"; the racy Pompeian murals in the bathrooms have bluenoses gasping "what next?"

Wente Vineyards S 25 25 24 $42

5050 Arroyo Rd. (Wetmore Rd.), Livermore, 925-456-2450

■ Chef Kimball Jones' "superb" regional Cal-Italian cuisine is "worth the journey" to Wente Vineyards in Livermore for a meal that beautifully complements the "wonderful wine list"; the "marvelous setting" with "outstanding views" is "perfect for a romantic night" and most repeat visitors "love it every time."

TOP 5 FOOD RANKING

	Restaurant	Cuisine Type
25	Santacafe	Eclectic
	Cafe Pasqual's	Southwestern
24	Coyote Cafe	Southwestern
	Carlos' Gosp'l Cafe	Sandwiches
	India Palace	Indian

OTHER IMPORTANT PLACES

El Farol	Mexican/Spanish
Geronimo	Southwestern
Inn of the Anasazi	Southwestern
La Casa Sena	New Mexican/SW
La Choza	New Mexican
Old Mexico Grill	Mexican
Pink Adobe	Continental/SW
Pranzo Italian Grill	N/S Italian
Rancho de Chimayo	New Mexican
Shed	New Mexican

F | D | S | C

Cafe Pasqual's S — 25 | 19 | 21 | $21
121 Don Gaspar Ave. (Water St.), 505-983-9340
There's "always a line" at this midpriced "funky and fun" Southwestern cafe a block south of the Plaza, but it's "worth the wait" for "the best people-watching in town" and creative cuisine like salmon burritos and "simply the best Sunday breakfast anywhere"; dissenters liken it to a "cattle call."

Carlos' Gosp'l Cafe — 24 | 16 | 21 | $9
125 Lincoln Ave. (bet. Marcy St. & Palace Ave.), 505-983-1841
A local favorite, this lunch-only soup and sandwich cafe with a "nice little patio" is renowned for dishes like Hangover Stew, the Alice B. Toklas sandwich and "the best lemon meringue pie anywhere"; it's "not fancy, just good."

Coyote Cafe S — 24 | 24 | 23 | $38
132 W. Water St. (bet. Don Gaspar Ave. & Galisteo St.), 505-983-1615
While some Santa Fe natives consider chef Mark Miller's place an "overrated" "tourist trap", plenty of "locals do dine here and love it", praising "the most creative menu in town" and voting it Santa Fe's Most Popular restaurant; his "innovative" Southwest cuisine, marked by "big flavors" and an original "use of chile", is "always a surprise" and, for most, "well worth the cost."

El Farol S — 20 | 21 | 18 | $24
808 Canyon Rd. (Camino del Monte Sol), 505-983-9912
A "heavy local scene" for "drinking and dancing", this cozy adobe Spanish-Mexican is a "classic" of its type and fun for solo travelers; the tapas are "interesting", "especially the calamari with romesco sauce", but "can easily become a very expensive meal."

	F	D	S	C
Geronimo S	24	26	22	$35

724 Canyon Rd. (Camino del Monte Sol), 505-982-1500
■ Housed in a "beautiful" 150-year-old adobe, this pricey "hidden gem" on Santa Fe's old artist road is "classy without being snobby" and offers what admirers call "the most creative Southwest contemporary cooking"; apart from a few complaints about service, most say it provides a "lovely experience anytime."

	F	D	S	C
India Palace S	24	21	23	$21

227 Don Gaspar Ave. (Water St.), 505-986-5859
■ "One of Santa Fe's best, most consistent and friendliest", this "absolutely great all-around" Indian serves what devotees call the "best curry this side of Bombay"; white tablecloths and candles give it a "special occasion" feel, although some note the "staff always seems to be better attired than the guests."

	F	D	S	C
Inn of the Anasazi S	24	25	23	$38

Inn of the Anasazi, 113 Washington Ave. (bet. Marcy St. & Palace Ave.), 505-988-3236
◪ Highlighting seafood and vegetarian specials, this "pricey but top-drawer" Southwestern a half block from the Plaza offers "imaginative, exquisitely prepared" "nouvelle and natural" cuisine; handcrafted elegance gives this inn the look of a "European hotel", and the food presentation is as "gorgeous" as the decor; dissenters find both food and service "uneven", but they're outvoted.

	F	D	S	C
La Casa Sena S	22	24	22	$30

125 E. Palace Ave. (Washington Ave.), 505-988-9232
◪ Yes, there was a fire, but the "charming decor" in this historic Sena Plaza casa has been preserved, and the New Mexican–Southwestern food has flair, with praise going to the trout cooked in clay and "heavenly" enchiladas; it "may be touristy, but it exudes charm"; waiters belt out "great tunes" in the adjoining cantina.

	F	D	S	C
La Choza	23	19	20	$14

905 Alarid St. (bet. Cerrillos Rd. & St. Francis Dr.), 505-982-0909
■ A "nice alternative to touristy New Mexican"; locals don't like to tell folks about La Choza (same owner as The Shed) and its "fabulous green chile" and red enchiladas – not to mention the mocha cake, all of which makes for a "good, inexpensive family dinner"; lunch lines are shorter than The Shed's.

	F	D	S	C
Old Mexico Grill S	23	18	19	$20

2434 Cerrillos Rd. (St. Michaels Dr.), 505-473-0338
■ "Fine dining in a strip mall" is what you get at this eatery with "no atmosphere, but who cares?" – its "open grill" turns out "true Mexican food" including "fantastic lamb dishes" and "the best fajitas"; according to surveyors, it's "like a visit to Mexico without worrying about any gastrointestinal consequences."

	F	D	S	C
Pink Adobe S	21	24	21	$27

406 Old Santa Fe Trail (Alameda St.), 505-983-7712
◪ Housed in a "cozy" old pink adobe, this "piece of history" with a Continental-SW menu still offers what some call the "best steak around", especially Steak Dunnigan (with mushrooms and green chile); "Gypsy Stew on a snowy day" can't be beat, but modernists say "they need to add to the menu" and some find it "too crowded."

	F	D	S	C
Pranzo Italian Grill 🅂	22	22	21	$23

540 Montezuma Ave. (Guadalupe St.), 505-984-2645
◪ "Best Italian for the price" say fans of this "consistent standby" offering "excellent value in a town where that's never the case"; "good pizza" and salads and service "without attitude" make it a "great local" resource; on the downside, it sometimes feels "too crowded and rushed."

	F	D	S	C
Rancho de Chimayo 🅂	20	24	19	$20

Santa Fe County Rd. 98 (¼ mi. off Hwy. 76), Chimayo, 505-351-4444
◪ "Not a restaurant – an experience"; drive to this New Mexican at sunset, sit on the terraced patio, have a blue margarita and the carne adovada burrito and you'll see why it's "an institution"; critics cite "average" food and say "beware of tour buses."

	F	D	S	C
Santacafe 🅂	25	25	23	$37

231 Washington Ave. (bet. Marcy St. & Paseo de Peralta), 505-984-1788
◪ With its Southwestern and "Asian slant" on Eclectic cuisine and "elegant", "minimalist decor", this favorite (rated No. 1 for Food in Santa Fe) is "still king of the hill"; fans love its "creative" appetizers, "superb wine list" and historic adobe setting with courtyard dining a block north of the Plaza; but a handful find it "overpriced" and "too snooty."

	F	D	S	C
Shed, The	21	20	19	$17

113½ E. Palace Ave. (bet. Cathedral Pl. & Washington Ave.), 505-982-9030
■ In a "great old building" (circa 1692) with "low doors and bright paint", this "adorable" New Mexican is a "local institution" and "perennial Downtown lunch favorite"; prices are low and its "red chile is the benchmark", so expect "long lines" – but admirers say "if you can get in, it's worth it."

TOP 15 FOOD RANKING

	Restaurant	Cuisine Type
28	Rover's	New French
27	Campagne	New French
	Shiro's	Japanese
26	Georgian Room	American/Continental
	Shoalwater	Northwestern
	Fullers	Northwestern
	Christina's	Northwestern
	Szmania's	Northwestern
	Wild Ginger	Pan-Asian
	Reiner's	Continental
	Relais	Classic French
	Kaspar's	Northwestern
	Dahlia Lounge	Asian/NW
	Cafe Campagne	French Bistro
25	Wildflowers	Northwestern

OTHER IMPORTANT PLACES

Anthony's Pier 66	NW/Seafood
Cafe Lago	N/S Italian
Canlis	Traditional American
El Gaucho	Steakhouse
Etta's Seafood	NW/Seafood
Flying Fish	Seafood
Il Terrazzo Carmine	N/S Italian
Lampreia	Eclectic
Marco's Supperclub	Eclectic
Palace Kitchen	Eclectic
Place Pigalle	Eclectic
Saleh al Lago	N/S Italian

F | D | S | C

Anthony's Pier 66 & Bell St. Diner S — | — | — | M

2201 Alaskan Way (Pier 66/Bell St. Pier), 206-448-6688

A bustling, bi-level class act on the waterfront, this high-end branch of the popular Anthony's HomePort chain provides high-quality seafood and service with a smile (despite swarms of tourists); downstairs is a casual, industrial-style diner (with a promenade-side fast-service fish bar); upstairs, there's a handsome NW–Pacific Rim dinner venue with a panoramic view.

Cafe Campagne S 26 | 23 | 22 | $22

Pike Place Mkt., 1600 Post Alley (Pine St.), 206-728-2233

■ "Been there, love that!" sigh regulars as they wait with tourists in picturesque Post Alley for a coveted table at the less-expensive, "me-too version" of its upstairs sibling, Campagne; Peter Lewis' charming French bistro "breathes Left Bank Paris" and features "the Market's best breakfast", "terrific roast chicken" and more.

Cafe Lago S | 24 | 19 | 20 | $23

2305 24th Ave. E. (bet. Lynn & McGraw Sts.), 206-329-8005

"Incredible" lasagna and other "superfresh pastas" result from the "apparent loving care" that Jordi Viladas and Carla Leonardi take at their "always packed" Montlake trattoria; a wood-fired oven produces "fantastic" thin-crust pizzas and the antipasti "sampler is amazing"; complaints are about "high wine prices", "small portions" and "long waits" because it's "gotten too popular."

Campagne S | 27 | 25 | 25 | $38

Pike Place Mkt., 86 Pine St. (Post Alley), 206-728-2800

"Peter Lewis and staff should be elevated to sainthood" say those who know that when you "want to be pampered", dinner at this "intimate", "Euro-elegant" French is "like one long caress"; chef Jim Drohman's "exciting" fare "keeps getting better", making this tops "for special occasions"; "overpriced", some claim, but "you get what you pay for"; "the bar is even more romantic."

Canlis | 21 | 23 | 23 | $43

2576 Aurora Ave. N. (Halladay St.), 206-283-3313

"Old Seattle goes to celebrate" at this culinary landmark with a "spectacular view"; dissed in the past as "dazzling in the '50s, faded in the '90s", this "survivor" with an award-winning wine list has had an extensive makeover, adding more private dining space while retaining its noted elegance; the Traditional American menu too has seen change, and is now tweaked with seasonal NW ingredients rather than the "Polynesian flavors" that helped make this haven for "expense-accounters" a "worthy institution."

Christina's S | 26 | 23 | 24 | $34

Porter Bldg., Main St., 2nd fl. (North Beach Rd.), Eastsound, Orcas Island, 360-376-4904

It's easy to think you're "in heaven" at Christina Orchid's "cozy", waterside Orcas Island "gem"; "creative", "contemporary NW cuisine", "the highest-quality seafood" (much of it local), "a great wine list" and "a beautiful outdoor deck" make for "sophisticated" fine dining that many rate "the best in the San Juan Islands"; "don't let the outside fool you" warn those who've climbed the stairway to heaven above this remodeled '30s gas station.

Dahlia Lounge S | 26 | 24 | 23 | $31

1904 Fourth Ave. (bet. Stewart & Virginia Sts.), 206-682-4142

"If an out-of-towner could spend only one night in Seattle, this is the place to eat"; "iconoclastic chef" Tom Douglas "challenges the palate" with "memorable" NW-Asian fusion food at this first of his Downtown ventures; a "hot spot for hot people", it has a "chic-o-rama" setting that's "perfect for business" or a date; a few find "too many tastes on the plate", but far more term it "totally satisfying."

El Gaucho S | – | – | – | E

2505 First Ave. (Wall St.), 206-728-1337

Retro viva! shout fans of Belltown's hip revival of the long-gone Gauch, where mink-lined booths and flaming shish kebabs reigned; owner Paul Mackay, who managed the original, sports a tux and his million-watt smile while overseeing one of the hottest tickets in town; piano jazz rules, as does a martini and steakhouse mentality, in a swanky, windowless, theater-in-the-round setting; the bar's a scene, as is the cigar lounge.

Etta's Seafood S

24 | 22 | 22 | $29

Pike Place Mkt., 2020 Western Ave. (bet. Virginia & Lenora Sts.), 206-443-6000

◩ "The Dahlia's little sister doesn't embarrass her" insist fans of the second of Tom Douglas' three Downtowners; drawing discerning crowds to its bustling Market location, it earns raves for "NW seafood as it should be", prepared with Pan-Asian flair and "unique execution unmatched in Seattle"; though "a tad too trendy" and "expensive" for some, the bar is "great for a solo dinner" or drink.

Flying Fish ◐ S

23 | 22 | 21 | $31

2234 First Ave. (Bell St.), 206-728-8595

◩ "People are flying in to try it" – the "fabulously creative" fish with "Asian overtones" that chef-owner Christine Keff whips up at this "colorful", "impressive" Belltown seafooder; her "beautiful presentations" taste "as good as they look", but to some the "portions seem small for the prices" and service seems "snooty"; the "deafening" decibel level comes courtesy of the open kitchen, crowded bar and high ceilings.

Fullers

26 | 24 | 25 | $42

Sheraton Seattle Hotel & Towers, 1400 Sixth Ave. (bet. Union & Pike Sts.), 206-447-5544

■ "Great for a power lunch" or "special occasion", the Sheraton's fine-dining room is "the ultimate in casual elegance" (though a bit "stuffy" to some), offering "wonderfully creative" NW fare that's "all about flavor"; however, a few say "too much fusion is more like confusion" and it's "best with someone else's money."

Georgian Room

26 | 29 | 27 | $41

Olympic Four Seasons Hotel, 411 University St. (bet. 4th & 5th Aves.), 206-621-7889

■ "When you want to pamper yourself or someone else", the "swank" Four Seasons dining room is "still the most elegant" place in the city; you'll "feel like a king" and you'll pay a king's ransom for chef Kerry Sear's "flawless", "beautifully displayed" seasonal American-Continental creations that are "sometimes too esoteric" for conservative palates; Sunday breakfast is a highlight at this bastion of "gracious dining for the Lexus set."

Il Terrazzo Carmine

25 | 24 | 23 | $33

411 First Ave. S. (bet. Jackson & King Sts.), 206-467-7797

■ A "sophisticated" "surprise in Pioneer Square", Carmine Smeraldo's "lovely, lively" Italian is perfect for a "leisurely lunch or romantic dinner", offering "great visuals" and a never-changing menu that's "heavy" but "stunningly good"; expect "impeccable service" from "white-coated waiters" bearing such "top-drawer" treats as "exceptional osso buco" and sweetbreads; surveyors have just one lament: "wish I could afford it more often."

Kaspar's

26 | 24 | 24 | $36

19 W. Harrison St. (1st Ave.), 206-298-0123

◩ "Kaspar Donier knows how to do it right" and he "gets better every year" at creating "sophisticated", "quintessential NW entrees" and "perfect" vegetables "marred only by a heavy hand with salt"; "the tablecloth would probably taste good" at his "elegant" Queen Anne location with "gorgeous decor", "European service" and "a wonderful wine bar"; a minority cries "overrated."

Lampreia
25 | 21 | 23 | $43

2400 First Ave. (Battery St.), 206-443-3301

◪ "Arguably the most talented chef in town", Scott Carsberg's devotion to fresh seasonal ingredients and "keep-it-simple" philosophy yields "serious" Eclectic fare for "serious diners"; "refined food and service", "beautiful presentations" and an "upscale", minimalist setting prove "too precious" for some, but to most, this Belltown "sophisticate" is "first-class all-around."

Marco's Supperclub Ⓢ
23 | 20 | 21 | $26

2510 First Ave. (Wall St.), 206-441-7801

◪ "Homestyle cooking with a Belltown beat" is the draw at this Eclectic bar/restaurant serving "imaginative food for the in-crowd" ("try the fried sage leaves" or "mighty roast pork"); "Marco is a sweetheart", as is his wife Donna, who runs this "crowded, smoky" yet "romantic" place with "mismatched china" and a "funky bar"; some say the ambiance "makes the food seem better than it is."

Palace Kitchen ◐Ⓢ
25 | 23 | 22 | $27

2030 Fifth Ave. (Lenora St.), 206-448-2001

■ "Tom Douglas further enriches the Seattle food scene" with this "worthy addition to the Dahlia tradition"; "lively to the point of being scary", this Eclectic "rocks" with theatrical decor, an enormous bar (where "fabulous appetizers make a satisfying meal") and an open kitchen with a wood-fired grill turning out a menu that's "heavy on meats"; "wish they'd take reservations" cry one and all.

Place Pigalle
25 | 24 | 23 | $29

Pike Place Mkt., 81 Pike St. (main entrance), 206-624-1756

■ A "unique bistro feel", "perfect location" overlooking Puget Sound and "lots of talent in the kitchen" make this "jewel in the Pike Place Market" "almost too good to be true"; the Eclectic menu takes a "seasonal approach" and makes "creative use" of local ingredients including "lovely mussels"; "polished service", a "marvelous bar" and "excellent wine list" complete the picture.

Reiner's
26 | 23 | 24 | $37

1106 Eighth Ave. (bet. Spring & Seneca Sts.), 206-624-2222

■ "Will it be as good without Reiner?" is the question on many lips since Reiner Greubel sold this "elegant", "art deco" Continental; so far most agree that new owner Hanspeter Aebersold (ex Rainier Club) has maintained the "classic European techniques" and "old-world charm" that make it a "special occasion place", but some find the "intimate" room too "stodgy."

Relais Ⓢ
26 | 24 | 25 | $49

(fka Gerard's Relais de Lyon)

17121 Bothell Way NE (near 96th Ave. NE), Bothell, 425-485-7600

◪ Gerard passed the torch to new owners, but continue to expect "Classic French" fare in the "formal setting" of this relais with many "tiny rooms" and a charming courtyard; despite the "unlikely" Bothell location, a "remarkable experience" can be had either à la carte or via the degustation – a "four-hour" feast that toes a fine line between "scrumptious" and "too heavy."

Rover's 28 | 23 | 26 | $49

2808 E. Madison St. (28th Ave.), 206-325-7442

■ "Charming" chef Thierry Rautureau "is a genius" whose "French fare with NW touches" and "attention to detail" are "over the top"; his "elegant" "country house" in Madison Valley earns Seattle's top food rating, and though some find it "fussy and expensive", most say the "superb food", "spotless service" and handsome remodel make it the "NW's top French" and worth every cent.

Saleh al Lago 25 | 21 | 24 | $35

6804 E. Green Lake Way N. (1st Ave. NE), 206-524-4044

◪ Chef Saleh Joudeh "is a perfectionist" and a "Seattle institution" say lovers of this "upscale Italian worthy of Milan"; "consistency" is the key to the success of such dishes as "calamari and veal to die for"; still, some "can't understand the praise" and think that this "too pink, California '80s" Green Lake favorite "needs a face-lift."

Shiro's S 27 | 17 | 22 | $29

2401 Second Ave. (Battery St.), 206-443-9844

■ "Shiro is a master" whose career has spanned decades; after a brief retirement, this sushi savant opened this "upscale" Belltown Japanese, which some find "too bright" and "cramped" but "otherwise lovely"; snag a seat at the sushi bar (tough to do) and you'll think you've "died and gone to Japan" thanks to "top-quality fish" and other "classical" fare; "pricey but terrific."

Shoalwater S 26 | 24 | 25 | $32

Shelburne Inn, 4415 Pacific Hwy. (45th St.), Seaview, 360-642-4142

◪ Vacationers have long come to stay at Seaview's historic Shelburne Inn, if only to dine at its "quaint restaurant" where the NW-inspired food is "almost better than the sex that follows"; some say the adjoining Heron and Beaver Pub "almost rivals the restaurant", which critics find "a little pretentious"; but most agree that owners Ann and Tony Kischner make it one of the area's best.

Szmania's S 26 | 20 | 23 | $30

3321 W. McGraw St. (34th Ave.), 206-284-7305

■ "Lucky Magnolia" say those envious of the neighborhood where Ludger Szmania creates "world-class cuisine" that borrows from the NW and his native Germany; the "simple" room has an open kitchen with counter seating, but those who say the decor needs help will like the remodeled room with its stone fireplace.

Wildflowers 25 | 23 | 23 | $26

2001 E. College Way (1 mi. east of I-5, exit 227), Mt. Vernon, 360-424-9724

■ "Surprise, no hick-town chow here" – this relatively "unknown gem" in Mt. Vernon is "intimate", "romantic" and "well worth a long drive"; wildflowers bloom outdoors and a "changing menu" of NW cuisine blossoms under the capable hand of chef David Day.

Wild Ginger S 26 | 23 | 22 | $26

1400 Western Ave. (Union St.), 206-623-4450

■ Seattle's Most Popular restaurant is a "sophisticated" Pan-Asian extravaganza, a "hip, exotic", "happening place" where you can "sit alone at the satay bar" and sup on "intensely flavored" soups and curries or "come with friends and share" "creative" seafood and meat dishes ("some bites are subtle, others are explosions"); it's "a place to wow visitors" and "Monday night jazz is superb."

TOP 15 FOOD RANKING

	Restaurant	Cuisine Type
28	Tony's	N/S Italian
	Fio's La Fourchette	French/Swiss
	Cafe de France	Classic French
27	Giovanni's	N/S Italian
	Al's	Steakhouse
	Zinnia	Californian/New Amer.
26	Gianpeppe's	Northern Italian
	Dominic's	N/S Italian
	Sidney Street Cafe	American/Continental
	Faust's	Continental/Eclectic
	Ritz-Carlton Grill	New American
	Seventh Inn	Continental
	Trattoria Marcella	N/S Italian
25	Malmaison	New French
	Kemoll's	N/S Italian

OTHER IMPORTANT PLACES

Bar Italia	N/S Italian
Cafe Balaban	Eclectic/New American
Cafe Mira	International/New Amer.
Café Provençal	French Bistro
Cardwell's	American/Californian
Crossing	New American
Harry's	New American
Harvest	New American
Morton's of Chicago	Steakhouse
Remy's Kitchen	Mediterranean
Riddle's Penultimate	New American

	F	D	S	C
Al's Restaurant	27	21	26	$44

1200 N. First St. (Biddle St.), 314-421-6399

■ "Superlative food, anything you want, any way you want it" explains sky-high ratings for the area's top steakhouse, an "old-fashioned", "club"-like Downtown "treasure" providing giant portions that earn it the nickname "Cholester-Al"; while some would "prefer a menu with prices" (it's a pioneer in the "raw meat as menu" concept), beef lovers agree it's "a wonderful experience."

	F	D	S	C
Bar Italia S	24	15	19	$19

4656 Maryland Ave. (Euclid Ave.), 314-361-7010

■ Legions of admirers appreciate the "excellent preparation of imaginative fare", "warm environment" and "great grappa" – and tolerate the "slow European service" – at this "fave" Central West End trattoria run by a "cool owner" from Eritrea; perhaps the "decor needs an upgrade", but "who cares, the food is wonderful", and while it's "cramped inside" the patio provides "outdoor dining at its best."

Cafe Balaban S 25 | 21 | 21 | $27

405 N. Euclid Ave. (McPherson Ave.), 314-361-8085

Balaban's Bistro 201 – | – | – | E

The Barn At Lucerne, 930 Kehrs Mill Rd. (Clayton Rd.), Ballwin, 314-391-9393

■ This "trendy" (some say "snooty") Central West End "landmark" is "like your favorite pair of shoes – comfortable and always a good choice"; fans find the "passionate" Eclectic–New American fare by chef David Timney – "superb jerk chicken", "fabulous BBQ salmon with Chinese mustard" – "worth every penny"; so the few who say it's "way overpriced" are clearly outvoted; the newer Balaban's Bistro 201, serving similar fare, opened post-*Survey.*

Cafe de France 28 | 25 | 26 | $39

410 Olive St. (bet. 4th St. & Broadway), 314-231-2204

■ "When you want to be pampered" head straight to this "formal", "romantic" Downtown French that's highly rated across the board; "a real treat to the palate and the eye" (translation: "superb food and service" and "lovely ambiance"), it's "everything an expensive restaurant should be"; not surprisingly, many consider it "in a class by itself" and a "great value – even at these prices."

Cafe Mira – | – | – | E

12 N. Meramec Ave. (bet. Forsyth & Maryland Ave.), Clayton, 314-721-7801

Mike Johnson's skill in the kitchen shows in a superior touch with spicing, a light hand with garnish and considerable imagination all through the New American–International menu; spare decor, hustling service and crowds eating red curry pork and chocolate bread pudding mark what may be the best of the Class of '98.

Café Provençal 24 | 16 | 21 | $22

40 N. Central Ave. (bet. Forsyth & Maryland), Clayton, 314-725-2755 S

427 S. Kirkwood Rd. (Woodbine Center), Kirkwood, 314-822-5440

■ The "tables are appallingly close together" ("sardines have more room"), the noise level is "deafening" and the decor is "spartan", yet diners can't stay away from this "very European" Clayton French; Eddie Neill's "fabulous food" at "reasonable prices" is the drawing card; customers also call the three-course prix fixe menu a "great buy"; N.B. the Kirkwood location is new and unrated.

Cardwell's 24 | 23 | 22 | $27

94 Plaza Frontenac (Clayton & Lindbergh), 314-997-8885 S

8100 Maryland Ave. (Brentwood Blvd.), Clayton, 314-726-5055

■ Both the Clayton original and the new Plaza Frontenac branch of this "noisier than hell but addictive" Cal-American satisfy nearly all diners with "beautiful presentation" of "imaginative" food served in a "gracious setting" (many prefer the "less formal" mall location); a few find the duo "pretentious" and "pricey", but they're outvoted.

Crossing – | – | – | E

7823 Forsyth (Central Ave.), Clayton, 314-721-7375

A pair of former New York chefs bring real style to another new Clayton entry; early (hopefully not too early) samplings reveal an American menu crafted with intense care and a nifty, imaginative look at fresh ingredients: beet salad, pureed parsnips, duck with three different styles of preparation and gingered crême brûlée are excellent introductions to Jim Faila's and Cary McDowell's cooking.

Dominic's 26 25 26 $40

5101 Wilson Ave. (Hereford St.), 314-771-1632

■ This "classy", "elegant" Italian on the Hill, one of the top-rated in the city, shines in every category: "outstanding food" (try the "best shrimp scampi in North America", "wonderful pasta", "great veal dishes"), "delightful decor" and "superior service"; some say it's "far too expensive" for the "small portions", but most tolerate the tab since it's "always excellent in every way."

Faust's S 26 26 24 $36

Adam's Mark Hotel, 315 Chestnut St. (4th St.), 314-342-4690

■ Expect "an evening of elegance" at the "romantic" dining room in the Adam's Mark; with "incredibly creative presentation" of "tremendous" Eclectic-Continental food ("missing the brunch should be illegal"), "pampering service" and an "excellent pianist", it "surpasses most hotel dining" and is "expensive but worth it for special occasions"; the few who find it "stuffy" and "snobbish" probably aren't used to dining in such a "classy" place.

Fio's La Fourchette 28 25 27 $44

7515 Forsyth Ave. (Lee), Clayton, 314-863-6866

■ Second only to Tony's, but not by very much, this Swiss-French winner is "worth breaking two diets for"; free second helpings of "consistently delicious food" (don't miss the "divine" dessert soufflés), "outstanding service" and "beautiful decor" in a new, slightly larger Clayton location combine to create a "superb and sublime" dining experience, eliciting the ultimate compliment "expensive yet a good value"; a recent sale to two long-standing employees doesn't seem to raise any storm warnings.

Gianpeppe's 26 23 25 $30

2126 Marconi Ave. (Bischoff Ave.), 314-772-3303

■ "Mom cooks every dish" and her son greets every customer at this small, "excellent but expensive" Northern Italian on the Hill that's "sort of secret" but "better than its higher-profile neighbors"; the result is "marvelous food" and "perfect service"; it's "elegant" and "romantic" despite somewhat "sterile decor."

Giovanni's 27 25 25 $36

5201 Shaw Ave. (Marconi Ave.), 314-772-5958

■ St. Louis' second-ranked Italian, where "they treat everybody like a special guest" and the "owner makes you feel like an Italian", rates raves for "excellent everything": "incredible food", "superb service", "warm" ambiance; but it may be "a little too pretentious" and "expensive" for some.

Harry's Restaurant & Bar S 23 24 21 $25

2144 Market St. (Jefferson Ave.), 314-421-6969
15415 Clayton (Kehr's Mill), Ballwin, 314-256-0221

■ A "gorgeous", "preppier-than-thou" New American offering a "sensational view" of Downtown that baits the "beautiful" crowd with an "imaginative menu", "cosmopolitan atmosphere" and "excellent outdoor patio"; only a few feel it "promises more than it delivers"; N.B. the Ballwin branch is new and unrated.

Harvest S — | — | — | E

1059 S. Big Bend Blvd. (Clayton Rd.), 314-645-3522

Notwithstanding its high sound level and an Everyone Who's Anyone reservation list, this hot New American newcomer has hit the pinnacle by virtue of more than mere fashion: namely, a strong kitchen and service that's settled down nicely; the food's stylishness matches the room, with oh-wow onion rings, fab fish, a wonderful wine list and lots of seasonal offerings; reserve or expect a wait.

Kemoll's S 25 | 25 | 24 | $32

Metropolitan Sq. Bldg., 211 N. Broadway (bet. Olive & Pine), 314-421-0555

◪ "Still excellent after all these years" is how many describe this "elegant", "expensive", family-run Italian that's perfect for "power lunch" or a "romantic dinner"; but there are those who think the food is "too rich", the portions "much too large" and it "lost something after the relocation" from North Side to Downtown.

Malmaison S 25 | 27 | 25 | $36

St. Albans Rd. (off Hwy. T), St. Albans, 314-458-0131

■ "There aren't enough superlatives to describe" this "lovely" French "hideaway" an hour west of the city, but respondents give it the old college try: "romantic as St. Louis gets", "you'd swear you're in France", "expensive and absolutely worth it"; the few nonfans in town say the "food is slipping."

Morton's of Chicago S 24 | 23 | 23 | $43

7822 Bonhomme Rd. (Central), Clayton, 314-725-4008

◪ "Morton's is about excess" – "either you like it or you don't" is how one respondent sums up this Clayton branch of the Chicago-based steak chain, where "good food" comes in "ridiculous portions at absurd prices"; despite lush decor, a "great wine list" and "red meat heaven", some roosters lament "definitely not a chick place"; in fact, it attracts "too many Clayton lawyers."

Remy's Kitchen & Wine Bar 22 | 20 | 21 | $22

222 S. Bemiston Ave. (bet. Bonhomme & Shaw Park Dr.), 314-726-5757

◪ A "palate pleaser", this Clayton cafe by Tim Mallett is "another gem", a "very creative", "marvelous Mediterranean" featuring chef "Lisa Slay at her best"; the "flights of wine are interesting" and a "great value"; for the majority it's an "admirable effort" that "gets better all the time", but for a few it's just too "weird."

Riddle's Penultimate S 23 | 14 | 19 | $20

6307 Delmar Blvd. (bet. Eastgate & Westgate), University City, 314-725-6985

■ "Another star in the Loop", this New American with "homemade food" and a "superb" selection of wines by the glass is a favorite for "seasonal specials", "great fish", "magical garlic potatoes" and "great ice cream"; it's "colorful and charming" and service is "excellent", but some say it "needs to spruce up the decor."

Ritz-Carlton Grill S 26 | 28 | 26 | $36

Ritz-Carlton Hotel, 100 Carondelet Plaza (Hanley Rd.), Clayton, 314-863-6300

■ "Ultra-elegant true Ritz style" is found in this "beautiful" room that rates No. 1 for Decor in the *St. Louis Survey*, a "very relaxing" "class act" featuring "great service" and an "excellent" dinner-only American menu; the "legendary Sunday brunch" is a favorite, and naturally, this "high quality" comes at a "high price", but in the final analysis, "it's the glitz of the Ritz" and "worth it."

F	D	S	C

Seventh Inn ◐ 26 | 26 | 26 | $39
100 Seven Trails Dr. (1½ miles west of Woods Mill Rd.), Ballwin, 314-227-6686
■ "Fit for a princess" sums up this "beautiful, romantic" West County Continental where everything is "always excellent" – from the "outstanding" food to the "wonderful atmosphere" to the "best" service; a small but vocal minority, however, sees it as "gaudy", "snooty" and "not worth the shock to your pocketbook."

Sidney Street Cafe 26 | 23 | 24 | $28
2000 Sidney St. (Salena), 314-771-5777
■ Always popular South Side American-Continental that lands in St. Louis' top 10 food rankings once again, winning accolades as "outrageously good", "always a treat" and "five-star without the fuss"; fans "can't say enough" about the "fabulous food", "cozy, romantic" atmosphere and "superior service" but wonder "why can't they have a printed menu?"

Tony's 28 | 26 | 28 | $48
410 Market St. (bet. Broadway & 4th St.), 314-231-7007
◪ This veteran Italian may have lost a star, but it's still one of the city's most popular restaurants and top-rated for food and service; "always superb", "worth every dollar", "a credit to our town" are the high notes in the chorus of praise for what surveyors call a "unique institution"; although some sniff it's "not as great as everyone carries on about", most say it's "hard to top."

Trattoria Marcella 26 | 16 | 23 | $23
3600 Watson Rd. (bet. Chippewa & Hampton), 314-352-7706
■ The lack of decor is the "only shortfall" of this "exciting" Italian newcomer on the South Side that cracks the city's top 15 with "innovative, delectable food" ("excellent risotto", "delicious pasta") and "enthusiastic service"; it even earns the ultimate compliment for a small place: "crowded, noisy and worth putting up with it!"

Zinnia S 27 | 21 | 24 | $27
7491 Big Bend Blvd. (Shrewsbury), Webster Groves, 314-962-0572
■ This flower in Webster Groves "blooms all year long" with a "tantalizing" Cal-American menu created by "one of the best young chefs in America", "excellent food", "knowledgeable waiters" and, of course, "fresh flowers"; only a few rebels write it off as "overpriced and overrated", and only a few fans request "lose the purple paint."

TOP 10 FOOD RANKING

	Restaurant	Cuisine Type
28	Mise en Place	New American
	Beach Bistro	Med./New American
27	Bern's Steak House	Steakhouse
	Blue Heron	Eclectic
	Euphemia Haye	Eclectic
	Bijou Café	Continental/New Amer.
	Michael's on East	New American
26	Ophelia's	Eclectic
	Morel	Eclectic/New American
	Armani's	Northern Italian

OTHER IMPORTANT PLACES

Café L'Europe	Continental
Ceviche	Spanish/Tapas
David Michael's	New American
Maritana Grille	Floridian/New American
Oystercatchers	Seafood
Salt Rock Grill	Seafood/Steakhouse
Shula's Steak House	Steakhouse

F | D | S | C

Armani's 26 | 28 | 27 | $46

Hyatt Regency Westshore, 6200 Courtney Campbell Causeway (Hwy. 60), Tampa, 813-874-1234

■ "Just the place to wear a little black dress", this "elegant" Northern Italian in Tampa's Hyatt Regency Westshore has it all: "terrific food", "classy atmosphere", "wonderful service" and "views to the nth degree"; but "don't forget your wallet", as this "premier dining experience" comes at a steep price – though the consensus is it's "worth it" for a "top-of-the-line" evening at one of the Gulf Coast's finest.

Beach Bistro S 28 | 23 | 26 | $41

6600 Gulf Dr. (66th St.), Holmes Beach, 941-778-6444

■ Foodies from Anna Maria and beyond can't resist this "intimate" New American–Mediterranean, a "restaurant with charisma" that offers "outstanding service", "fabulous" sunset views and "always remarkable" fare; true, it's "pricey" and "limited seating" might make it "too crowded" at times, but the majority feels it's "worth it" to enjoy one of the area's "best overall", a place that "would make it in Paris or NY."

Bern's Steak House S 27 | 22 | 27 | $42

1208 S. Howard Ave. (bet. Marjorie & Watrous Sts.), Tampa, 813-251-2421

■ Since 1956, this "national treasure for beef" in Tampa's Hyde Park has been gathering accolades for its "famous, fabulous" steaks and the "best wine list in the world"; while not everyone likes its "bordello-like", "red flocked wallpaper" decor, most give all-around high marks to this "dining event" and recommend you "tour the kitchen and wine cellar, then feast in the dessert room."

Bijou Café
27 | 23 | 24 | $34

1287 First St. (Pineapple St.), Sarasota, 941-366-8111

■ This "elegant little" Theater District place is Downtown Sarasota's "most sophisticated" cafe despite its unlikely location in a former "1930s service station"; "they work hard at" their "inventive" Continental–New American menu, turning out nearly "perfect food" that's enhanced by "excellent" wines and "gentle service"; though "jammed on opera nights", it manages to maintain a "lovely", "laid-back" atmosphere.

Blue Heron S
27 | 22 | 24 | $33

Shoppes at Clover Pl., 3285 Tampa Rd. (bet. Lake St. George & US 19), Palm Harbor, 727-789-5176

■ "A rare combination of food and sauces" distinguishes the Eclectic mix served by this posh Palm Harbor veteran (now celebrating its 10th anniversary), where a recent renovation is yet to be reflected in its already respectable decor score; devotees adore the "high-quality" cuisine so fervently that they beg "please open for lunch", but for the moment it's dinner-only.

Café L'Europe S
26 | 25 | 24 | $37

431 St. Armands Circle (Hwy. 41), Sarasota, 941-388-4415

■ The "grande dame of Sarasota" recently celebrated its 25th anniversary, and this Continental "fixture on St. Armands Circle" is "still tops", a "model dining spot for food, wines, decor and service"; this "haven" can seem "a bit fussy" and "expensive" (some call lunch "a better value"), but most think it's "worth it" for one of the "most romantic" experiences in town.

Ceviche Restaurant & Tapas Bar ◐ S
▽ 21 | 18 | 18 | $27

2109 Bayshore Blvd. (Howard Ave.), Tampa, 813-250-0203

■ A newcomer to Tampa's stylish SoHo (South Howard) area, this tapas bar draws crowds with its "interesting menu" of Spanish finger foods, despite its unconventional location in a Bay Shore residential high-rise; up-all-night types applaud the late-late weekend hours ('til 2:30 AM) and everyone finds the weekend flamenco dancers quite snappy.

David Michael's
26 | 20 | 23 | $36

328 John Ringling Blvd. (St. Armands Circle), Sarasota, 941-388-4429

◪ The "chef reaches for the stars with every dish" at this "quirky" little second-story cafe on Sarasota's swank St. Armands Circle, offering New American fare with a special flair for "unbelievable salads"; most commend the menu's "originality", and though doubters say it's sometimes "self-conscious" and "doesn't always succeed", ratings indicate that more often than not, "great presentations" of "imaginative cuisine" is the outcome.

Euphemia Haye S
27 | 23 | 23 | $41

5540 Gulf of Mexico Dr. (Gulf-to-Bay Rd.), Longboat Key, 941-383-3633

■ It's "hard to beat" this Longboat Key Eclectic for "world-class dining" in a "romantic" setting; it can be "cramped downstairs" ("hope you like your neighbors"), but claustrophobes can opt for the upstairs Haye Loft piano bar, where a "light menu" or a choice of "wonderful" desserts await; up or down, there's a "wine list that touches all bases" as well as "attentive" service.

Maritana Grille S ▽ 27 | 28 | 25 | $47

Don CeSar Beach Resort, 3400 Gulf Blvd. (Pinellas Bayway), St. Petersburg Beach, 727-360-1882

■ Experience "nirvana" at this Floribbean gem, the signature dining room of St. Pete's historic Don CeSar Resort, where beachside panoramas from the terrace and indoor saltwater aquariums stocked with indigenous fish make it one of the most striking rooms on it the Gulf Coast; the "fabulous, creative" fare, prepared over a pecan and cherry wood grill and accompanied by an extensive wine list, gives the view a run for its money.

Michael's on East 27 | 26 | 25 | $40

Midtown Plaza, 1212 East Ave. (bet. Bahia Vista & Prospect Sts.), Sarasota, 941-366-0007

■ Again voted the Gulf Coast's Most Popular restaurant, this "posh" New American has "just been redesigned" and its "drop-dead gorgeous" new look has also "greatly improved the noise level"; the "superb", "up-to-date" menu attracts a "very glitzy crowd" in search of "a special night" and though it can be a bit "pricey", most say it's "worth it" to savor Sarasota's "brightest star."

Mise en Place 28 | 24 | 24 | $35

442 W. Kennedy Blvd. (Grand Central St.), Tampa, 813-254-5373

■ "Incredibly inventive cuisine" at "fair prices" attracts gourmands to this Downtown New American, rated No. 1 for Food on the Gulf Coast; its "state-of-the-art combinations", "creative presentation" and "great wine selection" make this "as good as it gets in Tampa", and those who say the "only flaw is the wait" will be happy to know that it now accepts reservations.

Morel 26 | 20 | 24 | $33

3809 S. Tuttle Ave. (Bee Ridge Rd.), Sarasota, 941-927-8716

■ This "tiny" Sarasota Eclectic–New American thrills fans with its "memorable" cuisine and "superb preparation and presentation" ("smooth service" doesn't hurt either); though in a "very unlikely location for such a fine restaurant" – a "tacky storefront" "in a strip mall" – stalwarts say "this lovely little bistro" is always "pleasant" and "friendly"; dinner only.

Ophelia's S 26 | 25 | 24 | $35

9105 Midnight Pass Rd. (south of Turtle Beach), Sarasota, 941-349-2212

■ "Sit outside if you can" at this "pretty spot" on the Siesta Key waterfront and enjoy its "romantic atmosphere" and "views galore", plus an "exciting" Eclectic menu "presented in a very appealing way" with "some different choices" and "wonderful desserts"; it can get "pricey", but for "elegantly served, inspired cuisine", the overwhelming majority agrees that this "A-one" place is "worth it."

Oystercatchers S 26 | 26 | 25 | $35

Hyatt Regency Westshore, 6200 Courtney Campbell Causeway (Hwy. 60), Tampa, 813-281-9116

■ "A beautiful water view" of Old Tampa Bay and "very good" seafood that some rate "best in the area" await at this Hyatt Regency Westshore fish palace, where the open kitchen is proudly on display; a "great brunch" and one of the "best breakfast buffets" around are more reasons why fans pronounce this "special occasion" place simply "wonderful."

Salt Rock Grill S ▽ 26 | 28 | 23 | $33

19325 Gulf Blvd. (¼ mi. north of Park Blvd.), Indian Shores, 727-593-7625

■ Truly a "place to be seen", this "superb" surf 'n' turfer offers a "diverse", "interesting" menu from its open kitchen, a "great wine list" and stunning decor (including a cigar bar) that all merge to form the quintessential "yuppie hangout"; it's "noisy", but what else would you expect from one of Tampa Bay's most "popular" spots?

Shula's Steak House S 26 | 23 | 25 | $45

Wyndham Westshore, 4860 W. Kennedy Blvd. (Westshore Blvd.), Tampa, 813-286-4366

■ You can "eat like a football player" at this West Shore chophouse in the Wyndham serving "very, very good" food in huge portions that might be "too much" for the unathletic; decorated with memorabilia from Don Shula's coaching days with the Dolphins, this "men's club" delights the guys, who call the steaks "excellent" and the experience "wonderful", even if it's "overpriced, period."

TOP 10 FOOD RANKING

	Restaurant	Cuisine Type
28	Ventana Room	American/Eclectic
27	Janos	French/Southwestern
	Vivace	N/S Italian
	Le Rendez-Vous	Classic French
25	Gold Room	Southwestern
	Cafe Poca Cosa	Mexican
	Rancher's Club of Arizona	Steakhouse
	Tack Room	Traditional American
24	Sachiko Sushi	Japanese
	Mi Nidito	Mexican

OTHER IMPORTANT PLACES

Anthony's	Continental
Arizona Inn	New American
Cafe Terra Cotta	Southwestern
Cielos	New French/Spanish
Cottonwood Cafe	Southwestern
Daniel's	Northern Italian
¡Fuego!	Southwestern
Le Bistro	French Bistro
Nonie	Cajun
Oven's	New American
Pastiche	Eclectic/New American
Presidio Grill	New American

F | D | S | C

Anthony's in the Catalinas S — 24 | 27 | 24 | $36

6440 N. Campbell Ave. (Skyline Dr.), 520-299-1771

◪ This foothills Continental is a "gracious room with magnificent views" – "mountains out one window, city lights out the other"; admirers say the "views do not surpass the food" (don't miss the chocolate soufflé) and praise the "notable wine cellar", but foes find the cooking "tired."

Arizona Inn S — 23 | 26 | 24 | $27

Arizona Inn, 2200 E. Elm St. (bet. Campbell Ave. & Tucson Blvd.), 520-325-1541

◪ Dine alfresco at this "elegant", "vintage" in-town oasis with "finger bowl" service and a "top-notch" New American menu – "great" for power breakfast and lunch; however, some note that the "serene", "genteel" setting with "charming" gardens and fireplaces can sometimes "eclipse" the food.

Cafe Poca Cosa — 25 | 22 | 22 | $18

88 E. Broadway Blvd. (bet. Scott & 6th Aves.), 520-622-6400

Little Cafe Poca Cosa ⊄

20 S. Scott Ave. (Congress St.), 520-622-6400

■ "Changed the course of Mexican food in Tucson forever" declare Cafe Poca Cosa fans who plead "don't tell anyone"; but word of the "fresh", artful platters "bursting" with "brassy" flavors has spread so far that nonlocals say it's "worth a special trip" here to sample the "changing menu", especially the "chef's choice al día of three superb entrees" – best enjoyed with a 'rita on the "magical patio"; N.B. the casual Little Cafe is breakfast and lunch only.

F | D | S | C

Cafe Terra Cotta S
24 | 22 | 22 | $24

St. Philip's Plaza, 4310 N. Campbell Ave. (River Rd.), 520-577-8100

■ "Outstanding" and "still trendy after all these years", with a "clever" menu that leads in "defining SW gourmet" eats; the "great smells" from brick-oven pizzas "make spirits rise", as do "marvelous tortilla soup" and "wow desserts"; here you can "dine well at a variety of price points", catch "great people-watching" on the shaded patio, and on jazz nights, it's "nirvana."

Cielos S
– | – | – | E

Lodge on the Desert, 306 N. Alvernon Way (bet. Broadway & 5th St.), 520-325-3434

Executive chef John D. Harings and much of the staff from L'Auberge de Sedona, one of AZ's finest French restaurants, are setting this once-faded landmark resort on an exciting new culinary course, offering Spanish fare enlivened by a French twist; the Spanish-accented setting exudes old-world elegance yet remains comfortable rather than stuffy; look for brunch to be added soon.

Cottonwood Cafe ◐ S
23 | 26 | 21 | $22

60 N. Alvernon Way (Broadway Blvd.), 520-326-6000

■ This "new kid on the block", in a restored "Santa Fe–style" ranch house with a patio, is making quite an impression; the "innovative", "varied" Southwestern menu (from paella to sweet-potato chips) ensures that it'll remain "noisy" and "trendy" for quite a while.

Daniel's Restaurant & Trattoria S
24 | 24 | 22 | $33

St. Philip's Plaza, 4340 N. Campbell Ave. (River Rd.), 520-742-3200

◪ Admirers consider this Northern Italian a "classic" and "one of the good 'finds' in Tucson", citing its "fabulous", "haute" menu, "great wines" and "attractive", "relaxing" setting, including a patio; detractors find the menu "overwrought" and note "uneven" service, but it's "much improved with an ownership change."

¡Fuego! Restaurant, Bar & Grill S
24 | 21 | 22 | $29

Santa Fe Sq., 6958 E. Tanque Verde Rd. (Sabino Canyon Rd.), 520-886-1745

◪ Staking out culinary frontiers, this "noisy", "bright", clean-lined place has an "excellent kitchen" "bordering on outstanding", turning out "innovative", Southwestern nouvelle cuisine, with special raves for chef Alan Zeman's signature dishes; but some find it "pricey", "pretentious" and "trying too hard for exotic combos."

Gold Room S
25 | 26 | 25 | $34

Westward Look Resort, 245 E. Ina Rd. (east of Oracle Rd.), 520-297-1151

◪ Evocative SW-inspired fare and views of sunsets and city lights mark this "delightful mountain aerie" as a "Tucson classic", "redone to very nice result"; while most find the food "excellent" and laud a "lovely brunch", a few find service "patronizing."

Janos
27 | – | 27 | $39

3770 E. Sunrise Dr. (next to the Westin La Paloma Hotel), 520-615-6100

◪ Though newly relocated from a historic Downtown adobe to a tony resort setting with desert and mountain views (thus outdating our decor rating), this standout continues to serve "accomplished" cuisine blending Classic French sensibilities with SW flavors and regional ingredients; with sumptuous decor, first-rate service and a lovely patio, it should maintain the appeal that earned it the Most Popular title in our *Tucson Survey.*

Le Bistro S | 24 | 21 | 22 | $25

2574 N. Campbell Ave. (bet. Glenn St. & Grant Rd.), 520-327-3086

This "first-rate French" is "friendly and relaxed" and serves some of the "best bistro food in Tucson": "marvelous mussels", surprising salads and "fantastic" chocolate towers that make it difficult to "leave without dessert"; but while some call the setting "small and romantic", others find it "cramped."

Le Rendez-Vous S | 27 | 22 | 24 | $35

3844 E. Fort Lowell Rd. (Alvernon Way), 520-323-7373

Escape desert sun to the subdued light of this "authentic", "intimate" bit of France in Tucson where diners come to "relax and enjoy" "lovingly prepared" food that makes for "exceptional", "romantic" dining "à deux" that "never fails"; *bien sûr*, "don't miss the Grand Marnier soufflé" or you may hurt the owner's Gallic pride.

Mi Nidito S | 24 | 17 | 20 | $13

1813 S. Fourth Ave. (29th St.), 520-622-5081

It's "my little nest" and a lot of others' as well ("still Tucson's most crowded Mexican"); the reason: reviewers unanimously (at the exclusion of any mention of decor or service) cite "large portions" of "excellent", "real" Mexican food; unfortunately, they've removed the "great jukebox."

Nonie S | – | – | – | M

2526 E. Grant Rd. (Tucson Blvd.), 520-319-1965

This hot-as-a-pistol Cajun newcomer dishes up spicy New Orleans fare in a casual, bistro-like atmosphere; owned by Elmore Leonard's son and designed to capture the spirit of Bourbon Street, it seems to have taken the desert by storm.

Oven's Restaurant S | 23 | 20 | 21 | $20

4280 N. Campbell Ave. (bet. Limberlost Dr. & River Rd.), 520-577-9001

Leave the jacket and tie at home because this American bistro ("Cafe Terra Cotta clone") with a terrific patio is "supercasual"; the "friendly staff" serves "ample portions" of "outstanding" and "unusual" seafood and pasta to a "trendy", "yuppie" crowd.

Pastiche | – | – | – | M

3025 N. Campbell Ave., 520-325-3333

Cuisines from around the globe converge at this hip Midtowner, where painted concrete floors, colorful modern art and background jazz create a slightly offbeat ambiance that mirrors the Eclectic–New American menu; the food is enhanced by an excellent choice of wines by the glass and efficient service by a young staff.

Presidio Grill S | 23 | 20 | 21 | $22

3352 E. Speedway Blvd. (bet. Country Club Rd. & Palo Verde Blvd.), 520-327-4667

You feel like "you're back in TriBeCa" say displaced NYers of this "slick", "noisy", "big city" "bar hangout" serving "urban" New American fare; while some metropophiles thirst to sip the martinis, sample "sleek, imaginative food" (try the "roasted garlic and Brie") and check out the "in-crowd", others say the "iffy service" and "overpriced" menu are why they left NYC in the first place.

Rancher's Club of Arizona 25 | 24 | 25 | $37

Sheraton Hotel & Suites, 5151 E. Grant Rd. (bet. Craycroft & Swan Rds.), 520-321-7621

■ "Forget the cowboy steaks" – this "gem" of "Old West elegance" "hidden" in a business hotel is where diners sit beneath steer-horn chandeliers in soft leather chairs and receive "white-glove"-and- cloche service along with "fine steaks cooked over a variety of hardwoods" with "adventurous sauces"; there are veggies cooked right and perfect crème brûlée, accompanied by the nightly harpist.

Sachiko Sushi S 24 | 16 | 21 | $19

1101 N. Wilmot Rd. (Speedway Blvd.), 520-886-7000

◪ Fish and sushi fans flock to this "top" "neighborhood" sushi bar that also offers artful udon and tempura, making it our surveyors' pick for Tucson's "best Japanese"; "bright lights" and "lots of tables" don't win stellar decor scores, and some feel service could be improved, but the "excellent" food is "worth it."

Tack Room S 25 | 25 | 25 | $46

2800 N. Sabino Canyon Rd. (Tanque Verde Rd.), 520-722-2800

◪ Many still find this "lovely old ranch house" "close to perfect", with a "quiet elegance" that makes "you feel like a king"; its "superior" (albeit "pricey") SW-accented Traditional American menu, "outstanding service" and "strains of Chopin" from the piano make it a good place to take anyone from "your mother-in-law" to a "lover"; but with "more competition now", some say this "tack is not as sharp as it used to be" and "needs an infusion of pizazz."

Ventana Room S 28 | 28 | 27 | $44

Loews Ventana Canyon Resort, 7000 N. Resort Dr. (Craycroft Rd.), 520-299-2020

■ Nestled below granite peaks northeast of the city, this very "luxurious" American-Eclectic is acclaimed for its "spectacular" views (with shows of "summer lightning"), "gracious service" and, last but not least, "sumptuous", "savory" fare ("I learned to love caribou!") that earns Tucson's top food rating; it's a "top-notch" place for "gala dinners" that leaves just one regret: "wish we could afford it all the time."

Vivace S 27 | 21 | 24 | $27

Crossroads Festival Plaza, 4811 E. Grant Rd. (Swan Rd.), 520-795-7221

■ "Delightful in every way" sums up Tucson's top-rated Italian, which boasts a "stylish" "bistro atmosphere" and open kitchen that lets the high-energy crowd watch as chef Daniel Scordato ("terrific!") and his "enthusiastic" staff whip up creamy risotto, fabulous farfalle and other food that's consistently "excellent" and a "best buy"; a new, more intimate wine bar should satisfy those who find the wide open setting in need of "noise control."

Washington, D.C.

TOP 20 FOOD RANKING

	Restaurant	Cuisine Type
29	Inn at Little Washington	New American
28	Kinkead's	New American/Seafood
27	Makoto	Japanese
	L'Auberge Chez Francois	Classic French
	Obelisk	Northern Italian
	Gerard's Place	Classic/New French
	L'Auberge Provencale	Classic French
	Lespinasse	New French
26	1789	Regional American
	Galileo	Northern Italian
	Seasons	New American
	Prime Rib	American/Steakhouse
	Morrison-Clark Inn	New American
	Vidalia	Southern
	Four & Twenty Blackbirds	New American
	Melrose	New American
	Patisserie Cafe Didier	Bakery/French Bistro
	Nora	New American
	Sushi-Ko	Japanese
	Morton's of Chicago	Steakhouse

OTHER IMPORTANT PLACES

Ardeo	New American
Bombay Club	Indian
Bread Line	Bakery/International
Cashion's Eat Place	New American
Citronelle	Californian/French
DC Coast	New American
Duangrat's	Thai
El Catalan	Spanish
Georgia Brown's	Southern
Jaleo	Spanish/Tapas
McCormick & Schmick's	Seafood
New Heights	New American
Old Ebbitt Grill	Traditional American
Pesce	Seafood
Pizzeria Paradiso	Pizza
Red Sage	Southwestern
Sostanza	Italian/Steakhouse
Taberna del Alabardero	Spanish
Tahoga	New American
Villa Franco	Northern Italian

Ardeo S

– | – | – | M

3311 Connecticut Ave., NW (Macomb St.), 202-244-6750

The spring '98 debut of this smashing art deco Contemporary American in a duplex on Cleveland Park's restaurant row is yet another indication that this neighborhood has come of culinary age; its founder, Ashok Bajaj (Bombay Club, 701, Oval Room), knows what DC wants: interestingly seasoned, light tasting fare served in sophisticated settings; start-up problems can be expected, but it's likely to last.

Bombay Club S

25 | 25 | 25 | $36

815 Connecticut Ave., NW (bet. H & I Sts.), 202-659-3727

■ Beltway insiders and "unknowns" alike are "treated like rajas" at this "plush and hushed" Anglo-Indian power-dining room near the White House; a meal here is "elegant", "delicious" and impressive; in short, this place with "top-notch service" "gets everything right", causing one Republican to lament "too bad Clinton likes it."

Bread Line

21 | 13 | 14 | $11

1751 Pennsylvania Ave., NW (bet. 17th & 18th Sts.), 202-822-8900

■ Mark Furstenberg's "industrial chic" bakery/cafe near the White House raises "carryout to a new level" with Internationally inspired bread-based meals (empanadas, piadinas), "fabulous soups" and salads, plus "excellent" artisanal loaves; sure, you need "strong teeth" and high "tolerance" for lunchtime lines, but who else could make a "tuna sandwich remarkable?"

Cashion's Eat Place S

25 | 21 | 21 | $35

1819 Columbia Rd., NW (bet. Biltmore & Mintwood Sts.), 202-797-1819

■ At award-winning Ann Cashion's "refreshingly different" urban American bistro in Adams Morgan, you "don't have to dress up for great food" and "cosmopolitan" surroundings; they make everyone – from the President and parents with "teenagers in grunge clothes" to solo diners seated at the "happening" bar or sidewalk cafe – feel like "moving right in."

Citronelle S

24 | 23 | 23 | $48

(aka Michel Richard's Citronelle)

Latham Hotel, 3000 M St., NW (30th St.), 202-625-2150

◪ This posh Georgetown dining room is the "place to see the who's who of DC", and now that superchef Michel Richard is permanently "at home" in its kitchen, it is equally a place for "exquisite food" and expense-account pampering; given its spectacular multimillion dollar new look and its cutting-edge Cal-French cuisine, its already excellent ratings (which predated the redo) should soar and win over doubters who dub it "overpriced."

DC Coast

– | – | – | E

1401 K St., NW (14th St.), 202-216-5988

Airy, mirrored, polished and dramatically chic, this long-heralded Downtown newcomer looks every inch the power center it was designed to be; its art deco style matches its smooth personnel profile and, with the much-missed Jeff Tunks (ex River Club) turning out multiregional New American cuisine, it's also fulfilling its food destination destiny.

Duangrat's S | 25 | 21 | 22 | $25 |

5878 Leesburg Pike (Glen Forest Rd.), Falls Church, VA, 703-820-5775

■ The *DC Survey's* top Thai provides an "elegant" Northern Virginia backdrop for "skillfully seasoned" food; to say that its "brilliant" specials and "gracious" waitresses (in traditional dress) "make French food seem boring and Italian waiters seem rude" may overstate matters, but still, this place will "impress the boss" for a fraction of the cost of a comparable meal Downtown.

El Catalan | 21 | 25 | 17 | $37 |

1319 F St., NW (bet. 13th & 14th Sts.), 202-628-2299

◪ "Barcelona meets DC" at this "dazzling" evocation of Iberian rusticity, which was instantly annexed upon opening by Downtown VIPs; chef-owner Yannick Cam's "expertise" is reflected both in the refined barroom tapas and the dining room entrees; now that he has directed his attention here, early "kinks" – "inconsistent" dishes served so slowly diners suspect they're "individually shipped" from Spain – should smooth out.

Four & Twenty Blackbirds S | 26 | 22 | 24 | $35 |

Rte. 522 (Rte. 647), Flint Hill, VA, 540-675-1111

■ "Take the back roads" to this "gratifying" example of Virginia small-town rusticity for "superb country dining" and "attentive" hospitality; the setting may be "bucolic", but the "scrumptious" Contemporary American cooking, which relies on top-flight regional ingredients, and the power couple clientele are all quite urbane.

Galileo S | 26 | 23 | 23 | $52 |

1110 21st St. (bet. L & M Sts.), 202-293-7191

◪ "The Italian of choice" for "wonderful" food and wine in a star-studded setting; Roberto Donna, his "creative" executive chef Todd Gray and a "knowledgeable" staff "maintain standards" that win this "classy" Downtown restaurant national acclaim; go for a "fantastic" chef's tasting meal in the kitchen to understand why, even with "occasional lapses" and "pricey" tabs, it's "the most fun in town."

Georgia Brown's S | 23 | 23 | 21 | $32 |

950 15th St., NW (bet. I & K Sts.), 202-393-4499

◪ "Visually stunning" and lined with "lawyers and pols" who revel in its "huge portions" of "nouvelle" Southern cooking and "boisterous" bonhomie, this Downtown crowd-pleaser feels "truly" DC; sure, it's "too noisy for conversation" and sometimes serves "heavy" food that requires a "nap after lunch", but it's a surefire bet for spotting "dignitaries" and has a "spectacular" Sunday gospel brunch.

Gerard's Place | 27 | 22 | 24 | $55 |

915 15th St., NW (bet. I & K Sts.), 202-737-4445

■ With star chefs Jean-Louis Palladin (of the Watergate) and Jean-Pierre Goyenvalle (Le Lion D'Or) gone from the DC scene, attention is focused on Gerard Pangaud's "subtle" but "stellar" and "worth every dime" French on McPherson Square; his cooking is showcased in this "small, intimate dining room", with the "elegant" touches and "impeccable" service that make a "power lunch or romantic meal"; lately, he's been in and out (attending to his Georgetown bistro, Vintage), but it hardly seems to matter since surveyors say it's "always at least excellent."

Inn at Little Washington S 29 29 29 $96

Inn at Little Washington, Main & Middle Sts., Washington, VA, 540-675-3800

■ "Nearly perfect" scores make this the *DC Survey*'s No. 1 rated restaurant across the board and the "ultimate" Virginia country destination; chef/co-owner Patrick O'Connell's "spectacular" Contemporary American food, "opulent" appointments and the staff's constant "attention to detail" leave surveyors sighing "nirvana" that's "worth every penny"; N.B. try to reserve a chef's table in the state-of-the-art, multimillion dollar kitchen.

Jaleo S 23 21 19 $26

480 Seventh St., NW (E St.), 202-628-7949

■ The "atmosphere is electric" at this pioneering Penn Quarter trendsetter that "despite popularity, crowding" and "waits" just "keeps getting better"; most find it "impossible to get bored" with its Spanish tapas concept, which allows for the "pleasure" of sharing "great food" and offers "flexible" dining before or after MCI Center events.

Kinkead's S 28 23 25 $44

Red Lion Row, 2000 Pennsylvania Ave., NW (I St., bet. 20th & 21st Sts.), 202-296-7700

■ Almost 1,500 respondents rate Bob Kinkead's very '90s American bistro No. 2 for food and popularity in the *DC Survey*; his "brilliant innovation" – serving a "spectacular" seafood-oriented menu with "awesome choices" in handsome, "not too formal" settings – revolutionized DC "power" dining; "knowledgeable" service, an "excellent wine list" and "great jazz" are other reasons why most people feel "lucky" to "get in."

L'Auberge Chez Francois S 27 28 27 $50

332 Springfield Rd. (2 mi. north of Georgetown Pike), Great Falls, VA, 703-759-3800

■ There is "no more enjoyable place for a celebration" than this rustic French farmhouse in Great Falls, our DC surveyors' perennial favorite restaurant; lovingly managed by the Haeringer family in the "European" manner, its "hearty" Alsatian food is "plentiful, delicious" and gives "full value"; the "unique setting" down a "winding" country road is "less formal than you'd expect", with an utterly "magical" garden.

L'Auberge Provencale S 27 27 26 $64

L'Auberge Provencale, Rte. 340 (Rte. 50), White Post, VA, 540-837-1375

■ This "romantic getaway" near Virginia's horse country featuring a "creative, herb-enhanced [five-course] menu" and an "interesting wine list" makes "you think you're in a French Provençal hotel"; most find the effect "charming" and say "it's up there with the best."

Lespinasse 27 28 26 $75

Sheraton Carlton Hotel, 923 16th St., NW (K St.), 202-879-6900

■ "Elegance personified", this "exquisite", "impeccable" New French showpiece in a hotel near the White House is the ultimate indulgence when someone else pays and the site of DC's most "dazzling" (some say "ostentatious") "VIP business" lunch; but given its NY prices, many expect it to "walk on water" – and it merely glides; N.B. it sailed back from its summer '98 vacation with a new French chef, Sandro Gamba (who trained with France's Alain Ducasse), at the helm.

Makoto 🅂 | 27 | 24 | 27 | $44

4822 MacArthur Blvd., NW (Reservoir Rd.), 202-298-6866

■ "Exquisite little things just keep coming" during a "stunning set dinner" at this "sauna-sized" (four tables and 10 sushi bar seats) Palisades Japanese; one of the *DC Survey*'s top-rated spots, a meal here is an "aesthetically pleasing experience" that's reputedly "as good as all but the best in Japan" and for "one quarter of the price."

McCormick & Schmick's 🅂 | 22 | 22 | 21 | $33

1652 K St., NW (bet. 16th & 17th Sts.), 202-861-2233
11920 Democracy Dr. (Library St.), Reston, VA, 703-481-6600

◪ With their Victorian splendor (paneled booths and "private" snuggeries), corporate cordiality and "fresh fish", these Downtown and Reston "power spots" are "first choice" sites for doing deals, "family meals", happy hour and late-night snacking on $1.95 plates; however, while some say this "high-end" venture "handles crowds with aplomb", others claim diners can be "lost in the shuffle."

Melrose 🅂 | 26 | 25 | 25 | $47

Park Hyatt Hotel, M & 24th Sts., NW, 202-955-3899

■ One of DC's top "creative" Contemporary Americans, this hotel dining room has an "understated elegance" that makes it a "quiet oasis" and "escape from the city" right in the heart of the West End; with "excellent" food, well-chosen wines, "gracious" service and luxurious touches like fine art and a "cascading fountain" on the terrace, it's a "little pricey but perfect for a special occasion."

Morrison-Clark Inn 🅂 | 26 | 26 | 25 | $43

Morrison-Clark Inn, 1015 L St., NW (bet. 11th St. & Massachusetts Ave.), 202-898-1200

■ "A lovely restaurant with class, charm and the wonderful cooking" of Susan Lindeborg, one of the area's top chefs, who "imaginatively" "updates" "everyday" American food; while the "setting is elegant and refined", its "very professional" staff puts boldface names, "foreign visitors" and just-folks at ease; now that the nearby MCI Center is revitalizing what was an "out-of-the-way" neighborhood, its only "negative" becomes another plus.

Morton's of Chicago 🅂 | 26 | 22 | 23 | $49

3251 Prospect St., NW (Wisconsin Ave.), 202-342-6258
Washington Sq., 1050 Connecticut Ave., NW (L St.), 202-955-5997
Fairfax Sq., 8075 Leesburg Pike (Aline Rd.), Tysons Corner, VA, 703-883-0800

■ "Check your belt at the door" of these "macho" beefhouses and dig into a "steak as big as a house cat" and a baked potato that's the "size of Idaho"; the "cigar smoke", the "hustle", the "chatty waiters" and the bill are all "a bit much", but isn't that the point? N.B. they serve lobster, veggie platters and chocolate soufflés too.

New Heights 🅂 | 25 | 23 | 23 | $43

2317 Calvert St., NW (Connecticut Ave.), 202-234-4110

■ "Wonderfully seductive" and "original", this Contemporary American "pushes the creative envelope" with "gorgeous presentations", drawing a steady, discriminating clientele that "never tires of trying something new"; its second-story space, overlooking Rock Creek Park, is awash with art and "when the trees are in bloom" is "magical", but service, while "phenomenally nice", is a bit "slow."

Nora
26 | 24 | 24 | $47

2132 Florida Ave., NW (bet. Connecticut & Massachusetts Aves.), 202-462-5143

■ "DC's best combo of romance, fine food and unstuffy elegance", spiked with "guaranteed celebrity" sightings, is found at this "original" New American set in a "charming" carriage house near Dupont Circle; chef-owner Nora Pouillon practically invented market-driven menus featuring "natural" ingredients and her staff is "knowledgeable" too.

Obelisk
27 | 23 | 25 | $53

2029 P St., NW (bet. 20th & 21st Sts.), 202-872-1180

■ "Refined, understated and excellent" food makes Peter Pastan's "delightful little jewel box" off Dupont Circle the *DC Survey*'s top Italian; though the "prix fixe menu is limited", everything's "pure, simple, handmade" and hence "close to perfection"; since many maintain it's the "best high-end value in town", it's become a "favorite for spoiling friends."

Old Ebbitt Grill ● S
19 | 22 | 20 | $28

675 15th St., NW (bet. F & G Sts.), 202-347-4801

■ "Deservedly mobbed", this handsome Downtown "institution" is virtually a White House "annex" filled with a "who's who" of "journalists" and "wide-eyed out-of-towners" who find that its "celebratory" mood, "polished" manners, long hours and "serious" all-American food fit any occasion; it's "quintessentially DC" and "considering the quality", "you get your money's worth."

Patisserie Cafe Didier
26 | 15 | 17 | $17

3206 Grace St., NW (bet. K & M Sts.), 202-342-9083

■ Pâtissier Didier Schoner's "unsurpassed pastries" taste every bit as "wonderful" when he's at his "charming" Georgetown cafe/ bakery as when he's away teaching at NYC's prestigious French Culinary Institute – the stable high food rating tells the story; besides the "best choice of desserts anywhere", his international clientele "looks forward to" flavorful, airy soufflés, "delicious" little pizzas and "light", "lovely" lunch entrees.

Pesce S
25 | 15 | 20 | $33

2016 P St., NW (bet. Dupont Circle & 20th St.), 202-466-3474

■ One of the town's top seafooders, this "lively" urban bistro off Dupont Circle boasts an "original", "skillfully" executed, daily-changing menu featuring "fish that doesn't get better than this", a "wine list of wonders" and "attentive" help (when not "rushed"); the whitewashed "fish store" setting matches the "exquisite simplicity" of the concept; the only gripe is too bad it's so "small."

Pizzeria Paradiso S
25 | 17 | 18 | $18

2029 P St., NW (bet. 20th & 21st Sts.), 202-223-1245

■ "The epitome of pizza", "best anywhere", "no rivals" – once again, the *DC Survey*'s top pizza honors go to this whimsically decorated Dupont Circle denizen and its "perfect" pies, which are distinguished by "delicious, fresh toppings" and a "smoky", crispy crust; other pluses include sandwiches, salads and a staff that doesn't panic "even when it's packed", i.e. at peak hours.

Prime Rib 26 | 24 | 25 | $48

2020 K St., NW (bet. 20th & 21st Sts.), 202-466-8811

■ The "retro supper club appeal" of "blonds, booze", crab imperial, "exceptional" prime rib and getting "dressed up" keep this Downtown "art deco classic" steakhouse filled with distinguished-looking types; run by real pros who "treat you right", it's been a "quiet place to do [the nation's] business" for years.

Red Sage S 22 | 25 | 20 | $36

605 14th St., NW (F St.), 202-638-4444

◪ Mark Miller's "Southwestern circus" is enjoying a long run; located near big-name law and lobby palaces, the White House and the Mall, its "upstairs chile bar" "serves the masses" (not to mention "celebs and pols") casual bites of "exciting" regional cuisine in "electric" surroundings; even more "spectacular" is the "tumbleweeds-on-acid decor" in the down-under dining room; "if you can handle the spice", the downstairs price and having your waiter occasionally "disappear", by all means, go.

Seasons S 26 | 26 | 26 | $52

Four Seasons Hotel, 2800 Pennsylvania Ave., NW (28th St.), 202-944-2000

◪ An "opulent" "dream world" setting "overlooking lots of green", and equally "elegant" New American fare, help make this "luxurious" hotel one of DC's "best" for all seasons; it's a "great place for business meetings", "getting engaged" and "impressing your aunt", plus its Sunday brunch "buffet blitz" will bliss you out.

1789 S 26 | 27 | 26 | $51

1226 36th St., NW (Prospect St.), 202-965-1789

■ "Great everything" – "warm, inviting surroundings", "first-class" American regional food and "special guest" treatment for all; its chef, Ris Lacoste (ex Kinkead's), sparked a "renaissance" at this "historic", "romantic" Georgetown residence, putting it in the Top 10 for food, decor and service and causing hundreds of devotees to declare if you "have something to celebrate, do it here!"

Sostanza S ▽ 19 | 20 | 18 | $43

1606 20th St., NW (Q St.), 202-667-0047

■ "The more Vincenzo's changes, the more it stays the same" say surveyors about the recent rebirth of this gourmet "favorite" off Dupont Circle as a Roberto Donna Group Italian steakhouse run by Vince McDonald; the new menu features steak alla Fiorentina plus refined regional fish and pasta dishes served in a serene space.

Sushi-Ko S 26 | 15 | 20 | $29

2307 Wisconsin Ave., NW (south of Calvert St.), 202-333-4187

■ A post-*Survey* remake of DC's "drab" and "dated" "original sushi bar" into a sleek and tasteful retreat, plus the return of Japanese master-chef Tetsuro Takanashi, who first made it the local "gold standard for sushi", can only increase the above ratings.

Taberna del Alabardero 25 | 26 | 24 | $46

1776 I St., NW (18th St.), 202-429-2200

■ Diplomats and internationals in-the-know are utterly at home in this "beautiful" Downtown Iberian, as is anyone who delights in "refined" yet gutsy Spanish food, "lots of privacy" and "artful" service; a branch of one of Madrid's "world-class" restaurants, it lends a "sense of occasion" to a business meal or evening event.

Tahoga S | 23 | 21 | 21 | $40

2815 M St., NW (bet. 28th & 29th Sts.), 202-338-5380

■ "Great beginnings" made its "minimalist" Georgetown digs a stage set for the stylish, yet this New American "keeps working on getting it right"; despite a chef change, its "generally good" food is becoming "even better", and its sometimes "overconfident staff" is settling down; one of the "best new restaurants" in the area, it has a "hidden courtyard" that's the most romantic place in town.

Vidalia S | 26 | 23 | 24 | $43

1990 M St., NW (bet. 19th & 20th Sts.), 202-659-1990

■ It's not just the "namesake onions" that chef-owner Jeffrey Buben transforms into "glamorous" fare; his "imaginative" renditions of Southern classics have made his "sunny basement dining room" ("looks like Van Gogh by way of Valdosta") a "premier" M Street site for "expense-account comfort food"; be sure to ask about his "fine wines."

Villa Franco S | – | – | – | E

601 Pennsylvania Ave., NW (Indiana Ave.), 202-638-2423

Within sight of the Capitol and in the heart of happening Downtown, this smashing sun-washed evocation of an Italian villa is becoming a major dining destination; the light pastas and seafood grills are revelations to Americans accustomed to the red-sauced stuff that passes for Neapolitan cooking; the production is orchestrated by seasoned pro Franco Nuschese (Cafe Milano).

CITY ABBREVIATIONS

AC	Atlantic City	MI	Miami/Miami Beach
AT	Atlanta	MN	Minneapolis/St. Paul
BA	Baltimore/Annapolis	NJ	New Jersey
BO	Boston	NO	New Orleans
CH	Chicago	NY	New York City
CI	Cincinnati	OC	Orange County, CA
CL	Cleveland	OR	Orlando
CO	Columbus	PB	Palm Beach
DA	Dallas	PH	Philadelphia
DC	Washington, DC	PO	Portland, OR
DE	Denver Area	PS	Phoenix/Scottsdale
DT	Detroit	SA	Santa Fe
FL	Fort Lauderdale	SC	Salt Lake City
FW	Fort Worth	SD	San Diego
HO	Honolulu	SE	Seattle
HS	Houston	SF	San Francisco
KC	Kansas City	SL	St. Louis
LA	Los Angeles	TB	Tampa Bay/Sarasota
LV	Las Vegas	TC	Tucson

TYPES OF CUISINE

American (New)
American Rest., KC
Américas, HS
Anago, BO
Angeluna, FW
Anthony's, HS
Aquaterra, PB
Ardeo, DC
Arizona Inn, TC
Aubergine Cafe, DE
Aujourd'hui, BO
Aureole, NY
Bacchanalia, AT
Bayona, NO
Beach Bistro, TB
Biba, BO
Bijou Café, TB
Bistango, OC
Black Orchid Cafe, FL
Boca, CI
Boulevard, SF
Boulevard Grill, PB
Brooks, FL
Buckhead Diner, AT
Buffet at the Kimbell, FW
By Word of Mouth, FL
Cafe Allegro, KC
Cafe Aspen, FW
Cafe Balaban, SL
Cafe Chardonnay, PB
Cafe Mira, SL
Campton Place, SF
Canoe, AT
Cardwell's, SL
Cashion's Eat Place, DC
Cena, NY
Charles Court, DE
Charlie Trotter's, CH
Citrus, PB
Courtright's, CH
Cousins Heritage Inn, DT
Crofton on Wells, CH
Crossing, SL
Dandelion, DE
David Michael's, TB
David Paul's, HO
DC Coast, DC
dick & harry's, AT
Dilworthtown Inn, PH
Dining Room, NJ
Eddie's Grill, PS
Eleven Madison Park, NY
European Cafe, DE
Five Lakes Grill, DT
Food Studio, AT
Fork, PH
4 & 20 Blackbirds, DC
Four Seasons Cafe, AT
French Laundry, SF
Frog & the Peach, NJ
Gautreau's, NO
George's at the Cove, SD
Georgian Room, SE
Glitretind, SC
Globe, SF
Gordon, CH
Gotham Bar/Grill, NY
Gramercy Tavern, NY
Grand Finale, CI
Green Gables, NJ
Green Room, DA
Grille on Broadway, KC

Hamersley's, BO
Hampton's, BA
Handke's, CO
Harry's, SL
Harvest, SL
Harvest on Huron, CH
Harvey's Bistro, OR
Hawthorne Lane, SF
Hedgerose, AT
Highlands Garden Cafe, DE
Highlawn Pavilion, NJ
Himmarshee B&G, FL
House, SF
Icarus, BO
Inn/Little Washington, DC
Iron Horse, CI
Jake's, PH
John's, DE
Keystone Ranch, DE
Kinkead's, DC
La Réserve, HS
Le Parvenu, NO
Lindey's, CO
Linwood's, BA
Little Nell, DE
Loring Cafe & Bar, MN
Mainland Inn, PH
Mango, CH
Manuel's on 28th, OR
March, NY
Mariposa, SC
Maritana Grille, TB
Market Sq. Bistro, CL
Mark's, HS
Masquerade Cafe, PB
Max's Grille, PB
Meetinghouse, SF
Melrose, DC
Merlot, CO
Metropolis, KC
Michael's at Citadel, PS
Michael's on East, TB
Mike's on the Ave., NO
Mise en Place, TB
MoMo's, SF
Morel, TB
Morrison-Clark Inn, DC
Moveable Feast, DT
Mr. Stox, OC
Mumbo Jumbo, AT
Nana Grill, DA
Nemo, MI
New Heights, DC
No. 9 Park, BO
Nora, DC
one sixtyblue, CH
Opus One, DT
Opus 251, PH
Oven's, TC
Palace, CI
Palm Beach Tavern, PB
Pano's & Paul's, AT
Park Avenue Cafe, CH
Park Avenue Cafe, NY
Pastiche, TC
Pebbles, OR
Phoenix, CI
Pierpoint, BA
Piñons, DE
Plaza 600, CI
Polo Grill, BA
Presidio Grill, TC
Printer's Row, CH
Q's, DE
Rainbow Room, NY
Rattlesnake Club, DT
Redwood Grill, HS
Reflections, FW
Renaissance, DE
Rhapsody, CH
Riddle's Penultimate, SL
Ritz-Carlton Grill, PH
Ritz-Carlton Grill, SL
River Cafe, NY
Riverhorse Cafe, SC
Riverview Room, CL
Rococo, PH
Rouge 98, PH
Rudys' 2900, BA
Ruga, NJ
Saddle River Inn, NJ
Seasons, BO
Seasons, CH
Seasons, DC
Seeger's, AT
Sent Sovi, SF
Sevy's Grill, DA
Sidney St. Cafe, SL
Spruce, CH
Stolen Grill, KC
Strings, DE
Sweet Basil, DE
Table Of Contents, MN
Tahoga, DC
Tapawingo, DT
Tarbell's, PS
Tavern on the Green, NY
Terra, SF
32 East, PB
3 Doors Down, PO
302 West, CH
Too Chez, DT
Tribute, DT
Trio, CI
28, NJ
240 Union, DE
208 Talbot, BA
Union Pacific, NY
Union Sq. Cafe, NY
Van Gogh's, AT
Ventana Room, TC
Versailles, MI

Vesta Dipping Grill, DE
Vineyards, KC
White Dog Cafe, PH
White Rainbow, BO
Whitney, DT
Wildflower, DE
Windows on the World, NY
Wright's, PS
York Street, DA
Zealous, CH
Zinnia, SL

American (Regional)

Bayport Amer. Cookery, MN
Cameron's, CO
Charleston, BA
Craig's, PB
Dakota B&G, MN
Denver Chop Hse., DE
Entre Nous, CH
Fourth Story, DE
Goodfellow's, MN
Lakota, SC
Latilla Room, PS
Mariposa, HO
Matt's No Place, DA
Milton Inn, BA
Opus 251, PH
Orchids, CI
Oregon Grill, BA
Rainbow Lodge, HS
Reed's River House, FL
Rowe Inn, DT
Rowes Wharf, BO
1789, DC
St. Paul Grill, MN
Sundance Tree Room, SC

American (Traditional)

Bang!, DE
Brasserie Z, DE
Canlis, SE
Cap City Fine Diner, CO
Forge, MI
Grill, LA
Houston's, KC
Hugo's Cellar, LV
Hy's Steak House, HO
Kincaid's, MN
Lark Creek Inn, SF
Manor, NJ
Marconi's, BA
Mrs. Peter's, KC
Mr. Stox, OC
New Yorker Club, SC
Old Ebbitt Grill, DC
Palace Arms, DE
Peppercorn Duck, KC
Pike Street, DT
Prime Rib, DC
Ram's Head Inn, AC
Rib Room, NO
Ritz-Carlton Grill, DT
Rotisserie/Beef & Bird, HS
S & S Rest., MI
Shaw's, CO
Starker's Reserve, KC
Stephenson's, KC
Stroud's, KC
Swann Lounge, PH
Tack Room, TC
'21' Club, NY
Victoria & Albert's, OR
Worthington Inn, CO

Asian

Ambrosia, BO
Belvedere, LA
Blue Ginger, BO
Buddakan, PH
Cafe Japengo, SD
China Grill, MI
Chinois on Main, LA
Dahlia Lounge, SE
Five Feet, OC
Heights, MI
House, SF
Liberty, DA
Madame Ching's, LV
Mon Jin Lau, DT
Pacific Moon, CI
Phnom Penh, CL
Salamander, BO
Saucebox, PO
Shiro, LA
Susanna Foo, PH
Taka, SD
Wild Ginger, SE

Bakeries

BonBonerie, CI
Bread Garden, AT
Bread Line, DC
Patisserie Cafe Didier, DC

BBQ

Angelo's, FW
Goode Co., HS
Jack Fiorella's, KC
Johnny River's, OR
Montgomery Inn, CI
Railhead Smokehse., FW
Sonny Bryan's, DA
Tom's Place, PB

Belgian

Belgian Lion, SD

Brazilian

Blue Door, MI
Fogo de Chao, DA
Sergio's, CL

British

Barclays, DA

Classics, CL
Clive's, HS
Canoe, AT
Dining Room, NJ
European Cafe, DE
Faust's, SL
Five Crowns, OC
Flagstaff House, DE
Forge, MI
Fountain, PH
Four Seasons, NY
Georgian Room, SE
Golden Mushroom, DT
Grapevine, SC
Gustaf Anders, OC
Highlawn Pavilion, NJ
Hôtel St. Germain, DA
Hugo's Cellar, LV
Inn at Perry Cabin, BA
Johnny's Bar/Fulton, CL
Johnny's Downtown, CL
La Tour d'Argent, HS
Macaluso's, KC
Maison et Jardin, OR
Manor, NJ
Merlot, CO
Michael's, LV
Monte Carlo, LV
Moveable Feast, DT
New Yorker Club, SC
Nikolai's Roof, AT
103 West, AT
Orchids, HO
Palace Arms, DE
Palace Court, LV
Palm Court, PS
Pano's & Paul's, AT
Park Grill, SF
Peter Scott's, OR
Pink Adobe, SA
Pyramid Room, DA
Rancho Valencia, SD
Reiner's, SE
Rib Room, NO
Ritz, OC
Ritz-Carlton Buck. Cafe, AT
Rudys' 2900, BA
Seventh Inn, SL
Sidney St. Cafe, SL
Swann Lounge, PH
Terra, SF
Tio Pepe, BA
Tivoli Deer, DE
Vineyards, KC
White Rainbow, BO

Cuban

Cafe Havana, MN
Rolando's, OR
Versailles, MI
Yuca, MI

Delis

Brent's Deli, LA
Carnegie Deli, NY
Cucina, SC
Wolfie Cohen's, MI
Zingerman's Deli, DT

Desserts

Mademoiselle de Paris, PH
Patisserie Descours, HS

Dim Sum

Ocean Star, LA
Tropical Chinese, MI

Eclectic

Américas, HS
Bexley's Monk, CO
Biba, BO
Blue Ginger, BO
Blue Heron, TB
Boca, CI
Cafe Balaban, SL
Cafe Japengo, SD
Capitol Cafe, SC
Charles Court, DE
Chez Betty, SC
Chez Melange, LA
China Grill, MI
Clancy's, NO
Depot, LA
DeVille, HS
Drai's, LV
EatZi's, DA
Eddie's Grill, PS
EOS, SF
Euphemia Haye, TB
Faust's, SL
Frog & the Peach, NJ
Gary's Little Rock, AC
Golden Truffle, OC
Grand St. Cafe, KC
Grape, DA
Grape Escape, FW
Grill Room, NO
Handke's, CO
Hot Chocolates, FL
La Bettola, BO
La Caille, SC
Lampreia, SE
Lark, DT
L'Auberge, PO
Laurels, DA
Lockkeeper's Inn, CL
Log Haven, SC
Lon's at the Hermosa, PS
Mango, CH
Manuel's on 28th, OR
Marco's Supperclub, SE
Mary Elaine's, PS
Masquerade, PB
Mercer Kitchen, NY

Metropolis, KC
Metropolitan, SC
Mike's on the Ave., NO
Mixx, SD
Morel, TB
Mullane's, CI
Napa, LV
No. 9 Park, BO
Olives, BO
Ophelia's, TB
Palace Kitchen, SE
Pastiche, TC
Picasso, LV
Place Pigalle, SE
Rainbow Room, NY
Randall's Gourmet, FW
Rigsby's, CO
Salamander, BO
Santacafe, SA
Savaradio, AC
Sterling Brunch, LV
Stolen Grill, KC
Taka, SD
Tasca, HS
Tremont 647, BO
Trio, CH
Tutto a Posto, CL
Union Sq. Cafe, NY
Upperline, NO
Ventana Room, TC
Yia Yia's Eurobistro, KC
Zefiro, PO

Eurasian

Bali-by-the-Sea, HO
EOS, SF
Indigo, HO
Roy's, HO

Floridian

Astor Place B&G, MI
Maritana Grille, TB
Rest./Four Seasons, PB

French Bistro

Babette's Cafe, AT
Balthazar, NY
Bistro, AT
Bistro at Maison de Ville, NO
Bistro Banlieue, CH
Bistro 45, LA
Bistro Jeanty, SF
Bistro St. Tropez, PH
Brasserie Le Coze, AT
Brasserie Les Halles, MI
Cafe Bizou, LA
Cafe Campagne, SE
Cafe des Amis, PO
Café Provençal, SL
Chaya Brasserie, LA
Chez Georges, HS
Chez Gerard, DA
Chez Madeleine, NJ
Fringale, SF
Grand Finale, CI
Hamersley's, BO
Harvey's Bistro, OR
KiKi's Bistro, CH
La Brochette Bistro, FL
La Petite Maison, PB
Lavendou, DA
Le Bar Lyonnais, PH
Le Bistro, TC
Le Bouchon, CH
Le Coq au Vin, OR
Le Montrachet, LV
Metro Bistro, NO
Mimosa, LA
Patisserie Cafe Didier, DC
Pinot Bistro, LA
Pinot Provence, OC
Saint-Emilion, FW
Scala's Bistro, SF
Tapenade, SD

French (Classic)

Andre's, LV
Antoine's, NO
Arnaud's, NO
Belgian Lion, SD
Bistro 24, PS
Cafe de France, SL
Café des Artistes, NY
Cafe L'Europe, PB
Cafe 36, CH
Cellar, OC
Chez Alphonse, CI
Chez François, CL
Chez Nous, HS
Chez Vincent, OR
Christian's, NO
Ciboulette, AT
Cliquo, HO
Coventry Forge Inn, PH
Crozier's, NO
Daniel, NY
Deux Cheminées, PH
Diaghilev, LA
Dilworthtown Inn, PH
Earle, DT
El Bizcocho, SD
Fio's La Fourchette, SL
Fond de la Tour, CH
French Laundry, SF
French Room, DA
Galatoire's, NO
Gerard's Place, DC
Julien, BO
Kathy's Gazebo, PB
La Caravelle, NY
La Côte Basque, NY
La Grenouille, NY
La Mediterannee, KC
La Mer, HO

L'Antibes, CO
La Petite France, CI
La Provence, NO
La Tour d'Argent, HS
L'Auberge Chez Francois, DC
L'Auberge Provencale, DC
Le Bec-Fin, PH
Le Cirque 2000, NY
Le Festival, MI
Le Fou Frog, KC
Le Français, CH
Le Rendez-Vous, TC
Les Célébrités, NY
Les Nomades, CH
L'Espalier, BO
L'Orangerie, LA
Louis XVI, NO
Maisonette, CI
Maison Robert, BO
Michel's, HO
Montparnasse, CH
Pascal, OC
Pyramid Room, DA
Refectory, CO
Relais, SE
Ritz-Carlton, OC
Ritz-Carlton Atlanta Rest., AT
Ritz-Carlton Buck. Cafe, AT
Ritz-Carlton Din. Rm., BO
Riviera, DA
Tante Louise, DE
Tatsu's, KC
Tersiguel's, BA
Thee Bungalow, SD
231 Ellsworth, SF

French (New)

Ambria, CH
Ambrosia, BO
Aqua, SF
Aubergine, OC
Aubriot, CH
Baricelli Inn, CL
Bel-Air Hotel, LA
Belvedere, LA
Blue Door, MI
Bouley Bakery, NY
Brasserie Perrier, PH
Cacharel, FW
Café Blanc, LA
Cafe Bon Homme, DT
Cafe Louis, BO
Cafe Panache, NJ
Campagne, SE
Carlos', CH
Chanterelle, NY
Charles Nob Hill, SF
Chez Alphonse, CI
Chez Michel, SF
Chinois on Main, LA
Ciboulette, PH
Cielos, TC
Citronelle, DC
Citrus, LA
Clio, BO
Couvron, PO
Cypress Club, SF
Domaine Chandon, SF
El Bizcocho, SD
Elephant Walk, BO
Erna's Elderberry, SF
Everest, CH
Fleur de Lys, SF
Floataway Cafe, AT
Fountain, PH
Fromagerie, NJ
Gabriel's, CH
Gautreau's, NO
Gerard's Place, DC
Heathman, PO
Hôtel St. Germain, DA
Isabella's, PH
Janeiro, PB
Janos, TC
Jardiniere, SF
Jean Georges, NY
La Cachette, LA
La Colombe d'Or, HS
La Folie, SF
La Grille, OR
L'Antibes, CO
Lark, DT
L'Auberge, PO
Laurel, SD
Lavande, LA
La Vieille Maison, PB
Le Bernardin, NY
Le Cirque/Osteria Circo, LV
Le Palais, AC
Le Provence, OR
Lespinasse, DC
Lespinasse, NY
Le Titi de Paris, CH
Le Vichyssois, CH
Lutèce, NY
Mademoiselle de Paris, PH
Malmaison, SL
Masa's, SF
mc^2, SF
Mercer Kitchen, NY
Mille Fleurs, SD
Mirabelle, DE
Mistral, BO
Monte Carlo, LV
Montrachet, NY
Nan, PH
103 West, AT
Palace Court, LV
Pamplemousse Gr., SD
Papillon Cafe, DE
Parker's, CL
Patina, LA
Rest./Four Seasons, PB

Ritz-Carlton Atlanta Rest., AT
Ritz-Carlton Din. Rm., CH
Ritz-Carlton Din. Rm., SF
Riviera, AT
Rover's, SE
Rubicon, SF
Ryland Inn, NJ
Saddle River Inn, NJ
Sent Sovi, SF
Silks, BO
Susanna Foo, PH
Tallgrass, CH
Tante Louise, DE
Troquet, OC
231 Ellsworth, SF
Vignola, SD
WineSellar, SD
Zinc, BO

Greek

Black Olive, BA
Gardens of Salonica, MN
Milos, NY
Periyali, NY

Hamburgers

Kincaid's, FW

Hawaiian (Regional)

Alan Wong's, HO
Bali-by-the-Sea, HO
Maui Grille, FL
Ono Hawaiian Foods, HO
Sam Choy's Diamond, HO

Indian

Bombay Club, DC
Bombay Grille, CO
India Palace, KC
India Palace, SA
India's, DE
Taj Palace, CO

International

Bayona, NO
Bread Line, DC
Cafe Mira, SL
Hau Tree Lanai, HO
Hoku's, HO
Moshulu, PH
Orchids, HO
RoxSand, PS

Irish

Local, MN

Italian

(N=Northern; S=Southern; N&S=Includes both)
Abruzzi, AT (N&S)
Acquario, PB (N&S)
Acquerello, SF (N)
Antonello, OC (N)
Antonio's, OR (N&S)
Armani's, TB (N)
Assaggio, PO (N&S)
Babbo, NY (N&S)
Baci Trattoria, SC (N&S)
Baricelli Inn, CL (N&S)
Bar Italia, SL (N&S)
Barolo Grill, DE (N)
Barresi's, CI (N&S)
Boccaccio, BA (N)
Buca di Beppo, MN (S)
Cafe Arugula, FL (N&S)
Cafe Jordano, DE (S)
Cafe Lago, SE (N&S)
Caffe Abbracci, MI (N&S)
Caffè Mingo, PO (N&S)
Campagna, DE (N)
Campo di Fiori, DE (N&S)
Capriccio, AC (N&S)
Carpaccio, MI (N)
Casa D'Angelo, FL (N)
Chaya Brasserie, LA (N&S)
Chef Vola's, AC (N&S)
Ciao Mein, HO (N&S)
Coco Pazzo, CH (N)
Crescendo, CO (N&S)
Damian's, HS (N&S)
D'Amico Cucina, MN (N)
Daniel's, TC (N)
Dominic's, SL (N&S)
Earle, DT (N&S)
Enzo's on the Lake, OR (N)
Escopazzo, MI (N)
Floataway Cafe, AT (N&S)
Fratello's, CL (N&S)
Fresco Italian Cafe, SC (N)
Full Moon Grille, DE (N&S)
Gabriel's, CH (N&S)
Galileo, DC (N)
Gavi, CL (N&S)
Genoa, PO (N)
Germano's, CI (N&S)
Giacosa, MI (N)
Gianpeppe's, SL (N)
Giorgio, MN (N)
Giovanni's, CL (N)
Giovanni's, SL (N&S)
Giuseppe's, CO (N&S)
Grappa, SC (N&S)
Il Capriccio, BO (N)
Il Mulino, NY (N)
Il Tartufo, FL (N)
Il Terr. Carmine, SE (N&S)
Irene's Cuisine, NO (N&S)
Isabella's, PH (N&S)
Johnny's Bar/Fulton, CL (N)
Johnny's Downtown, CL (N)
Kemoll's, SL (N&S)
La Bettola, BO (N&S)
La Finestra, PB (N)
La Griglia, HS (N&S)
La Grotta, AT (N&S)

La Mora, HS (N)
La Piazza, FW (N&S)
La Riviera, NO (N&S)
Laudisio, DE (N&S)
La Veranda, PN (N&S)
Le Cirque/Osteria, LV (N&S)
Locanda Veneta, LA (N)
Lombardi Mare, PA (N&S)
Macaluso's, KC (N&S)
Marcuccio's, BO (N&S)
Medici, AC (N&S)
Mia Francesca, CH (N)
Mi Piaci, DA (N)
Monte Carlo Liv. Rm., PH (N&S)
Moro's Dining, DT (N&S)
Nick's Italian Cafe, PO (N)
Nicola's, CI (N)
Nino's, HS (N&S)
Obelisk, DC (N)
Oliveto, SF (N&S)
On Broadway, FW (N&S)
Osteria del Teatro, MI (N)
Palomino, MN (N&S)
Paulo & Bill's, KC (N&S)
Piero's, LV (N)
Pignoli, BO (N&S)
Pomodoro, BO (N&S)
Pomodoro, SC (N&S)
Pranzo Italian Grill, SA (N&S)
Primavera, FL (N)
Primavista, CI (N&S)
Rao's, NY (S)
Rigsby's, CO (N&S)
Rist. di Modesta, DT (N)
Rist. Di Palma, PH (N&S)
Rist. Luci, MN (N)
Rose Pistola, SF (N)
Saleh al Lago, SE (N&S)
Salvatore's, SD (N)
Saporito's, BO (N)
Scala's Bistro, SF (N&S)
Scalea's, CI (N&S)
Scalini Fedeli, NJ (N)
Sergio's, OR (N&S)
Simposio, HS (N&S)
Sostanza, DC (N&S)
Spiaggia, CH (N&S)
T. Cook's, PS (N&S)
Terrace Din. Rm., PS (N&S)
Terramia, BO (N&S)
Terrazza, LV (N&S)
Tony's, HS (N&S)
Tony's, SL (N&S)
Trattoria Marcella, SL (N&S)
Trattoria Roma, CO (N&S)
Tra Vigne, SF (N&S)
Tre Figlio, AC (N&S)
Tre Visi, LV (N&S)
Tuscany, SC (N)
Valentino, LA (N&S)
Va Pensiero, CH (N&S)
Veni Vidi Vici, AT (N)
Villa Franco, DC (N)
Vivace, SD (N)
Vivace, TC (N&S)
Vivande, SF (N&S)
Wente Vineyards, SF (N&S)

Japanese

Café Blanc, LA
Domo, DE
Ginza, BO
Hirosuke, LA
Ichiban, FL
Ichiban Sushi, SC
JoAn, CI
Jun's, KC
Kacho, HO
Kyo-Ya, HO
Makoto, DC
Matsuhisa, LA
Ninja's, NO
Nobu, NY
Origami, MN
Restaurant Japan, CO
R-23, LA
Sachiko Sushi, TC
Sagami, NJ
Sagami, PH
Sapporo Wind, CO
Shiro's, SE
Shuhei, CL
Soto, AT
Sushi Den, DE
Sushi Huku, AT
Sushi-Ko, DC
Sushi Nozawa, LA
Sushi Ota, SD
Sushisay, NY
Yohei Sushi, HO

Latin American

Latin Rooster, CO

Mediterranean

Acquario, PB
Aubergine Cafe, DE
Audrey Claire, PH
Azul, HO
Azzura Point, SD
Beach Bistro, TB
Bistro A, DA
Bistro Louise, FW
Cafe Arugula, FL
Caffe Bella, BO
Campanile, LA
Cascada, HO
Citricos, OR
Dmitri's, PH
Full Moon Grill, DE
Janeiro, PB
John's, DE
La Belle Vie, MN

Mexican/Tex-Mex

Middle Eastern

Moroccan

New Mexican

New World

Northwestern

Nuevo Latino

Pacific New Wave

Pacific Rim

Pizza

Russian

Sandwiches

Scandinavian

Seafood

Black Olive, BA
Bristol B&G, KC
Buccaneer Bay Club, LV
Cafe Pacific, DA
Cafe Pacifica, SD
Cantler's Riverside, BA
Dmitri's, PH
Doris & Ed's, NJ
Emeril's, LV
Etta's Seafood, SE
Farallon, SF
Fish, DA
Flying Fish, SE
Flying Fish Cafe, OR
Fulton's Crab House, OR
Grill 23 & Bar, BO
Hau Tree Lanai, HO
Hobo's Fish Joint, FL
I&J Station House, PB
Jax Fish House, DE
Joe's Stone Crab, MI
J's Fresh Seafood, CI
Kelly's Del Frisco's, HS
Kincaid's, MN
Kinkead's, DC
La Veranda, PH
Le Bernardin, NY
Legal Sea Foods, BO
Legend Seafood, HO
Lenny's Chop House, BA
Lombardi Mare, DA
Mainstream Fish Hse., DA
Manhattan Ocean Club, NY
Market St. Broiler, SC
Matsuhisa, LA
McCormick & Schmick's, BA
McCormick & Schmick's, DC
Milos, NY
Nick's Fishmarket, CH
Oceana, NY
Ocean Star, LA
Oyster Bar, NY
Oystercatchers, TB
Palm, AT
Pesce, DC
Pierpoint, BA
Prime, AT
Red Fish Grill, MI
Salt Rock Grill, TB
Savoy Grill, KC
Sea Grill, DA
Shiro, LA
Sierra Grill, HS
Spoto's Oyster Bar, PB
Striped Bass, PH
Sunfish Grill, FL
Tillerman, LV
Water Grill, LA
Young's, NO

South American

Churrascos, HS

Southern/Soul

Charleston, BA
Flying Biscuit Cafe, AT
Georgia Brown's, DC
Reed's River House, FL
South City Kitchen, AT
Sylvia's, NY
Vidalia, DC

Southwestern

Arizona Kitchen, PS
Armadillo Cafe, FL
Arroyo Grille, PH
Bar Abilene, MN
Cafe Annie, HS
Cafe Pasqual's, SA
Cafe Terra Cotta, TC
Chimayo, SC
Cottonwood Cafe, TC
Coyote Cafe, LV
Coyote Cafe, SA
¡Fuego!, TC
Geronimo, SA
Golden Swan, PS
Gold Room, TC
Heights, MI
Inn of the Anasazi, SA
Janos, TC
La Casa Sena, SA
Mansion on Turtle Creek, DA
Nava, AT
Pink Adobe, SA
Reata, FW
Red Sage, DC
Roaring Fork, PS
Ruggles Grill, HS
Sierra Grill, HS
Star Canyon, DA
Vincent Guerithault, PS
Windows on the Green, PS

Spanish

Cafe Seville, FL
Ceviche, TB
Cielos, TC
El Catalan, DC
El Farol, SA
Emilio's Tapas Bar, CH
Jaleo, DC
Marquesa, PS
Mesón Sabika, CH
Taberna del Alabardero, DC
Tapeo, PO
T. Cook's, PS
Tio Pepe, BA

Steakhouses

Al Biernat's, DA
Al's, SL
Bern's, TB
Bob's Steak, DA
Bone's, AT

Swedish

Swiss

Tapas

Thai

Vegetarian

Vietnamese

ALPHABETICAL PAGE INDEX

Wine Vintage Chart 1985-1997

This chart is designed to help you select wine to go with your meal. It is based on the same 0 to 30 scale used throughout this *Survey.* The ratings (prepared by our friend **Howard Stravitz**, a law professor at the University of South Carolina) reflect both the quality of the vintage and the wine's readiness for present consumption. Thus, if a wine is not fully mature or is over the hill, its rating has been reduced. We do not include 1987 or 1991 vintages because, with the exception of cabernets and '91 Northern Rhônes, those vintages are not especially recommended.

	'85	'86	'88	'89	'90	'92	'93	'94	'95	'96	'97
WHITES											
French:											
Burgundy	24	25	20	29	24	24	–	23	28	27	26
Loire Valley	–	–	–	26	25	19	22	23	24	25	23
Champagne	28	25	24	26	28	–	24	–	25	26	–
Sauternes	22	28	29	25	26	–	–	18	22	24	23
California:											
Chardonnay	–	–	–	–	–	25	24	23	26	23	22
REDS											
French:											
Bordeaux	26	27	25	28	29	19	22	24	25	24	22
Burgundy	25	–	24	27	29	23	25	22	24	25	24
Rhône	26	20	26	28	27	16	23*	23	24	22	–
Beaujolais	–	–	–	–	–	–	20	21	24	22	23
California:											
Cab./Merlot	26	26	–	21	28	26	25	27	23	24	22
Zinfandel	–	–	–	–	–	21	21	23	20	21	23
Italian:											
Tuscany	27	16	24	–	26	–	21	20	25	19	–
Piedmont	26	–	25	27	27	–	19	–	24	25	–

*Rating is only for Southern Rhône wine.

Bargain sippers take note: Some wines are reliable year in, year out, and are reasonably priced as well. These wines are best bought in the most recent vintages. They include: Alsatian Pinot Blancs, Côtes du Rhône, Muscadet, Bardolino, Valpolicella and inexpensive Spanish Rioja and California Zinfandel.